THIRTEEN CREATIVE STORIES THAT TAKE YOU TO OTHER WORLDS AND SHATTER THE BOUNDARIES OF IMAGINATION!

What would you do if . . .

Your only hope to save a human colony at the edge of the solar system against alien invaders was to become a robot?

You could travel through space to Mars and achieve immortality?

You had a cutting-edge time machine—or more than one for that matter?

Have you ever imagined . . .

Making a yearly 500-million-mile round trip through the cosmos—just to fulfill a promise?

Somehow escaping a brilliantly well thought-out plot to kill you devised by a newly discovered species?

Getting shipped to another galaxy because of your friendly personality?

Have you ever considered . . .

Saving the life of an alien because only you could understand him?

Inventing a pair of wings to save your ship from falling off the world and sailing into infinite space?

These are the award winners for the sixteenth year of the most successful contest for new writers. Let their exciting stories take you to unknown realms and the outer limits of space—guaranteed to be hard to put down.

Imagine that!

What has been said about the

L. Ron Hubbard
PRESENTS
WRITERS OF THE FUTURE
ANTHOLOGIES

"This has become a major tributary to the new blood in fantastic fiction."

GREGORY BENFORD

"From cutting-edge high tech to evocative fantasy, this book's got it all—it's lots of fun and I love the chance to see what tomorrow's stars are doing today."

TIM POWERS

"I recommend the *Writers of the Future*® Contest at every writers' workshop I participate in."

FREDERIK POHL

". . . an exceedingly solid collection, including SF, fantasy and horror . . ."

CHICAGO SUN TIMES

"A first-rate collection of stories and illustrations."

BOOKLIST

"It is rare to find this consistency of excellence in any series of science fiction and fantasy stories. The well-deserved reputation of L. Ron Hubbard's *Writers of the Future* has proven itself once again."

STEPHEN V. WHALEY
PROFESSOR ENGLISH & FOREIGN LANGUAGES
CALIFORNIA POLYTECHNICAL UNIVERSITY, POMONA

"The untapped talents of new writers continue to astonish me and every WOTF volume provides a well-spring of the greatest energy put forth by the ambitious writers of tomorrow."

KEVIN J. ANDERSON

"This contest has changed the face of Science Fiction."

DEAN WESLEY SMITH
EDITOR OF *STRANGE NEW WORLDS*

"Some of the best SF of the future comes from *Writers of the Future* and you can find it in this book."

DAVID HARTWELL

"Not only is the writing excellent . . . it is also extremely varied. There's a lot of hot new talent in it."

LOCUS MAGAZINE

"As always, this is the premier volume in the field to showcase new writers and artists. You can't go wrong here."

BARYON

"*Writers of the Future* is the leading SF pathway to success."

ALGIS BUDRYS

"This contest has found some of the best new writers of the last decade."

KRISTINE KATHRYN RUSCH
AUTHOR & EDITOR

"I have been fortunate enough, myself, to make use of L. Ron Hubbard's *Writers of the Future* anthologies for a number of years in my own classroom, and my students have learned much about what constitutes good writing."

DR. JOHN L. FLYNN
ENGLISH PROFESSOR
TOWSON UNIVERSITY, MARYLAND

SPECIAL OFFER FOR SCHOOLS AND WRITING GROUPS

The thirteen prize-winning stories in this volume, all of them selected by a panel of top professionals in the field of speculative fiction, exemplify the standards which a new writer must meet if he expects to see his work published and achieve professional success.

These stories, augmented by "how to write" articles by some of the top writers of science fiction, fantasy and horror, make this anthology virtually a textbook for use in the classroom and an invaluable resource for students, teachers and workshop instructors in the field of writing.

The materials contained in this and previous volumes have been used with outstanding results in writing courses and workshops held on college and university campuses throughout the United States—from Harvard, Duke and Rutgers to George Washington, Brigham Young and Pepperdine.

To assist and encourage creative writing programs, the **L. Ron Hubbard Presents Writers of the Future** anthologies are available at special quantity discounts when purchased in bulk by schools, universities, workshops and other related groups.

For more information, write

Specialty Sales Department
Bridge Publications, Inc.
4751 Fountain Avenue
Los Angeles, CA 90029
or call toll-free (800) 722-1733
Internet address: www.bridgepub.com
E-mail address: info@bridgepub.com

L. Ron Hubbard

PRESENTS

WRITERS of the FUTURE

VOLUME XVI

L. Ron Hubbard

PRESENTS

WRITERS of the FUTURE

VOLUME XVI

The Year's 13 Best Tales from the
Writers of the Future
International Writers' Program
Illustrated by the Winners in the
Illustrators of the Future®
International Illustrators' Program

With Essays on Writing and Illustration by
L. Ron Hubbard • Michael H. Payne •
Judith Holman • Algis Budrys

Edited by Algis Budrys

Bridge Publications, Inc.

Home Grown: © 2000 William Brown
Like Iron Unicorns: © 2000 Paul D. Batteiger
Atlantis, Ohio: © 2000 Mark Siegel
A Conversation with Schliegelman: © 2000 Dan Barlow
In Orbite Medievali: © 2000 Toby Buckell
Guildmaster: © 2000 Dan Dysan
An Essay on Art: © 2000 Judith Holman
Skin Song: © 2000 Melissa J. Yuan-Innes
As the Crow Flies: © 2000 Leslie Claire Walker
Mud and Salt: © 2000 Michael J. Jasper
The Quality of Wetness: © 2000 Ilsa J. Bick
Your Own Hope: © 2000 Paul E. Martens
Pulling Up Roots: © 2000 Gary Murphy
Fame? Fortune? Chocolate? © 2000 Michael H. Payne
Daimon! Daimon! © 2000 Jeff Rutherford

Illustration on page   8 © 2000 Troy Connors
Illustration on page   20 © 2000 Samantha Miceli
Illustration on page   45 © 2000 James T. Johnson
Illustration on page 125 © 2000 Deth P. Sun
Illustration on page 160 © 2000 Yana Yavdoshchook
Illustration on page 187 © 2000 Frank Wu
Illustration on page 257 © 2000 Jayson B. Doolittle
Illustration on page 278 © 2000 Steelee Faltis
Illustration on page 296 © 2000 Jayson B. Doolittle
Illustration on page 322 © 2000 Justin Phillips
Illustration on page 387 © 2000 Troy Connors
Illustration on page 415 © 2000 Katalin Sain
Illustration on page 451 © 2000 Judith Holman

Cover Artwork: © 2000 Bridge Publications, Inc.

ISBN 1-57318-203-6

Library of Congress Catalog Card Number: 84-73270
First Edition Paperback 10 9 8 7 6 5 4 3 2 1
Printed in the United States of America

CONTENTS

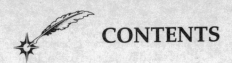

INTRODUCTION by *Algis Budrys* 1

HOME GROWN *William Brown*
Illustrated by Troy Connors 3

LIKE IRON UNICORNS *Paul D. Batteiger*
Illustrated by Samantha Miceli 15

ATLANTIS, OHIO *Mark Siegel*
Illustrated by James T. Johnson 40

SEARCH FOR RESEARCH
by L. Ron Hubbard 104

A CONVERSATION WITH
SCHLIEGELMAN *Dan Barlow*
Illustrated by Deth P. Sun 120

IN ORBITE MEDIEVALI *Toby Buckell*
Illustrated by Yana Yavdoshchook 155

GUILDMASTER *Dan Dysan*
Illustrated by Frank Wu 182

AN ESSAY ON ART
by Judith Holman 243

SKIN SONG *Melissa J. Yuan-Innes*
Illustrated by Jayson B. Doolittle 252

AS THE CROW FLIES *Leslie Claire Walker*
Illustrated by Steelee Faltis 273

Mud and Salt *Michael J. Jasper*
    Illustrated by Jayson B. Doolittle 292

The Basic Basics of Writing
    by Algis Budrys 308

The Quality of Wetness *Ilsa J. Bick*
    Illustrated by Justin Phillips 317

Your Own Hope *Paul E. Martens*
    Illustrated by Troy Connors 383

Pulling Up Roots *Gary Murphy*
    Illustrated by Katalin Sain 410

Fame? Fortune? Chocolate?
    by Michael H. Payne 440

Daimon! Daimon! *Jeff Rutherford*
    Illustrated by Judith Holman 446

L. Ron Hubbard's Writers and Illustrators of
the Future
    by Algis Budrys 493

Contest Information 498

INTRODUCTION

Written by
Algis Budrys

With Volume XVI of *L. Ron Hubbard Presents Writers of the Future*, we have now presented one hundred and ninety-two prize winners in the Contest from which this book derives. We have also presented a fair number of runners-up. There are, as well, a fair number of runners-up we have not presented, who came close, though not quite enough, but who got notes from us . . . which struck so close to home that the recipients promptly sold books, and thus rendered themselves ineligible for the Contest.

Of the nearly two hundred prize winners, one hundred and thirty-odd have gone on to sell stories and books in significant numbers, among them Dave Wolverton, Robert Reed, Nina Kiriki Hoffman, David Zindell, Dean Wesley Smith, K. D. Wentworth and on and on. In other words, L. Ron Hubbard's *Writers of the Future* Contest is an extraordinary success—in fact, the most acclaimed merit competition of its kind in the world.

We are, quite justifiably, proud of that record. But make no mistake—what we did was to find these writers and call public attention to them, but the talent and the hard work of writing were up to the writers and no one else.

Which is the reason for the Contest. L. Ron Hubbard did not labor under the delusion that he created artists out of whole cloth. But he wanted to give talented people a conspicuous place "in their creative efforts to be seen and acknowledged" and he did just that, with outstanding results.

The Contests—two, actually, since we are also talking about L. Ron Hubbard's *Illustrators of the Future* Contest—are open to new and aspiring writers and illustrators, and each offers between $500 and $1,000 to three quarterly winners. Annual winners in each Contest receive a further cash prize of $4,000 . . . along with a prestigious L. Ron Hubbard Gold Award. The judges who assist in achieving the aims of the Contest—as you can see by a glance at the cover of this publication—are among the top names in the field.

In addition to the Contest cash awards, each winner is invited to a week-long Writers' Workshop utilizing articles written by Mr. Hubbard and taught by some of those very names listed on the cover of the book. Then there is the annual awards event and publication in an anthology such as the one you are holding now.

At no time do the entrants pay any money. These Contests are financed by the estate of L. Ron Hubbard. They are not funded from entry fees. And no one but the Contest Administrator knows who the entrants are . . . and she's not talking. Only when the First, Second and Third Prize winners for the quarter are determined does the Contest Administrator reveal the names. That is basically how it works. For more information, see the complete rules published in the back of this book.

And if you want to see the latest in stories and illustrations from the next generation of promising artists, read this fine book.

HOME GROWN

Written by
William Brown

Illustrated by
Troy Connors

About the Author

William Brown has lived all his life in the San Francisco Bay Area. His love for speculative fiction goes as far back as he can remember. He is an active member of Critters, an on-line writers group (www.critters.org), which he credits with giving considerable valuable feedback to "Home Grown."

He has been married five years, and he and his wife have two small children. William works for a software consulting firm, designing and implementing applications for Fortune 500 companies, and he has spoken numerous times at software conventions.

About the Illustrator

Troy Connors lives in Deerfield Beach, Florida, with "the two most wonderful women in the world"—his wife, Sonia, and their daughter, Chloe.

Troy is currently working on a new-concept graphic novel called "Steel Fields." He has been at it for three years, using his talents as an illustrator, inker, painter, designer, publisher and publicist. Overwhelming but insufficient thanks should be given to those who have supported him.

Sprawled in his overstuffed chair, Tyler stared into the garden and watched the naked Dryad suck mold and fungus from the marble statue's flat stomach and heavy breasts, licking her delicate hands and feet. Behind him, Butler softly coughed.

"Yes?" Tyler said, glancing backwards.

"The gene-broker has arrived. He landed his bumblebee in the clearing. Shall I send a wisp to guide him to the house?" Butler asked.

Butler stood tall and impassive in the doorway. Dark eyes stared without blinking. Thick black hair combed straight back offset the pale, flawless skin. Butler wore black slacks and a shapeless gray housecoat.

Tyler nodded and turned away.

"Sir," Butler said, "your guest is not here to purchase the Dryad or myself, is he?"

Tyler turned back and spoke carefully, watching for a reaction. Butler had never asked a question not directly related to the running of the house. "No, you're safe. Don't worry, I'm not going to sell you. He's here to purchase your template, your gene pattern, nothing more."

"And the Dryad, she is safe as well?" Butler pushed on.

Tyler frowned. "Why do you ask?"

"There is a certain familiarity that I find comfortable, sir."

Tyler stared and felt his stomach turn over uneasily. You're not built that way, he thought.

"We can talk about this later. The visitor is very important. So let's keep any feelings quiet for the time being."

Tyler turned back to watch the Dryad finish cleaning the statue of the naked woman. He had purchased the statue as a gift to himself; she stood with her arms at her sides, palms facing out and lifted slightly away from her body. A bowed head obscured her features, but closer one could see a hint of a smile. Straight hair fell midway down her back. Perfect, ample breasts blended into a strong broad chest. Carved muscles appeared to move and slide under the cool, white marble skin.

The Dryad's chameleon skin bleached white to match the statue's marble. Now Tyler could see the Dryad's body and her striking resemblance to the statue.

Climbing off the statue, the Dryad gathered leaves and weeds into a small, neat pile. Tyler strained to spot her, with her chameleon skin now mimicking the garden's greens and browns. Only her slow arm movements, from the yard waste to her mouth, betrayed her presence. She chewed each mouthful thoroughly while staring at the house and windows where Tyler watched.

The idea for the statue had come to him while he watched the Dryad clean the pond near the edge of the landscape. Her skin had rippled against the green water, and, for a brief moment, as her face mimicked the yellow sandstone, Tyler imagined the Dryad was human.

Finished, the Dryad stood next to the statue, leaving herself clearly visible, and cast an unreadable look at the house before vanishing into the landscape.

• • •

Tyler summoned Butler and pulled his cat robe on. The robe flowed over his body, reading the skin's slight bumps and raised hairs. It thickened to cover and warm where he felt chilled.

Butler appeared silently in the doorway.

"Get the house opened up for the day and change into something a bit more formal," Tyler said.

Butler's eyes closed in concentration. Under his silent command, the house's muscles contracted. The curved walls and arched ceilings rippled and peeled away, revealing the house's shimmering membranes and the thin, arching skeleton. After the sheets of skin and muscle folded themselves away, Tyler watched as Butler's jacket lapels broadened and coattails dropped down. A cummerbund oozed out from his stomach. His jacket and pants darkened from light gray to dark and then to a deep, flat black. A tie snaked around his neck and began consuming itself, forming a tight knot. Minutes after the order, Butler stood in a well-fitting tuxedo.

"Anything else, sir?"

Tyler grinned broadly and marveled at his work. I'm going to be rich.

"You must be hungry. Get some ATP from the house teat. Our guest will probably want to see that trick." Adenosine triphosphate, the cell's primary source of energy, was today's trade item. If you could not grow it, you traded for it. A clever designer could build anything with enough ATP and raw materials.

• • •

The gene-broker had facetiously introduced himself as Gene. His heavyset face was still flushed from the short walk up the hill.

Illustrated by Troy Connors

Tyler almost asked why, in an age where biotechnology could sculpt your body, Gene kept himself heavy. Gene laughed at Tyler's stare. "Want to know why I look like this? It's a strict program of benign neglect. Believe me, it's harder than it looks. But enough chitchat. Let's do business.

"Impressive-looking, but what does it do?" Gene asked, as he paced around Butler.

"Everything. Everything within the walls of this house." Tyler waved his arms to indicate his home. "He is the entire house interface. In fact, he is the house. No more awkward chemicals or controls to use. After the house is planted, with the right material and enough energy, the house gives birth."

"Good. Must be energy intensive. Only the rich can afford it, but that's fine with me. We can charge a premium. But what's with the tuxedo?"

"That's why I insisted you come. The shining jewel. The new concept I wanted to show you." Tyler paused and smiled. "Camouflage. Make everything blend together. I used a lot of human gene stock. As far as anyone else is concerned, he is a human servant. All the status but almost no overhead, just the original design."

"Looks human." Gene stepped closer and shut his eyes. He inhaled deeply. "Good, even smells human. Ought to fool most people. But you said there were two things to show me."

"Come outside, I'll show you the next step."

● ● ●

When Tyler called for the Dryad, she peered around the broad redwood tree. Her deep, green eyes were surrounded by skin colored a dark reddish brown resembling the tree bark.

"Come out," Tyler called. He then turned to his guest. "She's skittish. That's part of the camouflage. Keeps her out of sight."

Slowly, the Dryad emerged from her hiding place. Standing against the tree, one side of her body blended into the tree's rough reddish bark. The other matched the flickering golden greens of the crackle bush behind her.

"Incredible." Gene's voice was barely audible. He took three quick steps toward her.

The Dryad trembled and her eyes flickered toward Tyler, who paced behind Gene.

"Timid thing," Gene said and held his hand out to her. "Here, step away from the tree.

"She's amazing," Gene said, as the browns faded and her torso flushed with the greens and golds behind her. "Strong as hell," he remarked, studying her broad shoulders, muscled arms and legs. Gene ignored both Dryad's and Tyler's flinch as he caressed her right breast, which mimicked his skin color, revealing a faint pink nipple.

"A nipple?" Gene squatted down and forced the Dryad's legs apart. He stroked her trembling thigh. "Hairless, but seems functional. Can she reproduce?"

"Yes, with the right chemicals and conditions. Please don't do that. It . . . it bothers her."

Gene wiped his hand on the grass. "You're being awfully protective of your creations. I think our friend is too," Gene said, glancing backwards at the house.

Tyler turned. Butler stood at the door, watching them with his flat, expressionless eyes.

"If I didn't know better, I'd say he's angry. Looks like he wants to run out here and stop me."

"I told you," Tyler said, focusing on Butler, "he's part of the house. He can't leave it."

"Really. So . . . he can't stop me from doing this."

"I said stop it. Leave her alone." The Dryad backed away until she pressed up against the tree. "I may need to do something about Butler," Tyler muttered.

"No," the Dryad croaked out with a long-disused voice.

"She can speak?" Gene asked.

"Damn it, you've scared her." Pause. "Yeah, enough to do her job."

"Let's take her inside then. I'd love to see these two together."

"Can't, the house won't let her in. I wanted to restrict them to their designed roles."

Gene whistled and said, "That's got to be the strangest relationship I've ever heard of."

Following Tyler inside, Gene glanced backwards, but he could not spot the Dryad; inside, Butler was nowhere to be seen.

•••

Tyler glanced at the slip of paper Gene had pushed across the table. His eyes widened and a broad smile broke out across his face.

"Well, then I guess we have a deal." Tyler shoved his hand across the table.

Gene pointedly ignored the offered hand. "Almost. I want the Dryad. For good faith, and customers are going to want to see her." Gene stood, placed his hands flat on the table and stared at Tyler.

"I don't think that would be a good idea. I'm not really ready . . . she's not ready. . . ."

"I know better than that. If you weren't ready, you wouldn't have contacted me. Just bud yourself a new one. And," he paused for emphasis, "if you refuse, I'll blackball you so hard, you'll never market another genotype. You're not established enough to cause problems."

Tyler looked up and said, "That doesn't leave me much of a choice. But look, maybe . . ." Butler stalked from around the corner behind Gene. For a moment their eyes met, and Tyler stopped himself from calling out, then Butler slammed a heavy tree branch against the gene-broker's head.

•••

"That takes care of the broker's bumblebee," Tyler said, carrying his kit of chemicals, hormones, and virus-delivered gene splices. "Scrambled its memory and navigation brain. It will fly until it's tired and crashes someplace."

Butler sat at the table.

"Are you finished with him?" Tyler asked.

"This is the remainder of the gene-broker." Butler took a bloody femur off the table and gnawed at it, gulping down the bone fragments and marrow.

Holding a tiny metal cylinder, Tyler walked behind Butler. "Can't have you going around killing people. Even if they deserve it. Now what am I going to do with you?" Tyler asked. He pressed the cylinder against Butler's atlantooccipital joint where the neck joined the skull.

The chemicals leached into the bloodstream. Soon the voluntary nerves temporarily stopped transmitting signals from the brain. Paralyzed, Butler slumped over the table. His unblinking eyes stared across the room.

"Now to make sure nothing like this ever happens again."

As he shone a small light into Butler's eyes, Tyler heard a rustle behind him. He spun around, dropping the kit of hormones and gene splices. Metal tubes, clear bottles, and tools tumbled from the kit and scattered across the floor. Dryad stood in front of one broad window. The house's reflected light painted her body with twisting shadows.

With Butler incapacitated, the doors would not flex open. Tyler pushed through the house's thick membrane until he stood a few feet from Dryad.

"Brought food from the garden, for dinner. Where is Butler?" Dryad peered into the house. At her feet rested a simple wooden bowl filled with breadfruit, apples, and a small pile of butterfly beef. Just a few of the items that the Dryad's garden supplied to the house.

"Thank you, I'll take it in." Tyler tried to block Dryad's view into the house.

"Butler sick?" Dryad asked.

"No, no, he's fine. He'll be fine."

Dryad nodded and shrugged.

Heat flooded Tyler's chest and groin as Dryad's gesture made her appear even more human. She knelt on one knee and picked up the bowl of food.

"Thanks, I . . . I have a few things to do." He took the bowl from her. Briefly, their hands touched and Tyler flinched as if shocked.

Inside, Tyler placed the small bowl near the spring fed from the house's taproots and took an apple from the bowl. After picking up the spilled kit from the floor, he started to work on Butler.

Deep in thought, Tyler took a bite from the apple. He chewed while preparing a drug to shut down Butler's limbic system, stopping most emotions and sociability. Later, a retroactive gene splice carried on a virus would make the alteration permanent. If other symptoms occurred, he would root those out as well.

While preparing the shot, he noticed that the apple had a bland, flat taste and soft, fibrous flesh. As Tyler picked up the half-eaten apple, he remembered studying the days when fruit spoiled or came tasteless from the store. Pressing his fingers into the apple, he realized the damp flesh resembled a mushroom the way it crumbled and flaked away.

Tyler's heart hammered against his ribs, and he fought for air as his throat clamped shut. His vision faded and his knees buckled forcing him to the floor. Distantly, he felt his bowels and bladder explode. A few inches away, hidden just under a table, was the branch Butler had used to kill the gene-broker.

Suddenly Tyler understood where the branch had come from. Long ago, he had turned the garden over to the Dryad for care. Tyler never dreamed that she might improve his garden, change it. Even fashion weapons.

Tyler arched his back so he could stare out into the garden, Dryad's garden. The Dryad stood close to the house, her skin colors dancing with the reflection of the wind-tousled bushes behind her.

• • •

The house and lands continued on despite losing their master. Three times a day, the Dryad brought food to the house, placing the bowl within Butler's reach. Butler would watch her approach, and they would both stand there for as long as they could, until their instinctive duties called them away. If the house was not spotless or the landscape not quite manicured, there were good reasons for it.

LIKE IRON UNICORNS

Written by
Paul D. Batteiger

Illustrated by
Samantha Miceli

About the Author

Paul D. Batteiger was born in Columbus, Ohio, twenty-seven or so years ago, spent his childhood in York, Pennsylvania, and has lived in the Midwest since the age of thirteen. He left college at twenty-three, without a degree, to pursue writing.

He has been a landscaper, a waiter, a picture framer, a tech writer, a janitor, a bus driver and a bookstore clerk—the usual run of jobs for a writer. He lives in Tulsa with his wife, an iguana, six rats, three cats and seventeen snakes. The genesis of Like Iron Unicorns *was one too many rereadings of Michael Shaara's* The Killer Angels . . . *and a broken word processor.*

About the Illustrator

Samantha Miceli was born in Boston in 1976. She graduated from the Rhode Island School of Design in 1998.

She currently lives in San Francisco, where she is working toward a master of fine arts degree in 3D computer arts.

When he dreams, now, it is always this: He is crouched in a graveyard as he imagines they must be on Earth. The stones stand ranked in the sunset light, the air is cold. And he listens closely, for he hears it coming. The dream is vivid. He does not float; time is steady if slow. He can feel the firmness of the consecrated earth, see every cruel leaf of the holly bush before him, the lowering sun molds everything with a sullen gold.

The sound begins with exquisite softness, so quiet it barely comes across the silence. The footfalls build slowly as they near him. Each carries in its heart a soft, brushing ring like steel whisked over skin. They are not the footsteps of a man. They are hoofbeats. He hunkers lower to the ground, pressing one palm against the stiff brown grass and cold earth for balance. Breath lies slack in his lungs as he stills himself completely. The bushes rattle though there is no wind. His vision distorts in time with his forgotten pulsebeat. And the sun slips below the clouds and lights the sky above with flame.

It steps into view with a grace like the sea. It is all of wrought iron, black and gleaming, its skeletal shape embellished with flanges and curls from some forger's vision. It moves smoothly without joint or seam, unheeding and complete. Its horn is a fluted spiral upon its noble skull, black as the line that cuts night from day.

He watches, unbreathing, unthinking, unmade. It crosses the graveyard before him. Its footfalls are loud, solid, real. He breathes now, astonished. The air curls up before him like smoke. The unicorn's head inclines soundlessly, as though it can hear him. He watches it turn delicately and pass with stately tread through ranks of headstones until it comes to a small white one that lies flat and worn. The sun falls away and suddenly all the world is blue and deep.

The unicorn lifts its slender leg and sets one sharp hoof on the gravestone. He hears the tiny bell-sound of iron on rock, and then the sound grows, courses up through the earth, and finally thunders through him like a bellowing engine. He whips in a vast wind, and wakes.

•••

He wakes in his seat on the shuttle, neck stiff from dozing. The port beside him is covered, and there is a shudder below. They are entering the atmosphere. Falling to Earth from Moscva station 15. He has slept through free-fall, and now Earth's gravity is sinking into him, making him heavy. Accustomed as he is to Mars' lighter pull, the grasp of his birthworld seems strong. The transport from Phobos was kept at a steady 1G for most of the trip inward, but he isn't yet accustomed to it.

Reaccustomed, he thinks almost sadly. It's been fifteen years since he set foot on Earth. It doesn't seem like home anymore, and he isn't even there yet. Beneath him the shuddering stops and there is a slow lurching as the shuttle goes from falling to flying. The pilot comes on the intercom as the port shields slide back to reveal a world of cloud. It will be twenty minutes until they land in Flagstaff. He has never been in the Americas before. Half a day on the bullet train and he will be in Pennsylvania, another place he has never been to.

Looking down at Earth he can see the curve of the horizon arching up into the starry night. The world below seems very large, twice the size of the red world he now calls home. He wonders if that is over, and he wonders why he is really doing this. Does it mean enough to him to spend his whole leave on Earth? He avoided telling his friends where he was going without really knowing why. It was too complicated to explain.

He rubs his eyes, shuts the port cover to close off the earthlight. He pulls the discbook from his bag, enjoying the vinyl smell of newness. The disc he wants is in it, so all he needs to do is open, and read.

•••

"Only in retrospect is it plain that the Armies of the Potomac and Northern Virginia were moving inevitably toward collision in June of 1863. Lee's invasion of the North had carried his forces well into Pennsylvania and the Union army had not yet managed to confront him. Intelligence reports at the time were often extremely poor, relying entirely upon direct observation and hand-delivered messages. General Lee received no information for several days and so was unaware of the proximity of his foe. Almost by accident, the two forces closed in on the small town of Gettysburg, where battle was joined on the first of July.

"To modern sensibility, the armies that fought that war must of necessity seem extraordinarily strange. The high officers on both sides had nearly all attended the military academy of West Point together, and most were at least familiar with the men who opposed them. Many of the generals who faced one another across the battlefield had been friends, and remained so. Congenial reunions of old comrades under flags of truce were far from rare.

Illustrated by Samantha Miceli

"Yet for all this, it was a brutal war. No mercy was shown on the field of battle, both soldiers and officers cut down by snipers and artillery. The toll of dead all the worse for being mourned on both sides of the struggle."

•••

He shuts the book as the shuttle begins its final approach. Air pressure stuffs his ears and he yawns and swallows, blinking. He tries to picture it: the old black-powder rifles spitting great puffs of smoke, the noise and acrid smell. The antique cannon with their roaring and flame, making great clouds of gun smoke for men to march through, bayonets dark at the ends of their rifles. Horses, he thinks, trying to imagine that. Men mounted on horses, brandishing swords. He laughs softly and the man in the next seat glances at him, sees the uniform and the bars of a colonel, looks away.

He grimaces. A sympathizer. He tries to ignore it, but the man is a kind he has come to loathe. One of the soft ones. A fat-waisted man who frowns at the war from a distance and agrees with his friends how terrible it all is, the bloody price of imperialism. David puts his discbook away and folds his hands in his lap, staring at the closed port but not wanting to open it. He is not ashamed of what he is; he will hold his head up and not look away from those who may sneer at him, may call him fascist or worse. He is a soldier of Mars, he is loyal. And he will fight the rebels though many are known to him, and were his friends.

But it is hard, he thinks, remembering Olympus. It is very hard. He remembers the feel of the storm. The pushing and twisting of the thin air. The sky's red light dim and darkened. The rebels attacked in the night, the

dark and the spring dust storm rendering the command
center on the north rim of Olympus Mons' ancient crater
all but blind. He remembers waking in the dark of his
room, hearing the distant thumping of artillery over the
wailing alarms.

They formed up in pitch darkness by the swinging
beams of flashlights. Jerking on their survival suits,
hooking up respirators and IR visors, grabbing weapons
from the racks where they crouched like insects. The
center was running on emergency power only. The main
generators were a torn-open hole. They followed the
muffled sounds of fighting to the surface locks and tried
to prepare. They had no heavy weapon support, no
visibility. The satellites were blinded by the storm and
there would be no intelligence of enemy strength, no
target spotting. They were blind and up against it, hard
and cold.

The outer lock door looked like something dead
under the crawling lights. It was ridged and contoured
and it looked like a rib cage. He could dimly hear it
clatter as it slid up, letting the billows of dust swell
inward on the angry wind. They went to infrared and
could see nothing, no enemy, no threat. The men looked
at him, and he nodded.

The surface of the red planet at night is brutally cold.
Each of the men wore an insulating suit to allow him
to survive the –80°C temperature. The suits were also
designed to mask what body heat did escape, making
infrared spotting much more difficult. With their lights
out, racing over the rocky ground, David's men should
have been all but invisible.

The rebels were waiting. Just as the last men were
dashing from the lock, a ripping wave of gunfire washed
over the division. In the thin air it sounded distant, but
the hot traceries of bullets in infrared were very close.

All around them a net of fire wove itself, seeming to pause here and there to tear men to pieces. The smell of filtered air in his mask burned as he ran, hit the ground screaming, firing. He couldn't see anything. There was nothing on infrared but fire and darkness. He closed his eyes, breathing hard, shaking.

•••

The woman at the counter looks hard at the silver Maltese cross on his collar as she keys in his credit numbers. He doubts she has ever seen an Olympian Cross before. He blinks at her round face, the tight gray bun, and he wants to tell her what it means. There is no higher honor in the Martian armed forces, but for the Shield of Ares. She slides the rental car keys across the counter and he takes them silently. He hates his uniform, his decorations. He is ashamed to wear them. Or rather, he is ashamed of his pride, which he feels he does not deserve.

He does not know Gettysburg, but the sat-link in the car will take him where he needs to go. He taps in the address he wants and sits back, letting the car run itself in the controlled lane. He doesn't mind going slow. The town looks odd to him; he had not expected it to be modern, which in hindsight is silly. Of course time has not stopped here, nor anywhere.

It is a hot day, and he is sweating. He is surprised it is so warm this far north; he has always thought of Pennsylvania as being cold. It is July, and humid. David rubs the back of his neck and watches the city roll by. So much time. He has been reading so much about this place, about what happened here almost 250 years ago, that he expected to feel some resonance, some echo of the familiar, but there is nothing. Here and there some remnant of the past peers out at the world—an old house, or a dull metal cannon. But they look artificial, without meaning or time, as if they've been pasted on a flat image of a place that never was.

The map in the car tells him he is no more than a block from the graveyard, so he stops and gets out. He wants to approach on foot, to try to feel the time and distance and sworn duty that has brought him here, to this most unlikely of places. He walks under the July sun with his shadow beneath him. There is a little breeze. It is strange for him to not hear the wind bellowing outside. Strange to walk free under the sky without suit or mask. It is a heady feeling. Free.

The graveyard is not disappointing, for all that it is different from his vision. It is larger than he had imagined, and more open to the sky. The stones do stand in clean rows, but there are no bushes or trees among them. The grass is even and very green. From where he stands he can see that there are buildings on all sides of the graveyard, and he is surprised to find himself saddened. Once this place was on an open hill beside a great battlefield. Now it is surrounded—cut off from the strength of its origin, its reason. He walks quietly among the graves and reads the names on the stones. There are people here from many different times. This may have begun as a war cemetery, but it grew from what it was to encompass many things. He crunches a leaf underfoot and wonders if that means something. For the first time since landing he puts a hand in his pocket and touches the piece of paper there. On that paper is a number. If he calls it he will speak to a man who can make him disappear. If he pays the price that is asked he will never have to return to the war. David Shah will drop from sight and fight no more forever.

At the north end of the cemetery is a large stone monument to the fallen soldiers; when he steps around it he sees the woman coming and they nearly collide. She has been crying. Her eyes are red and swollen, and she holds one hand curled in front of her mouth. She almost does not see him and flinches away when she does. He holds out his hands as if to steady her, stepping back to show he means no harm. She wipes at her face and sniffs loudly. He wants to turn away and give her privacy. But she is small and pretty in a gentle way that draws his eyes.

"I'm sorry," she says, swiping under her nose with a ragged tissue.

"No, no," he says, wishing there were something meaningful for him to say. Her obvious hurt has moved him. He struggles with his words. "I should—well, I mean . . . I wasn't watching where I was going."

"No, it's . . ." she sniffs again, "it's all right." She looks away. "I was just . . ." Her face begins to crumple again and she visibly controls herself, wrenching her eyes away from whatever they saw. "I was just . . ." She shakes her head, and he sees that she is alone, and does not wish to be.

"I'm David." He says it softly, so as not to frighten. A bird sings vividly somewhere behind her. She looks at his outstretched hand for long heartbeats of time before she pockets the wadded tissue and takes it. Her hand is warm and slightly damp, and very small. He smiles at her, and she almost smiles back. She has straight brown hair and dark eyes. She is very thin.

"I'm Marcia." She sniffs again and they both laugh lightly at the sound.

• • •

Lunch is a pair of roast-beef sandwiches in a small café they find well away from the graveyard. She eats quietly and does not mention his uniform. As she eats she slowly regains her composure, so that soon she looks him in the eye with only a trace of her earlier nervousness. He eats faster than she, accustomed to a mess hall, so he stirs his coffee and watches her eat.

"What brings you to Earth?" she asks between bites and he drops his eyes. Of course she has noticed his uniform. He should have changed before he came. She smiles at his hesitation. "Family?"

He shakes his head. "I'm doing a . . . favor, I guess. For a friend." He stops her other questions with one of his own. "What about you?" He winces at the oafishness of his tone.

She looks away. "My . . . my husband died a year ago tomorrow. I was coming to see him." She works her lips as she controls a little sob. "It's just been hard for me. . . ."

He waves her off. "Hell, I'm sorry. I didn't mean to—shit." He ducks his head into one palm and rubs at his scalp. He feels like an asshole.

"He died last year in Anatolia. He was with the forensic unit investigating the war crimes." She speaks as if she has not heard him. "They were always finding land mines left over from the war. He called them care packages." She laughs but her eyes are bright. "I guess he wasn't careful enough." She shakes her head. "I'm sorry. I shouldn't ramble."

"No, no. I'm sorry. I shouldn't have asked." He wants to look at her, but he's embarrassed to.

"I'm glad you did. I want to talk about it." She smiles. "It seems like I think about him more now he's gone." Another bite of her sandwich. "Who did you come to see?"

"I . . ." Now that he has to talk about it, it seems dreadfully thin. A poor excuse for all the trouble. He sips his coffee, laughs as if at himself. "Oliver Wilcott. I'm here to put a bottle of rum and a Bible on the grave of Oliver Wilcott." He meets her gaze as if daring her to laugh at him. "He died here on the second of July at the battle of Gettysburg. On a hill called Little Round Top."

She looks puzzled, her gaze slips sideways and she watches a waiter bus the next table over. "Oh. Was he an ancestor of yours?"

David folds his arms. "Nope, no relation. A friend of mine asked me to do it for him. It's a tradition in his family, even though he's no relation either. I guess it's been passed down from person to person ever since the battle—to come here every year and do this." He snorts. "Kind of silly, huh?"

"What about your friend; why isn't he here?" She is nibbling at her sandwich, not looking at him.

David clenches his hands in his lap, staring hard at the smooth white table. "He can't do it anymore. He's gone." He tries not to remember, but it does not help.

●●●

He remembers lying in the dust, seeing nothing but the red lightning of gunfire. They were pinned down and helpless. He rolled left to get better cover. The rebels were firing from above, on the ridge. He could not see their heat. Distantly there was the shudder of explosions. In the thin Martian air sound does not carry far; they were close to the attack point. He could hear nothing over his radio but screaming. Pain, fury. He turned on his back and fired at the ridge, watching the jittering bright needle trace across the barely visible rock

face twenty meters up. The answering fire sprayed
down around him. Dust churned up and rocks split
open. He dug his feet into the shifting sand, crabbing
backward frantically. He screamed and kept firing
blind, willing the bullets to strike. His rifle shook in his
hands as he emptied it. A large rock sheltered him from
the attack. He was shaking unstoppably, breathing in
huge gasps. His teeth chattered and he could not hold
his rifle. He felt so cold he thought he must be dying. His
last two fingers on each hand were numb and tingling.
He lay mashed against the stone, unable to draw even
an inch away from it. Through the earth he felt the
vibration of the approaching ground transports. His
squadron was cut to pieces; the lock was unprotected.
Olympus was wide open. The rebels were rolling in, and
he was all alone.

● ● ●

When he dreams this time, all is still. He stands in the
cemetery of his mind and looks up at the unicorn. It
stands atop the low white gravestone and it is as utterly
still as if it had never moved. There is snow on the
ground and he can hear it crunch softly beneath his feet
as he turns slowly in a circle, eyes wide, for he hears
them coming.

There is a trembling time of waiting, with nothing
but the sound. It comes from all sides. A soft pattering,
like rain, but made of iron. His hands are cold. The
breath in his chest billows out in clouds of white. The
sky is gray and low. And when the first of them steps
into sight it makes him shiver. The branches of holly part
and they step through, as stately and full of grace as
their kindred upon the white stone. Black unicorns of

iron and stillness that march nonetheless. Slowly. In their numbers they have an aura of forbidding that one alone did not possess. There is menace in them. Purpose in their inexorable tread, dark cloven hooves touching lightly the ground and leaving no trace.

They are all around him. He turns and turns but there is no escape, no break in the ordered precision of their advance. Their horns are stark against the gray light. Bayonets in a sea that washes toward him without pause. Slowly, they continue. Stopping here and there to take sentinel upon a stone-marked grave. But the others come onward and he shrinks from them, cowers down, arms crossed over his head. He waits without breathing, in the timelessness of dream, for the touch of a horn.

• • •

He wakes in the darkness of the hotel room and does not know where he is. He twists and looks at the clock and for long moments the numbers have no meaning for him. Beside him in the dark, Marcia stirs and he knows himself again. The world falls into place and he sighs, sinking back into the pillow. He waits to see if she will wake, but she makes no sound. He tries to get comfortable without moving too much.

He does not know how he feels about sleeping with her. It had been so long since he'd even had sex that he had almost forgotten who she was while they coupled; he had been lost in the sensations, the heady closeness with another human being, the smell of her. When it was over she had been quiet and he'd almost left, feeling like an intruder. But they'd slept, without touching, as if alone. He wants to leave now but doesn't, not wanting her to think poorly of him when she wakes. It will be plain enough in the morning if she wants him to go. He knows he is just a substitute for someone else, someone she can't have anymore.

He breathes in deeply and lets it out. Good to be here, he thinks. It is good to be in bed with a pretty woman. Good not to be alone. He thinks on these things and tries to be content for the moment. Tomorrow there will be other things to think on, other things to remember. But not now. No, not now.

●●●

The battlefield looks very different than what he has been envisioning. It is larger, and more open, and filled with so many memorials and monuments that it almost seems like a cemetery itself. He looks at the cheap paper map in his hand and tries to relate it to what he is seeing, but he cannot. It is an alien place to him, separate from everything he knows. He can see vultures circling on the other side of Little Round Top, holding their black wings in wide V's. He wonders what is dead over there. There would have been more of them, on that day. The sky would have been filled with scavengers and smoke.

This flat-topped, rocky hill was the extreme flank of the Federal line. Some of the bloodiest fighting of that long-ago war took place on the far side of this mound of earth. He stares at it, wanting to see the smoke, the little fires of rifles being discharged, the dark tide of gray men swarming across the place where a peach orchard once stood, to attack an impossible position. What were they thinking? An uphill march on an entrenched position, with no such thing as air support or even accurate artillery. General Lee must have been a bloodthirsty madman.

He sits on a low stone and listens to the starlings. The fleshy smell of dogwoods drifts uphill to where he ponders a distant day of slaughter. His discbook is in his pocket. He opens it, and reads.

•••

"On July second, the second day of the battle, Lee ordered a general assault upon the western flank of the Federal army. The forces of his trusted second, General James Longstreet, moved south along the Union line and attacked fortified positions at Devil's Den and Little Round Top. It was intended that a feint on the eastern flank would draw reinforcements and supply in that direction, thus allowing Longstreet to smash through and flank the Union army, forcing them to retreat or even into open rout.

"Bad timing certainly played a part in the failure of this en échelon attack, but perhaps the deciding factor was the determination and courage of the Federal troops holding the crucial hilltop positions. Outnumbered and, by afternoon, desperately short of ammunition, the Union soldiers fought off wave after wave of rebel troops. Of especial note was the action of a Colonel Chamberlain, of the 20th Maine Regiment. Out of ammunition and in danger of being overrun, Col. Chamberlain ordered a bayonet charge by his decimated regiment and succeeded in routing the attackers and driving them back down the hill in disarray. He captured five hundred enemy prisoners without firing a single shot. Afterward, he was awarded the Congressional Medal of Honor for what President Lincoln termed his `unswerving and leonine courage in the face of the enemy.'"

•••

He remembers the rumble in the Martian soil beneath him as the ground assault vehicles closed in. His rifle was empty. His regiment was gone; hiding like him or torn open and frozen in the red sand. The radio in his ear was screaming static-laced questions and orders from the command center. They were blind and outflanked with the chain of command collapsing all around them. No one was reporting in, no one knew what was happening, except him. Once the rebels were in the main lock there would be no stopping them. The few men inside had no idea the mountain was about to be breached. They would never know what hit them.

The ground was shuddering. He could hear the thump of artillery very close now. Crimson dust gyred all around him and he had never felt so completely alone, on the edge of the world. He called into his radio, speaking carefully so that he could not be mistaken. "Olympus control. Olympus control. This is Colonel Shah. I have a hard target at zero three one six. Repeat: I have a hard target at zero three one six. Do you copy that?" He was shivering. It was so damned cold out here!

"We copy, Colonel. What the hell is going on?" The voice was young, almost panicked. Some baby-faced lieutenant. David could almost see him.

"Did you hear me?" He was bellowing over the roar of the wind. "I have a hard target now! Take the shot! Zero three one six. *Now!*" He could see the shadows of the armored troop carriers through the driving dust, their engine signatures bright as day.

"Roger that, Colonel." It was a different voice now, older. "Are you requesting a thunderbolt?"

"Yes!" He rolled on his back and stared up at the invisible sky, wondering if he would see the flash of the orbital laser before he was wiped from the face of the earth. He shouted into the wind, every nerve stretching tight for the final moment. "Yes!" He shouted—he was almost laughing; he was sure he was going to vomit. *"Bring me my thunderbolt!"* The first troops were pouring out of the rebel transports. The doorbusters with their shaped charges and laser cutters. He could barely see their heat ghosts. There was a light. The sky above turned from blowing dust to churning fire and David threw himself flat behind the rock, screaming. And the world burned with light and a thunder, like iron on stone.

•••

It is afternoon now, and he is with Marcia at her husband's grave. It is a modest stone with a Star of David the size of his palm etched on the smooth marble. He stands at an awkward distance while she prays softly in Hebrew. He did not know she was Jewish, and wonders what she would say if she knew his last name ended with an *H* rather than a *W*. He has little of the look of his Palestinian parentage, but the blood between his people and her own is long and bitter. He has already decided he will not say anything. There is no reason to.

She caresses the headstone almost lovingly, running her hands across the polished stone, the careful letters that are still sharp and clear. She asked him to come, to be with her, but he feels out of place. He has a bottle of rum in a plastic sack in his right hand, in his pocket is a real paper Bible—not as easy a thing to find as he had expected. It took him most of the morning. The sun beats down on him and he turns his face up to it, eyes closed. Just after lunch he dialed the secret number in his pocket, listened to it ring twice before hanging up. It made him feel dirty just to try the call. But now, here under the blue sky, he thinks it would be worth anything, any price, to be free.

Marcia begins to cry softly and the way she turns her head away tells him she does not want him to see this, that these tears are not for him. So he turns and steps away without a sound. There are bees humming in the summer light like tiny motes of gold. He paces the rows of graves until he comes to the oldest part of the cemetery, where the identical white stones stand ranked as though for battle. Down the green path he follows, reading each name as he passes it. Samuel Cobb. Joseph Wilson Gray. Louis Garret. Nathaniel Porter. Oliver J. Wilcott. Here.

There are no photographs of this man, nothing remains of who he was or what he did; except that on the second day of July in 1863 he charged down a hill called Little Round Top under the command of a man named Chamberlain, who won the Congressional Medal of Honor. Oliver J. Wilcott received nothing but this tiny plot of ground, with a stone to mark it. David takes out the bottle of rum and sets it gently in the grass, leaning it against the headstone so it will not fall. He puts the Bible beside it and stands back up. He wants to say something to the dead man, but would feel ridiculous if he did. So, not knowing what else to do, he salutes. This is important, he thinks. He could not explain the feeling to anyone else, but it gives him pride to be a soldier and do this small thing for another soldier who is long dead. He promises himself he will do this again next year, and the next, every year until there comes a time when he cannot, and must pass it on to another.

•••

There is always a stretched feel of waiting to military hospitals, something purgatorial and expectant. In the weeks after the assault he did little but lie in his bed and think of nothing. General Plath, his C.O., came often to visit him but never seemed to know what to say. He was aware in a vague way that he was a hero, and that people were afraid of him. The blast from the orbital laser had been mostly eaten by the mass of silicate in the lower atmosphere, but the pressure wave from the expanding, superheated air had proven more than destructive enough. The rebel insurgents had been shattered, and no one would be using that part of the Olympus complex for a while.

The rock that David had hid behind so avidly had saved his life, shielding him just enough. Only his left leg and half his ribs had shattered, instead of his whole body. The rest of his regiment was gone except for a handful. No way of telling which had been dead already and which he had killed himself. There was talk of giving him a medal—an Olympian Cross, or even the Shield of Ares—with a half-dozen crimson sashes or so for wounds in the line of duty. The other patients in the ward knew what he had done and looked at him strangely. They wondered what kind of man could knowingly kill his own troops to get at the enemy, what was in this man that could call down a thunderbolt on his own position.

After two months he was well enough to walk, and requested permission to visit the POW ward, where those of his enemies who were not dead lay recovering, awaiting imprisonment. He went in and walked down the long hallway with its bolted doors, looking at the names printed on them. There was only one he knew.

The man's face was half crushed in and twisted by burns, but David still knew him. "Hi, Nate, how's the head?" The small hissings of the machines keeping Nate alive were almost unbearable. The mutilated skull shook gently from side to side. The nurse came in and checked some things, shook his head discreetly at David, and was gone again. David looked at the floor. Nate had been his roommate at the academy, and he wasn't going to make it. How many of the other unnamed dead had been known to him? How many of his own soldiers had he smashed away into nothing? What was left of Nate's red-blond hair was very thin, cut so short it was almost invisible.

There were so many things he had wanted to say, but had not. The reasons why they had come to this would not be found, and would not matter anyway. He sat and watched his friend die, until Nate's one surviving green eye focused blearily and the lopsided mouth made sounds past the hiss of the respirator. "There's somethin' you gotta . . . do for me."

David clasped his hands and felt cold and unfeeling; he flinched for no reason. "What?"

Hiss. Hiss. Hum. "You have . . . to go . . . to Earth. . . ."

•••

He remembers it all from a cold distance, because he cannot stand to remember it too well. When they gave him the medals he was proud, and ashamed of his pride. He sits now in the dark of his own room and stares at the vidscreen without seeing it, the bluish light making his skin look wasted and pale. Tomorrow he will have to go; his leave is almost up. Tomorrow he will have to make the call, or not. He will have to decide.

He does not want to think about that, about going back to Mars, about the war. He had so hoped it would all be over by the time he was out of the hospital, but now the rebels have dug in at Tharsis and the war looks to be long, longer than he can tolerate. All the wounded, all the dead, each face, it seems, a face he knows. The discbook is beside the bed, but he does not want to read it. He doesn't want to know any more about Gettysburg and the battle that made it famous. All it has done is make him see that nothing is different. Brother is still set against brother and friend against friend, and there is no purpose and nothing to show for it but death. And that feeling that came when the sky lit up over his head and fire charged down from the heavens. That feeling.

He wonders how that man Chamberlain felt when he charged down Little Round Top. Did he feel alive when he drew his sword and cried for bayonets? Did he feel alive? David turns off the vid and lies back, staring into the dark, his brain seeming to hum as it grinds against itself. He lies there, seeing the light in his mind's eye. It is this that tears at him: That final moment, when he lay in the red soil and waited to be destroyed, was the most perfect, blazing moment he has ever felt.

•••

The shuttle port has the breathless feeling of a place of movement; no one stays here, everyone is coming or going. He watches the people go by, hurried or slow, and wonders what it is like to be each one. What burdens do they carry? Marcia coughs and he looks down at her. They are both leaving. He has three hours before his ride out of the well; she is boarding an LEO shuttle in ten minutes that will take her back to Haifa.

She has noticed his distraction, misreads it as impatience. "Here," she says. "This is my net address. Call me sometime and let me know how you are." She smiles. "Thanks, David, I'll remember you." It's not true. But she tells it well. He takes the proffered paper and gives her a quick kiss on the cheek.

"I'll drop you a line when I can. If you're here next year I'll see you then." Another lie, a sweet one. Good to think of the two of them meeting here each year—a gentle fantasy. "I won't forget you either," he says, and this, at least, is truth. They say more goodbyes, kiss one more time, and then she is gone and both of them can breathe relief. Now it is over, and neither of them has to pretend to be anything other than what they are.

After a while he goes to a public phone, takes the piece of paper out of his pocket and stares at it. After Olympus he had wondered at his action, trying to decide why he'd done what he'd done. And why it had felt so good to do it. He still does not know, but it doesn't really matter. Rare for a man to have a choice like this; to be able to decide what will happen to him, and how he will be remembered. He crumples the paper into a ball and tosses it away. And when his flight is called he is the first man on it. Because, for him, there is no other way.

• • •

This dream he dreams one final time, and it is this: The cemetery is gone, instead there is a rocky broken hillside where long ago men fought and died for an ideal no one remembers. He stands among the trees and stones and looks uphill through the blowing fog that he sees is not fog, but smoke. There is thunder, and again. He can smell the sting of burning powder and hear the blasts of the cannon deep in his chest. Far away someone screams for bayonets.

He stands so still, unafraid. And in time they come. The shadows slip through the smoke and become real men like himself, in faded blue uniforms with rifles held ready, bayonets like dark horns. There is fear in them, there is sadness, but onward they come. Like iron unicorns, their virtue leading them to slaughter; with eyes set and horns uplifted, free from the possibility of grace.

●●●

David Shah returned to duty with the 9th Legion, Mars Authority Forces, on July 21, 2115, and went on to become the most honored soldier in the Ranger Corps. Decorated for heroism no less than eleven times, he was awarded the Shield of Ares in January of 2116. He died in action at the assault on Tharsis on the fourth of July 2116, two days before the end of the war. His body was never recovered. And so even though his name is one of the highest on the War Memorial, no stone marks his final resting place.

ATLANTIS, OHIO

Written by
Mark Siegel

Illustrated by
James T. Johnson

About the Author

Mark Siegel was born in Buffalo, New York, but has moved a lot since then. He won a BA in political science from Williams College, took a masters in creative writing at the State University of New York in Buffalo, a PhD from the University of Arizona, taught American culture as a visiting professor in Japan, and was elected chairman of the English Department at the University of Wyoming.

This does not touch on his career as a developer in Los Angeles, a publisher, and a lawyer in Phoenix, or his non-fiction writing career, which involves a dozen books and more than a hundred articles. "Atlantis, Ohio," is his first success with fiction.

About the Illustrator

In 1968 James T. Johnson was born in a tent, in the backwoods near Bonanza, Oregon. He spent seven years in the army and works as a mechanic, but his father's love of reading cultivated his own love for science fiction. On reading A Princess of Mars *by Edgar Rice Burroughs, he became enchanted with the cover art. Now he strives to create art as captivating as that first book's cover.*

I was wondering if the end of the world was always so cold and clear, when Lemon shuffled across the deck in his characteristic blind man's crab-walk, his head completely enshrouded in what looked like aluminum foil. I squinted against the antarctic glare as he joined me at the rail, finding and grasping it with only the slightest hesitation. Of course, he could have been peeking out from under the contraption, if he'd ever had eyes to peek with. "Jake? Did you get the tape?"

"How'd you know it was me? My mildew-scented aftershave?" It was standard issue for the entire crew on this glorified salvage scow, but it stank a little different on everyone.

"Notice anything different about me?" Lemon somehow pirouetted without letting go of the rail.

"You're disguised as a TV dinner. Just remember to take the foil off before you climb into the microwave."

"Microwaves, exactly," he chortled. "I can feel a difference already."

"You've probably had a stroke." Tormenting Blind Lemon had been a preoccupation ever since I'd been assigned to nursemaid him on this polar expedition, my punishment for not playing well with others in the Navy hierarchy. Lemon took it in good humor, and got his revenge in other ways.

"This is the place, Jake. I can feel it."

"Sure." The robot probe had confirmed it was *the place* where the *SeaFort*, a Navy Explorer, had sunk into a ring of active volcanoes twelve hundred feet under the sea. But that's not what Lemon meant.

Incessant volcanic activity beneath these waves had created the wickedest currents I'd ever experienced—hell, that I'd ever heard of. The *SeaFort* had been dispatched to this remote shelf in the Antarctic to investigate an inexplicably persistent low-frequency rumble reported by SOSUS, the global network of deep-sea microphones originally developed by Naval Intelligence to track Soviet subs, now used primarily to track geological activity. The perimeter of rushing water they found was a quarter mile thick, with a core strip a few hundred yards across moving at over forty knots and riddled with undercurrents and whirlpools.

This unprecedented oceanic anomaly was the product of a five-mile-wide circle of active underwater volcanoes just a little over a thousand feet down, unusually close to the surface. We'd almost capsized ourselves a dozen times coming across the perimeter. Even as we lay at anchor over an enormous underwater mesa that rose to within a few hundred feet of the surface, our salvage vessel slowly rotated counter-clockwise. It wouldn't make you sick, unless you intentionally stood at the bow and stared out at the glacial landscape.

I'd been staring for about an hour now. The surface was plankton rich and sea life abounded in the un-naturally warm water. Floating pods told us we were anchored above a kelp forest. Dolphins, which shouldn't have been this far south, were constantly underswimming the prow of the *Revelation*, and I'd seen what looked like a couple of small whale surface in the distance just long enough to catch a blow. One or more of the dolphins would stop occasionally to stare up, as if contemplating whether the shiny buttons of my shirt might be edible, or at least fun to play with, if I could be persuaded to fall overboard. The sun was brilliant today, warming the air just a tad as it reflected off the glaciers. The breeze riffled through my open parka, exposing the sidearm I carried, standard issue only to a SEAL. I wondered what kind of fish I could shoot from the bridge.

"Mostly mackerel or big-eyed jack," Blind Lemon said.

"What?" I studied his baked-potato visage for a moment. If you think epicanthic eyelid folds and high cheekbones make someone inscrutable, try staring at tinfoil. "How'd you do that?"

"Atlantean technology," was Lemon's muffled reply.

"Don't go *X-Files* on me, Lemon." *That's* how Lemon got back at me. "Anyway, I'm glad to see your mojo's working. Your Atlantean technology lock on to any freeze-dried sailor brains yet?"

"Can't read dead men," he told me with a metallic rustle of foil.

I sighed. "You're not supposed to say that. You are here because of your proven psychic ability to locate lost airmen. People might believe it even works on lower forms of life, like sailors, but everyone knows there won't be any survivors from the *SeaFort*. Your briefing included the fact that the *SeaFort* was not a sub, right?"

"And why are you really here, Jake?"

"When I was passed over for promotion this time, they mentioned poor people skills. I guess that comes from thinking of them as targets."

Illustrated by James T. Johnson

"Ah, so this is a learning experience for you. I'm your goddamn albatross, O my mariner!" Lemon chuckled and flapped his arms, a sight that would have scared away the most competitive pelican. "Naval Intelligence sent you because of Connor's sub, right?"

"Lemon, you need to stop pestering Lieutenant Connor. As a civilian, you're not even supposed to know about the minisub, much less be lobbying its pilot to scrap his orders and explore where you want him to."

"But he's looking in the wrong places! The voices are right below us! He's looking for sulfur-based life forms thriving around volcanic vents. Hello! Not deep enough! He's looking for an interface with Dark Life where there is none."

Around this time, I was looking to interface with dark beer.

"Jake, you have to get Connor to listen to me. You can tell him you got secret orders from some organization known only by its initials—"

"No!" I needed to disengage before Lemon cornered me, or read my mind, or whatever he did. "Look, Lemon, I'm sorry I've been acting like an asshole."

"That's OK. It's not easy for people to . . . be around me."

"Why? 'Cause you're a hideously ugly geek? Shit, half the guys I started out with in Nam looked worse than you when they went home. I'm acting like an asshole because I'm fifty years old and too stubborn to retire and I'm being fucked over by people I once commanded. It's got nothing to do with you. You're just in the line of fire."

"Forget it. Just tell me you got the tape."

Crewmen were shouting orders as the probe came up over the side of our vessel, but everything seemed orderly enough. The *Revelation* was an ASR, specially built to find and salvage sunken property of the U.S. military, from submarines to satellites. A relatively small ship, a single-decked 250-footer, with a lot of lift-cranes and other topside equipment, there was barely room on deck for our special twenty-foot minisub. Because the Navy did a great deal of underwater charting and, since the regrettable end of the Cold War, often leased out their equipment to civilian ventures, a fleet of ASRs and their double-bodied pontoon-style cousins were busy all over the world. We, however, had one of only two existing minisubs, and Captain Nelson hadn't wanted to jeopardize it in these currents until he first tried the robot probe.

The sea at the center of the volcanic circle was clear as glass except for the swirling business. The nausea effect, unfortunately, seemed to be lost on the blind. Or maybe it was just lost on Lemon. When our Submarine Rescue Ship was being torn in the trough of the current and most of the Navy lifers were retching, praying, or counting life jackets, I'd found Lemon braced against the walls of the forecastle, straining his attention into the wind, intent on some whisper in the wail.

Lemon pulled the hood off his head, pressing his horrible, grinning face into the wind, just as I was. He had no eyes at all, just the briefest indentations under a huge, bulging forehead. "Like a dolphin," he reminded me.

Like a dolphin from hell, I thought. It was a face only a mother could love, and then only if the mother's last name was Pumpkinhead. "Yeah, I have the tape."

• • •

Used to following mental mazes, Lemon could traverse the uniform corridors of the ship better than most sighted sailors. There was only a single level below deck, but when you sleep fifty men, there have to be a lot of similar-looking doors. When Lemon suddenly turned away from the particular cul-de-sac in which our cabins were located, I decided to pretend I didn't know what was up.

"Lemon, that's not the way to our cabins."

"I have a spare room, Jake. Didn't you wonder where I got the microwave helmet?"

"I thought it came free with your white cane from QVC." Of course I was aware of the room. The captain had informed me, and I'd watched Lemon sneak in there more than once. I'd stopped short of breaking in mostly because of my own despondency.

Tapping a security code into the steel door frame, Lemon let us into a locked room filled with computer equipment. I mean filled. I whistled in appreciation.

"The military has the best toys," Lemon confirmed. Sliding his hands in front of him, he set himself into a chair at a computer console with an oversized monitor, flipped it on, and began typing away. The keys emitted a concert of chirps and whistles, his performance evocative of a concert pianist. Occasionally, Lemon would hit what must have been a playback button. Then he listened to the tonal sequence and, if satisfied, entered it.

I had assumed the monitor was for my benefit until Lemon hit another switch and the entire field turned into a video thermogram. Lemon apparently had no difficulty distinguishing the varying degrees of heat with his fingertips as he touched the screen, felt the outlines and grazed over the center, then switched it back to normal visual mode. "Ready?"

"This isn't going to cook the tape, is it?" I inquired as I handed it to him.

"Is this a scornful look?" Lemon twisted up the corners of his mouth and waggled his tongue at me. "We'll run it on normal video first, so the tactually challenged can give me his impression."

We did, but after a few minutes I had to tell him it was pretty poor quality. "The robo started taping just before it was lowered into the water, and that looks normal. But as soon as it got down fifteen or twenty feet, the water started to get real murky."

"Volcanic ash?"

"Don't think so. Looking down from the bow of the ship, the ocean looks clear. You can see the shadows of a kelp forest in some places. But this looks inky, like the robo is dropping through some sort of cloud you can't see from the surface. I think they were able to make out the kelp just enough to keep from getting tangled up, but that's about it."

There was an occasional flicker of fin from an inquisitive fish, rarely enough of it visible for identification, and tangles of kelp, enormous green stalks buoyed along their hundred-foot lengths by coconut-sized pods filled with air. Then there was a sudden jump in the tape, as if robo had hit something, and the camera angle swung wildly, showing a brief jumble of rock, only to be swallowed up again in the cloud and kelp a few seconds later. "We hit the mesa; the camera is all over the place." From that point on, down to the ocean floor, I could barely make out anything. A few hundred feet below the mesa, the water cleared and robo's lights pierced the blackness for maybe thirty feet, great if you liked looking at black water. Then I was looking at the hull of the *SeaFort*, as if we'd been led there on a string.

"There's a big hole punched in the side. It may have been thrown into a glacier by the current. Or maybe the hull breached when it hit bottom. But it's in one piece, sure enough."

"What do you see in the way of sea life?"

"Not much. An occasional shape just out of range. Sea bass, maybe, grouper. Nothing unusual."

"See any sharks?"

"Not a one."

Lemon nodded to himself as if this confirmed something. "What about rock or coral formations? Anything out of the ordinary?"

I reported in the negative. I didn't think coral grew a thousand feet down, but I didn't say anything.

Lemon sighed and sat back in his chair. After a moment he said, "Rewind to where we hit the mesa."

I did as I was told.

"Freeze frame when you get to that `jumble of rock' you mentioned. Any place where there's a clear frame of anything but kelp."

I rewound. "OK, I think I've got something caught in robo's headlights. But it's kind of distant."

"See that enlarge button?" But he went ahead and hit it himself, and the screen divided itself like graph paper. "Use the mouse to select a quadrant, then hit the enlarge button."

"Wow," I said a moment later. "You should see this coral reef. At least I think you'd call it a reef. It's got all kinds of intertwined arches. Looks kind of like . . ." I stopped before I said it.

"A cathedral?"

"Lemon, you have the soul of a poet trapped in the head of Wes Craven's favorite nightmare."

But he wasn't listening to my cruelty. Instead, Lemon was back at his own PC station-cum-calliope making weird music. A minute later, I found myself looking at an archeological dig, and at what at first appeared to be a robot with a pointed head. Actually, it was some kind of pyramid helmet, more of Lemon's eclectic headgear. "*Enchanté*," I remarked, from my limited vocabulary of fashion compliments.

"Never mind Your Hero Astride the Dig," Lemon rebuked me. "What can you make out of the pit itself?"

"Bones and rocks. Leaving out the dirt and some jerk wearing a pyramid on his head."

"How about fossil bones and fossilized coral?"

"You were about to enlarge some part of this for me."

"Right." And he did. First he showed me what looked like the broken remains of a bizarre hollowed-out coral reef. The next image was a fossil reconstruction of what could have been a dolphin with a disproportionately large head.

"Striking resemblance. A Lemon family photo?"

In response, Lemon showed me an artist's reconstruction of the fossil as a dolphin. "It's about twenty feet long."

"How old?"

"Four, five million years old."

"They haven't changed much, have they?"

"As far as we know, bottle-nosed dolphins have been pretty stable for the past ten million years. This one, however, is physically larger, and has a proportionately larger cranial capacity. Probably had some birthing problems, which accounts for their relative scarcity."

"Where'd you get all this shit?"

"A little town in Ohio. See this?" Lemon pianoed up a map of North America, except it wasn't the North America I pledged allegiance to.

"What's that solving the problem of fresh seafood in the Midwest?"

"The Western Interior Cretaceous Seaway. Seventy million years ago, during the Cretaceous period, it divided North America into two landmasses, over the interior of the U.S. between the emerging Rockies and the old, eroding Appalachians. The last of it didn't drain until around three million years ago. In between, glaciers made a pretty good mess of the place. The dolphin civilization was pretty much eradicated."

Lemon was an entertaining SOB, the Quentin Tarrantino of sea salvage. "Civilization, Lemon?"

"Think about it, Jake. Even today, dolphins exhibit complex social behavior. Spinner dolphins control entire harbors with a militia of male dolphins working in formation to keep out sharks. They make our fighter pilots look like kites with tangled strings."

"And ancient dolphins, or at least the Big Head, were smarter? So smart they developed a civilization? So where's the proof? Where are their buildings, their technology?"

"That's what I'm trying to show you." He was back into his archeology file, and brought up an image of the fossilized wreckage from his dig. It was weirdly different from coral formations I had seen before. Much of it was hollowed but not dug out, with shafts of coral forming arches, walls, and nooks. Some of it could have been statuary sculpted by an alien hand, an alien mind. "Our reconstruction makes it out to be about the size of the Colosseum. The coral was coated with some sort of alkaloid we haven't fully identified, but which seems to account for its preservation. The cathedral you're looking at existed entirely underwater, several million years ago."

"So that coral thing, you're telling me it's—what—natural?"

"Absolutely not."

"This thing is built? By dolphins? What did they use for tools?"

Lemon gave one of his shrugs. "Their teeth. They also probably used other breeds of sea animal, especially those that burrowed or secreted various substances. Think it out, Jake. They may have spent hundreds of years constructing it, just as we did some of our cathedrals back in the Renaissance. Maybe it took thousands of years, unless they developed a method for accelerating coral growth. You wanted artifacts, Jake. Well, here it is."

I sighed at the sheer lunacy of it—and then sat bolt upright in my chair. I had virtually forgotten where all this had started.

Lemon must have heard my chair swiveling back to the dive tape. "So, are you looking at a second cathedral, or what?"

"What I'm looking at on the robo tape is a brief fragment of weird-looking reef. Period. I'm not buying into a theory of lost dolphin civilization based on that."

"Don't go Naval Intelligence on me, Jake."

•••

I went back out on deck to purchase joke insurance before giving Lemon's story serious consideration. It was ridiculous, but I was bored. So bored that I thought

I detected the slightest something different in our antarctic surroundings. I was still trying to figure out what it was when there was a lurch.

Nothing apparent loomed over the ship. I looked around to see if we had hit an iceberg. There were no ice cubes on deck, no waltzing socialites or other telltales that we were about to become another *Titanic*. In fact, I began to wonder if I'd imagined the whole thing. If we'd hit anything—

Then I realized what had been wrong. When I'd been on deck earlier, the ship hadn't been rotating, for the first time since we'd entered this circle of fire. Now we were moving again.

I went back to where all the salvage activity was and had a sailor confirm the rotation had in fact stopped during the robot probe descent and had just commenced again. "That's why we bashed into the mesa," he added. "We'd calculated for a pendular movement, and then the rotation stopped on us just a minute or so after she started going down."

"The rotation just stopped?"

He shrugged. "Maybe one of the volcanoes went off," he said with a malicious grin. "The enlisted will be the last to know, sir."

I thought of something else that was suddenly different. "Where are the dolphins?"

"You'd have to ask in the com room, sir. Maybe they're tracking them on sonar." He knew they were, of course, but he was cautious about compromising his informants.

Preparations for the raising, simple as they promised to be, were bustling along. Back in the late sixties, when the Navy had found the twisted and imploded remains of the *Thresher*, they'd been working a mile and a half down. The *Titanic* had been salvaged at two miles. By comparison, raising the *SeaFort* with the minisub was going to be like rolling up one sleeve and reaching into the bottom of a dirty bathtub.

The crowd around the minisub hid a bizarre little machine about twenty feet long, eight feet wide, and ten feet high. It had two large mechanical arms, six feet long but folded up now, giving it the look of a really fat praying mantis with tractor treads on the bottom. Clearly the thing was designed less for diving than for crawling along the ocean floor and poking around with the long-armed pincers. There was just a single tiny port in front and another in each side, but there were numerous stubby indentations and projections which provided various sensory data to the occupants.

At the same time the minisub was being prepared, a crew was assembling the cranes and rigging that were to be used in bringing up the *SeaFort*. Everyone was confident. The seas were calm.

And Lemon was over on the other side of the sub conferring with that innocent young Lieutenant Connor again.

"Captain Walker!" Connor saluted me, and I tried putting him at ease by directing my ire at the man who I knew deserved it.

"Lemon, you're not pretending to give this gentleman orders, are you?" I asked. There were little mechanical fingers on the ends of the robot arms, whirring melodically as they were tested out in three-hundred-sixty-degree spins.

"Jake—"

"Lemon, let's you and I wander your ass away from this top-secret equipment and talk about it."

He said his goodbye to Lieutenant Connor, protesting his innocence until we were out of earshot. "Jake, how could I be spying on Navy hardware when I can't even see?"

"Cut the crap, Lemon. I saw you touching the machine. For all I know, you could have bugged the lieutenant's uniform. Or been scaring the shit out of him with one of your fish stories."

"Would it be so bad if he looked around a little, while he was down there? Took a few soil samples? If this is an ancient ecosystem, even the microorganisms might be worth knowing about—"

"I thought you wanted to talk to dolphins. Why can't you do that from up here? They're not going to be a thousand feet down."

He hesitated for a fraction of a second, a worried expression on his already catastrophic mug. "The thing is, they're not talking to me. Not even the usual chirping stuff. It's like they're scrambling their signals intentionally."

"How would they even have any clue that there was someone up here trying to read them?"

He didn't respond right away.

"Is my little blind buddy holding out on me?" I asked sternly.

"I tried broadcasting," Lemon said finally, when we were settled back at the railing around midship. "I had some phrases in the Old Tongue—that is, what I think was the Old Tongue—that I tried. That's when they started to scramble."

"Whoa. The Old Tongue?"

"Smart animals talk, Jake."

"If they were so smart, what happened to 'em?" I caressed my gun reassuringly.

Blind Lemon wrinkled his snout. I'd tried to spare myself the sight by teaching him to shrug like a sighted person early in our voyage, but he hadn't taken to it. "Let's say the smart ones were geographically limited."

"Like kangaroos in Australia?"

"More like engineers in Silicon Valley. The Western Cretaceous Sea was probably a pretty nifty place for smart sea mammals: temperate climate, protection from extreme ocean weather, plenty of inlets and coastline."

"More easily defensible," I added before I could stop myself. Then I frowned.

Lemon apparently caught the frown vibes and smiled. "More easily cut off, when an ice age or a big quake hits and the Sierras pop up out of nowhere. Dolphins can't cross even a narrow land bridge. The population was trapped. Then, over the course of hundreds of thousands of years, the sea dried up, extinguishing the subspecies, except for a handful that had fled earlier. Then, millennia later, disease or some new predator—man, for instance—got what was left of them."

"So, a few million years ago, these rare big-headed dolphins were running the show, but then suddenly became extinct from some disease?"

"Why not? Neanderthal may have been superior to Cro-Magnon in every way except his ability to resist a certain disease."

"Lemon, don't you think this is pretty far-fetched? You're just piling speculation on top of speculation."

Lemon leaned toward me confidentially. If he'd had eyes, he would have been staring into my lapel. "How do you think I found that fossil big-head dolphin?"

"Go ahead and goof on me."

"A dolphin told me. While I was out in the North Atlantic, on one of your rescue missions."

"I thought you only got beeps and chirps."

"Except from this Elder."

"Right. The Elder." Lemon tried to fill my silence with one of his grotesque displays of facial and body language. "Maybe what you showed me in that excavation is a single mutant whale and the remains of a coincidentally unusual coral reef. Or maybe not even that; maybe just some graphics you doctored for my benefit? Lemon, you made this whole goddamn thing up for some other nefarious purpose, didn't you?"

"You didn't let me get to the best part, Jake!" Lemon laughed.

"What's that?"

"You were supposed to ask me the name of the place we excavated."

"The name of the lost dolphin kingdom?"

"Atlantis, Ohio." Lemon snorted and moved off toward the lower deck. It was a minute or two before I realized that he'd successfully evaded my questions about his interest in the minisub.

Whatever else Lemon was accomplishing, he was making me nervous. I just hadn't admitted it until I found myself in the communications center watching the remote video of the minisub's descent.

At first the water turned cloudy, just as it had for the robo; but when the craft changed course, the ocean suddenly cleared, and the remote camera treated us to a view of fleeing flashes. "Look like squid," Lieutenant Connor's voice advised as the sub swung back under the *Revelation* to avoid stretching out the salvage cables it was guiding down. "There must have been a crowd of them around the boat, attracted to our leavings."

"Bullshit," I found myself announcing to no one in particular. "The robo's too big to eat. Why would they follow it down two hundred feet, instead of just squirting and fleeing?"

To avoid tangling its lines, the sub stayed clear of the kelp forest surrounding the mesa. The video feed switched perspective every few minutes, alternating at irregular intervals between at least four different cameras set around the sub. Occasionally we would get a glimpse of a larger fish or a dolphin on the fringe of the sub's light perimeter, but even our bright lights created no more than twenty yards of real visibility.

I watched the initial sighting of the *SeaFort* and a few moments of the laborious hookup operation. The sub was using its extension claws to secure the cables to various parts of the sunken ship, but apparently didn't need to blast anything out of the way.

When the sub began its ascent, the captain appeared in the com room to take a report on the procedure. Suddenly there was a shout, both from the sub crew and the com operators. Everyone rushed forward. There was static in the video feed, clearing rapidly, except for one of the cameras that was apparently no longer functioning. Someone in the com room was shouting at the sonar man: "What was that? What have you got?"

"Looks like a small whale," sonar reported. "It came in fast from behind the mesa, and it's headed back there now. I think you scared it off."

"Then it's mutual," Connor responded from the sub, sounding a bit relieved. "That sucker packs a wallop."

"Probably territorial," a self-appointed expert offered from the back of the room.

"I just hope this isn't mating season," Connor responded. I imagined him smiling.

There was no leakage. Apparently the crew's reaction had resulted more from surprise than any real threat; but whatever else the attack had accomplished,

it took away any desire the sub crew had for unsched-
uled exploration of the mesa, which I imagined had been
Lemon's purpose in talking to Connor earlier that day.
Connor surfaced quickly and docked alongside the
Revelation, in case the sub was needed during the raising
operation scheduled for the following day.

• • •

Nothing about the incident was deemed worthy of
delaying the raising of the *SeaFort.* The sub hull was
tough stuff indeed, and the damaged camera, which had
protruded only slightly, probably could have been re-
paired if they hadn't had a replacement ready to drop in.
I did manage to borrow the tape from the damaged
camera, which I immediately smuggled down to Lemon's
dungeon laboratory-cum-Radio Shack.

"What kept you?" Lemon grimaced. Although I
hadn't said a word to him and as far as I knew there was
no reason anyone else would have reported the whale
attack to him, he had all his machines fired up and his
translator programs loaded.

"Laws of space and time," I replied. "Unlike you, I'm
bounded by them."

"You've got to stop thinking like a government
employee, Jake."

It was simple to run the video tape backwards from
the moment the camera had gone out, in order to get a
glimpse of what had done the damage. Of course, it
would have been nice if the monster had swum straight
into the camera from a distance instead of coming down
on the sub from above in a side-swiping attack, and for
a moment I thought Lemon was going to send me back
down to the sub to purloin the rest of the videos from its

other cameras. But eventually we isolated a couple of pretty clear frames in which part of the beast was within the light perimeter and not so close as to be blotting out its own shape.

"If that's a whale, I'm Captain Fucking Crunch."

Lemon played his hands across the thermal display, that ghastly smile cracking his jaw line. "As long as you're down here, let me show you something else we found in the dig." It turned out to be another of his artistic recreations rendered over skeletal remains. The thing was not an ocean creature I'd ever seen. It looked more like a torpedo with teeth.

"What the hell is that?"

"Lemonoryx. Your basic antishark weapon."

"Let me guess: you got to name it. It's the only one ever found. The question is, was it ever found anywhere but on this computer?"

"A confirm on the only identifiable skeleton guess. So thirty feet may not even be its maximum size. Look, Jake, have you done any research at all on deep-sea recovery? Every time they send that little sub down a couple miles to volcanic rifts, they find completely isolated colonies of life, some of such primitive variety that we thought they'd been extinct for millions of years. And they find new species, things that haven't evolved anywhere else."

"Lemon, you're talking about bacteria, tubeworms, shit like that. And at two miles, you're talking about a completely isolated ecosystem, because nothing can leave the volcanic area without freezing to death. This thing you're showing me here is a highly evolved mammal. It can't hide down there. It has to breathe."

Lemon smirked like a gargoyle who's just tongue-snatched a pigeon off his own upper lip. I'd fallen into his little logic trap. "You're absolutely right. The reason you've never heard of the antishark is that it has no evolutionary history. Usually a new species like this one would have evolved over millions of years, leaving some sort of fossil record. An elongated killer whale in one geological strata. A million years later, maybe we'd see this recession in the dorsal fin or that peculiar cranial formation. A million years after that, maybe a nearly complete prototype. But this thing seems to have appeared out of geological thin air."

"So probably it's a random mutation, or something like that, not a real species."

"Or an antishark mammal developed by dolphin eugenics. They could have done it over a few hundred or a thousand years, with a very controlled breeding program, which would also explain why there were only a few of them."

"Dolphin eugenics? Lemon, there is no evidence of a dolphin civilization."

"This is the only kind of evidence there'd be, Jake! What are they going to use buildings for? To stay out of the rain? And how could they manipulate tools without digits? Think about what dolphins need, and what they could do better to meet those needs."

"Food. Protection." I shrugged and rolled my eyes, putting one over on the blind man.

"Let's suppose that during the Pleistocene, when most of the smaller sea game on which dolphins now feed became prevalent and many of their larger predators died off, these big-brained dolphins were active in both areas. You think that's a coincidence?"

"I've heard the same argument made for twenty-four beers in a case, twenty-four hours in a day."

"You at least can't rule out the possibility that they were practicing husbandry and had made some advancements in self-defense. Simple genetic selection, making sure specific schools interbred and that others were destroyed."

"Too bad you can't find a live shark-killer and just ask it."

Lemon sighed apologetically. "I don't expect to. There probably haven't been any sharks on this mesa for a million years, so there wouldn't be much use for the antishark."

"There isn't a square foot of habitable ocean anywhere that's shark-free for more than five minutes."

"My guess is this cylinder of water has been completely isolated for millions of years. Before that, the big-brained dolphins had chosen this site for breeding experiments because of its isolation. And since they became extinct and the current worsened because of some natural cataclysm, nothing has gotten in or out. So no sharks."

"Bullshit."

Lemon's smile was pure Halloween. "Have you seen any sharks in these waters?"

"No, but that only means I haven't seen them."

"And neither has anyone else. And you won't."

"Lemon, the whole scenario is impossible. Volcanoes don't erupt continually for a million years. This place can't have been isolated for that long."

"What about a series of volcanic vents sitting over the equivalent of a south magnetic pole, so that the forces effecting eruption—movement in the tectonic plates, changes in the earth's magnetic field—are uniquely stable?"

"My only degree is in shooting people, with some postgraduate work in road rage. But from that, I can tell you what's absent here is common sense."

"The sharks are absent. You know that."

"Maybe the thing that hit the sub was some kind of shark."

"So now you're a marine biologist," Lemon chuckled. "Get any tissue samples off the side of the sub?"

"You're telling me that if I had, you could analyze them?"

With uncharacteristic modesty, Lemon admitted he could not. "But when we get back, I could have it done."

I sighed. "They probably hosed the thing down already. You know how the Navy is about hosing things down."

"They're very neat," Lemon agreed. "But probably they didn't hose down the camera they replaced, and this thing smacked right into it."

"So you want me to go back down there and break into a top-secret vehicle and steal a classified piece of equipment so that maybe, sometime in the future, you might be able to analyze a piece of whale blubber?"

"You have to take the video tape back anyway," Lemon pointed out. "Pleeeeaaase, Jake! They're going to raise the ship tomorrow and then we'll leave, and I won't have a single goddamn piece of physical evidence to prove what we both know is going on here. Without it, I'll never be able to get the funding for a return trip."

I sighed and picked up Lemon's tinfoil hat and put it over my own head. It was dark and hot and made my hair stand on end.

"What are you doing?" he asked suddenly at my silence.

"I'm trying to read my own mind," I said. "I think I'm going nuts."

•••

As luck would have it, I did not have to get myself thrown in the brig to get Lemon's tissue sample. Lieutenant Connor was talking to a security guard at the head of the gangway to the sub, and when I offered him the tape and explained what I wanted, he invited me down into the heavily insulated seven-foot ball that amounted to crew space.

He was a lonely guy, common in the Navy, and wanted to chat about his family. I pretended to empathize as best I could while we took some pretty good-looking scrapings off the camera lens, which had been stowed in a sealed bag. But then came the inevitable question: What about me? No wife? No kids, parents, or friends?

"I've got Lemon. Who needs friends?"

"He must be awfully lonely," Connor supposed. "Imagine going through life looking like that."

I shrugged. The sub made me feel like I was in my own head talking about myself. In constant danger of destroying valuable (and top-secret) stuff with my skull, I hunched around with my knees bent, trying not to touch either of the walls that were constantly at my elbows.

"It looks more complicated than it is," Connor assured me good-naturedly. "Most of these dials are exploratory measurement readouts. Sonar. Video. There's a laser sighting system that will recreate a virtual-visual of your surroundings more than ten times further out than you can see with the lights. We even monitor radioactivity. You actually drive the thing pretty much like a tractor. Forward, reverse, digging speed. Up, down. Here are the grips for the mechanical arms. Look out for that doomsday button over there."

"You have a self-destruct on this thing?"

Connor shrugged. "Don't want it to fall into enemy hands."

"What's that console back there, under the porthole?"

Connor turned with me, and even managed to squeeze past to a panel that was completely locked down.

"Laser cannon, technically for undersea excavation, but it has a pretty high range. You could excavate a whole damn mountain with it. Or bore through twenty-four-inch steel plate."

I was about to ask him the next question he wanted to hear, when suddenly he jumped back right into my arms.

"Jesus Christ!"

It wasn't Jesus having taken a misstep while out walking on the water, but a pretty good-sized fish eye, magnified enormously, staring in the convex porthole at us.

Connor let out a little laugh. "Sorry, Captain. It's just a dolphin."

"Looks like it," I said. Its eye was clear and very, very cold.

• • •

The raising commenced on schedule the following morning. The cranes hummed gigantically, the lines tightened a foot at a time, then, it seemed, an inch at a time until they were taut and straining.

Lemon accompanied me to the com room to eavesdrop on the process, making occasional inquiries of the sonar man as to fishy activity in the area. There seemed to be none of that either, beyond the usual dolphins underswimming the *Revelation*.

"I don't like it," Lemon informed me quietly. "We should stop this thing and send the sub down again."

"You don't like it because it means we'll be out of here soon and you didn't get as much exploratory data as you'd hoped. Everything's going like it's supposed to. The hull of the *SeaFort* is holding, the lines are holding, she'll be on the surface in an hour, and then we can patch and refloat her." How they were going to get her through the current was another matter, but not really my concern.

"No! Listen, Jake, why isn't there more aquatic activity around the rising hull? The dolphins should be curious as hell—"

"Forget it, Lemon. I'm not going to help you sabotage the raising so you can have the sub go down again."

In the end, when the *SeaFort* broke the surface to cheers, I agreed to accompany the repair crew that was going over to patch the hull, lace the already visible deck with inflatable pontoons, and pump out the ship—and to see if I could salvage any specimens for our blind psychobiologist.

It was a welcome relief to put on the tank, heavy-duty dry suit, spear gun, and the rest of my gear. Although the water outside the five-mile Circle of Fire was better suited to a snowsuit and ice pick, I was looking at what was for the ocean a relatively warm sixtyish degrees Fahrenheit. I'd surfed in colder, and my muscles ached for the opportunity to finally do more than hold up my uniform.

A crew of ten swung over to the deck of the *SeaFort* on crane lines before descending down the sides of the ship to inflate pontoons and install pumping equipment in the holds that still might be airtight. When these were dry, the *Revelation* would be able to lift the *SeaFort* a little more, and we would repeat the process until the rip in the hull could be sealed completely and the sunken ship floated once again. A couple of the ten men went down to the rip immediately to measure the work ahead and cut off jagged bits with underwater torches. I started out sloshing my way through the six inches of water on the top deck, looking for stairs that would take me below into the flooded compartments that might contain Lemon's specimen.

The deck itself was surprisingly free of material. I had expected crustaceans, if nothing else, but even these were scarce; so I stuck my regulator in place and moved down belowdecks, into the galleys. There I had a little better luck, spearing an odd-looking sea bass in the thirty-pound range. It was so slow moving and meaty that it was difficult to imagine how it could survive predators of any size. I ignored everything I recognized as mundane, but also managed to sample-bag a long green thing the likes of which I'd never seen before. It was spongelike, somewhere between flora and fauna, but at least it didn't bite, strangle, or poison.

I was down for less than twenty minutes. But when I surfaced, the first thing I noticed was that the activity on the deck of the *Revelation* had changed considerably. Before my descent, there had been a few casual observers lining the deck. Now a dozen men, some of them with hand-held communication devices, were straining over the rails, trying to peer down into the water. Only our crew leader was outfitted with a regular radio, the other divers only requiring emergency beepers for sudden location and retrieval purposes. Five of the repair crew were standing on the foredeck, next to the crane line, and I shut off my regulator and dragged my catch over to them.

"What's up?"

"Smith and Shavers—the two men who went down to the hold—haven't resurfaced. The beepers aren't functioning. We sent another man down after them a few minutes ago, and he hasn't come back up either. The captain ordered everyone else back up here until the sub can take a look, but two of the men installing the air pump in Hold Four haven't shown yet. I beeped them, but got no response."

"What's the sub going to do? We're only talking about twenty feet below the surface. . . ." But I knew the captain was right.

We were in an emergency drill. "How much air do they have?"

"Another twenty minutes. But our orders are to stay clear, sir."

"Right. How do I get to Hold Four? The sub can't get in there." I dropped my specimen on the deck next to him and was back down into the galleys, looking for a hatch to Hold Four—which happened to be right next to the cargo bay that had been torn open in the wreck.

It's hard to proceed in complete silence while you're blowing bubbles, so I told myself *that* was why I was holding my breath. The submerged hallways were barely wide enough for a man to swim down with his spear gun in front of him, so I was hoping I wouldn't turn a corner and accidentally impale an absent-minded sailor, struggling to finish up his pump installation. Some of the doors lining the corridor were open, some were closed. I closed the ones that were open as I passed. Maybe it didn't make sense, but I wasn't about to be flanked by anything lurking inside a supposedly vacant room. This went on until I reached a door that couldn't be closed, because it had been broken in.

I was about ten feet from the end of the corridor, which I expected to branch off immediately into Hold Four; where I expected to find two guys connecting a stubborn pump—where I should have expected to find two guys connecting a stubborn pump.

Of course, the door could have been broken in by a panicked seaman when the *SeaFort* went down. But why would it have been broken in rather than out?

And why, with the entire crew of the *SeaFort* missing, hadn't I come across a single dead body so far?

I pressed my back against the wall opposite the open door and brought myself even with the opening, spear gun pointed straight at the darkness.

Movement. Just enough of a flash so that I had no idea if it was another fatty sea bass or Moby Dick having crammed himself into the cabin like in that Marx Brothers' movie. And a sound.

It was the pump. It was working, slowly, just around the corner, but they had gotten it up and running. With a sigh of relief, I slid around the corner.

The pump was there, and operative, but the divers weren't. I was thinking they had gone up on deck through the rear stairwell while I was coming down the front, when I saw the thing I suddenly knew was a piece of a man bobbing up in the corner of the hallway.

My gag reflex on overdrive, I spun back around in the direction of the open door—and then dove gun-first at the shape that was emerging from it. Surprised by my aggression, the enormous eel-like head with extruding fangs retreated into the gloom, and I was by it, swimming on back with the gun pointed behind me at the door. Halfway down the hall, the head pushed out again, wicked-toothed jaws that could have severed a horse's head from its body, an enormous killing machine being pushed toward me on an elongated, snakelike body. I shot the fucker right in the neck, then dropped the gun and swam for my life without waiting to see how badly it had been hurt.

•••

Pandemonium was breaking loose on the deck of the *Revelation;* controlled, military pandemonium, but the real thing, nevertheless. I was the last one up the crane line, the others already having evacuated.

As I reached the deck, I was informed that the captain wanted to see me at the same time I became aware of Lemon scuttling along the side of the ship, one hand on the railing, shouting my name. I grabbed him and turned him around in mid-"Ja——." I knew I was going to regret this later, but I figured the captain ought to hear this insanity from the Yahoo's own mouth.

The other divers were still in their wet suits when we reached the briefing room. The crew leader was reporting that there had been no sign of any of the missing men.

"Did one of the guys at Hold Four have a red beard?" I asked. I thought the severed head I had seen bobbing in the corner of the hallway had had a red beard. Of course it could have been the blood. His eyes had been open, and I tried to remember their color. I couldn't help thinking they were startled eyes, with the look a fish has the moment it is hooked and yanked into the air, and somehow retains when it is mounted. I told them what I had seen, leaving out some of my more personal reflections.

"You're telling me that a giant wolf eel has moved into the *SeaFort* and is attacking the crew?" Captain Nelson scoffed in disbelief. He was a sturdy six-footer in his mid-forties, but already grayer than I was. I respected his no-nonsense attitude.

"No, I'm not," I responded. "It couldn't have taken out the three men outside at the same time it was devouring two inside."

"Smithson," the captain asked his comm officer, "could somebody have a nuclear sub around the other side of that mesa without our detecting it?"

"If they're lucky and spending all their time dodging us, just maybe. But who the hell would it be?"

Somebody suggested terrorists or pirates who had been using the Circle of Fire as their private harbor.

"They're here," Lemon interrupted quietly.

"Pirates?" the captain asked in surprise, appearing to notice Lemon for the first time.

"Mr. Lemon has an interesting theory, Captain," I explained. "Although his official purpose is to aid in the recovery of lost seamen, he's been conducting some experiments for Naval Intelligence. While we don't have any proof of anything—"

"They're here, Jake. You know they're here."

I breathed deeply and let it all out. "What Mr. Lemon means, Captain Nelson, is that he believes there is highly intelligent marine life, sort of mutated dolphins, actually, who consider this territory their domain—"

"They're in the hold of the *SeaFort*," Lemon interrupted. "They came up directly under that ship, one at a time, during the raising, and went in through the hole in the hull. That's why you haven't detected them on your sonar. That's why they killed the divers who went down there. They've hid in there, hoping you'd drag them through the current that holds them captive."

"Dolphins need air, Mr. Lemon. Don't these things?"

"Perhaps less than we'd suppose, but yes. And that's precisely their problem. When you sent repair people down instead of immediately hauling a half-floated ship, one filled with both air and water, through the current wall, they started to panic. They realized they would have to drown or attack. But then the pump was installed in Hold Four, next to their cargo bay, giving them some breathing room, so to speak."

"So, in your theory, all we have to do is turn the pump off and they'll have to get the hell out of there, sooner rather than later? Then we can get on with our work?"

"They're not going to give up that easily, Captain. They've been trapped here for a very long time, and the *SeaFort* was probably the first indication they had that there was even a hope of breaking out of captivity. They must have studied the ship as it lay on the bottom and begun planning. I've heard you say that not a single *SeaFort* sailor was found. They must have removed them."

"What for? Food?"

Lemon shook his head. "Psychological factor is my guess. They didn't want the dead bodies to scare us away. What they're doing isn't spur of the moment, and as the business with the air pump shows, they're flexible thinkers."

The captain smiled. "We can find out about that. Carruthers, shut off the pump to Hold Four."

"That may not be such a great idea, Captain," I found myself interrupting. "You're forcing them to act before we're ready to react."

The captain looked from me to Lemon and back for a moment. "You want me to drop the *SeaFort* back into the sea, abort this mission in panic, and flee from a bunch of fish, Captain Walker?"

I knew Lemon was about to say yes, you bet your sweet flannel ass, so I interjected again. "I think, Captain, that what Mr. Lemon is suggesting is that we just maybe are making contact with the Other Intelligent Species on our planet for the first time, and we're doing it under very poor circumstances. We could

withdraw and send in a military mission, including a
carrier outside the circle to provide air support. Under
those circumstances, you'd be considered a hero, not a
goat. You won't have killed any of them and soured the
negotiations, but you also won't have jeopardized this
ship, lost any more sailors, or allowed the others to
escape into the ocean at large."

Allowed them to escape: I hadn't really thought about
that myself before now, because I hadn't really believed
in them, not seriously, until I'd watched them operate.
So I added one more bit of theory for Captain Nelson
to consider.

"The dolphins don't know exactly how we think,
although they've been watching us, looking for clues,
ever since we arrived. But they can only surmise that we
think a little like them, and a little like the other fish in
the sea. And they're aware of Mr. Lemon here. He tried
communicating with them, and they not only refused
to respond, but immediately shut down all their communications and changed their language code. They
clouded the robot probe's view on the way down to
prevent us from gaining information about them. They
risked a single encounter with the minisub to test its
defenses. They removed all the bodies from the *SeaFort*
because they didn't want to scare us away. In other
words, they're treating us like smart sea food. This all
amounts to a very single-minded and determined military operation. My training, Captain—and this is the
area I am trained in—my training tells me these creatures will only use negotiation or attempts at
communication as part of their military objective to
escape from this place. Maybe they will listen to negotiations some time after that; but by then, they, and not
we, will hold the upper hand. They will be loose in a
world that is three-quarters ocean. So I would second

your suggestion that we drop the *SeaFort* to the bottom and withdraw until the proper task force is assembled."

"Interesting, Captain Walker. Do you or Mr. Lemon have a single shred of physical evidence to support any of this science fiction?"

I held my breath for a moment, praying Lemon wouldn't go into his conversations with the Elder, whoever the hell that was. Neither of us said anything, and after a moment the captain came to his own conclusion.

"Let's float the *SeaFort* with pontoons and move this ship away from her. Get me a satellite linkup. Frankly I think this is crap, Captain Walker, but I'm not willing to call you a liar. I understand from your silence that Intelligence must have based your mission here on something, even if you're not allowed to reveal it to me. So I'm going to let people who are in possession of all the facts make this decision."

Lemon beamed beatifically, the way fallen angels did.

"That was great, Jake," Lemon congratulated me as soon as we were out of the room, heading back up to the deck to watch the detachment. "I knew you were a believer."

"Nice story, Lemon. But it's all conjecture. I've never talked to a dolphin. I have no proof there are intelligent dolphins down there plotting to overthrow the government of the United States. I didn't even see a goddamn dolphin while I was down there, just an eel with a head bigger than mine."

"Security, Jake. The eel doesn't need air, so they stuck him in there before the raising began—"

"Give it a rest, will you? All I know is that five men have been killed and that I don't have a rational explanation for it, so I panicked and put my career on the line for a blind lunatic—no fucking offense. What do you suppose the captain is going to do when he gets through to Naval Intelligence and discovers there is no secret paramilitary operation? No well-developed analysis of a convincingly high pile of preliminary data suggesting super-intelligent dolphins?"

"It won't matter," Lemon said, matter-of-factly enough to stop me in my tracks.

"Why not?"

"Because the captain shut off the pump, remember? The dolphins are going to show themselves any minute."

I swore colorfully, my years as a sailor not having been entirely wasted, and escorted Lemon to the railing to watch. I could see the captain up on the bridge, although we had the better view of the side of the *SeaFort* from which the dolphins, or whatever was in its hull and breathing air, were likely to emerge. The pump already had been turned off, but there was still plenty of noise as the crew worked to remove the crane and other lines securing the two ships.

Suddenly the deck of the *SeaFort* began to vibrate, and then the ship itself began to twist in the current. "Jesus," I reported to Lemon. "Whatever is in there is powerful enough to move the ship." And, too late, I recalled the *Revelation* inexplicably stopping in the current's rotation for a few hours. The dolphins had been experimenting.

Evidently, the captain had observed this as well, and he ordered the *Revelation* to full power, readying to move off as soon as we were free of the *SeaFort*. And that's when we first saw them.

The dolphins began to pour out of the damaged hull, at least a hundred of them. They were bigger than the ones that had been underswimming the *Revelation* for the past week. I could swear that an inordinate number of them looked up at where Lemon and I stood on the deck. "Can you hear anything?"

"Yeah. They're full bore. I don't know what they're saying, but by the way they're broadcasting, I'd say they were calling in reinforcements from some distance."

That's when we saw the whales coming around from where they must have been hiding on the other side of the mesa. Almost immediately, the captain decided we ought to be full-speed-ahead for the current wall.

Just then there was a terrific lurch, and the deck of the *Revelation* pitched. If Lemon hadn't been a habitual rail-holder, he would have accompanied a half-dozen unfortunate sailors overboard. My hip slammed into something as a sailor slammed into me from behind, but I held tight. "What's happening?" Lemon shouted over the din of sirens suddenly going off.

We hadn't been hit by anything I could see. "I think the dolphins may have tangled the salvage cables around our steerage. We're out of control." Worse yet, I could no longer make out the captain on the bridge. Had he been injured when the ship lurched?

"But we're moving!" the blind man advised me.

"Yeah. No one's given the order to shut down the power."

"Where are we heading?"

I looked around our arcing course and described the iceberg to Lemon. "I'm going to put you in the galley and get to the bridge. Strap in. You'll be safe there if we hit."

He protested, so I half carried, half dragged him across the rolling deck and strapped him up with enough life vests to make him look like an orange zeppelin. Then I tied him to a stationary chair, so he wouldn't get thrown around. He was plenty pissed, and so was I.

There was a second terrific lurch, and by the time I got to the bridge, I realized we had tried to reverse our engines and lost them too. In fact, I was informed, the steel salvage cables had pretty much destroyed the props. A white wall of ice loomed in front of us. Captain Nelson's body was being removed.

His neck had been cut nearly through by broken glass from the observation window. The bridge was awash with his blood. "Goddamn fucking bastard fish!" the second-in-command was screaming.

"They're not fish," I pointed out, only to try to calm him.

"Goddamn fucking right!" he screamed, rushing up to me, then backing away when he realized what he was doing, wheeling around and shouting, "They're Satan's swimming dogs!"

"They're the enemy," I said. "That's all. Now how do we stop the boat?"

"We're dead!" he hissed. "We're going to be eaten by fucking sharks!" And this was, in fact, when we hit the iceberg.

Our hull grated horribly. I wondered if that's what the sailors on the *SeaFort* had heard just before they went down.

But almost immediately, there was a series of secondary bumps, and suddenly we were floating free of the berg. Over the shouts from Damage Control reporting that the hull had been seriously compromised, I heard something about the whales.

When I went to the railing, I could see at least a half-dozen of them crowding every inch of our hull, shoving us away from the iceberg. And picking up speed again, as we headed for the current wall. Driven by demons, all right, I thought.

I estimated it was more than a mile away and that we were taking on a considerable amount of water. Even if the whales got us moving at ten knots or better, we had a little time—but to do what? The comm officer had already been arranging the satellite uplink before the attack had commenced, so we were screaming for help with the best of them, but I couldn't imagine anyone could get here in time to do us any good. Helicopters could only lift so many sailors to safety, and fighters weren't going to be able to pick off the whales without punching even more holes in our hull.

More holes. The dolphins weren't just trying to sink us. They were going to get our speed up as much as they could and then jump in through our hull and try to ride us through the current wall. Then they would let us sink—while they swam out into an unwary world for the first time in three million years. In a world that was more water than land, what might the impact be of a demonstrably ruthless species that had been perfecting itself for longer than humans had been able to count their toes?

Yeah, OK. Forget about preserving the primacy of *homo sapiens;* I was pissed off. I pulled the enormous automatic pistol from my shoulder holster and headed for the *Revelation*'s flooding hold, where, now or later, I expected to find Flipper's evil twin, Alexander the Fish, Genghis Guppie, Adolphin—whoever, whatever, shooting fish in a barrel was my sport.

The problem was going to be keeping my powder dry.

Traffic, not surprisingly, was against me. When I finally got belowdecks, I discovered the entire quadrant of the ship had been sealed off, so I came back up and started looking for a cargo door that would let me look down into the gushing hold. By now, sailors were milling about the deck, looking to abandon ship—but none too happy at the prospect of lowering the lifeboats onto the backs of whales that were rushing us toward the worst currents in the Antarctic. Of course, they could shoot the whales, and then lower the lifeboats into the bloody water and wait for pissed-off relatives to arrive. . . . With the captain gone, they were not hearing a lot of great contingency plans or inspired improvisation. Still, they were American Navy, and discipline was holding. Not that I expected it to do any good, except to keep people out of my way.

Pushing the straps of a small cargo crane aside, I pulled up the hatch nearest to the breach in our hull and looked into the rushing water, now about twenty feet below me. I didn't see any of the antishark things, or even a dolphin for that matter, but what I did see had the gun back in my holster and me running back down the deck to the galley faster than you can say Chicken of the Sea.

Why was I going back for Lemon? A lot of people were going to die here, and I didn't see a way to save more than two of us. Maybe it was that simple piece of math, Lemon being the only likely number two. And he was in my care, and he was blind, and I had left him tied up. And he had tried to warn me about this, and I had ignored him.

He wasn't in the galley. The life jackets were, but he had slipped out of them. I headed for his private command post belowdecks.

In the gangway of the lower deck, water was already a couple inches deep. Lemon was sitting in it, scrunched against the bulkhead outside his door, bleeding from his massive forehead. As I watched, he drove an ice pick into his own hand. Stupefied, I continued to watch as he screamed and thrashed around on the floor, and then, with a slower agony, pulled it out and prepared to strike again.

I grabbed his wrist and wrestled the pointy tool away from him. "What the hell are you doing to that ice pick, Lemon?"

"Jake?" He sat there panting, bleeding from a gash across his forehead as well as wounds in his hand, arm, and leg.

"Isn't there a simpler way to change the oil in the old brain radar?" Actually, I was wondering if the old "braidar" might not be out of action for good following that assault, but after a moment he whispered something.

"It *is* their Australia," he said softly. I caught it the second time.

"Well, something just pushed us into the iceberg. Something is pulling us back into the current while we sink. Aliens, dolphins from Atlantis' second, isolated colony—I just want to shoot the sons of bitches."

"You don't get it," he sighed. "This place was the dolphin version of Australia. A place of exile for criminals."

"For millions of years?"

"They're pretty pissed," Lemon said.

"But Australia today is cool," I pointed out, inspecting his head, hand, and leg, and applying a bit of pressure to the worst wounds as best I could without letting go of the ice pick. Gray shit was oozing out of the head one. Keep him talking, I thought, keep saying the kind of glib, dumb-ass things he'd expect me to say.

"The people the British sent to Australia had stolen loaves of bread. Dolphins don't have possessions. And they probably bred soldier dolphins for certain qualities, remember? Like violence, strength, discipline—"

"So your theory goes." The talking had calmed him down. I let go of his wrist to see what would happen, and he seemed all right, except for the convulsions.

"Well, now's your chance to check it out," he said with one of those Blind Lemon smiles. "You wanted to shoot something. They're in the lower hold. Just don't get within about ten feet of the surface of the water."

"How many?" I asked, patting my pockets. Of course, I hadn't taken any back-up shells to shoot at the iceberg.

"About thirty so far. It'll be wall-to-wall, with more of them coming in the lower we sink."

"They're using the ship to break through the perimeter, to get out into the free ocean?"

"Yeah. Isn't that what you'd do?"

"You're asking me because I'm the psychotic criminal type?" I shifted my crouch, but didn't rise yet. "Lemon, are you going to do anything bad to yourself before I get a chance to do it to you myself?" Wincing, he shook his head. "Why were you stabbing yourself?"

"I was trying to slow them down. I thought if I could broadcast a lot of pain, maybe it would hurt them."

"Did it?"

"Couldn't tell. They're too desperate. For them this is Armageddon and Rapture rolled into one."

"You're done hurting yourself, then, right?"

"What would be the point? We're all going to drown in a few minutes. Did I tell you I can't swim? I suppose that will make me better at drowning than the rest of you."

"I don't mean to diminish your last triumph, but I think I have a way out. Let me get you up to the cargo door."

Draping his arm over my shoulder, I dragged Lemon through the corridor, back up onto the deck, and toward the hold, trying not to look at the men I was deserting. The box control for the little crane was easy enough to figure out. I sat Lemon in the straps as if it were a playground swing, and started lowering him into the hold.

"Ah, Jake? You remember what I said about no swimming?"

"Relax, Lemon. I'm not planning to drop you all the way in. But how am I gonna know if there are any killer fish down there if they don't have a decoy to snap at?" When I had him positioned where I wanted, about six feet over the water, I shut down the crane, grabbed a ten-foot grappling hook, and climbed down the chains after him. There was less than ten feet of air between the rising seawater and the deck, which was now our ceiling. And only about a foot between our dangling toes and where the hull of the minisub would be, assuming I could snare it with the grappling hook. Somehow it had avoided being crushed between the iceberg and the *Revelation*, but had then been sucked inside the hull when the water rushed into the gaping hole.

I leaned out with the grappling hook, Lemon bitching at me the whole time about one thing or another, and finally got a grip on one of the camera ports. I drew it to us, and when the topside hatch was just below our feet, I handed the hook to Lemon with instructions not to poke himself in the head with this one, and stepped down onto the hull. Holding on to Lemon's straps with one hand while the rushing current tried to pull me away from him and unbolting the hatch with the other was no mean feat, and I made Lemon admit it before I lowered him through the hatch into the sub.

The lights in the hold flickered off and then on again. The emergency generators wouldn't last for long if the ship were being flooded. In the flickering lights, I was straddling the hatch, still hanging on to the crane belt with one hand, about to lower myself down, when Connor appeared from the shadows about twenty yards away.

"Holy Christ."

"What are you looking at, Jake?" Lemon shouted up.

"It's Connor, the sub pilot. He's, ah, walking on water." Actually, he was waist-deep in it, but he had to be walking on something. The water in here was fifteen feet deep.

"It's not Connor, Jake."

"He looks pissed," I added, trying to see if his twisted expression was just an effect of the strobing lights. "I think he wants the sub for himself." Connor started to move slowly toward me in a series of movements that were both flowing and hesitant at the same time. His eyes were open, but they weren't looking at me. Blood and drool trickled from the corner of his mouth. The lights flashed off for a full second, and when they came back on, his body seemed to have hunched a bit.

"It's not Connor!" Lemon was still shouting that when Connor stopped staring at me and suddenly rushed across the space between us at an incredible speed, his fingers trailing in the water.

I screamed—why the hell not?—and flung the grappling hook with all my might right at where I imagined his balls would be, just under the surface. He jerked, but kept coming, smashing into the side of the sub. The impact nearly pitched me off, and I nearly threw myself off in revulsion as his cold dead arms brushed my own. Instead I flung myself down the hatch.

I was back on my feet in a flash, one hand going to the shoulder holster, the other reaching upwards to pull the hatch down. This time when I poked my head out, it wasn't Connor waiting for me, but a piscine face with an enormous beak full of razor-sharp teeth. It had the familiar rictus grin of a dolphin, but its eyes were clear and very, very cold.

It wasn't there just to stare me down, so I shot it in the head four times, point-blank, dropped the gun, and slammed the hatch down over my head.

"It's not Connor," I confirmed for Lemon. "He must have come down here to get the sub, and they were waiting for him."

"Classic predatory behavior," Lemon pronounced. "They used his body like a decoy duck to attract more of us."

I fired up the sub, and after a minute had it pointed in the direction of the breached hull. I couldn't see much on the surface and so submerged us a couple feet. The flank of a whale blocked our exit. "If these fish from hell are smart enough to try something like that—if they can be that ruthless, can plan for something like this—if they think of us as game fish rather than equals with feelings—"

"Welcome to Atlantis, Australia."

"Well, this is Australian for *fuck you*." I aimed the laser cannon at the whale blocking our exit and fired.

Unlike Connor, I didn't think the cannon was originally designed as a weapon. It's aiming mechanism was too cumbersome; you practically had to point the entire sub to line up a shot. On the other hand, hitting a whale at twenty yards was not a problem.

There was a flash, and suddenly the water at the breach was pink and murky with bits of flesh. I did not wait for the others to react, but gunned the sub forward, or tried to, anyway. The engine strained against the water rushing in. At full throttle, I was creeping forward, trying to match the sub's snout to the bouncing hole that was my goal. We were being shaken like a maraca. Finally, I edged out into the opening, and a minute later the crosscurrent rushing along the outside of the boat caught us—and flung us against another whale that had been coming up to replace the one I'd shot.

We bounced off—Lemon was holding on for his life, having been unable to find the seat-belt straps on his own. But at least we were out of the ship and into open water. Then, as we descended, I waited to see if they'd chase us.

They didn't seem interested. I let us plummet aimlessly for a moment, and then took control of the dive, sending us steadily down. Lemon was a mess, but I talked him into a chair and harness. "You think this will get through the current wall?" he asked.

"Would you let me enjoy my action high?" I snapped. "I just saved our butts. I don't want to hear `What do we do now?' quite yet."

"You don't have a plan, do you?"

"To actually extend our lives beyond the"—I tapped a gauge—"twenty hours of oxygen we have? No." Depression and elation danced in the mosh pit of my head.

"So, can this sub get through the current wall?"

"Good question. Probably not."

"Ever been swallowed by a whale?"

"Personally? No. But I see where you're going with this. The Jonah bit, where we get ourselves swallowed by something in this prison break and then blow our way out of it as soon as we're on the other side, right?"

Lemon sighed. "Unless volcanoes have underground passages. Do you know? After three million years, these desperados would know about a tunnel or a weak point in the current if there was one, so that's out. But we have a greater heat tolerance—not to mention the sulfides in the volcanic water are probably toxic—so maybe we could make our way through the heart of the volcano itself, and come out with a tan on the other side of the wall."

"Lemon, how does a blind guy read so many comic books?"

"Can you make a volcano erupt by blasting it with the cannon?"

"Right. Then the chain eruption would kill all the dolphins, alter the current, or both, and we'd be home free. So what, if that hasn't happened in three million years.

"Isn't it about time for you to get in touch with the Elder?" I asked in my turn. "Or at least tell me about it?"

"There is no Elder. I made him up to explain what I thought I knew from the Atlantis dig."

"Ha! Shit. And I was counting on that to get us out of here."

We shared some silence for a moment. The engine of the little sub thrummed dully, a cheap little car idling on the ramp of a freeway packed with speeding semis. We were going to die. The crew on the *Revelation* was going to die. The vicious fishes who were trying to escape were going to be pureed. But Lemon, sitting there with brains and blood dripping from his forehead, smiled a little nearly normal smile. "So we have time on our hands?"

"Twenty hours. And there's food here somewhere."

He sighed and said, "Since we're going to die anyway, let's take a pass at the mesa. I'd really like to see Atlantis."

"Why the hell not?" Lemon was not the company I would have imagined for my Last Voyage. I had always imagined I'd be alone.

●●●

I have spent a good deal of my life in the water, but not much under it. When we pierced the kelp that had hidden the mesa from view, even without the greenish glow of the thallium iodide searchlight mounted on our snout, looking out of the little sub at the mesa was eerie, like peering out of some giant's eyes at his own alien landscape. The mesa was perhaps a mile across, but it took just one glance to realize the entire thing had been well inhabited for a very long time. There were no buildings, of course, but the coral had been nurtured and clipped in sheets and arches and towers, some of them rising fifty feet toward the surface. The kelp forest, which had surrounded the perimeter from which we'd approached, had been allowed to grow in discrete patches throughout the city proper, like greenways occupying a few percent of the mesa's surface area. The coral arches, in golds and pinks and blues and grays, dominated the landscape, reminding me of nothing so much as a grove of enormous pastel bonsai trees that had taken thousands of years to grow.

And the parallel to a Japanese garden did not stop there. Rocks and shells had been pushed and planted to create patterns both clearly artificial and perfectly harmonious with the landscape. The effect was one of simplicity rather than clutter, of order but not regimentation.

There wasn't a sign of a single dolphin.

I described to Lemon what I saw, while he told me what he felt. "Nobody's home," Lemon confirmed from what must have been left of his brain radar. Without having made a conscious notation, we had slipped into talking about this place as we would have a human village.

"They're all off watching the greatest battle of their lifetimes, eh? They're not going to make it, you know. the *Revelation* won't survive, and neither will anyone or anything in it."

"The females and children were evacuated," Lemon informed me, "in case we counterattacked."

That made sense. This place would have been impossible to defend. And then I found myself thinking about the fact that, despite the immense effort and endless millennia Atlantis had taken to build, its inhabitants cared far more for the safety of their children—and the ongoing genesis of their race—than for the material world they had built. It was worth knowing that about your enemy, I thought reflexively.

With my limited knowledge of marine biology, I catalogued what I could for Lemon. There was a great variety of bottom dwellers, particularly crustaceans and mollusks. Hundreds of blood sea stars were paired and arched like multiplex McDonalds. ("The cleaning crew in heat," Lemon informed me.) A yellow tube sponge over six feet high beckoned like Mickey Mouse's four-fingered fist to a Disneyland of fantastically colored coral and vegetation. While the mammals may have taken a powder, they'd left part of the food supply behind; an incredible swarm of big-eyed jacks swam in a tight spiral about a dozen feet across and a hundred feet high, a living tornado of silver fish. ("Can't pen them," Lemon informed me, "so they probably use young adults as shepherds to train the food stock to stay in one place.") At one point a leafy sea dragon floated out of the kelp and browsed our porthole. I tried describing its golden sea horse body ribbed in fluorescent white, turning to vegetable at every appendage like a thing enchanted or cursed. "It's about a foot long, kind of funny looking, slow moving."

"A pet or toy for dolphin calves," he mused.

There were relatively clear areas studded with towers and low arches, some of them color coded, that may have been playgrounds or training fields. Otherwise, what I took to be artwork dominated the floor of the mesa. The shells comprising most of the various shapes and images were themselves unbelievably beautiful, but the artwork of which they were a part was breathtaking. I've heard speculation that truly alien art would be incomprehensible to humans, the psychology of shape and color so different that we would experience nothing of its pleasure. What I saw on the mesa cut me to the soul. I don't know if these creatures were Spawn of Cain or Fish in the Iron Mask. I don't know if they were so like humans in their thought that their lives were not so alien from ours, or if the experts are simply wrong, that there is a common aesthetic, universal in intelligence itself, or based on the commonest of experiences, of needs, or desires.

For me, death had never been a contemplative sport, and my gauges predicted I wasn't experiencing oxygen deprivation, yet my reverie was only deepened as we moved further around the perimeter of the mesa. We found a cave nearly big enough to squeeze into, but stopped when its interior suddenly began to blink furiously with hundreds of colors. "I think we've found those squid," I informed Lemon. "Of course, it could be a single giant. They go well over sixty feet in our own oceans. Probably, though, from what we saw on that video tape, we're looking at a school of Humbolt. Not that it matters much. Even Humbolt squid go six feet and a hundred pounds, so I think we'll stay out of there." Thankfully, hating light as they did, the squid stayed inside and away from us.

"Anything in particular you'd like to, ah, visit?" Of course I knew Lemon's ultimate interest, and, from the robo-dive photos, where we were likely to find the cathedral.

Lemon launched into a lecture. "It has some extremely interesting spatial properties," Lemon informed me. "What it boils down to is tonal properties. At least that's what we've been calling them. We don't have it entirely figured out, because a lot of the finer elements of the cathedral couldn't be recreated and we have to guess. But what we do have is a structure that reverberates and reflects waves in a very unusual way. The reverb apparently alters some of the tonal properties. The reflection is also a refraction, so that distorted parts of sound waves recombine as they sweep back and forth across the cathedral space."

"So it's not a temple but a concert hall for fish?"

"I believe it's both. I think that the cathedral was designed not merely to magnify the usual echolocations and communications of the dolphins that used it, but to enhance another subsonic wave-form. An energy wave-form that bore the equivalent information values of telepathy."

"So dolphins came here to get telepathic?"

"Maybe some of them did. Maybe that's why they built it."

And built it they had. The cathedral's spires dominated the mesa's southeast quadrant. Elliptically shaped and a hundred yards in length, it was the only thing we'd seen approximating a human structure in size and shape, and was all the more startling for that. Skeletal though it was, the naked ribs and Moebius spirals seemed very much alive—and, in a sense, they were. As we edged the sub carefully through the coral maze, I told Lemon that I thought I was seeing areas where repairs were in progress. In smallish patches, living coral, extending polyps into the current to feed, stood out from the bulk of the polished structure. The living coral was sometimes surrounded or checked in its line of growth by venomous-looking sea urchins, which Lemon assumed provided the means to sculpt the living coral into the desired shape.

"Well, is your telepathy enhanced at all by Charlie Tuna's Temple of Doom?"

"I'm hearing . . . something." Lemon's own voice was awed. I couldn't bring myself to make fun of him, even though our deaths were imminent and I might not have another chance.

"Take some samples of the living coral, Jake. I bet it's super-fast growing, like nothing we've seen. But don't hurt anything, OK? And get everything on videotape."

"It's been running ever since we left the *Revelation*. I think it's automatic while the monitors are on." Mentioning the ship gave me an odd feeling, like talking about a dead person in front of her still-open casket. "But I don't know how much tape there is left." They probably needed to be changed every four hours at least, I reasoned, so I sank the sub onto the floor of the cathedral to prevent it from drifting into anything it might wreck, and began to dig around in the various overheads for spare tapes.

"Can we take audio recordings?" he inquired, while I was at it.

"I don't know how, but the sonar is working. I think a record of that is kept on one of the sub's directional computers."

"We've got to get some measurements. Is there something out there you can use to provide a photographic perspective?"

Finally I paused. I believe in enjoying your final moments to the greatest extent possible, but there's a limit to my capacity for self-delusion, at least where sex isn't involved.

Lemon may have read my thoughts, or may simply have known they were the same as his own. "Someone else may recover the sub, Jake. Or the records and samples at least. We could tie them to a dive marker or a balloon or something."

"The dolphins will see them on the surface. They may not know what they are, but they'll recognize them as an attempt to communicate with other humans, and they'll destroy them."

"What'll we do, Jake?" Lemon's voice was almost panicky for the first time since we'd set out from San Diego. "Someone has got to learn about this. About . . . them."

"Even if the *Revelation* never got through on the satellite uplink, the Navy is going to be pretty damn cautious after losing two ships in the same area. They'll figure out, at least roughly, what's going on here."

"And then?" Lemon asked.

I stared at him for a moment. "Will they nuke it? Is that what you're asking? I don't know. Probably not." Well, maybe not.

"Jake, we've got to stop it somehow. You can't just destroy an intelligent species. *The* only other intelligent species on this planet. The only other intelligent species man may ever encounter."

"That intelligent species is probably eating your fellow crew members at this very moment. Unless they decide to save a few—to study, I mean." What I meant was, to stake out. `Honey pots,' the Viet Cong used to call the wounded American soldiers they used to draw other Americans into ambush.

But I knew what Lemon meant, especially after immersing ourselves for the past hour in a world that, albeit unspoiled by actual pain-in-the-ass inhabitants, seemed somewhere between pastoral and fairy-tale fucking wonderful. He was silent now, reverential. As I continued to describe both what I observed on the cameras and what I read on sonar, I caught Lemon, out of the corner of my eye, pressing his massively deformed forehead to the little porthole. I could have imagined tears streaming down his face, had he had something besides the newly drilled holes in his head for tears to come out of. I imagined how Lemon must have wanted to press himself right through that glass, to become a part of what was on the other side, to dissolve into pure thought that might join and resonate forever with the million years of prayer that had been offered up in this cathedral. Lemon could not even cry, and I felt sorry for that.

That reflection led me to an obvious question: since he couldn't be looking at anything, why was his face pressed against the porthole at all? I stared at the hideous forehead reflected in the plexiglass for a full ten seconds before realizing that what I was seeing was not the reflection of his own forehead at all.

"I thought you told me there was no one home," I whispered from his shoulder. The dolphin drew back a foot or so from the other side of the window as Lemon pulled back to let me have a look. The creature appeared to be an oversized bottlenose with an enormous head, furrowed around the eyes. It was the eyes themselves that made the most difference. They were bottomless and clear, and in their distance you could see the beginnings of creation.

The beast backed away a little further, and turned sideways, as if to give me a profile, and I gained from this view, from the slackness of the skin and a certain stiffness in its movements, a sense of tremendous age. Now that it had backed up, I was able to check out alternative views on a couple of the monitors that confirmed this impression. It occurred to me that the animal was nearly as big as our sub. "Are you talking to him?"

"Her," Lemon corrected. "She stayed behind to see us."

"Lemon, are you communicating with that fish, or are you reading seaweed leaves, or what?"

"I don't know," he whispered. "Since we came in here, I've been hearing . . . things. I can't tell you why I think I understand them, but a while ago I started to feel I did understand one particular voice, or sound, or song. I have a sense she has been waiting for us. She's been watching, I guess, to see if we were safe to approach. When the males planned their attack, she supervised the evacuation of the females and the calves, but she knew she would stay. She expects to die, Jake. She expects us to kill her. But she is near death anyway, and she wanted to see—what her ancestors have waited to see since the dawn of their history."

"Us?"

"Well, intelligent creatures. She's in no position to split hairs."

"Thanks, Lemon."

"She wants to know how the two of us manage to live in the same shell. I told her you're not that bad."

"Lemon—"

"Just kidding, Jake. I told her the shell is only temporary, that we sometimes use it to explore."

"Look, Lemon, I need to know if you're really talking to her. We shouldn't be telling her too much about us. Nothing about the number of people we have on the *Revelation*. Nothing about our own armaments or capabilities. Nothing about the cannon or how long we can stay down—"

"Jake, everyone's dead. What's the point?"

I looked out the port at the dolphin. She was starting to drift away.

"She needs air," Lemon said. "She's weak. I don't think she'll be coming back."

We followed her out of the cathedral into a central courtyard, and, on the cameras, watched her spiral slowly up and out of sight, her outline visible for some time in the dim light that penetrated the ocean above. I felt an absence in the pit of my stomach, and identified it just as she disappeared from sight: she'd never tried to speak to me.

We sat in silence, Lemon with his head bowed. His blindness seemed almost a blessing at the moment. I am not good at prayer, and soon found myself examining the place in which we now found ourselves—a large, open space, perhaps a public gathering place for the dolphins. The very center of it was decorated in the largest example of public art I had seen so far, a circle of four spiraling displays composed of coral and shell, each of them at least twenty feet across.

Each display looked like a map of creation, with lines of force flung outward in an expanding spiral toward something unknown even to God. Five star-shapes were interwoven near the perimeter of the work. Next to one spiral picture there was another and another, four in all, each similar enough in pattern to be generations of the first one. I looked more closely at the detail, trying to compare the variations. And suddenly, as I was describing it all to Lemon, I realized what I was seeing.

"I have a plan now," I said, pulling some charts from the overhead.

"If it's not a good one," Lemon said, "you can leave me here."

But I knew he wasn't serious.

•••

We retreated down the less- and finally uncultivated coral canyons of the mesa, down the thousand feet to the ocean floor, angling outward, away from the mesa, until we approached the current wall. On the floor of the ocean, the current was a wall of sand and debris that, from a distance, looked solid. We were approximately a mile from the nearest volcanoes, and I carefully steered among roiling volcanic vents and chimneys three or four stories high, raising the water temperature so that it rippled and shimmered in our lights, sometimes colored yellow or red or black or white by the various oxides they were spewing out. When we were not directly over hardened lava flow, enormous mounds of mineral deposits, like brains the size of football stadiums, attested to just how long these vents had been in operation. And while the sulfurous composition of the water in this area obviously deterred not only the dolphins but most other common forms of sea life, the area swarmed with groves of tubeworms, many of them three or four feet high, waving tulip-shaped lips into the noxious night.

The dolphin map had directed me to a point that was one of the farthest reaches between volcanoes on the circumference of this formation—the place at which the current shifted the most. Before we were anywhere near it, the water became cloudy with debris. I experimented with the laser-sighting screen Connor had shown me, and, sure enough, the current wall showed up on it as a blurred, shape-shifting semisolid object. The minisub felt the pull of that current from a quarter mile away, and I used the virtual imaging to nudge our way into its deepest fold of relatively calm water—always conscious that the fold could collapse in on us at any moment.

The force of the flow seemed narrower and more intense on the floor of the ocean, and must have been better than fifty knots at the center of the current. I found an area free of both lava and the mineral pillows and put the sub on the ground. Activating the tank treads, I fought in closer to the current wall, until I was finally pointing the sub at an angle to the onrushing water. The wall didn't appear solid now, but it remained opaque, its obscurity broken only by the occasional rushing object large enough to identify. I told Lemon I thought I'd seen a small dolphin, dead of course, suspended in the maelstrom.

"Do you suppose they've hit the wall yet?" Lemon asked. He meant, Are they all dead now, humans and dolphins alike? I wondered if we'd be seeing pieces of the *Revelation* any time soon in this mosaic wall of death.

When I felt the hurricane-force current lifting our front treads, I started firing the cannon into the ocean floor directly in front of us. Again I fired, and then again. The debris was immediately lifted off by the current, but I had to continue to fire swiftly to keep my excavation from filling in with current deposits. Ten minutes later, I had hollowed out a stone grave. A minute after I'd backed us into it, the debris already was building up on top of us, starting to bury the sub. I shut our exterior lights and drive motor off and let the darkness outside become complete. The terrific erosive power of the current leveled the ocean floor right over us in less time than it had taken to dig the hole.

And throughout my maneuvers, the barely tolerable current in which we sat was getting stronger. That's what the dolphin maps had predicted.

•••

I wasn't too worried about our hull being breached. After all, the minisub was designed for depths of over two miles, a lot more pounds per square inch than we currently endured from a few yards of dirt and rock. Well, from what I assumed were only a few yards of dirt and rock. Inside the sub, we suffered an immediate and complete blackout, but just for a moment as the sub's lights flickered, went out, then came back on. I could not tell whether the thunder above us bespoke creation or destruction. That was for finer ears than mine, perhaps for ears like Lemon's. My job, as always, was to do my job, so I unstrapped myself and went about tending Lemon's wounds. They were terrible but didn't seem life threatening. He didn't complain once. He seemed goddamn cheerful.

"You know, Lemon, you're a tough little bastard."

"Have to be, Jake. How else could a freak like me survive?"

I thought about that. I remembered Connor, who had barely spoken with him, observing the hideous blind man's loneliness, and I felt ashamed. Only I had an inkling of the exquisite torment of Lemon's isolation, cut off from humanity in so many ways, yet always haunted by the voices in his head. I was reminded of a child, locked in a darkened closet, hearing the laughter of a world forever beyond his reach.

"Hey, Jake, what are you doing?"

"Just checking you for chills," I said, removing my arm from around his shoulder. "I'm surprised you're not in shock after what you've been through."

He didn't say anything, but suddenly shook as if he in fact was chilled to the bone. A moment later, when that subsided, I asked, "What did she want to know about us?"

"She wanted to know where our children were. Do you have any children, Jake?"

"No." This was not the best time to think about that. "How about you?"

"No." His sigh had a note of finality to it, but then he continued. "She must have thought we were a war party because we came without women or children."

"Maybe she thought exploration rather than war," I suggested. "We've done a pretty good job proving how dangerous that can be. So maybe she knows we didn't come here to kill them."

"I hope so." Lemon's forehead was soft and pulpy to the touch. It felt more like a foam bumper than flesh and bone. I wondered if it could have been surgically altered to make him look more like a normal human being. Assuming he wanted to look like a normal human being.

I persisted clumsily, "I mean, what did she think of us?"

Lemon made a face that was inscrutable even to me. It made me realize how much I wanted his wildest fantasies to be true. I wanted to know that one of us had communicated with an alien. I wanted to know how something truly alien appraised us. Before I died, I wanted to know—

"You want to know what God thinks of us, Jake?"

"Stop reading my mind, Lemon, and tell me what you read in hers."

He reflected for a moment. "She thought we didn't seem so bad."

"Well," I said softly, pressing myself into the padded back of my chair, "I'm glad we didn't blow up the cathedral or anything." Then I stopped talking and thought about how Lemon had made contact with two intelligent species and I not even one.

The storm raged above us. Though buried, the sub vibrated, hummed, trembled, at its proximity, and I cursed my stupidity. We might have had some chance of outlasting—or being ignored by—the dolphins if we'd surfaced. Assuming the *Revelation* had gotten through to somebody before its demise, we could have prayed for an airlift. Instead, we would be buried forever down here, or suddenly uprooted and torn to pieces in the current. I was seized by an ironic sense that, in some way, this burial was similar to what the folks in Atlantis, Ohio, must have experienced millennia ago. But in another sense, it was not. Whatever befell Lemon and me, it would be of little consequence. Try to conceive not just the matinee poster of falling temples and togaed beauties fleeing nowhere beneath a flaming sky, but the thought of an entire civilization falling into the sea—or rising from it and drowning in air. A culture, a language, a way of life— a way of being. How can we comprehend the loss of something like this when we cannot even adequately, cannot ever, come to grips with the inevitable loss of our own small lives?

• • •

By the time the roar above had ebbed and my watch concurred it was time to start digging ourselves out of the dirt, I had explained to Lemon that the four huge shell works we'd found in the middle of the mesa were, quite naturally, dedicated to the most important phenomenon in the lives of these creatures, the current wall that delimited their world. Each of the shell diagrams was a detailed map depicting that wall during one of the four tidal periods of the day—of this day, in particular. My guess was that they kept a library or calendar predicting the precise position of the current. And, I hoped, updated the big pictures—their version of the clock in the middle of the town square—each day.

By overlaying the sub's charts of the ocean floor, I had been able to locate a place where the current fluctuated several hundred yards between high and low tide. I'd hedged my bet by burrowing in as far as I could to narrow the space the core current would have to cross in order to leave us on the other side when we popped up out of our hole.

Of course, if I was wrong, we'd be ripped to bits.

"What the hell," Lemon said generously. "Let's take a look."

And so we did. I fired the cannon, and waited. The cameras were out of action, of course. They were covered with dirt, even if they weren't completely smashed, and we could see nothing through the porthole. I fired a second time, and activated the tank treads, trying to follow upwards from our grave the tunnel I hoped I was making. There was a grinding sound, a brief lurch, but no real forward movement.

"When we get out of here, Lemon, is anyone going to believe us anyway?"

"I hope not," he grinned, reminding me again of how much he looked like a dolphin. I fired again, wondering how much power the cannon retained. Then I shifted the treads into gear and pushed forward. There was only the grinding—and then suddenly something outside broke loose, and we were moving forward.

And I felt something break loose inside of me at the same moment, and begin to rise to the surface.

SEARCH FOR RESEARCH

Written by
L. Ron Hubbard

About the Author

L. Ron Hubbard's adventurous life and remarkably versatile and prolific career as an internationally bestselling author have become legendary in their dimensions and far-reaching creative influence. Though always, quintessentially, a writer's writer, his exploits, travels, unquenchable curiosity and richly diverse talents led him to exceptional achievements in other professional fields as well—as an explorer and ethnologist, master mariner and pilot, photographer and filmmaker, philosopher and educator, composer and musician.

In a career spanning over half a century, he also enthusiastically shared his energies, time and knowledge with other writers, especially beginners, helping them to become more proficient and successful at their craft.

L. Ron Hubbard grew up in the rugged frontier country of Montana, was riding horses by the time he was three, and by the age of six had been initiated as a blood brother of a Blackfoot Indian medicine man. While still a teenager, before the advent of modern commercial air transportation, he journeyed more *than a quarter of a million miles by land and sea—including stints as a helmsman and supercargo—into areas of the Far East rarely visited by Westerners, broadening his knowledge of other peoples and cultures.*

Later in his storied life, as a master mariner licensed to operate ships in any ocean, he led three separate voyages of discovery and exploration under the flag of the prestigious Explorers Club. He also served with distinction as a U.S. naval officer during World War II.

It was on his return to the United States from the Far East in 1929, however, that Mr. Hubbard entered the George Washington University where he became president of both the Engineering Society and Flying Club, and wrote articles, stories and a prize-winning play for the school's newspaper and literary magazine.

A daredevil pilot, he barnstormed across the United States in gliders and early powered aircraft, becoming a correspondent and photographer for the Sportsman Pilot, *one of the most distinguished national aviation magazines of its day. And at the age of only twenty-five, his reputation as a writer of popular fiction already prominently secure, he was elected president of the New York chapter of the American Fiction Guild, whose membership at the time included Dashiell Hammett, Raymond Chandler and Edgar Rice Burroughs. He also worked successfully in Hollywood, writing the original story and script for Columbia's 1937 box-office-hit serial* The Secret of Treasure Island *and as a screenwriter and script consultant on numerous films for Columbia, Universal and other studios.*

All this—and much more—over the breadth and scope of his professional career found its way into his writing and gave his stories a memorable authenticity and a stirring sense of the textures of life, and of the way things credibly might be in some possible future or alternate dimension or in the deep vistas of space, that continue to captivate and excite readers everywhere.

Beginning with the appearance in 1934 of his first published adventure story, The Green God, *in one of the hugely popular all-fiction "pulp" magazines of the day, L. Ron Hubbard's outpouring of fiction was prodigious—often exceeding a million words a year. Ultimately, he produced more than 250 published novels, novelettes, short stories and screenplays in essentially every major genre, from action and adventure, western and romance, to mystery and suspense, and, of course, science fiction and fantasy.*

Mr. Hubbard had, indeed, already attained broad popularity and acclaim in other genres when he burst onto the landscape of speculative literature with his first published science fiction story, The Dangerous Dimension. *It was his trendsetting work in this field from 1938 to 1950, particularly, that not only helped to vitally enlarge the imaginative boundaries of science fiction and fantasy, but established him as one of the founding architects and creative wellsprings of what continues to be regarded as the genre's golden age.*

Such enduring L. Ron Hubbard classics of speculative fiction as Final Blackout, Fear, Ole Doc Methuselah *and* Typewriter in the Sky, *as well as his precedent-setting capstone novels, the epic saga of the year 3000,* Battlefield Earth, *and the ten-volume* MISSION EARTH® *series, continue to appear on bestseller lists and to garner plaudits in countries around the world.*

The single biggest and one of the bestselling science fiction novels in history—and now a major motion picture— Battlefield Earth *was given hallmark recognition, among its many other accolades, when it was voted the #1 science fiction novel of the twentieth century by the American Book Readers Association.*

At the same time, an original L. Ron Hubbard screenplay about look-alike spies, Ai! Pedrito!—When Intelligence Goes Wrong, *novelized by Kevin J. Anderson, was published in 1998 and immediately became a* New York Times *bestseller. This was followed the very next year by the publication of* A Very Strange Trip, *an uproarious L. Ron Hubbard screenplay of time-traveling adventure, turned into novel form by Dave Wolverton, that also became a* New York Times *bestseller directly after its release—the fifteenth Hubbard fiction title to do so.*

The culmination of L. Ron Hubbard's lifelong commitment to actively fostering the work of new and aspiring writers of demonstrated ability came, meanwhile, with his establishment in 1983 of both the Writers of the Future Contest, now the largest and most successful merit competition of its kind in the world, and the L. Ron Hubbard Presents Writers of the Future annual anthology of the winning best new original stories of science fiction, fantasy and horror. The anthology also provides an influential showcase for winners of the companion Illustrators of the Future Contest, inaugurated in 1988.

Mr. Hubbard's earlier work with fledgling writers, however—undertaken while still in his twenties—was marked by lectures he gave at such schools as Harvard and George Washington University on how to get started as a professional.

He also began, as early as 1935, to publish incisively practical "how to" articles and essays about writing as a craft and profession, which appeared in major writers' magazines and continue to be used today in writing courses and seminars, and as the basis for the coveted Writers' Workshops held each year for the winners and published finalists of the Writers of the Future Contest.

All of us want to sell more stories and write better ones. It is hard to believe that there exists a writer with soul so dead that he would not. But, from careful observation, I have come to the heartbreaking conclusion that while writers usually want to do this, they generally fail to try.

Writers are the laziest people on earth. And I know I'm the laziest writer. In common with the rest of the profession I am always searching for the magic lamp which will shoot my stories genie-like into full bloom without the least effort on my part.

This is pure idiocy on my part as I have long ago found this magic lamp, but not until a couple years ago did I break it out and use the brass polish to discover that it was solid gold.

This lamp was so cobwebby and careworn that I am sure most of us have not looked very long at it in spite of its extreme age and in spite of the fact that it is eternally being called to our attention.

The name of this magic lamp is RESEARCH.

Ah, do I hear a chorus of sighs? Do I hear, "Hubbard is going to spring that old gag again." "What, another article on research? I thought LRH knew better."

In defense I instantly protest that I am neither the discoverer nor the sole exploiter of research. But I do believe that I have found an entirely new slant upon an ancient object.

In Tacoma a few months ago, I heard a writer sighing that he was having a hell of a time getting plots. This acute writing disease had eaten deeply into his sleep and bankbook. It had made him so alert that he was ruined as a conversationalist, acting, as he did, like an idea sponge. Hanging on and hoping but knowing that no ideas could possibly come his way.

As usual, I injected my thoughts into his plight—a habit which is bad and thankless.

I said, "Here's an idea. Why not go out and dig around in the old files at the library and the capitol at Olympia and find out everything you can on the subject of branding? There should be a lot of stories there."

He raised one eye and leered, "What? Do all that work for a cent and a half a word?"

And just to drive the idea home, I might remark that one day I happened into the New York Public Library. Crossing the file room I slammed into a heavy bulk and ricocheted back to discover I had walked straight into Norvell Page[1] and he into me.

I gaped. "Page!"

"Hubbard!" he whispered in awed tones.

Solemnly we shook each other by the hand.

---

1. **Norvell W. Page:** is best known to SF audiences as the author of "But Without Horns," one of the finest "superman" stories of the golden age, in *Astounding*. Most of his production at the time LRH bumped into him, however, went to *Astounding*'s companion magazine, *The Spider*.

CHORUS: Well, this is the first time I ever saw a writer in a library!

These two instances should serve to illustrate the fact that research does not rhyme with writer no matter what kind of mill[2] you pound.

Research is a habit which is only acquired by sheer force of will. The easy thing to do is guess at the facts— so thinks the writer. When, as a matter of fact, the easy thing to do is go *find* the facts if you have to tear a town to pieces.

Witness what happened last summer.

Staring me in the face were a stack of dangerous profession stories which have since appeared in *Argosy*. At that time they were no more than started and I sighed to see them stretching forth so endlessly.

I chose *Test Pilot* as the next on the list and started to plot it. I thought I knew my aviation because the Department of Commerce tells me so. Blithely, thinking this was easy, I started in upon a highly technical story without knowing the least thing about that branch of flying—never having been a test pilot.

For one week I stewed over the plot. For another week I broiled myself in the scorching heat of my self-accusation. Two weeks and nothing written.

Was I losing money fast!

There wasn't anything for it then. I had to find out something about test pilots.

Across the bay from my place in Seattle is the Boeing plant. At the Boeing plant there would be test pilots. I had to go!

2. **mill:** typewriter (1930s writer slang).

And all for a cent and a half a word.

I went. Egdvedt, the Boeing president, was so startled to see a real live writer in the place that he almost talked himself hoarse.

Mitchell, the chief engineer, was so astounded at my ignorance that he hauled me through the plant until I had bunions the size of onions.

I sighed.

All for a cent and a half a word!

I went home.

About that time it occurred to me that I used to write a lot for the *Sportsman Pilot* and, as long as I had the dope and data, I might as well fix the details in my head by writing them an article.

That done, I suddenly saw a fine plot for my *Argosy* yarn and wrote that in a matter of a day and a half.

Two months went by. Arthur Lawson came in as editor of Dell and promptly remembered *Test Pilot* in Argosy and demanded a story along similar lines.

In two days I wrote that.

A month after that, Florence McChesney[3] decided that she needed a twenty-thousand-word flying story.

"*Test Pilot*," says I, "do your stuff!"

Each and every one of those yarns sold first crack out. Article for the *Sportsman Pilot,* short for *Argosy,* short for *War Birds,* twenty-thousand-worder for *Five Novels*.

One day of research = several hundred bucks in stories.

---

3. **Florence McChesney:** editor of *Five Novels Monthly.*

This naturally made me think things over and, not being quite as foolish as editors think writers are, I added up the account book and promptly went to work. Thus, the moral is yet to come.

On the dangerous profession stories which followed, I almost lost my life and broke my neck trying to make them authentic. On each one I kept a complete list of notes and a list of plots which occurred to me at the time. There is enough writing material in that file to last me at least a year. It is the finest kind of copy because it is risky in the extreme, full of drama and high tension. I haven't any fears about mentioning this, as any writer who is crazy enough to go down in diving suits and up in spar trees[4] deserves all the help he can get.

But research does not end there and that is not the point of this article.

A short time ago I began to search for research on the theory that if I could get a glimmering of anything lying beyond a certain horizon I could go deep enough to find an excellent story.

I stopped doing what I used to do. There was a time when I expected a story to blaze up and scorch me all of its own accord. I have found, however, that there is a premium on divine fire and it is not very bright when used by a pulpateer. This gentleman has to write an immortal story about once every three days to keep eating.

On this plan I began to read exhaustively in old technical books, ancient travel books, forgotten literature.

4. **spar trees:** the treelike arrangement of the round timbers used for extending sails on masts of multi-masted vessels.

But not with the idea of cribbing. I wanted information and nothing else. I wanted to know how the people used to think here, how the land lay there. Given one slim fact for a background, I have found it easy to take off down the channel of research and canal-boat out a cargo of stories.

In other words, I have no use for an obvious story idea as laid out in *Popular Mechanics* or *Forensic Medicine*. I want one slim, forgotten fact. From there a man can go anywhere and the story is very likely to prove unusual.

In one old volume, for instance, I discovered that there was such a thing as a schoolmaster aboard Nelson's ships of the line. That was a weird one. Why should Nelson want a schoolmaster?

Answer: Midshipmen.

When did this occur?

Answer: The Napoleonic Wars.

Ah, now we'll find out how those old ships looked. We'll discover how they fought, what they did.

And there was the schoolmaster during battle. Where? In the "cockpit" helping hack off arms and legs.

Next lead indicated: Surgery during the Napoleonic Wars.

Wild guess in another allied field: Gunnery.

Again: Nelson.

A battle: On the Nile.

A ship or something strange about this battle: *L'Orient*, monster French flagship which mysteriously caught fire and blew up, throwing the weight of guns to Nelson.

Incidental discovery: "The Boy Stood on the Burning Deck" was written about the son of *L'Orient*'s skipper.

Back to midshipmen, the King's Letter Boys: They were hell on wheels, arrogant, ghastly urchins being trained as officers.

And with all this under my mental belt I girded up my mental loins. Complete after a few days of search I had *Mr. Tidwell—Gunner*, which appeared in *Adventure*.

All that because I chanced to find there was a schoolmaster aboard Nelson's ships of the line.

This is now happening right along because I haven't let the idea slide as my laziness dictated I should.

The final *coup d'état* arrived last winter.

Boredom had settled heavily upon me and I sat one evening staring vacantly at a shelf of books. They were most monotonous. Whole sets stretched out along the shelves with very little change in color or size. This annoyed me and I bent forward and took one out just to relieve the regularity.

It proved to be Washington Irving's *Astoria*, his famous epic of the fur trading days.

It had never been brought home to me that Irving had written such a book, and to find out why, I promptly started to read it. The result was, of course, a fur trading story. But the method of arriving at this story was so indirect that it merits a glance.

Irving only served to call to my attention that I was out in the fur trading Northwest and that I had certainly better take advantage of the history of the place.

I roved around, found very little because I had no direct starting point. I went to the *Encyclopaedia Britannica* to discover a bibliography of such source books and started out again to ferret them out.

All these books were contemporary with fur trading days, all of them written, of course, by white men. But everywhere I kept tripping across the phrases "The Warlike Blackfeet," "The Bloodthirsty Blackfeet."

This finally penetrated my thick skull. I did not like it because I thought I knew something about the Blackfeet.

Were they as bad as they were represented?

Into the records. The real records. Into Alexander Henry's Journal. Into this and out of that until I had a stack of material higher than my desk.

And then I capped the climax by locating a young chap in Seattle who happens to be a blood brother of the Blackfeet. Lewis and Clark's Journal contained about five pages concerning the circumstances which surrounded the killing of a Blackfoot brave by Lewis.

The way this suddenly shot down the groove is remarkable to remember. The Hudson's Bay Company, the Nor'Westers, the Blackfeet, John Jacob Astor . . . The story pieces dovetailed with a click.

Coupled with years of experience in the Northwest, these hundred sources jibed to make the story.

The result was *Buckskin Brigades*, a novel being put out this summer by Macaulay.

Buckskin Brigades came to life because I happened to be bored enough one evening to sit and stare at a line of books on a shelf.

This account of researching is not complete unless I mention a certain dogging phobia I have and which I suspect is deeply rooted in most of us.

H. Bedford Jones mentioned it long ago and I did not believe him at the time. But after rolling stacks of it into the mags, I know that BJ was right as a check.

He said that it was hard for a person to write about the things he knew best.

This gives rise to an ancient argument which says pro and con that a writer should write about the things he knows.

Witnesseth: I was born and raised in the West and yet it was not until last year that I sold a couple westerns. And I only sold those because somebody said I couldn't.

Know ye: The Caribbean countries know me as El Colorado and yet the only Caribbean stories I can write are about those countries which I have touched so briefly that I have only the vaguest knowledge of them and am therefore forced to depend upon researching the books and maps for my facts.

Hear ye: I wrote fine Hollywood stories until I came down here and worked in pictures. I wrote one while here and the editor slammed it back as a total loss.

There are only a few exceptions to this. I have been able to cash in heavily upon my knowledge of North China because the place appealed to me as the last word in savage, romantic lore. The last exception seems to be flying stories, though after flying a ship I can't write an aviation story for a month.

The final proof of this assertion came in connection with my Marine Corps stories. Most of my life I have been associated with the Corps one way or another in various parts of the world and I should know something about it.

But I have given up in dark despair.

He Walked to War in Adventure was branded as technically imperfect.

Don't Rush Me in *Argosy*, another marine story, elicited anguished howls of protest.

And yet if there is any story in the world I should be qualified to write, it is a marine story.

These are my woes. The reason for them is probably very plain to everyone. But I'll state my answer anyway.

A man cannot write a story unless he is deeply interested in it. If he thinks he knows a subject, then he instantly becomes careless with his technical details.

The only way I have found it possible to sidetrack these woes is by delving into new fields constantly, looking everywhere for one small fact which will lead me on into a story field I think I'll like.

This is not very good for a writer's reputation, they tell me. A writer, it is claimed, must specialize to become outstanding. I labored trying to build up a converse reputation, hoping to be known as a writer of infinite versatility.

I did not know until two years ago that the specializing writer is *persona non grata* with an editor. Jack Byrne, for instance, rebuilt Argosy with variety as a foundation. And once I heard Bloomfield[5] sigh that he wished some of his top-notchers would stop sending him the same background week in and week out.

Maybe I am right, possibly I am wrong.

---

5. **Howard Bloomfield:** editor of *Adventure* magazine.

A CONVERSATION WITH SCHLIEGELMAN

Written by
Dan Barlow

Illustrated by
Deth P. Sun

About the Author

Dan Barlow was born in Massachusetts, but now lives in Durham, North Carolina, with his wife, Jennifer, and his son, Stephen. He studied writing at the University of North Carolina in Chapel Hill.

He has worked as a stand-up comedian, and he won the 1980 National Open Cribbage Tournament. He has had several humorous essays and cribbage strategy articles published. However, since marrying Jennifer—a fantasy writer and fan—Dan has been inspired to try the field of speculative fiction.

About the Illustrator

Deth P. Sun is a student at the California College of Arts and Crafts, studying painting and thinking of double majoring in printmaking. He is originally from Southern California.

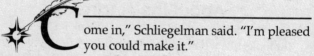

ome in," Schliegelman said. "I'm pleased you could make it."

"What's this all about?" I asked.

"I have something to show you. Something astounding. Follow me."

Schliegelman closed the door behind me, and I followed him through his living room to a small room at the back of the house. "This is my study," he said, "or rather, this is the room which my realtor, twenty years ago, suggested would be a fine study, but which has remained empty all that time, save for this small book-case." The bookcase stood flush against the right wall, crammed with physics books, most of them written by Schliegelman.

There was one other item in the "study," one which Schliegelman now pointed out to me, not that I could have missed it, for it filled fully a third of the room. "Well," he asked, "what do you think?"

"Incredible," I said. "What have you built this time?"

"No, no, I didn't build it."

"Well, it didn't come through that door. How did you get it in here, and what is it? Is this one of your puzzles, Schliegelman?"

"It's a puzzle, to be sure, but not one of my making."

"I still recall that contraption you brought into your physics class once. It had more dials and switches than a 747 cockpit."

"Ah yes. I challenged the class to tell me what it was. There were guesses from a laserscope to a magnetron to an X-ray diffractometer."

"And it turned out to be a toaster."

"Yes. Made excellent toast," Schliegelman boasted.

"I'm sure it did," I said. "So, Professor, what is your *new* toy? A blender?"

He laughed. "Possibly, but I don't think so."

"It looks like a bathysphere with legs," I said. "How *did* you get it in here, by the way?"

"I didn't. It simply appeared here yesterday morning."

"Appeared? What do you mean?"

"I mean," he said, "it wasn't here yesterday at 7:30 when I walked past this room, but when I passed by again, at noon, here it was. I'm reasonably certain that if a crew of workmen had come into my home and built the thing, I'd have noticed them. Thus I can only surmise that it appeared out of thin air."

"I'm skeptical," I told him, "but I'll play along. Do you know what it is?"

"Yes. I've given it a lot of thought, and there is but one possibility: a time machine."

"Impossible," I declared.

"That's what I thought," Schliegelman said, "but what else? Surely it wasn't beamed here from the transporter room of the *Enterprise*."

"Obviously not. A time machine is much more logical."

"Despite your sarcastic tone," Schliegelman said, "you're right. It's the *only* logical explanation."

"Schliegelman, ignoring the purely scientific objections to time travel, has it occurred to you that if time travel were possible, we undoubtedly would have had a visitor from the future by now? That there would be historical records of visitors from the future?"

"Yes, I thought about that. I couldn't get past it for the longest time. A code of laws restricting time travelers to a role as secret observers was my first theory."

"But one which fails to consider man's historic inability to keep anything secret," I said.

"Precisely," he agreed. "I then theorized that perhaps time travel was allowed only into the future, for fear that travel to the past might alter history adversely. I was satisfied with this theory, until yesterday, when I suddenly realized why we've had no visitors from the future."

"Enlighten me," I said.

"The time traveler must reappear in the same place from which he disappears!" Schliegelman explained.

"Your point being?"

"I don't mean the same place on Earth. Why should time travel be subject to Earth's gravity? I mean the same place in the universe. If the Earth and the solar system and the galaxies were all stationary, all would be well. But everything is constantly moving. Moving very fast, as you know. When the time machine rematerializes at its new time, the Earth is nowhere to be seen, and the time traveler is marooned in outer space. Go forward in time a single day, and when you reappear, the Earth is more than a million miles gone."

"I see," I said. "So those who have traveled through time have ended up in space, with no hope other than that of returning to the exact time they left?"

"Correct. And I sincerely doubt the controls of such a machine could be that accurate. To be off by only a few seconds might mean materializing within the Earth's

Illustrated by Deth P. Sun

crust, or beneath an ocean, or, once again, in outer space."

"Interesting," I said. "But your theory leads me to a rather obvious conclusion. Since the Earth has never before been at its current location, and never will be again—you agree, Schliegelman?"

"Odds are certainly against it."

"This object before us cannot be a time machine!"

2

"Coffee?" Schliegelman asked.

"Yes, please, black," I requested.

"You've overlooked something," he told me.

"About the coffee?"

"The coffee? Yes, it's already brewed, I'll be right back."

With Schliegelman out of the room, I took the opportunity to examine the latest addition to his furnishings. It was gray and metallic, and about seven feet tall. The body was nearly spherical, and rested on four stout legs, each two feet high. There were no windows or openings which might afford a view of the inside, but a circular groove around the top suggested a hatch of some sort, though I could see no means of opening this hatch, if such it was. Footholds up the side of the object strengthened my belief that the groove marked an entrance hatch. Theorizing that I was seeing a holographic projection, I kicked one of the legs, but succeeded only in bringing minor pain to my toes.

"Solid as a rock," Schliegelman said, entering the room. He handed me a mug. "What have you concluded in my absence?"

"I first concluded that you had this house built around this object twenty years ago, and that you waited all this time to reveal it, merely for the pleasure of hoodwinking me."

"Ha! I do love a good practical joke!"

"However, I then decided that you could not have resisted this long. Ten years maybe. Fifteen tops. But not twenty. My second guess was that the object has been here since you purchased the house, but that you first noticed it yesterday morning. This seemed a much more plausible theory, for you do tend to be preoccupied much of the time, Schliegelman."

"Most amusing," Schliegelman said.

"Thank you. My final conclusion, however, is that the object has always been here, but has been invisible to you. In some sort of dimensional warp."

"Dimensional warp?" Schliegelman laughed. "You've been reading too much science fiction. The only relevant dimension here is the fourth dimension. Time. The fifth dimension, as you are undoubtedly aware, exists only in used-album stores."

"Very funny. You were telling me that I'd overlooked something."

"Yes," Schliegelman said. "Go over what we know so far."

"We know two things: one, that this thing materialized here yesterday morning; and two, that this is impossible."

"Assume that this 'thing' is a time machine."

"Okay, we know that this *time machine* materialized here yesterday morning. And, based on your theory, we know that it took off from the spot in the universe that this room occupied sometime yesterday morning. Do time machines 'take off,' Schliegelman? Or is there a more accurate term?"

"It's called a chrono-launch."

"Sorry I asked."

"Your conclusion?"

"My conclusion? I conclude that some other planet will pass, or did pass, through the exact spot the Earth occupied yesterday morning, and at that precise moment, a time machine will be, or was, put into service—"

"Chrono-launched."

"There is no such word as *chrono-launched*, Schliegelman. You made it up a minute ago. Admit it."

Schliegelman laughed. "I confess."

"And, incredibly, that time machine materialized right here on Earth, in your study."

"Ridiculous," Schliegelman scoffed. "Do you have any idea what the odds are of two planets with intelligent life passing through the exact same spot in the universe through all eternity?"

"Yes. A trillion times a trillion times a trillion to one."

"Not nearly that good."

"Okay, I give up. How do *you* explain the time machine?"

"You were close, but you failed to consider the obvious: the time machine was chrono-launched—sorry—the time machine took off . . . from a spaceship."

"A spaceship which just happened to be, at some point in time, at the exact position in the universe that your house occupied yesterday morning, when someone decided to . . . chrono-launch a time machine?"

"Highly unlikely. No. A spaceship which was—or will be—*intentionally navigated* to the exact position in the universe my house occupied yesterday morning."

3

"Excellent coffee," I said.

"Thank you," my colleague replied. "It's from Jamaica, a gift from a friend."

I took a sip, and said, "Schliegelman, I got lost three times trying to find your street. Yet you seem confident your house can be found from decades into the past or future. I bow to your expertise in all matters scientific, as you know, but . . ."

"Surely you aren't suggesting that the location of my house cannot be extrapolated by any competent mathematician, given the Earth's speed of rotation, its path through space, the movement pattern of the galaxies, and an accurate road map?"

"Of course not," I lied. "But is there really such a creature as a specific place in the universe?"

"Yes, there is. There are many. There's the North Star. There's Wrigley Field. And there's my study, which has recently become either a time machine landing strip, or a repository for the scrap metal of an advanced civilization."

"You know what I mean, Schliegelman. The universe itself could be rotating or shifting, and this would be undetectable. There needs to be a fixed reference point if one is to locate a specific place in which to land a time machine."

"Ah, but there *is* a fixed reference point," Schliegelman told me.

"And what is this immovable, unshifting, immune-to-all-forces point?" I demanded.

"Why, the time machine itself," Schliegelman stated gleefully. "Or rather the point from which it chrono-launches."

"I don't get it."

"We've already declared that the time machine always 'lands' at the same spot from which it departs."

"True, or not, we have declared it," I confirmed.

"Suppose a time machine is sent to the past or future, programmed to return two seconds later than the time it was sent. Using the astronomical data at their disposal, scientists determine the expected position of their spaceship, relative to the position of the time machine, which they know will reappear in the same place where it vanished. If they expect their spaceship to have moved two kilometers from the time machine, and it has, then they know that the rotation of the universe does not exist, or has no effect on the time machine. However, if they find that they've moved ten kilometers from the time machine, they assume the discrepancy to be the result of the universe's movement."

"So they make allowances for the extra eight kilometers. But in what direction, Schliegelman? There is no directional bearing in the universe."

"True, but suppose they send out two time machines, or ten. With several fixed points, they employ standard triangulation methods, adjust their coordinates, a little trial and error to confirm that they got it right, and *voilà!* Provided they can get their ship to the right location, they can send the machine anywhere, anytime."

"Even to your study."

"Yes, though I suspect they were aiming for my kitchen."

"That *would* make more sense," I agreed. "One would work up quite an appetite on a voyage of several centuries."

"I've worked one up myself," Schliegelman said. "I'll get us some fruit and cheese."

4

I stood alone in a room, with the most remarkable discovery in the history of mankind, and all I could think was what a boon it would be to the package delivery industry. *Federal Express: When it absolutely, positively has to be there three decades ago.*

What else was it good for? You couldn't go back and murder Hitler when he was a child, or hunt tyrannosaurs. To do so would apparently require loading the time machine on a spaceship, and traveling to the point the Earth occupied in 1895, or in the Cretaceous period. Too much trouble. Yet someone had taken the trouble to get this time machine into this house. Why?

Schliegelman brought in some sliced Jarlsberg and some bread and grapes, and placed them on the bookshelf. "What do you make of it all?" he asked.

"I'm ashamed to admit I was thinking how useless it is," I said.

"Ha! I had the same reaction. Figured it would be great for the witness relocation program, but what else?"

"How about tourism?"

"Wouldn't be cost effective. *Relive the '60s, only a trillion dollars.*"

"I've concluded, on a more serious note," I said, "that the machine has come from the future, rather than the past."

"Ah! I agree with your assessment," Schliegelman told me. "What was your reasoning?"

"For one thing, whoever sent it knows you live in this house. Until twenty years ago, you didn't live here. Even if they sent it from five or ten years ago, you could have moved, or died. For them to know with certainty that you live here at this time, would require them to have knowledge of your life at this time, knowledge they could only get in the future."

"I see. Anything else?"

"Yes. Finding the spot the Earth occupied yesterday would be easier from the future, as there'd be astronomical data. But from the past you'd have to *predict* Earth's position. A comet or asteroid could pass through the solar system, its gravitational field affecting the Earth's path enough to throw off the accuracy of the prediction."

"Excellent. But you have forgotten one thing about the beings with the time machine."

"What's that?"

"That they are beings with a time machine. They have the ability to come forward in time, confirm my address and the Earth's location, and to then proceed with their plan."

"True, I didn't think of that. But I'm not finished. I figure travel to the future is more dangerous. What if you materialize on Earth in the year 2200, only to find that there's a nuclear war going on? You could be killed instantly. Going back in time you can choose a time and place you know to be peaceful."

"Irrelevant. If they need something from the future, they aren't going to go to the past just because it's safer. Besides, you're assuming that the time machine must be manned. Certainly if they have the ability to send an unmanned time machine, programmed to gather data and return, they would do so before risking lives. And you must admit that the adventure of time travel would induce many to take such a risk anyway."

"First you agree with my conclusion, then you shoot holes in all my reasons for it. What makes *you* think it has come from the future?"

"I'll get to that in a moment, but first, since you do assume a manned time machine, I'm surprised you have yet to speculate on whether this particular time machine might be occupied."

"This one? Why . . . I naturally presumed that if it were occupied, its occupants would have made an appearance by now. Or we'd have heard some noise from the inside."

"Ah, but perhaps the occupant has determined that he cannot survive in our atmosphere, or that bacteria in our air would be fatal. Perhaps one must be placed in suspended animation for time travel, and he's still under. Perhaps time travel itself renders one temporarily unconscious, or . . ."

"Perhaps there's more than one occupant, Schliegelman. Perhaps there are three, and they got out of the time machine before you discovered it, and are somewhere in this house, watching us, waiting for just the right moment to spring their diabolical trap!"

"Ha! You've got the makings of a scientist!" Schliegelman told me, and I gushed with pride, though I knew he was being sarcastic.

"You were going to explain why you believe it's from the future," I said.

"Yes, well, that is merely a hunch, a hunch based on their motive in sending the time machine."

"Their motive? You know their motive?"

"No, but I have conjectures, as I'm sure you would if you gave it some thought."

"Well, it's obviously not a coincidence that the thing landed in the home of the greatest theoretical physicist on the planet."

Schliegelman agreed, both with my statement and my flattery. "And based on that premise," he said, "there are three possibilities. Number one, someone wants something from me."

"Probably some rich kid from the future wants you to do his math homework."

"If I may continue? Either they've sent someone to get what they want, or they expect me to figure out what it is and send it to them."

"In other words, to solve some problem, put the solution in the time machine, and send it back."

"Or forward, as the case may be. Correct. Or to put *myself* in and go back or forward to provide assistance with some seemingly insurmountable problem. Possibly even a problem I myself caused. Or will cause."

"Of course they could have made this easier for you," I said. "A user's manual, or a door. Or a can opener."

"True. But perhaps their intentions will be made known by the passenger, if one eventually emerges. A second possibility is that the time machine is a gift, or contains a gift, some means of showing appreciation for some future accomplishment of mine."

"Interesting. *Schliegelman's theories on time travel changed the universe, but he never lived to see the fruits of his work. Let's travel to a spot the Earth occupied during his lifetime and ship him a silk tie as a thank-you gift.* I like it."

"A third possibility is that this is meant to inspire me to direct my future work toward time travel. By showing me that this is a viable pursuit, they hope research will push ahead, and that time travel will become a reality sooner."

"Sounds like a military conspiracy. Someone lost a war they'd have won if they'd had time machines to go back and kill the enemy leaders' grandparents. If, thanks to your research, time machines are coming off the assembly line twenty years sooner, maybe the Mutalians rule the Galaxy, instead of the Vorelli. Personally, I think you should stay out of it. The Vorelli may be vicious killers, but the Mutalians have horrible table manners."

"Yes, well, I've made my point. If the time machine is a gift, it must be from the future, as I've done nothing up to now that would inspire such gratitude. If it's meant to direct my future research, it's unlikely to be from the past, for those in the past would not benefit from my work. And if it's an attempt to secure my assistance on some pressing problem, it is unlikely to be a request from the past, or why not travel an extra two hundred years into the future and get someone far more qualified?"

"Maybe they didn't have enough fuel to get to wherever Earth will be in two hundred years."

"They somehow managed to get here. Chances are they can get wherever they need to."

"Maybe they didn't have time."

"When you have a time machine, you have all the time in the world. I'll admit nothing I've said is proof, but each of the three possible motives points to the future as the source of our mystery."

"There is a fourth possibility, Schliegelman, perhaps the most likely motive of all, yet you seem to have completely overlooked it. Or perhaps you simply *wanted* to overlook it."

"I'm listening."

"Suppose your future work is destined to cause some sort of tear in the very fabric of the universe, one which threatens all life in all galaxies. Would they not send someone back to your past to eliminate you?"

"To rub me out, you mean? A time-traveling hit man? That's your theory?"

"Yes, Schliegelman. And the sad part is, if the hit man is inside that time machine, unconscious, and unable to carry out his task, I'll have to kill you myself. For the good of the universe, you understand."

"Of course. But how will you know the hit man wasn't sent by the bad guys?"

"The Mutalians?"

"Yes, to prevent me from creating Goodness, Truth and Wonderfulness Elixir."

"Good point. Okay, you can live. I'll kill the Mutalian in the time machine instead."

"Thanks. More coffee?"

"Please."

"I'll brew some more. If the intergalactic hit man comes out while I'm gone, tell him I died of a heart attack when I saw the time machine appear."

5

As I awaited Schliegelman's return, I considered the possibilities he had suggested. A gift? Nobody's that generous. That would be like spending a trillion dollars to go back in time and present Gutenberg with a Xerox machine. A nice gesture, but of little value.

An attempt to inspire Schliegelman to work in the time travel field? I wasn't buying that either. If you want time machines available earlier, why send one to Schliegelman? Why not just send one to whomever you want to have it? Not only does that make it available, it makes it available only to your chosen recipients, not an entire planet full of rip-off artists and industrial spies.

That left the possibility (assuming it wasn't a hit man) that someone needed Schliegelman's help. But why Schliegelman? Why not some super scientist from the twenty-second century?

Maybe there *was* no twenty-second century. Maybe time machines were being sent to all the great minds, so they could be brought together to solve the twenty-second century mystery of the vanishing galaxies. Maybe Schliegelman's work *caused* the vanishing galaxies, and they wanted to tell him to retire now and take up the cello.

I popped a couple grapes into my mouth. Annoyingly, they had seeds, which I spit into my hand. There was no wastebasket, so I pressed the seeds into a thick piece of cheese, gambling that my actions were not being monitored by a hidden camera on the time machine. I started to put the cheese into my pocket, but fearing Schliegelman would notice the smell or the grease stain, I left the room to flush it down the nearest commode. The coffee had left me needing the facilities anyway.

When I returned to the study, Schliegelman was back. He was sitting on the floor in an apparent state of grogginess.

And the hatch on the time machine was open.

6

"Schliegelman!" I cried. "What happened? Are you all right?"

"Why . . . yes, I think so. What time is it? Have I been here the whole time?"

"I was under the impression you were in the kitchen, brewing coffee. However, I see no coffee. Are you sure you're okay?"

"I'm not sure of anything anymore. But I may have just visited the future."

"You've been in the time machine?"

"I have."

"I was in the bathroom five minutes at the most, Schliegelman. Are you saying that in that short time, you returned to the room—perhaps to ask if I'd like crumpets with the coffee—that you found the time machine open, climbed inside, went into the future, had some wondrous adventure, returned to the exact time you left, and climbed out of the time machine? Granted, you could have been in the future, or the past, any length of time, even decades, as long as you returned to the time when I was out of the room. However, I assume, from the fact that you don't look any older, that you haven't been gone more than a few years. Your hair looks no longer, leading me to believe that you've been gone less than a week, though of course there are probably barbers in the future. I suddenly realize that you are wearing the same clothing. This does not surprise me, for to the best of my knowledge, you always wear a white shirt and black pants. However, none of your clothing appears inordinately wrinkled, which leads me to believe you've been gone no more than a day. Or that there are fabulous dry cleaners in the twenty-fifth century. How'm I doing, Schliegelman?"

"Your deductive powers are fascinating. However, there are two questions I would like to have answered before we continue with this discussion."

"I feel I'm the one who should be asking the questions, but go ahead."

"Number one, how did you know this was a time machine? And number two—and please don't take this the wrong way, my friend—what are you doing in my house?"

I paused, stunned by Schliegelman's questions. Had time travel robbed him of his memory? If so, how much of it? "Are you sure you're all right?" I said. "You still seem a bit woozy."

"I believe I'm okay now. I apparently blacked out while in the time machine, and only recovered moments ago."

"Can I get you some water? Or a stiff drink?"

"No, I'll be fine. Just help me up, will you?"

I assisted Schliegelman in standing, then said, "I don't quite get the drift of the questions you asked me. Are you unaware of the fact that I was present in this house before you entered the time machine?"

"To my knowledge, you were not present."

"Were you time traveling long enough to have forgotten the circumstances under which you left? Or has the experience affected your memory?"

"I have no idea how long I was gone, nor even *if* I was gone. And I distinctly remember being the only person present when the time machine opened."

"That's because I was in the bathroom. But surely you remember inviting me to come and see the time machine?"

"I'm quite sure I *would* remember that, if it had happened."

"I'm not making all of this up, Schliegelman!"

"Of course not. There has to be an explanation. I can, in fact, think of two. Tell me something: when did the time machine first appear?"

"Have you forgotten that too? According to you, it happened sometime yesterday morning."

"I see. My first guess is that everything happened as you claim it did. That I entered the time machine while you were in the bathroom, traveled through time, and returned. However, I returned to the wrong time. I returned to yesterday morning. You were then summoned, arrived and were greeted by me. Not the 'me' in the time machine, mind you, for I was still unconscious, but the 'me' who phoned you."

"Your evil twin?"

"Yes. Look at it this way. I'm in the house at two o'clock and at three. At three I take off in the time machine, and return at two. Is the 'me' who was in the house at two still there?"

"Good question. If he is, we can assume that the 'you' who invited me here today will walk through that door any second, holding two cups of freshly brewed coffee."

"And, in all likelihood, drop them on the floor in shock. I don't actually believe this possibility is likely, however, as I have no memory of your being here before I entered the time machine. Perhaps the memory has been expunged from my brain, but I doubt it."

"You said you had two possible explanations."

"Yes. The second is somewhat similar, but more likely. Suppose sometime in the future—it could be tomorrow, or years from now—a time machine somehow arrives in my study. I board it, black out, and the time machine eventually carries me to yesterday morning. I remain unconscious, while you are summoned to this house. I then awaken and emerge from the time machine just before you walk into the room, moments ago."

"In this case, once again, the other 'you' is about to come in and spill coffee on the floor."

"Yes. I'm afraid the carpet is doomed, no matter which theory proves accurate."

"There is a problem with both possibilities, Schliegelman. According to you—the other you—an attempt to return to the same spot you took off from, which was off by even a small amount of time, would leave the time machine in outer space, as the Earth would have moved."

"That is true. For me to be on Earth at a time earlier than that at which I left, I must have been transported to a spot the Earth previously occupied."

"That would require incredibly fast transportation."

"Or a means of transportation that is, itself, capable of time travel. Send the vehicle back in time far enough, and it has plenty of time to get where it's going."

"I see. So, do you have any memory of arriving on a space vehicle, and being transported anywhere?"

"None. As far as I know, I was unconscious the entire time I was inside the time machine." ·

"So, to summarize your hypothesis, some beings sent you a time machine. You got in and it chrono-launched, and—"

"'Chrono-launched?' Where'd you come up with that?"

"Never mind. You became unconscious, went back in time to a ship, which then itself traveled back in time before taking you to the spot the Earth occupied yesterday morning and sending you forward in time, in the time machine, to your own house. You lay unconscious in the time machine until five or ten minutes ago, at which point I left the room and you regained consciousness and came out."

"So it would seem."

"So the big question is, Why?"

"Yes, why? Errr . . . why what?"

"Why has someone apparently taken great pains to arrange a meeting between you . . . and yourself?"

"Ah. Yes, it's a mystery."

"You'd think they'd have placed a clue of some sort in the time machine with you."

"Perhaps they did. I didn't inspect my surroundings when I awoke. I'll take a look."

Schliegelman climbed up the side of the time machine and peered inside. "Most interesting," he said, and he disappeared into the interior.

"What do you see?" I asked.

"I'm not sure what to make of this. Just a moment."

I waited, and as I did so, I heard the sound of footsteps in the hallway. With Schliegelman number two out of sight, perhaps the carpet would be spared after all.

7

Schliegelman number one entered the room, holding two cups of steaming coffee. I took mine from him and suggested he set his on the bookcase. "Something extraordinary has happened," I said. "Look!" I pointed toward the time machine, noting with alarm as I did so, that the hatch had closed.

"What are you pointing at?" Schliegelman asked. "Has something changed?"

"It opened! While you were out of the room!"

"Ah! And? Did anyone come out? A Mutalian? A hit man? A Mutalian hit man? They're the worst kind, you know."

"It was you, Schliegelman!! *You* came out! The future you!"

"Me? Incredible."

"It *was* incredible. But I saw you with my own eyes."

"I just want to know one thing. In the future, do I still have my hair?"

"Schliegelman!"

"You're not joking, are you? I naturally assumed you were putting me on. So where am I?"

"You went back inside, just a minute ago."

"That's good news. You're aware, I assume, of the old superstition. If a mad scientist emerges from a time machine, and sees his past self . . . two more weeks of nuclear winter."

"Will you get serious, Schliegelman! I tell you, your future self is inside the time machine! He's obviously here for a reason. We have to do something."

"Maybe we should lock him in. I'm not sure it's a good idea to meet myself. Not that I think it would tear a hole in the universe or anything, but you never know. I mean, can two of Schliegelman's brains exist at the same time, in the same room, when there's really only one Schliegelman?"

"God help us all if they can. But unless you were a zombie while you were making the coffee, both your brains *can* exist at the same time, Schliegelman, if not in the same room."

"Did he . . . did I . . . say anything?"

"Yes. We had a long discussion. We were trying to figure out why he was sent here to confront you, and he decided to look inside the time machine for the answer. He sounded like he'd found something interesting. For Pete's sake, let's get him out of there!"

I stepped close to the time machine and banged on the outside. "Schliegelman?" I called out. "What are you doing?"

Silence. I climbed up to the hatch. "He may be unconscious again," I said. "There has to be a way to open this from the outside." I banged on all sides of the hatch, to no avail. Leaning toward the rear of the time machine, I discovered on the back of the hatch, near the hinge, a keypad with three buttons, which I commenced pressing randomly.

"Don't bother," Schliegelman said. "I tried every conceivable pattern yesterday morn—"

The hatch began hissing, and slowly opened.

"I'm not sure this is a good idea," Schliegelman said. "I don't think Miss Manners covers this. What does one say upon meeting oneself?"

"If it were I, I'd start by apologizing for being a jackass most of my life," I said.

"Not a bad suggestion."

"Schliegelman," I said, "meet Schliegelman."

No Schliegelman emerged. I leaned forward and looked inside the time machine. It was empty.

8

"Huh?" I blurted. "It's empty! But . . . I saw you get in! I don't get it!"

"Empty, you say? Strange. Most perplexing. Are you sure you weren't hallucinating when you—"

"Quite sure, Schliegelman."

"So I've vanished. Perhaps it truly *is* impossible for one being to exist twice in the same place at the same time. When I entered the room, POOF! My future self could not exist here."

"And went back to his own time?"

"I hope so. Either that, or simply vanished."

"That's a scary thought. To be responsible for your own obliteration just by walking into the room. At least you aren't doomed to keep doing it over and over, because next time the time machine appears, to the future you, you'll remember this and you can stay out of it."

"Actually, it may have already appeared. Who's to say it won't be sitting here for as long as I own this house? If so, the future has been altered irrevocably by this event."

"Unless the time machine disappears, and we develop selective amnesia with regard to it."

"Yes, well, in any case, there are other possibilities, as usual. And I believe they are more reasonable than the 'poof' theory."

"I can think of one myself," I said. "Perhaps the Schliegelman whom I saw enter the time machine was a holographic image being projected by the time machine itself. It was showing you what they want you, yourself, to do—namely, get in."

"An interesting theory. But one thing bothers me about it."

"Besides the fact that *you* didn't think of it?"

"Yes. It's the fact that it's preposterous. I thought you said you and 'I' had a lengthy conversation. Unless the hologram were brilliantly programmed, you undoubtedly would have suspected it wasn't alive at some point."

"That's true, I suppose. Come to think of it, I touched him when I helped him off the floor. Okay, so what is *your* explanation?"

"One possibility is that the time machine took the future me to another time, and then was sent back to this time."

"But it never disappeared. Not even for a second."

"How can you be sure? If it disappeared into the future, but returned and rematerialized at the exact same time at which it disappeared, we would have no way of knowing it ever left."

"Mind boggling."

"However, I note that there are no impressions in the carpet to indicate the time machine's former position. Which means it must have returned to the exact same location, not even a few millimeters off. Pinpoint accuracy. Not impossible, but . . ."

"You're debunking your own theory?"

"Not entirely. Merely expressing a preference for my second theory, if you'd care to hear it."

"By all means."

"The time machine does not itself actually travel, but merely transports its occupant, much like the *Enterprise*'s transporter, but through time rather than space."

"But we've already hypothesized that time travel, if not accurate to the second, could leave the time traveler stranded in outer space, or perhaps within the wall of a building, or a mile above the planet's surface. Obviously without the time machine to protect the traveler, the whole experience would be unacceptably perilous. Besides, it wasn't just you who appeared out of thin air, Schliegelman. The time machine did travel here."

"Ah, but suppose it was transported here by a larger time machine, one which remained at its home, just as this one remained here when I (the future I) left. You place a small time machine inside a large one, and send the small one to the time you wish to visit. It's actually an ingenious method of setting up two-way transportation. In fact, it's the only way for time travelers to get back where they started, if the time machines themselves don't travel through time."

"Expensive, however. Once you send one some-where, you can't get it back."

"Nonetheless, I like this theory," Schliegelman said.

"And I like your other one," I countered.

"Perhaps both methods are feasible. I see only one way to settle this. One of us is going to have to operate the time machine."

9

"One of us, Schliegelman? Meaning, possibly me? I'm shocked to think your scientific curiosity would not drive you to insist on being the one, assuming there's to be a 'one.'"

"I'll admit that the prospect intrigues me, but it also concerns me. Suppose I get in the time machine, and the beings who control it . . ."

"The Vorelli."

". . . take me back to two days ago. The 'past me' will find the time machine, possibly summon you here, and we'll repeat the scenario that played out today."

"You're saying we'll be trapped in a never-ending loop, repeating our actions over and over as the calendar goes backwards for us?"

"Not *never-ending*. It'll last about twenty years. Eventually we'll get back to the day before I owned this house, and when I emerge from the time machine, I'll find my realtor staring wide-eyed at me. Or I'll find Scully and Mulder here in my study, having been summoned by my realtor."

"Scully and Mulder didn't exist twenty years ago, Schliegelman."

"Scully and Mulder don't exist now."

"Oh yeah. Right."

"Of course, the process doesn't have to take twenty years to play out. If the time machine goes back a month at a time, rather than a day, it would be a mere seven months or so before government agents got hold of it and started their insidious experiments."

"How does all this change if *I* operate the time machine?"

"The only way to break a time loop is to do something differently than it's been done the other times through the loop. And the only way to be sure we're doing it differently is to do something totally outlandish, something we're unlikely to ever repeat."

"Like sending *me* off in the time machine."

"Yes. Suppose that when the time machine opens, *you* come out! The loop is surely broken! Imagine the situation. I'm making coffee. You are in the bathroom . . ."

"I return to this room and discover, sitting on the floor, my twin. In this case he might be dressed differently than I, though not necessarily."

"And how would you react?"

"I would probably reach the conclusion that you had invited me here to show me the results of your cloning experiment. I would be somewhat upset with you for cloning me without my knowledge, of course, and in a fit of anger, I would murder the clone. When the 'clone' later turned out to be my future self, I would be overcome with remorse. I would climb into the time machine, in an attempt to escape the memory of what I'd done, and be transported another day into the past. I'd then get trapped in a time loop in which I kill my future self every day. Twenty years from now, I'd finally meet Gillian Anderson."

"By then you'll be twenty years older, and she'll be twenty years younger."

"How sad. Guess it wasn't meant to be."

"If we can return to reality for a moment?"

"We're standing in front of a time machine, Schliegelman. And you speak of this as reality?"

"Here's what might happen after you discover your future self in the time machine. He doesn't get back in the time machine. If he remembers this conversation, he tells us what's going on and we break the loop. If he *doesn't* remember, we are left to try to determine how *he* came to be sent here in a time machine. Why you, and not me. Perhaps we figure out that it is our own doing, and we end the loop."

"Of course, in all likelihood, there is no loop at all, Schliegelman, and the time machine will take me to the transporter room of a Vorellian cruiser, where either they'll perform probing experiments on my body, or they'll say, 'Who the hell are you? We were expecting Schliegelman!'"

"Probing experiments?"

"Of course, they normally pluck nitwits out of Arkansas trailer camps for their probing experiments. Most likely they'll send me back to get you, and you'll go to the Vorellian cruiser."

"Where they'll perform probing experiments on *my* body?"

"Exactly."

10

"Schliegelman, something bothers me about this time loop theory. In order for the loop to continue for twenty years, the Vorelli have to keep transporting you to the place the Earth occupied the day before. They would have to do this every time you get in the time machine, possibly every day, right?"

"Yes."

"Over and over and over, right?"

"What is your point?"

"Why should they? Wouldn't they give up after a few tries? Or a few hundred?"

"There are two reasons they might not give up," Schliegelman said. "One, they are desperate to convey some information to me, but cannot do so while we are trapped in this time loop. They keep hoping one of these times we'll break the loop."

"I suppose if the fate of the universe rested with our breaking the loop, it would be worth their time and effort. What's the second possibility?"

"The second possibility is that the Vorelli are caught in the same time loop. That they will keep transporting me, because they are unaware that they've done so already, many times."

"So if we can end the loop, we're not only saving ourselves from the loop, we're saving the Vorelli."

"Depending on the nature of their mission, we may be saving the entire universe. Let's not forget that this whole thing started when they sent a time machine to the future me. They didn't go to all that trouble on a lark."

"True. Okay, Schliegelman, let's say I get in the time machine. One of two things will happen. If we *are* caught in a time loop, I will end up on a spaceship and will then be transported, within a time machine just like this one, to this room, but a few days ago."

"If so," Schliegelman claimed, "I will undoubtedly realize we're in a loop as soon as you come out of the time machine."

"If we are *not* caught in a time loop," I continued, "I will end up on a spaceship, and will impersonate you, assisting the Vorelli or the Mutalians in saving the universe."

"Or destroying it."

"Right. Eventually they'll realize I'm not you, assume I took your place in an attempt to foil their plans, and vaporize me with phasers. Listen, I hope you won't think any less of me, Schliegelman, but I don't really want to travel through time until it's been okayed by Ralph Nader."

He laughed. "Understood. I'm sure we can come up with something else."

"Why don't you get a Magic Marker and write on your shirt *Time Loop!*

"Then *you* do the time traveling. If you come out of the time machine with that written on your shirt, we'll obviously suspect a loop."

"Hmm. You know, that's not a bad idea."

"Really?"

"Simple, yet effective, assuming I'm still wearing the same shirt when I return. I'll get a Magic Marker. You see if you can get that hatch open again."

Schliegelman left the room and I climbed onto the time machine. Before I could touch the keypad, the hatch began hissing. I jumped to the ground and gaped upward as the hatch slowly opened.

"Schliegelman!" I called, running to the door, but the man had disappeared from the hallway. I turned back into the room and saw, stepping down the footholds on the side of the time machine, Schliegelman! He stepped down to the floor and turned toward me. On the front of his shirt, printed in Magic Marker, were the words *Time Loop!*

11

"You're here!" Schliegelman said. "Thank God!"

"Thank God? Why?"

"I believe I was caught in a time loop. One can never be certain, of course."

"Hence the words *Time Loop!* on your shirt?"

"Yes. A simple yet brilliant idea, if I do say so myself."

"Yes, only a true genius would think of it. So you aren't in a time loop?"

"If I was, it's been broken."

"How can you know that?"

"I can't, definitively, but I was here once before, and you were in the bathroom when I arrived. Now I'm back, and you're here. It's different, so I assume it's new. Besides, it's not like time loops develop every few minutes. I expect they're rather rare."

"Does that mean *we* aren't in a loop either?"

"We?"

"Me and the other Schliegelman. *My* Schliegelman. The one from this time. By the way, if you'd be so kind as to stick around till he returns?"

"A highly intriguing invitation. However, I'm expected elsewhere, and the fate of the universe is at stake. Nothing for you to worry about, I assure you. It's centuries down the road. And now that the loop is broken, we can get on with our work."

"We?"

"Me, Einstein, a few beings from other galaxies." He climbed up the side of the time machine. "Say hello to me when I get back," he said, "and if I'm responsible for breaking the time loop, thank me." He descended into the time machine and the hatch silently closed.

Schliegelman—*my* Schliegelman—entered the room moments later. He had printed *Time Loop!* on the front of his shirt.

"Must you always be gone when you're here?" I complained.

"What does *that* mean?"

"Your future self came out again. He just now left to go save the universe. He said to thank you if you were responsible for breaking the time loop."

"Hmm. Perhaps I was, by inviting you here. Or perhaps *you* were, by coming. Perhaps in all the other loops, you decided you were too busy to come view another Schliegelman discovery."

"So, I'm responsible for saving the universe?"

"I said 'perhaps.'"

"Let me see if I've got this straight, Schliegelman. The future universe was in danger of ceasing to exist. Time machines were sent to your future self, and to a bunch of other scientists, all of whom are now trying to solve this problem. Or will be in a few centuries. Somewhere along the way a time loop formed, trapping the future you and threatening to disrupt his crucial role in preventing the destruction of the universe. Meanwhile, by recognizing the possibility of a time loop, you—the present you—took steps to break it, and now your future self can go on to play his part in seeing that life goes on."

"For once, you make perfect sense."

I thought it over for a few moments. "Of course there's another possibility, Schliegelman."

"There always is."

"Suppose this apparatus before us is actually an elaborate magician's illusion, one which allows you to seemingly vanish, but to actually slip into another part of the house. Suppose this entire afternoon has been a brilliant hoax you've subjected me to, for your own sadistic amusement."

"An interesting theory. Not impossible, from your point of view, I guess. I don't recommend testing it however."

"Why not?"

"The Vorelli, or whoever arranged this party, are decades, or centuries, in the future. Now that the loop is broken, they have no reason to always keep their ship in the exact location *our* Earth occupies. If you were to enter the time machine, seeking mirrors and trapdoors, you might find yourself transported, not into my basement, and not into a larger time machine aboard a Vorellian cruiser, but into barren, empty outer space, billions of miles from the nearest Dairy Queen. Whereas, if you get into your car, you can drive a mere two miles to the nearest Dairy Queen, and reward yourself for saving your children's children's children's universe."

"That does sound better."

"I, meanwhile, shall attempt to dismantle this hunk of metal before curiosity compels anyone to climb inside. Once it's no longer operational, I believe I'll convert it into something useful."

"Such as?"

"Why, what else? A clock!"

IN ORBITE MEDIEVALI

Written by
Toby Buckell

Illustrated by
Yana Yavdoshchook

About the Author

Toby Buckell was born in the Caribbean and grew up spending time on Grenada and the Virgin Islands. When Hurricane Marilyn destroyed the boat he and his family were living on, they moved to Amish farmland in Ohio, where Toby is currently finishing up at Bluffton Liberal Arts College.

He has a story in Science Fiction Age, and another due in Nalo Hopkinson's anthology of Caribbean Fabulist Fiction, tentatively titled "Whispers from the Ceiba Tree Root." Many years ago, while Toby was a sophomore in high school, L. Ron Hubbard's Writers of the Future Contest was the first place to which he ever submitted work.

About the Illustrator

Yana Yavdoshchook lives in Lugansk, Ukraine. Her style is highly reminiscent of other artists from the Ukraine, where apparently the professors of art believe that you cannot draw something until you have closely studied a model of it. For "In Orbite Medievali," Yana did an outstanding job.

In a letter to Queen Isabella:

"Whereas, Most Christian, High, Excellent, and Powerful Princes, King and Queen of Spain and of the Islands of the Sea, our Sovereigns, this present year 1492, after Your Highnesses terminated the war with the Moors reigning in Europe . . .

"Your Highnesses, as Catholic Christians, and Princes who love and promote the holy Christian faith, and are enemies of the doctrine of Mahomet, and of all idolatry and heresy, determined to send me, Cristóbal Colón, to the above-mentioned countries of India, to see the said princes, people, and territories, and to learn their disposition and the proper method of converting them to our holy faith; and furthermore directed that I should not proceed by land to the East, as is customary, but by a westerly route, in which direction we have hitherto no certain evidence that anyone has gone." — Cristóbal Colón, 1492

The rim of the earth flashed past them as they fell. The edge of the world looked rather like the cliffs of Gibraltar—tall edifices of solid imposing rock. Only here the basalt stretched to the left and the right as far as the eye could see and, when they looked up, ran what seemed like miles above them. Finally it disappeared into roils of mist and clouds.

Once they had fallen past the edge it started to dwindle into the distance above them.

Sheets of seawater still cascaded down with the ship.

Pedro Yzquierdo used his knife to dig the bone out of the piece of meat in his stew. Already he'd made a mess, wobbling the bowl and causing its contents to ooze out into the air. He finally got the bone out. It spun away to hit the mast. Pedro retrieved it, throwing it out, away from the ship.

"Caca." Heavily salted meats, shriveled peas, stale water, and when he tapped his hardtack biscuit, weevils wriggled out into the air. The tossed bone passed the railing, and flew up past the ship's masts as the flat side of the bone caught the wind rushing up the sides of the hull.

Pedro noticed Rodrigo Gellego begin to shudder and heave.

He's seasick, Pedro thought. Or at least just sick. It had nothing to do with the sea, really. The seawater near them now just hung in curtains.

Rodrigo threw up. The bland results of dinner floated out in pasty globules. Several members of the crew swatted at the liquid in disgust with empty plates, trying to redirect the nasty-smelling bile over the decks and out across the ship's railing. It helped some. But if they hit it too hard it splattered and spread instead, making a worse mess.

"Mierda," someone muttered from inside steerage, the rear area of the deck covered by the quarterdeck. They started making similar sounds. Pedro sunk his knife into the mast and pushed off over to the sick man.

"Rodrigo," he yelled. The sound of the wind singing through the rigging and rails forced him to project his voice. "Stay near the edge. You'll have everyone else sick at this rate."

Rodrigo shook his head.

"No. I won't go near the edge. Dios mío, no! Give me a sack, Pedro, but do not make me do that."

"We can tie you to the rails . . ."

"It's windy. It's loud. Leave me here en la calma," Rodrigo pleaded.

Diego de Arana, master-at-arms, leaned over the quarterdeck. "What happens here?" he demanded. Rodrigo twisted in the air to look at him.

"He's sick," replied Pedro.

"Put him in a hammock. He shouldn't eat for a day."

"Señor Diego . . ."

"No buts, Pedro. He will keep throwing up if we feed him. Do you remember what you were like the first time you put out to sea?" Diego de Arana smiled. "He *will* get accustomed to it, just like you got accustomed to being at sea. Some people get used to the sea faster. Eh, Pedro?"

Pedro nodded.

"Verdad, señor. But none of us have ever fallen off of the edge of the world before." He tugged on Rodrigo gently, towing him towards steerage. Here, underneath the quarterdeck, all the other men huddled, strapped into their hammocks.

"Pedro," Diego said, "don't say that; we have not fallen off of the edge of the world. Don't be an ignorant peasant. Agilipollao!"

Pedro guided them both through steerage, looking for an empty hammock and a sack for Rodrigo. Diego could call him an ignorant peasant, a stupid fool, but Pedro did not care. It still didn't make sailing off of the edge of the world any stranger than it was.

Rodrigo stopped gagging.

"Do you really think we have fallen off of the edge of the world?" he asked. Pedro realized that Rodrigo

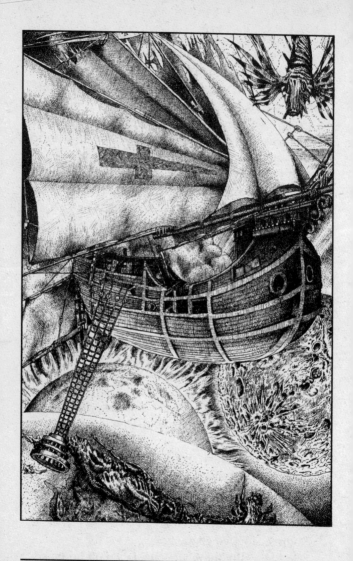

Illustrated by Yana Yavdoshchook

was scared. Many of the men strapped into the hammocks were miserably sick, but they all tilted their heads towards Pedro to hear what he had to say.

"Look around, no? It is obvious." Someone moaned. Others swore and crossed their chests.

"It is unnatural."

"We have been cursed."

"In Palos and Genoa, everyone says the world is round." Rodrigo pulled himself into the hammock. "I believed them when they told me to look at the ships coming into port. I saw myself that the masts became visible first, then the hull. As if obscured by a curve."

Pedro shrugged.

"Then maybe God made the world slightly curved."

"Sí. That makes sense." Rodrigo started to dry heave, finding nothing left in his stomach but acid. Pedro remembered his first three days at sea.

"Por supuesto." Of course he made sense. "Mira, get some rest, try to sleep." Unlike the rest of the crew Pedro could move around, not affected by their sudden predicament.

"But what will become of us? What madness have we been tricked into, coming on this voyage? We will die horribly, no doubt." Rodrigo shuddered.

"If you pray," Pedro said, "then ask our Lord to deliver us from this strange event."

As Pedro made sure that Rodrigo was tied into his hammock, he glanced past the varnished tiller arm. Useless, it vibrated madly from the rush of wind. Through the hole in the back to allow the tiller in, Pedro could see the two other ships. Two tiny caravels maybe half a mile away, floating suspended in the air, just like Pedro was. A light mist obscured them slightly.

It was the eighth of Octubre, anno Domini 1492. The nao *Santa Maria* and her two escorts, along with tremendous amounts of ocean, fish, and floating weeds, had been falling off of the edge of the world for almost a day.

•••

Pedro Yzquierdo pushed his way forward out towards the forecastle. The quarterdeck had steps coming down from either side, but steerage opened right onto the main deck between the raised forecastle and quarterdeck. Underneath the forecastle, ship's boy Paolo de Terreros tried to bank the cooking fire. The teenager, frustrated by a lack of progress, struck at the sand and ashes with a curse. The spherical flame, fueled by blackened pieces of wood nailed to the deck, refused to be quenched.

"Caray!"

"Paolo, easy." Pedro pulled the boy down from the end of his makeshift tether. "Don't strike things so violently. You'll push yourself out away from the boat."

"The fire, it doesn't work right. Even cooking is almost impossible."

"I'll take care of the fire. You should go now."

Paolo's thatch of midnight black hair floated like a halo of seaweed about his face.

"Gracias, Pedro. Perdoname."

"Bueno." Pedro looked at the ship's fire. Sand scattered on the deck, as well as the damp state of the deck, prevented a ship fire. The iron pot, ingeniously lashed above the fire by Paolo, had been redesigned to allow cooking in the constant floating. Pedro suspected the ship's cooper had done it.

"Mire esta," he said to himself. Look at that.

The sides of the bulbous pot now had latches to snap the top on. The two holes drilled into opposite sides, Pedro guessed, allowed steam to escape and food to be fed in. One hole had a piece of cloth tied on to prevent any food from blasting out, but allow steam through. A simple bellows stuck out of the other hole, allowing ingredients to be fed in without floating back out.

Cooking had now turned into something rather more complicated than the ship's boy had anticipated.

Juan Sánchez, the ship's physician, watched him with an owl-like eye from the railing of the forecastle. He had lashed himself there.

"Pedro Yzquierdo. You seem to grasp some of the aspects of our situation."

Pedro shook his head.

"I am just another traveler in God's world," he said. "I live where he puts me."

The cooper, Vizcaino, usually made sure all the casks in the hold stayed watertight and stout. Doubtless a frustrating job. Now the cooper's job took a turn for the interesting. What an ingenious mind, Pedro thought.

"I do not pretend to understand the world around me," Pedro continued, realizing that Juan waited for more conversation. "I only accept it."

Pedro took a sack of water and circled the spherical fire. He squeezed the sack slowly and started kicking himself around the fire in a circle. As he planned, using more and more force in his squeeze, all the water arrived at once. It quenched the flame satisfactorily.

"But look, Pedro." Juan wobbled until he lay in the air only inches away, parallel to the deck. His tiny pointed beard just scraped the musty deck. Juan dramatically extended only a finger, and pushed off upwards.

He slowly began to rise from the deck, inch by inch.

"It is incredible, Pedro. Think about it. Once I have pushed away, nothing will stop me from moving like this."

Pedro reached out and stopped him.

"There, you are at rest."

"Exactly," Juan floundered excitedly. "And anything at rest should stay at rest. Unless pushed by some force. I never thought of these things. But why do you stay on the Earth? Why do things fall?"

"God wills it."

"Maybe he does," Juan nodded. "But there is a force, a great attracting force that is pulling everything down to the ground, an outside force. A something falling out of a building should stay there, but it is pulled down. I wonder what all this is. . . ."

"You tire my imagination, Don Sánchez." Pedro started to swim away. "I'm a sailor. I know of many things, but mostly boats. I'm sure you could talk further with others."

Pedro made his way towards the edge of the deck where the wind howled. He looked out.

The *Pinta* and the *Niña* fell with them in varying heights, not more than a mile away. The *Niña* leaned a bit to her starboard. Then as wind hit her staysail, still up, her masts shivered and she leaned towards the port.

Pedro craned his neck along the edge of the ship, the wind tugging his cheeks back. He looked down past the stern at the cascade of water and mist in the distance, the waterfall at the edge of the world, miles upon miles wide. Down, he could see nothing but a haze. Far above, hidden in the clouds around the distant rim of the world, he guessed the sun still blazed away. Here though, light seemed to filter in from all sides equally.

The gray haze would fluctuate all the way to darkness, still in keeping with the cycle of the sun.

Pedro, not a fanatically religious man, found himself offering a prayer on behalf of his crewmates. May they all receive the mercy of his Lord, he prayed, for now their predicament lay well outside of the hands of men.

•••

On the second day, after the dark gave way to the gray haze, El Almirante Cristóbal Cólon himself came out of the cabin and looked around the ship. Pedro looked at their leader and admired his aquiline nose, massive build, and fair skin.

"There. It is Cólon," Rodrigo muttered from the iron pot. "I would give my right eye right now to be back in Cadiz. Pedro Yzquierdo, I should not have joined on this journey. I could be home with my Maria."

Pedro ignored his complaints.

El Almirante found the loose stores and general tidiness of the ship lacking, and wished to somehow bring the ships together. He charged Diego de Arana with making it happen, then retired into his cabin once more.

"Do you think maybe he's sick from the falling?" Rodrigo asked.

"Maybe. ¿Y qué?" So what?

Diego de Arana pulled himself down the stairs and pointed at one of the seamen floating carefully around steerage.

"You, take a rope, and jump out between the ships."

"No."

"If you fall, we can pull you back in on the rope," Diego assured him. The ship creaked and groaned. The wind still howled.

"You cannot make us. It's suicide."

"Restless men," Diego yelled. "You disobey my orders?" He pointed out Juan Sánchez. "This man of science assures me you will make it across."

"We are paid sailors. We are not mindless soldiers, or navy men," they replied. "Even if there were a holy man aboard we wouldn't jump."

Diego let it drop.

Juan Sánchez saw his opportunity, as he floated closer in from his perch on the forecastle.

"We can use cannon and rope," he said. "It'll reach."

"Then do it," Diego said.

Pedro helped Juan move the cannon around to face the *Niña*. They coiled rope next to the small weapon. Juan placed a brand to the touchhole and it fired; the pulleys took up the recoil. The coiled rope whipped out of the port, burning as it rubbed against the wooden sides. Juan Sánchez looked triumphant.

"It's curving up," Diego shouted. Juan, puzzled at first, turned, then struck his forehead with the flat of his palm.

"Mierda. The wind. I didn't think it would affect the thin rope and cannonball."

They both pushed out to the rail just in time to see the cannonball strike the topmast of the *Niña*.

"Ah," Juan said with satisfaction. "But it still works."

They fired another cannonball, this time at the *Pinta*, and then slowly pulled the ships together. The two distant caravels got larger and larger as they were pulled out of the haze. The hulls creaked and splintered when all three ships finally roped to each other.

The officers all immediately wiggled into the quarter-deck cabin.

•••

It took three days before everyone on board started moving around confidently. Pedro, not really wishing to dwell on his circumstance, took up much of his time tying knots in spare pieces of string.

Others began to mutter.

The *Santa Maria*, the *Niña*, the *Pinta*, all caravels, together had enough provisions and water for a year of travel. But the crews of all three ships worried about what would happen next, now that they had fallen over the edge of the world.

"Can we ever get back to España?" another crew-member, who shared Pedro's name, asked quietly.

"I don't know," Pedro replied honestly.

"Are we falling towards hell?" Rodrigo asked.

"You shouldn't talk of such things. Trust in the Lord. Somehow he will see us through."

A devout follower, Pedro found men talking to him. He prayed with them, calming them. They told him about their minor sins, such as "hacerse una paja," whispered to him with a descriptive flick of the wrist. Pedro didn't know how evil masturbation was, but he said he would pray for them.

For some unstated reason Cristóbal had not taken any holy men aboard for the journey. Pedro was the next best thing.

•••

Pedro could not say that things ever fell into a routine. There never felt like any time for that. He watched the physician floating at the edge of the crowd of men clustered around the mast on the main deck. Juan Sánchez was wrapping twine around something Pedro could not see.

"We will never get back to España. Not unless we demand that Cristóbal step down," Rodrigo announced one day.

"Rodrigo!" Pedro made to grab the boy by the ear, but Juan de la Placa grabbed his hand.

"Let the boy be."

Rodrigo glared at Pedro. "He is cursing us all, no?" Others in the crew agreed. Pedro saw Alonso Clivijo nodding.

Antonio de Cuellar, the carpenter, spoke up. "Maybe if he takes away the title, and renounces his title as Admiral, we will find ocean again. Take this curse away from us!"

The crew started yelling, loud enough to bring El Almirante floating out of his cabin. He spoke over the scream of the wind. Pedro felt his heart race.

"We aren't many leagues from the Canaries," El Almirante said. Confident, he continued. "I expect land soon. For the first man to sight land there will be, not only the reward of the Queen, but a silk jacket. Provided by me. Men, soon we will find new lands, and gold."

With that he returned to his cabin.

Pedro thought he caught a hint of trouble brewing in El Almirante's eyes, but he did not say anything.

Some of the crew grew quiet, thinking of gold. Others still protested.

"We have been falling for days!" Rodrigo said, still angry. "We should do something."

"You should obey Colón," Pedro snapped, and received a jab to the ribs from Antonio. The fools could not mutiny! It would be pointless; they were all in the same situation together.

Juan Sánchez shouted and got their attention.

"Mira." He hoisted the carcass of a bird up above his head. The bird's wings were forced open by small struts made of whittled plank. Twine dangled from its beak. The crew watched as Juan tossed it into the sky, snapping back on the twine as it flew up into the air.

"A kite," someone laughed.

Sánchez tugged, and the seagull dipped and dove around the boat, effectively distracting the crew's mind from thoughts of mutiny.

Pedro winced when the bird finally twisted off of the twine and fluttered away into the distance.

"We can imitate that," Juan Sánchez said, his dark eyes dancing with delight.

Pedro offered up another prayer for their safety.

• • •

El Almirante summoned both Juan Sánchez and Pedro into his quarterdeck cabin. His piercing eyes, Pedro thought, seemed worried. Cristóbal carried an aura of driven intensity, a man of purpose. It worried Pedro to realize that El Almirante was a man. Nothing more.

"I saw your demonstrations, and thought long about our predicament," El Almirante said to Juan. "Por favor, tell me if you think that it's really true we can mimic the flight of a bird."

Juan fidgeted in the air for several seconds.

"It will take some doing, Don Cristóbal. I will need canvas to replace feathers, and strong spars. We will need to get rid of much of the weight of the boat." He spoke quickly and with excitement.

El Almirante considered it for several seconds, floating calmly in the cabin. Pedro looked around. The officers sharing the cabin with Cristóbal had spread out, sleeping on the roof of the cabin as well. It made no difference what part of the room one slept on. The wall, the roof, the floor; it all seemed the same.

"Use whatever materials you must from the *Niña* or *Pinta,* Don Sánchez, to undertake this transformation of the ship."

"Señor. It will be done."

"It will be done quickly," Don Cristóbal Colón, El Almirante, continued. "I wish to resume this appointed journey with all possible haste."

After they left the cabin, Juan Sánchez turned to Pedro.

"The other captains, Martin and Vicente Pinzon, they are scared too. They want Colón to step down and admit he made a mistake."

"I pray they are the ones in error."

"You pray; I have other ideas. Hopefully between the two of us something will happen."

• • •

Juan had the resources of the crews from all three different ships.

"Lope the joiner, Antonio de Cuellar the carpenter, and Domingo Vizcaino," he called out from the quarterdeck. The physician floated above the railing, tied to it with a long piece of rope. He held a roll of parchment in his left hand.

"What is this?" they complained.

"We are going to fly," Juan Sánchez said.

"We're already floating."

"Be quiet. I need all the canvas you can find. All the sail, and the lightest woods. Lope, give men needles and stout threads."

Eight men drifted over from the main deck and down into the hold of the *Santa Maria* to look for canvas. More men drifted over the rails onto the other ships. Lope headed off to find his toolbox.

"You men," Juan pointed at a group tied to the mast. "Your job is to empty the *Niña*'s holds. Antonio, after they scoop out all the water, rip out as many of the extra bulkheads as you can. Then you will need to chop off the quarterdeck and forecastle."

"Why?" Antonio asked.

"Because we need the *Niña* to be as light as possible."

Don Vicente Pinzon stuck his head out of the corner of his cabin as men swarmed over his ship. Under Antonio's orders they began to hack out the rails with axes.

"What are you doing!" he cried out, pushing off to stop the nearest axe.

"Let them continue." Cristóbal pushed into the air.

"This is my command," Pinzon shouted.

"No. It is mine," Cristóbal said. Pinzon glared for a moment, then slumped in midair.

"I will get my things from the cabin." Pinzon pulled his way back in. The sound of axes hacking at timber resumed.

Juan Sánchez paused briefly. "Pedro. We need all the rope you can find," he said. "Go in the hold and see what extra you can find."

Pedro nodded and kicked off to land by the hatch. He looked in. It was dark and smelly, and he could hear the high-pitched squeals of dying rats and laughing sailors. He waited for them to move yards of yellowing canvas up through the hatch before he went down to look for rope.

• • •

The gray haze had melted into dark night. Pedro rested, tied to netting against the side of the ship.

"Someone, come quick!" Cristóbal's voice, unmistakable even above the ever-constant roar of the wind, pierced Pedro's ears. He untied himself and pushed back along the torn deck, past the huddle of tired, sleeping men. Off to the right the *Niña* did not resemble anything of its former self. The two boxy structures on either end were gone. No railing, no masts, no tiller or rudder, it looked nothing like a ship. Hundreds of yards of canvas stitched together sat bundled across the long flat deck.

In the dark, Pedro could barely make out Cristóbal's figure, and almost ran into him.

"¿Sí?"

El Almirante turned to Pedro excitedly.

"Look, over the edge, I think I can see a flicker of a light."

Pedro looked, squinting hard against the wind. Maybe. It eluded him. Hearing speech, Diego de Arana joined them.

"A light?"

He also leaned over.

"Do you see anything?" Don Cristóbal demanded.

"I think so. Yo miro, sí." Diego's voice sounded breathless with hope.

El Almirante looked pleased.

"Have someone stay on watch. Tell me of everything."

"We will see land again," Diego said, his voice choking somewhat. Pedro found himself trembling despite himself.

"Thank God," he said. "Our prayers are answered."

"Indeed," Diego said. "Thank God." He wandered back, and Pedro could swear he heard a choked sob come from the master-at-arms.

Pedro trailed away, choosing instead to lean over and look at the *Niña*. The bundled length of canvas was attached to various points of the *Niña* by the ropes Pedro had collected.

Juan Sánchez had shown him a drawing. When the canvas was released it would fly up over the ship like a massive sail.

"Sails catch the wind," Juan explained. "This will be similar. Only much larger. It will catch the wind coming from below, just like the wings of a bird, or the sails of any ship." He beamed.

Pedro marveled at the physician's mind. How he came up with such things!

•••

By morning Cristóbal ordered everyone over to the strange remains of the *Niña*. The flicker of light now revealed clouds beneath them that stretched far out in all directions, the haze having been swept away sometime in the night by better weather conditions.

"Cut loose the other two ships," Cristóbal said. And as the ropes were slashed the *Santa Maria* and the *Pinta* drifted away.

"Pedro Yzquierdo!" Juan smiled and floated over. "We almost have the wings done. Soon we can extend them fully, and see if we can fly."

"It would be a wonderful gift," Pedro replied.

Pedro wondered if the clouds were a result of the waterfall of ocean hitting the fires of hell. But as a fundamentally good man, and a follower, he had trouble believing that God would have condemned him to hell in such an obtuse manner.

"Would you like a prayer, Juan?"

Juan laughed. But it sounded hollow and forced.

"You take yourself too seriously, Pedro. Have some hope. We'll try soon and see what happens."

Pedro nodded. As the rest of the crew asked, he would pray for them too. Although he did not have the official blessing of the church, he did remember a Bible verse quoted by a bishop he traveled once to hear speak: Wherever there are more than one gathered, there also would the spirit be.

He felt it a major oversight on El Almirante to have forgotten the holy men. Maybe some of this would not have occurred if it weren't for that arrogance.

"The clouds are approaching," called the watch, peering over the side of the ship. Juan held up an arm and shouted a command.

"Ahora, sí."

"Hang on, Pedro Yzquierdo," Juan said. Then, "Throw it out!"

Crewmen cut the ropes, and suddenly the world turned dirty gray as canvas snapped and billowed up past them. Ropes sizzled and whipped past. Out of the corner of his eye Pedro saw Andres de Yruenes caught by the leg with coiled rope. Like a puppet he was snatched up screaming with the canvas.

"Wahhh . . . " He lost his leg and spun out of their sight still screaming.

Then the rope snapped short as the canvas reached the ends. The jolt shook every bone in Pedro and smacked his face against the deck. The *Niña* screeched and splintered in protest. Ropes snapped, hemp fibers filling the air and making breathing almost impossible.

Pedro realized he now lay on the floor, and when he tried to move, he could feel his weight pressing against him. He sat up, wincing from bruises, blood flowing down his upper lip. He smiled.

He looked up and saw nothing but the dirty gray canvas, with wooden ribs running from fore to aft to keep it open and stable. It creaked and groaned, but stayed. Moans from crewmen drifted around as they passed through the clouds.

Pedro liked it, a sudden wet feeling, like passing through a fog, and then just as suddenly they were through. He looked back up at the underside of the clouds, just as someone near the prow of the ship yelled.

"Land ho!"

•••

Juan and Cristóbal ordered all the men down into the hold.

"I'll stay to help you," Pedro offered, then scrabbled his way to the edge and looked out.

A marvelous sight.

Green and brown patches spread out in patterns over the land. It reminded Pedro of looking at a map; in the same manner he could perceive coastlines, bays, inlets, even towns. He saw ocean.

The *Niña* aimed for the ocean, away from the land.

"If we could touch the sea, and sail again, we aim for one of those bays," Cristóbal announced.

The land slowly rose to meet them. Juan and Pedro grabbed the ropes on the left, all wrapped around a series of ten pulleys, and used the capstan to winch them in. The *Niña* shook and shivered and began to slowly spiral.

"Let it out!"

They reversed their path and the *Niña* straightened out, presumably for land. The wind rushed fiercely across the deck, tearing Pedro's eyes.

And now Pedro could see wave tops, and sea foam.

Not such calm sea, as it had seemed from further up, but still very easy.

Pedro felt a surge of relief. They had come home, back to a more normal world. The one to which he belonged. This wasn't hell.

The wave tops came closer, and Pedro suddenly realized that the *Niña* was moving forward too fast. Faster than any ship had the right to go. The wave tops blurred.

Pedro's pulse raced.

They hit.

• • •

The impact stunned and deafened Pedro. It seemed like the world moved away. He pitched across the length of the deck, hitting fractured planks. Water rushed up through the floorboards, the hold, and he could distantly hear screams of human anguish over the shattering *Niña*.

It was the canvas that saved him. He was flung and bounced in an instant over the deck, and then out into midair. The large soft billowing canvas caught him, and even then it knocked him out.

Pedro woke up a second later underwater, trapped in swathes of restricting material and rope. He fought to escape. He fought for what seemed forever, but was probably only a minute. When he finally broke the surface he gasped for air, black spots dancing across his vision.

Pieces of plank floated all over, as well as dead bodies. But Pedro barely noticed. He grabbed ahold of a large piece and then passed out again, his entire body numb from pain.

•••

Pedro could not lay claim to understanding the darker-skinned men around him. He knew they had washed up in Gujarat, a land of Saracens, followers of the doctrines of the prophet Mohamet. They had translators who spoke European languages, and the ruler of the city granted them the hospitality of his own palace guest rooms, as well as his best doctors. Pedro was surprised they did not outright kill him for being a Spaniard, and a Christian. Pedro pointedly avoided any talk of doctrine, choosing instead to relate only his fantastic voyage.

It took two months before Pedro recovered enough to stand on his own. His legs, fractured by the impact, would have been amputated back home, but miraculously he had them. He still bore marks all over from bruises. Every once in a while he still suffered from dizzy spells and fainted.

Once he recovered his health, he made a point of seeking Juan Sánchez out one last time. Pedro found him in a large marble-tiled room surrounded by parchments laid on shelves, an ecstatic look to his face.

"Juan. ¿Cómo está?"

"Good, thank you, Pedro." He set down the parchment scroll in his hand. "And you, you are making plans to leave, no?"

"Sí. Verdad. I betray God every day I stay in here. The sheik gave me leave, and a 'Bat,' to travel to Turkey with. And then from there I'm hoping to find a merchant to take me to Italia."

"A Bat?"

"A tribe of men, the sheik tells me, who keep you safe by killing themselves on the point of a knife if you are harmed in your journey. The attacker is cursed by the suicide and their sons and family will be killed. It's a strange land, Juan."

"Indeed, Pedro Yzquierdo, but so much can be learned from them."

"I don't share your enthusiasm. Please, Señor Sánchez," he dropped into the formal, "you must return to España. Leave these unholy parchments alone. Our Holy Father didn't spare your life so that you could convert to these people's ways." And Pedro believed more than ever before. He was alive, he'd been chosen. His faith had carried him here.

"No, Pedro, I'm staying here. There is a great deal of important work to be done. Look." Sánchez showed Pedro a piece of parchment. "See this strip of parchment?"

"Sí."

"Imagine it's the world. Edges, here, and here. Now imagine you are sailing across the surface."

"You would fall off the edge."

"Verdad, Pedro, but listen further. No interrupting, por favor." Sánchez drew the edges of the paper slowly together, forming a ring. "Imagine that once the world was flat, or slightly curved, but now it is slowly being drawn together as our sailors begin to move out towards the Canaries, and even further out towards the West. We left to explore too soon, too hastily. We fell in between the edges, back into the world underneath."

Sánchez straightened up.

"God would not have made our world imperfect, and been forced to correct his mistakes only now that we begin to explore it." Pedro shook his head. "That is blasphemy. Begging your forgiveness, señor, you are much more learned in such matters. God isn't capable of error. And if the world is curved in this manner, why can't we look up and see the other side?"

"You are not thinking right, Pedro Yzquierdo. We live on the outside of the ring."

"I do not believe these things you say."

Medic started bending the paper, forgetting Pedro stood there.

"Even as we begin to explore South and North, He will have to bend the ring of the Earth until it becomes a globe. In the end, as we ask these questions and explore our world, we begin to shape it," he muttered, still fooling with the paper. "I think I finally understand how we ended up on the right side of the Earth's ring."

"Tell me," Pedro said, finding no harm humoring the physician. After he left, the man would have no fellow Christian soul to speak to.

"We fell out of the plane of the ring"—Medic made a motion with his finger—"and we passed by the other side, still falling mightily without realizing it. Then, that force which attracts things down to the Earth reasserted itself and we fell back down, this time approaching the right side, directly, while we were making our wings. We fell with the monsoons." Proud of himself he wiggled the ring of parchment. "Incredible."

"Sí. I must leave now, Señor Medic."

"Ah, Pedro, I will miss you. Has Cristóbal left?"

"¿El Almirante? He left many days ago, speaking of making more flying ships. He is a determined man. Who knows what he will do? Vaya con Dios, Señor Sánchez."

"Vaya con Dios, Pedro. Please, would you take this letter with you? To deliver to the Queen."

"I will."

Pedro left the room with a heavy heart.

● ● ●

In a letter to Queen Isabella:

"It is not an easy decision for any seriously minded Christian to make, to stay in the lands of the infidels and heathen such as these; yet, in speculative reflection, I have found a certain fascination in my dealings with the learned men of the area, particularly in their manner of treating melancholies, wounds, infections, and other violations to the body, particularly also in respect to several theories of the mind and, further, additionally to many other theories of the physical world held in the highest regard by the respected sages I have had the occasion to be spoken to of.

"It is furthermore drawn to my attention by our gracious host that word journeys here of several trips and discoveries of

new lands found by the Englanders to the North of our esteemed Admiral's westerly route, and of lands discovered to the South by the Portuguese; and it is my firm belief that we, in our infinite ignorance of the geography, were unfortunate enough to sail between, much like the banks of the river that turns into a waterfall, the two continents that lie on the edge of the Western world, and it is my firm recommendation that Your Gracious Majesty send no more ships seeking a western route until it is verified that the two ends of the Earth are joined together in a manner as to allow such a journey.

"But I will now write no more of this, leaving the telling of the account of the journey to the able seaman Pedro Yzquierdo, who is the deliverer of this sealed letter."—Juan Sánchez, Ship's Physician, 1492

GUILDMASTER

Written by
Dan Dysan

Illustrated by
Frank Wu

About the Author

Dan Dysan was born in La Crosse, Wisconsin, forty-five years ago, and lives in Madison with his wife, Sandy. He works as a computer programmer/consultant.

He has been writing seriously since he was forty, and pursues a number of hobbies, including blacksmithing, armoring, swordsmithing and shooting black-powder guns, which provide the background for his story. Usually, he sets his stories in the central Wisconsin countryside.

About the illustrator

Frank Wu is a science fiction, fantasy and horror illustrator, physically working in the San Francisco Bay area, but residing mentally in various diverse realms scattered throughout time and space.

Winning the Illustrators of the Future *award* marked an important point in his life. The work that won him the award was a culmination, in a way, of many years of study and hard work. Frank had taken piles of art classes, some as part of an undergrad degree in English (concentrating in medieval studies). He also earned a Ph.D. in bacteriology and was working in patent law, specializing in biotech. All that science and literature came together in his science fiction art. In 1997, Frank made a serious commitment to himself to really work on his art. Part of that commitment was attempting to win the Illustrators of the Future *Contest*. It took three tries, but he made it.

In addition to his artwork, he's also dabbling in writing and has several scientific and science humor writing credits to his name. The latter include various pieces on how Jell-O killed the dinosaurs; a scientific correlation between tornadoes, mobile homes and camcorders. The last was cited in *Atlantic Monthly*, which dubbed his work on the causes of hurricanes "vortigenetics." Frank's plan is to keep writing science humor and science fiction, and another dream is to eventually write and illustrate his own books.

His proudest moment is receiving the following message from a fan: "You're like the Frank Zappa of the art world!"

You Can visit his Web site at http://www.frankwu.com.

Part 1 — Survival

"Load!" the lieutenant shouted.

Twelve dragoons pressed their clips home with a click and slammed the M-16 bolts closed.

"Aim!"

Wade Thompkins stared down the muzzles. All he could think was "So, here it ends." He was almost too exhausted to care.

"Doctor, pharmacist, nurse, veterinarian . . ." The lieutenant read from a list in a bored voice, moving his finger down the sheet as he went. When finished, he'd give the command to fire. Wade had been a computer programmer before the Smash-up, a skill no longer in demand. He doubted if there was a working computer anywhere on the planet.

". . . potter, blacksmith, cooper, wheelwright . . ."

"ME!" screamed Wade. "I'm a blacksmith! Don't shoot, I'm a blacksmith!"

The lieutenant stepped up to Wade, staring him in the eye for an endless minute. "You a blacksmith?"

Wade nodded.

"You better not be lying to me. If you ain't a blacksmith, you'll wish we shot you clean. There's always bayonet practice."

"I'm a blacksmith."

"Private Thorne, take this man to the Lord Planner."

•••

Fourteen-year-old Nick Baker stopped work for a moment to wipe the sweat from his eyes. One slip of his sledgehammer and the six-year-old holding his chisel would be minus a finger or two. It was a point of pride with Nick that his holders never lost their fingers.

Just then he heard a volley from the execution wall. The shooting went on for some time as the dragoons had their fun. Another bunch of vagrants dead, just like his mother. She had been too weak and not attractive enough to take as a slave.

"Get back to work, trash." The overseer had noticed.

"Ya, Boss!" Nick roundhoused his sledgehammer and made the chisel ring. Another chunk split off the foundation of the toppled grain silo. With rapid blows of his hammer, Nick began squaring the irregular chunk into a block fit for the city wall. Out of the corner of his eye he saw a dragoon escorting a single vagrant back from the execution wall. Odd, why had they decided to spare one skinny bum? Oh, well. None of his business.

"You Sparta guys have really cleaned up. You got most of the rubble out of the main streets. Looks a lot better than any of the other towns I've seen." Wade tried a conversational gambit. The dragoon didn't bother to reply.

He took Wade to a waiting room in the town hall. Three hours later the receptionist announced, "The Planner will see the prisoner now."

The Planner was a hawk-faced man, about Wade's age, with a full head of silvery gray hair. A big man, he showed no sign of ever having suffered from short rations. His suit was clean and unmended.

He presented quite a contrast to Wade, cadaverously thin from years of near starvation, hair wispy gray, teeth going from poor nutrition. Wade's clothes hung from his gaunt frame in dirty tatters. He stood before the Deputy Planner almost barefoot, the soles of his boots flapping loose, the uppers rotting away.

The nameplate on the Planner's impressive desk read *John Shinka*. Close at Shinka's hand was a Colt .45 service pistol, hammer back, ready to use. Wade noticed bullet holes in the wall behind him and bloodstains on the floor in the spot where he was standing. The penalty for failing this interview would be substantial. He stood straight, waiting to be noticed.

After a bit, Shinka leaned back in his chair, picking up the pistol as he did so. He eased the hammer down and cocked it two or three times before he looked at Wade, pointing the pistol at him. "You say you're a blacksmith, is'at so?"

"Yes, sir!"

"Convince me; I'm waiting." The Planner set the pistol down, still pointing at Wade.

"In my bundle, two knives, a folding knife, and a hunting knife—I made 'em; there's no manufacturing marks. Your people took 'em." A frown from Shinka prompted him. "Ah . . . sir!"

Shinka snorted. "Knives?!" He waved the pistol. "I've had people claim they could make knives before. Those guys gave me crappy things that bent and wouldn't hold an edge. Now they're slaves working the wall."

"I can give you good knives—hard, sharp knives. I can make most of my own tools out of junk. It won't cost you much of anything, sir."

The Planner considered; the pistol vanished into a drawer. "I think I'll take a look at those knives you made."

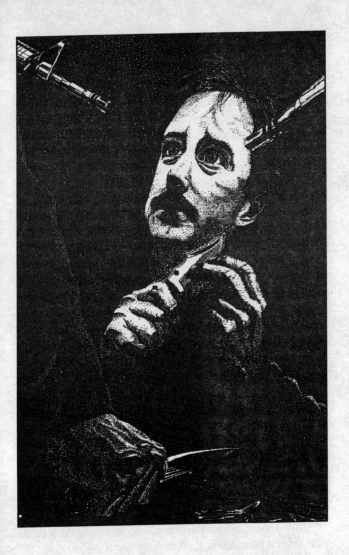

Illustrated by Frank Wu

Wade was taken to a cold cell in the basement, empty of furnishings or blankets. The only concession to comfort was some dirty straw in the corner. At least it gave him a place to sit that wasn't directly on the damp concrete floor. The only thing he could see out the tiny window at the juncture of the wall and ceiling was a small patch of typically gray sky; a light drizzle patterned the window glass.

For two years after the meteor impact it had rained. Crops failed, flooding became a major problem on every river, lake, and stream. Now, after nine years, it only rained about twice as much as before the impact. Prime bottomland had gone to swamp while farmers now planted hilltops.

Sparta, Wisconsin, survived better than most towns, thanks to Fort McCoy. In the first week of the disaster, ninety percent of the troops stationed at McCoy climbed into trucks headed south.

They never returned.

Two months later, the remaining troops at McCoy reached agreement with the city of Sparta. The city acquired a fighting force and access to a mountain of supplies. The troops gained a respected place in the elite of the new society. But more importantly, they gained access to local women.

After a few hours, his jailers fed Wade, a good sign. It had been two days since he had eaten and he was weak with hunger. The stew was cold, larded with congealed grease, the bread coarse and stale. Wade ate with enthusiasm. He could not remember a better meal.

With food, energy returned, and Wade faced a decision. Hope was a fraud. Planning for the future didn't work anymore, not since the Smash-up. All his plans hadn't saved his wife Samantha or Bobby, his son, or his parents or friends or anyone he knew. Dead, all dead. Why wasn't he? It was tempting to give up. But he was too stubborn to quit. Wade's mind began to turn, seeking a way out.

The light through the little window dimmed, leaving the cell heaped in gray shadow. With his arthritis, Wade couldn't do more than a few hours of work. What could he offer Sparta that would be worth his life? He rehearsed a speech in the dark cell.

About the time Wade was getting his dinner, Nick was having seconds on his dinner. More accurately, Nick was taking dinner away from Timmy Stevens, his chisel holder. "Give it over, punk. Half your food if you want to go on holding my chisel for me. How long do you think you'll keep your fingers with someone else? You know what happens to boys who can't work." He mimed shooting a rifle. "It'll be the firing squad for you, kid."

Stevens handed over the rest of his dinner.

Wade was sitting in the corner, arms wrapped around himself for warmth, when they came for him. He found himself blinking in the light of a camping lantern in the Planner's office. Sitting on Shinka's desk was an array of knives of various descriptions.

"Pick out yours." The Deputy, sitting behind his desk, waved a hand at the assortment. Wade noticed that the pistol was not in evidence. With two armed guards standing by, Shinka didn't feel the need to threaten him personally.

Wade stepped to the desk and, moving carefully so as not to alarm his guards, picked out two blades and set them aside.

"These were mine, sir. May I look at the others?" The Planner nodded. Wade rummaged through the pile, testing the edges and sorting them into two groups. He picked out a knife from the "bad" pile and tested its edge against his own hunting knife, taking a gouge out of the other knife.

He held up the gouged blade. "This is junk, sir. The temper is bad, wrong steel for the job—it's a toy, no good." He pointed to the other pile. "There's some real quality stuff there, see."

He selected one knife with simple lines. "This is Damascus steel—the best, a work of art." He put that blade to the side.

The Planner made a small gesture and the guards grounded their rifles; tension in the room relaxed. "Please," Shinka smiled, "sit down, Wade. Jack, Sam, wait outside." The two guards shuffled out of the room.

"All right, you know a lot about knives. Now tell me what you can do for me and why I should let you live." The Planner leaned back in his swivel chair, opening the desk drawer to reveal the pistol.

Wade moistened his lips nervously and took the plunge.

"Sir, blacksmithing is a craft that existed for thousands of years. I've taken a copper disk and hammered it into a vase—with just a hammer, no soldering. I've taken a nine-inch steel bar and pulled that nine inches into a three-foot sword. Smithing moves metal like clay; it's a skill that's almost lost now."

Shinka's face was unreadable. Wade couldn't tell how he was doing. At least Shinka didn't interrupt.

"Until the 1920s, every community had a blacksmith. Today, there are none. You could create a monopoly and it would cost you virtually nothing. All I need for supplies is junk: old steel—car leaf springs and the like—some hammers and pliers, charcoal or coke for fuel. I can train you a generation of blacksmiths."

The Planner shifted his weight, leaning forward and resting his elbows on the desktop. "Okay, I'll try you out, but you'd better produce. You've got a month to prove yourself."

Wade broke into a cold sweat. This was it, Shinka had taken the bait; but could Wade land him? The next few minutes would tell.

"Sir, I've got arthritis. I can't do production work."

"WHAT?" Shinka was on his feet, fumbling in the pistol drawer. "You can't cut it? You've wasted my time with this crap and you can't deliver?" He centered the pistol on Wade's head. "You trashy, low-life son of a bitch!"

"Please, sir, hear me out!" Wade's hands came up as if to block the slugs. With a conscious effort he forced his hands back to his side, accepting Shinka's power over his life.

"I can't do the work myself but I can teach! Give me apprentices—I'll train them. I know the secrets; I'll pass them along. Don't lose this opportunity—you'll have the only blacksmiths in the area—maybe in the world. You can set up a guild system. Anybody wanting to be a smith will have to come to you."

Wade desperately hammered his main points. "It won't cost you, just fuel and boys—and time, sir, time to train the boys. Low overhead; *big* payoff—in time, sir." Wade looked down the barrel and waited for his world to end. He could see wheels turning behind Shinka's eyes, weighing factors, calculating costs, payback.

The pistol returned to the drawer. Shinka paced behind his desk, back and forth and back, three laps; he turned and pointed a finger (not the gun) at Wade.

"Okay, smart guy, a trial period. You get the boys, fuel, and two troopers to keep an eye on things—so don't try to pull a fast one."

Shinka called in the guards. "This guy," he hooked a thumb at Wade, "is on the payroll; you're assigned to him. He's got trustee status, treat him nice; but if he escapes, you take his punishment, understand? He can go anywhere he wants, but never alone—always one of you with him. Make sure he gets what he needs.

"Now, take him out'a here; he stinks. Clean him up, feed him, get him some decent clothes."

Shinka wrote up an authorization for the slaves he needed for his blacksmith project and took it into Lord Mayor Vance's office for a signature. The Lord Mayor was passed out across his desk again, an empty bottle of the local rotgut in his hand. Shinka repressed the urge to kick the drunken sot, shaking him gently instead. Vance still served his purpose.

"Wake up, Ralph. More papers to sign. That's right. You sign and I'll get you a new bottle." That got the old drunk's attention.

"Is'at you, John? What do you want?" Obediently he signed in exchange for the bottle. "Stay and have one with me, John?"

"Not now, I still have work to do. I'll come back soon."

Lord Mayor Vance nodded absently as he fumbled with the bottle stopper, knowing Shinka wouldn't be coming. Councilman Koslowski expected to assume the mayorship in a few years, but Shinka was planning an accident for Koslowski. As long as the Lord Mayor stayed drunk and left decisions to Shinka, the Lord Mayor had nothing to fear. Lord Planner Shinka was content to let Vance drink himself to death before assuming the title that went with the power.

•••

Next morning, Wade woke in a real bed, covered with a real blanket, for the first time in years. He dressed in clothes only slightly worn. His room opened into the one where his guards were staying. Sam was on duty; Jack was sleeping.

Sam eyed him sourly. "Where da ya think you're goin'?"

"Nowhere without you, I figure." That was the right answer.

"Just so's you know." Sam smiled and got to his feet. "Lets go find some breakfast." Wade noticed Sam left his rifle leaning in the corner of the room.

Over the next two days, Wade was assigned shop space and six apprentices. The first day was spent examining possible sites; privacy was an important factor, so was living space. There must be room to house Wade, the apprentices, and the guards. Wade wanted to build a tribe; living together would help.

He selected a well-ventilated shop with attached office space that would provide room to live. Best of all, there was a yard surrounded by a high board fence for privacy.

That night, lying on his cot in the new blacksmith shop, Wade tried to understand everything that had happened. Just thirty-six hours earlier, he had been a condemned man. Since then, he had passed through prisoner status to trustee. Tomorrow, he would start a new career as "Guildmaster." It sounded pretty good.

He'd hoped to buy time, but he'd never expected this. This went beyond survival, an opportunity to make a place for himself. So far, he'd survived day to day. That wouldn't work anymore. In order to live, he had to make himself vital to Shinka. That would require thinking.

He got out of his cot and found a candle and a piece of paper, making notes and listing supplies he'd need. As the hours passed, the notes became plans and time lines. It was a long night.

●●●

Nick saw the guard named Sam talking to the overseer one noon. "Planner needs some kids for a special project. Who's good with a hammer?" The overseer pointed to Nick.

Sam marched Nick and five other wall slaves to an abandoned factory west of town. Nick was the only hammer man, the others were all chisel holders. As Sam and another guard lined them up in the factory yard, Nick recognized the man in charge as the bum who'd escaped the firing squad day before yesterday. He'd been cleaned up and given nice clothes, but it was the same man, Nick was sure.

Wade looked over his new apprentices, as the boys assembled under Sam's watchful eye. They were a sullen-faced lot, with calloused hands and scarred backs. Sam looked at Wade and shrugged.

"Good luck with this trash; you'll need it!" Over the past two days Wade and his guards had come to an understanding; Sam and Jack decided that duty assigned to Wade was easy duty, much better than living in the barracks under the sergeant's thumb. They wanted Wade to succeed.

"They'll do fine." Wade walked up and down in front of the line of boys, hands clasped behind his back, examining them from all angles.

"You boys have been selected as blacksmith's apprentices. You'll serve under me; I'm Mr. Thompkins, the Mastersmith. You will start as apprentices. After you learn basic skills, you will become journeymen, ready to do useful work. Finally, if you prove your skills to me, I can make you a Master, with the right to train apprentices of your own.

"Now you are slaves belonging to the Lord Mayor and the city of Sparta. As apprentices, you will belong to the Guild of Blacksmiths. And who is the Guild? We are the Guild!"

Wade stopped before the tallest boy in line, doing his best drill sergeant imitation, poking him with a blunt forefinger. "You, what's your name, how old are you?"

"Nick Baker, I'm fourteen."

"SIR!" roared Wade, sticking his face into the boy's until their noses almost touched. "'Nick Baker, SIR!' 'I'm fourteen, SIR!' SAY IT, SAY 'SIR'!"

The boy flinched. "Sorry, SIR! Nick Baker, SIR!"

"Nick Baker, if you join the Guild, your life will belong to me and the other boys here today. Will you take the oath or will you go back to being a slave on the wall?"

Nick decided fast. "I'll take the oath, sir!"

"You don't know what it is yet."

"I know working the wall; I'll take the oath. I want'a be a 'prentice." After a short pause, "SIR!"

Wade stepped back from Nick and addressed the group again. "The skills and knowledge of the art of blacksmithing must remain secret." He focused on Nick again. "Come here!" Wade laid his hand on the rusty anvil he'd found in town.

"Place your hand on that! Swear by the anvil—repeat after me: I swear on my life that I will obey the lawful orders of the Blacksmith's Guild and its Guildmaster. I pledge my life that I will protect and hold secret all the methods of the blacksmith's art, the secret of working steel. On this oath I pledge my life, my soul, and my sacred honor!"

First Nick, then each boy in turn, placed his hand on the anvil and swore the oath. When the last was done, Wade lined the boys up again. "You came here as slaves, but you're slaves no longer. You are now apprentices, Guildbrothers—you belong to me and I belong to you. The bond cuts both ways.

"Anyone who betrays the Guild betrays us all! The penalty for betrayal is to be crushed on this anvil on which we swore the oath." Wade snatched up a sledge maul and slammed it down on the anvil, making it ring.

"Crushed like that—first his hands, right and left, which learned the smith's skills. Then the oath breaker's head, which conspired to betray the Guild. Your Guildbrothers—the men you betrayed—will hunt you down and bring you to justice if any of you betrays the secrets of the Blacksmith's Guild."

The boys were obviously very impressed, even though the whole ceremony was an outrageous crock. Wade had borrowed it from the Mafia initiation sequence of a bad movie.

It had the desired effect on the apprentices, though. The kids had been slaves with absolutely no status; this was a major improvement. What's more, they couldn't remember the pre-disaster world. The oldest of them had been no more than five when the meteor shattered civilization. They'd had no exposure to such nonsense, taking it at face value.

• • •

Nick turned on his cot in the makeshift dormitory, pulling the blanket up to his neck. A whole blanket. He was used to sleeping under old sacking. And tonight's dinner—unbelievable. There had actually been more food than Nick could eat. Never in his entire life could he remember having his fill. What's more, there was even meat.

Any way you looked at it, this was better than working the wall. As he listened to the steady breathing of the other boys, Nick realized he had it made. He'd already established he was number-one boy in the place. His only potential rival, a kid named Slater, was now sporting a black eye. After that, the others fell into line. Good food, clothes, and a decent place to live—he was going to like it here.

Not that Nick believed any of that bull the new boss was handing out. The little kids might buy that crap about secrets and belonging to each other, but not Nick; he knew the score. The only way people belonged to each other was the way Sparta owned his ass.

He had a lot to think about. They weren't chained up the way they'd been on the wall gang. There were only two guards and the boss to watch over them. Escape was a possibility. But escape to where? He didn't have anywhere to go.

On the other hand, this looked easy. He'd run the dormitory, but he didn't want any trouble. With luck, he'd make the black-eyed kid his stooge and leave the strong-arm stuff to ol' Black Eye; or if not Black Eye, some other kid.

He rolled over and settled in to sleep. As long as the food was good, he'd play their game.

• • •

Wade wasn't sleeping that night. He kept remembering the view down the barrel of Shinka's pistol. Here he was, sitting under his own roof (sort of), Guildmaster. And he was no safer from Shinka's pistol now than he was three days ago.

Things went from one extreme to another. Before yesterday he'd had nobody to worry about but himself. Now he was responsible for half-a-dozen boys. This was more than just his last chance; it could well be their last chance too.

Lord Shinka was also awake. A new, very attractive slave had been captured two days earlier. Since they'd executed her husband, she was now unmarried. Lord Shinka did not mess with married women. His assistants had worked her over for two days, being careful not to mark her permanently. Now she was in a state of terrified surrender, ready for him.

She was serving him a late dinner, starting to relax, thinking she was safe for the moment. He'd have her for dessert. She wouldn't expect that.

Shinka was a man with a simple philosophy—a finger in every pie. From time to time, it was necessary to bake a new pie. The ingredients for blacksmith pie were cheap enough. As he waited for the right moment, he mentally tallied his gains and losses. "Two guards, six slaves, and an empty shed."

"What, sir?" The terrified-rabbit look was back in her eye.

"Nothing, I was thinking out loud." He looked her up and down. Suddenly, he was in the mood for dessert.

"Come here, girl."

Part 2 — The Guild

The next week was spent salvaging abandoned farms in the area. Each farm had a toolshed or small machine shop for day-to-day repairs. Along with the useless power tools was older equipment from a previous century.

There were anvils in all sizes, leg vises, and several three-foot-diameter foot-treadle grinding wheels. Lots of smaller items too: hammer heads, chisels, punches, drifts, and even hardy tools were found in odd corners and drawers. Many of these objects were covered with corrosion from decades of neglect; however, they were built to take it and recover.

After a week of work, the yard was cluttered with piles of rusty salvage. Wade put some of the boys to work cleaning and oiling the salvage while he and the oldest two boys built forges from automobile wheel rims. The next project was to develop working bellows.

Lessons in smithing began eleven days after Wade's capture. On that morning, the apprentices gathered around, watching Wade demonstrate. The first lesson was how to fire up the forge.

The fire smoked horribly at first as the wood chips caught and spread to lumps of pea coke. One boy pumped the bellows until sparks began to fly. Wade placed several rusty steel bars in the fire to heat.

"You all saw how rusty that stuff was; let's clean it up." The fire was hot now; the bellows pumped showers of sparks higher and higher as Wade shifted his bars around. He pulled one bar out of the fire, satisfied with the bright orange glow.

"Keep your metal clean. In the regular course of forging, you will keep building up a layer of burned crud on your steel. Clean it like this."

Holding the cool bar end in his gloved left hand, he scrubbed at the orange bar end with a steel brush. Sparks flew and big flakes of black stuff came off the bar. "Now this is clean. Remember, if your work gets dirty, take a cleaning heat and scrub it good."

Wade pulled another bar out of the center of the fire. The end of this bar glowed white-hot, difficult to look at; sparks cascaded in all directions. "This is burning steel— look at it! See the sparks—it's wrecked—no good, see?"

He scrubbed at the white-hot end with the wire brush, causing more sparks to fly. Wade held it up for all to see as it passed through orange toward dull red. Quenching the bar in a tub of water, releasing a cloud of steam in the process, Wade cooled it enough to pass around to his students.

"You see how the bar is burned and pitted. The carbon cooked out of that steel, changing it to iron." He retrieved the ruined bar and stuck it back into the fire, selecting another bar.

He held this bar up too, showing the yellow-white color, the occasional spark emitted from the hot steel. "This is what common steel should look like when it's ready to work." Quickly, he stepped to the anvil and held the bar at a shallow angle to the face of the anvil.

Whap, whap, whap, whap, clang! In five blows, rotating the bar a quarter-turn between each blow, he brought the bar to a point. Moving to the horn of the anvil, and striking with the wedge-shaped back of the forging hammer, Wade necked the bar in five inches behind the point he had forged. He scrubbed the cooling steel with his wire brush, examining it closely, satisfied with the results.

"Just one heat and I moved a lot of metal. That's the trick, move the metal. Machinists think in terms of removing metal. Blacksmiths move metal." He placed the worked bar back in the fire and took the burned one.

The burned end of the bar was yellow-white, the proper temperature. "Now we get rid of the burned piece."

He placed a "cutoff," a chisel-shaped hardy tool, in the square hardy-hole in the anvil face. Resting the hot steel on the edge of the cutoff, he hit it once, twice, a third time, splitting the steel against the cutoff until it was attached by a thin tab of metal. He rapped the bar against the anvil and the end broke off. Wade picked up the hardy tool and quenched it.

"Heat changes metal hardness, its temper. Don't let your tools get hot or they'll go soft on you. Sudden cooling makes steel hard and brittle; heating and gradual cooling makes steel soft and workable with a file." He held up the bar. "The bad bit is gone, the rest of this bar is good steel."

He returned to the forge and pulled out the partially shaped bar. The pointed end was white-hot, burning and spitting sparks. "I let the point get too hot. It's thin here at the tip, heats up faster, burns faster." He scrubbed at the end with the brush.

"It's not too far gone; this can be saved. Another minute and it would be too late. This is what they mean when they say 'too many irons in the fire.' If you work too many pieces at once, you'll burn some—that's for sure. This is a rule: Work only one piece at a time until I give you permission to work more."

While he talked, the color dropped back to yellow. Wade went to the anvil and, with four blows from the flat of a six-pound maul, flattened the end into a leaf shape. Sticking the bar back into the fire he commented, "It's easy to keep your steel in the working temperature range; keep it in the fire as much as possible. When you take it out to work, work fast, then return it."

He retrieved his piece and laid it flat along the top of the anvil with the glowing end projecting over the side. He struck it twice, bending the bar at a right angle conforming to the corner of the anvil.

Wade quenched the steel and held it up for the apprentices to see. "This is a fire rake now; each of you will make one for yourself. In fact, you will be making the bulk of your own tools: tongs, chisels, punches, drifts, and hardy tools. Now let's go over basic hammer techniques."

For the next three hours, Wade demonstrated the basics of forging, showing his apprentices how to use the wedge-shaped peen of the hammer to stretch and pull the steel, how to use the flat peen to spread and flatten. He showed how to punch holes in hot steel and drift the holes wider.

Wade worked until the tingling in his wrists turned to screaming pain. Then, he watched his boys trying to copy his actions. Standing close by them, he corrected their mistakes and gave advice.

"Let the hammer's weight do the work, don't try to power the blows. Lift and let the hammer drop. Hold it farther back on the handle, don't choke up on it. Work from the elbow, not the shoulder."

At the end of the day, each boy had spent at least an hour at the forge working the glowing hot steel. Each had taken the first step toward becoming a blacksmith. Wade gathered them together.

"You will practice what you learned for the next three days. By that time, I think you'll be ready for the next lesson. Now put away the tools, police the smithy, and get yourselves cleaned up for dinner."

Actually, it would take all of that time for Wade's hands to recover enough to teach again. The pain continued to get worse as the evening wore on and numbness was replaced by agony.

Next morning, Wade watched his boys fire their forges and get to work. Some were showing promise. Nick in particular had strength and skill with a hammer from his years on the wall. He had absorbed most of the first lesson and was ready for more. Even though it hurt to raise a hammer, Wade guided him through the steps to make a pair of blacksmith's tongs.

"This is a vital tool and we'll need about a dozen pair. I'm giving you the job and assigning two boys to help you."

Wade stayed around long enough to watch Nick make one of the tong halves (each pair of tongs consisted of two halves). As soon as he could manage it, Wade retired to his room. He didn't want his boys to see him in this condition. His pain was tempered by a sense of accomplishment. His boys were making great strides, especially Nick. It was a case of teaching the teachers; Nick would pass his lessons on to the younger boys.

On the next day that Wade had planned to lecture, his hands weren't up to it. He pulled Nick aside. "I want you to teach the boys today. Show them how to make the tongs. Keep them working all day. I'm going back to my office. I'll be around later to check on things."

Nick returned to the shop whistling and took over, putting the younger boys to firing their forges. Things were going better and better. Soon he'd have ol' Wade's job. Guildmaster Nick had a nice sound to it.

Wade was soaking his hands one evening, ten days after his first lecture, when the summons from Shinka arrived. Sam escorted him to the town hall, where Shinka kept him waiting for twenty-five minutes.

Shinka enjoyed these cat-and-mouse games, but it wasn't just for his own amusement. It was vital in order to maintain the *fear* in his underlings.

Once, a million years ago, before the Smash-up, Shinka had managed a small factory. He hadn't hated his underlings until the bastards had gone out on strike. The ingrates refused to see reason, objecting to a combination of employee pay cuts and executive bonuses. Living expenses were rising; executives like him needed their bonuses. And the laborers' wages were not competitive with those paid in Mexico. Still the workers refused to give in.

Shinka proposed moving the operation out of the country; upper management listened. They closed the plant, ending the strike, and moved south—without Shinka. He got his pink slip along with all the rest. The disloyal scum had cost Shinka his job.

Now Shinka could run things his way, introducing the work-or-die policy for captured vagrants. These were great times for management.

When Wade was finally called into the lantern-lit office, the first thing he did was look for the pistol. It wasn't in sight. Shinka got up to meet him.

"You're certainly looking better. The new job must agree with you." Shinka wrapped Wade's hand in his own and squeezed, flexing his grip, grating the bones of Wade's hand against each other. "Getting everything you need?"

Wade gasped, his face white, concentrating on keeping his feet until Shinka released his hand. "Thank you, sir. Everything's just fine. Thank you."

Shinka spoke in conversational tones, a big smile on his face. "Listen, you trashy low-life scum, I want you to understand this. You've got one month, thirty days, to produce. Got that? The countdown's started and I'm watching the clock!"

Wade's reply was equally calm and measured. "It can't be done."

"You'd better do it or you'll be facing a firing squad in thirty days."

"Shoot me now and let's be done with it." Wade realized with mild surprise that he meant every word. A week ago he'd have agreed to anything Shinka said.

"What?" This was the last response Shinka had expected.

"My boys aren't ready; they burn more steel than they work. If I promise you production in a month, when the month passes and there's nothing to show for it, you'd be twice as mad. If you shoot me now, it saves me a month of demonstrating—that's a lot of pain in the hands for nothing."

This wasn't going right. Shinka had broken dozens of people the same way; give them something, then threaten to take it away. Right now, Wade should be crawling and begging for his life. Something had changed.

"I'll give you more boys if that will speed things up."

"It takes a woman nine months to have a baby. Can nine women have a baby in one month?"

"How much time do you need?"

"I don't know. Nobody's done anything like this in centuries. It will take time, months at least. Less than a year, I hope. You want a good product. I want to give it to you."

Was this guy sassing him? "If I think you're jerking me around, I'll make you pay double for it. Nothing clean like a firing squad!"

"Believe me, sir, when I tell you that I understand my life depends on keeping you happy."

Shinka realized that was as good as he'd get out of Wade. "Sam, we're done here. Take him back."

Wade felt odd on his way back to the smithy, floating on air. He'd dodged the bullet one more time. Until he produced something of value for Shinka, though, he continued to be in danger, he and his boys too.

● ● ●

Nick stirred his bar in the forge the next afternoon, pulling it out to check the color: not quite right, too orange. A minute later, when the bar was almost white-hot, he took it to the anvil. In one heat, he made a clean shoulder, laying the hot iron against the edge of the anvil and pounding on the portion over the face. Then back to the fire.

The iron had cooled against the anvil, but it took only minutes to return to working temperatures. Nick turned the bar on the anvil so that the shouldered end extended over the edge and shouldered it again. Then he quenched it in the water tub.

There, the hard part was done; one half of a pair of blacksmith's tongs. All he had to do was draw out the end to form the handle. That and punch and rivet the two halves together.

"How'd ya do that so fast, Nick? And the shoulders are so clean. It always takes me four or five heats to do a shoulder and it's all jagged—looks like hell. How'd ya do it?"

Nick turned an angry scowl on Stevens, the ten-year-old working the bellows. "Shut yer yap. I showed ya how once. Just shut up and pump the bellows." Stevens flushed and looked stricken, but complied, pumping furiously, producing a flurry of sparks.

Stupid twerp. That was his problem, the kid took too many heats. A shoulder was best done in one heat with a few powerful blows. The kid's biggest problem was that he was too small; he'd have to grow into it. But Nick wasn't going to explain that.

The boss, ol' Wade himself, had assigned Nick to do the first assignment, tongs for the shop. Now, while the other boys were practicing lessons, Nick was doing a man's work. His skill with the hammer was appreciated.

What's more, ol' Wade was too crippled up to spend much time in the shop. The day after demonstrating a lesson, Wade could barely lift his spoon. Because Nick ran the day-to-day lessons, he could do as he pleased. Wade needed him too much to make a fuss.

When Nick was quarrying blocks for the wall, nobody cared if he was any good or if his chisel holders kept their fingers. Here, everyone knew that he was the best. He wasn't going to help any of the others surpass him. Let 'em figure it out for themselves if they were so smart.

Sam was the daytime guard; Wade got to know him over the weeks. Wade tried to invite Sam to his quarters for breakfast, but Sam always refused. That was because Sam had a supply of coffee that he didn't want to share. As a guard, he was a valued employee of the Lord Mayor and entitled to coffee. Wade didn't rank so high.

Shortly after Wade returned to his rooms one morning to soak his hands, Sam dropped by with a thermos of coffee.

"Got some good news," Wade greeted him. "We found a supply of borax yesterday." Wade fumbled painfully with a towel, drying his hands. "You can't forge-weld without flux to keep the oxygen out. Borax is a good flux. Borax was used as a laundry additive, softens water or something. Since it isn't edible, nobody bothered to salvage it. Borax doesn't rot. We found plenty in the abandoned Quick-mart."

"Can you work with your hands like that?" Sam was horrified at the thought of losing his gravy train; if Wade couldn't work, then the blacksmith job was over.

"It's not like I have a choice. Shinka's patience won't last forever; I've got to make him happy."

"Geeze, do you want some coffee?" It was the only thing Sam had to offer.

"God, yes! I'd kill for coffee; it's been years since I had some." With his gnarled hands wrapped around a hot cup, Wade drank his coffee. First a sip, then a big gulp. He shuddered, his eyes popped open and bugged slightly. "It's show time!"

Sam laughed. "Yeah, I saw that movie too. Seems like a million years ago. It's instant, you know. The Lord Mayor and his council have ground coffee. They took tons of the stuff from McCoy."

"Well, this is good enough for me. It's a real help too; haven't felt this good in years." Wade set his cup down and flexed his fingers.

"I've got to teach these boys before my hands give out. It's a race and there's a lot riding on it. If I fail, the game's over for me and the boys. I figure you're giving Shinka ah . . . status reports. I want this to work, you want this to work, we can get along. I don't want you to lie to Shinka, just put the best possible spin on things."

Sam looked unhappy. "You're a nice guy, Wade. But I can't let you mess up my situation here."

Wade finished his cup; Sam refilled it. "Sam, does it look like I'm trying to mess up anyone's situation? I've got a situation here myself. For the first time in my life,

I'm building something, doing something worth doing. I'll do anything to make the Guild work."

They finished their coffee in silence before Wade got to his feet. "I'm not asking you to violate any loyalties. I just want you to think about the situation, where your best interests lie. The Guild might turn out to be something big, something you want to be part of.

"Well, it's time for me to begin the lesson—today's tool steel. Come on back anytime; you're always welcome, especially when you bring coffee."

Sam had a lot to think about, walking back to his room with the empty thermos.

Nick did well enough drilling the boys on basic techniques. Most of the apprentices were ready for the next lesson. Slater, the next oldest boy, tried hard but showed no aptitude at all. The boy burned more and produced less than anyone else.

Despite the progress the other boys were making, Wade wasn't happy. He didn't like the atmosphere around the shop. The boys weren't pulling together. Nick kept order, but he ruled through fear, encouraging Slater to pick on weaker boys.

It reminded Wade of working at an office where a dictatorial boss ruled through intimidation, pitting employees against each other and keeping vital information to himself. It resulted in wasted effort, rumors, mistrust, and confusion.

Wade couldn't have that. He'd have to talk to Nick. If he could train just one boy before his hands gave out, one smith able to teach others, the Guild might succeed. Nick was that boy. But it could all be poisoned if Nick proved to be a bully.

"Today, we start on tool steel—high-carbon steel— which presents its own set of challenges. Tool steel, commonly available in the form of automobile leaf springs, must be worked at cooler temperatures. Orange to high red is the proper temperature range. Too hot— yellow—and the carbon cooks out. Too cool—dull red—and the steel cracks."

Nick was one of the last apprentices out of the shop. Wade stopped him at the door. "Just a minute, Nick. You've been doing a fine job teaching the boys, but there's a problem shaping up and I want to nip it in the bud. Sometimes you're too sharp with the boys. When they make mistakes, and they're going to make plenty of them, I don't want you jumping on them. Remember, they're younger than you and they're not as strong. Go easier on them. Okay?"

Wade smiled his brightest while Nick glowered at the floor, scuffing his feet, shoulders hunched, hands thrust deep in his pockets. His face was carefully blank.

"Uh-huh. Sure, Boss. Whatever you say."

Wade watched him and wondered if he'd done any good. He had no experience dealing with orphans scarred by world disaster. It seemed to help during the week; Nick ran daily classes while Wade recovered enough to teach the next lesson.

For that week, the apprentices worked on tool steel, forging knives, chisels, spear points, and arrowheads. The demand for these last two items was high. Bullets were getting scarce everywhere but in the Spartan Dragoons. Hunters were reverting to simpler technologies.

Wade's next demonstration was of critical importance. "Working tool steel is only half the battle; the real secret is tempering. This is the core of what we do, the secret of giving steel the proper amount of hardness. Too hard and the steel shatters like glass, too soft and the steel bends and won't hold an edge."

Wade showed them how to harden steel by heating it to a low white heat, testing it with a magnet. "When the steel is no longer attracted by the magnet, then it's ready. The crystals in the metal are randomized. That's when to quench the metal."

There were tubs of water, brine, and oil. "Water quenches fast, conducts heat away the fastest; oil quenches slowest, the metal cools more slowly. The edge cools fastest because it's thin; fast cooling makes the edge the hardest. The back of the blade or the shank of the tool, where the metal is thick, that area cools more slowly and stays softer."

Wade showed them how to temper by watching the color in the metal. "Quench the edge and clean the metal with a file. Watch the colors form and flow from the hot metal towards the cold edge. Dark blue is fine for knives, punches, and hammers; chisels and axes should be a straw color. When the color reaches the edge, it's time to quench."

After the lesson, while they were cleaning the shop, Wade threw out a question. "Boys, what does Sparta need? Shovels, hammers, pickaxes, what?"

Nick spoke immediately. "Chisels. They need stone-cutting chisels to make blocks for the wall."

Wade studied Nick thoughtfully. "And you know about chisels, don't you?" He was thinking about the broken jackhammer bits he'd found at one of the farms they'd salvaged. "Okay, we'll give it a try."

For the next demonstration, the class watched Wade and Nick make chisels. Nick acted as Wade's assistant, standing by the anvil with a twelve-pound sledge maul, instead of watching with the other apprentices. Wade heated the metal, bringing it to the anvil. Wade swung a light hammer. Every time he struck the metal, Nick immediately hit the same spot with his maul. As Wade turned and positioned the steel on the anvil, each one of his blows was mirrored by Nick.

It was a fast way to move metal and Nick learned a lot. They finished four chisels before Wade's hands gave out. Nick held the bar for the fifth one, directing the blows of Curt, third oldest at eleven. Nick was fourteen; big for his age, he already stood five foot ten. Curt, a smaller boy, lacked Nick's skill with a mall. He frequently missed the indicated spot. One blow landed too high on the piece, knocking the bar from Nick's hand.

"You stupid jerk." Nick gathered a handful of Curt's shirt and lifted him off his feet, shaking him. "You trying to kill me?" He tossed him against a workbench.

"That's enough, Nick. Go sit down. Right now." Wade was there, on the spot. He didn't stand any taller than Nick, but his authority was unquestioned. Nick obeyed. Wade turned to help Curt back to his feet. "Pick up your hammer and we'll finish this chisel."

With obvious pain and difficulty, Wade and Curt finished the fifth chisel. "I'll be tempering these tomorrow. Curt will be my fingers and the rest of you will watch. Except for you, Nick; you're excused from lessons until further notice. You're on shop clean-up duty instead. Report to me in my room after you've finished here."

Nick cleaned the shop after the other boys had left. He was in real trouble, that was obvious. The others were careful not to talk to him as they left. When he reported to Wade's rooms, he found Wade soaking his hands.

"Sit down, Nick. It's time we had another talk. You're the best smith I've got. You're a natural. You've learned a lot in just a few months. You'd be the perfect head apprentice, except for one thing. You're a bully. I can't have that."

Wade got up to pace. "Nick, you know more black-smithing than all the other boys put together. You really try hard and put a lot of work into it. But you don't share your skill. A good head apprentice is like an older brother to the younger boys. He helps them, teaches them.

"You are a bad influence on the boys. I know that you encourage Slater to pick on the other boys. That's got to stop right now. Until I figure out what to do with you, you will not be coming to lessons and you will continue to clean out the shop. I'll talk to you again soon."

Nick decided to hang tough. "You gonna boot me out? Send me back to the wall? What about all that brother crap?"

"Don't worry, Nick. You're Guild now—in for life. If you don't make it as an apprentice smith, there are other ways to serve the Guild. Get used to it; we're stuck with each other."

Nick digested that information for a bit. When he spoke, his voice was a little less hostile. "Who's doing the lesson tomorrow? You?"

"That's not your worry. Go get cleaned up for dinner now. You don't want to be late."

Wade did teach the lesson the next morning, with Curt's thumb-fingered help. Wade was obviously in pain. It almost made Nick flinch to watch it. Almost. Wade couldn't hold out very long.

But he did.

Every day Wade demonstrated, or he guided Curt through a demonstration, or he watched and guided the boys through their work, moving from boy to boy. As the new head boy, Curt got much better in a hurry. It went on that way for another week.

None of the boys would talk to Nick.

Wade requested an interview with Lord Planner Shinka. Since the death of Councilman Koslowski, Shinka could have moved to a larger office. He preferred the office with its trophies—bullet holes and bloodstains. Wade entered Shinka's office acutely aware of the pistol in the desk drawer.

"Lord Planner." Wade bobbed his head in a little bow. How long, he wondered, would it be before he would be tugging his forelock in the presence of the nobility?

"You brought me something? Something I'll like, I hope, for your sake." Shinka pointed an index finger at Wade, cocking a thumb. "Bang!"

"Yes, sir." As long as the pistol drawer stayed shut, Wade didn't care if Shinka wanted to point at him. "I brought you these. They were Nick Baker's idea, chisels for the block cutting crews. He told me that the original chisels wore out long ago, ground down past their temper points. These should speed things along."

He laid a bundle of five three-foot chisels on the desk. "And this." He laid a knife blade on the desk beside them.

Shinka picked up the blade first. It was bare of hilt or pommel. He tested the edge with his thumb and swore when the blade bit. "It's sharp enough, I'll admit. Still, it's not properly finished and you had four months to make it."

"No, sir. But it's a plenty good blade; the first of many. There'll be a lot more of those coming soon. They're not finished because I wasn't sure of your intentions. I assume that you plan to sell them. Do you want them as finished knives, or as finished blades?"

Shinka didn't have an answer for that. He hadn't expected this pie to yield a plum so fast. He stalled for time to think. "You must want something from me. Nobody comes to see me unless they want something."

"Yes, sir. I want more boys, three or four if you want finished blades, more if you want finished knives. And I want permission to make one of my boys into a guard. We need another guard and Slater didn't work out as a blacksmith, hasn't got it in him."

Shinka waved a dismissive hand. "Send him back to the wall. I'll send you another guard."

"No, sir. I can't send him back to the wall; he's in the Guild now. It's not his fault; he can serve the Guild some other way. We owe it to him."

"Huh?" Shinka looked at Wade as if he were crazy.

"He knows too much. Once you're in the Guild, once you know the secrets, we don't ever let them out. It's all part of keeping the secret."

"Oh. Why didn't you say so? Okay, make him a guard. I'll send you six boys. Give me finished knives and blades. And leave that one behind. I'll look after it."

Once Wade had gone, Lord Shinka examined the knife again in the light streaming through the window. As he turned it in his hands, the polished metal reflected a beam around the room. Shinka went to the door of his office and bellowed down the corridor.

"Take these chisels to the crew cutting blocks for the wall. I want a report on how well they work."

The foreman himself returned with the report. "These things are great! I haven't seen a chisel cut so well in years. Somebody stumble over a cache of pre-disaster tools?"

"Oh, these are an improvement?" Shinka inquired blandly.

"Gods, yes. They're hard and sharp, not worn out. They really cut. We've been doing most of the work with hammers, just bashing old foundations apart. Half the work went into squaring rough chunks of concrete into blocks. Very wasteful. With these we can cut the blocks, goes faster."

Harder, sharper tools; there was a fortune to be made here. His small investment was paying off. That gimpy bum Thompkins really did know his stuff.

"Bring your old chisels to the blacksmith's for sharpening."

When Wade returned to the shop, he called in three people. First Sam, then Slater, and finally Nick Baker was called. Nick arrived in time to see Slater and Sam leave Wade's rooms together. Then it was his turn.

"Sit down, Nick. This is that talk I said we'd have. Paul Slater has decided to become an apprentice guard. He'll be working with Jack and Sam from now on. He's still part of the Guild, of course.

"How about you? You like to throw your weight around, maybe you'd be happier in security. You chum around with Slater; you could go work with your buddy."

"No, please, sir. Let me be a smith again. I don't have to be head 'prentice, I can take orders from one of the other boys. Only please, let me be a smith. You said I do good work. I'll keep my yap shut and help out and anything. Please!"

"Okay, I'll give you another chance—as head boy. We're getting six new boys tomorrow. You're going to train them. You've got three months to turn them into proper smiths. I don't know if my hands would stand training up a new batch. I'll give lessons to all of you from time to time."

Nick found himself on his feet and pumping Wade's hand. "Thank you, sir. You won't be sorry, sir. I'll teach 'em everything I know and then some." He stopped when he noticed the pain his grip caused Wade. "You won't be sorry, sir."

On his way back to the dormitory, Nick couldn't believe his luck. Wade had forgiven him. Sucker! Wade was a pushover for a sob story.

He'd had a chance to think about things while he was in the doghouse and this time he'd be more careful. This wasn't like working the wall. There nobody cared how you treated people. Here, things were . . . civilized.

He'd pushed too hard, moved too fast. This time Nick would play Wade's game. Wade always seemed to talk his way to where he wanted to get. Nick could learn to do that. He'd be nice to the kids and show 'em his tricks. He'd dress his orders up with "for the good of the Guild."

What's more, Nick didn't want Wade's job anymore, at least not right now. Let Wade do all the hard work. Wade had to take the lumps if Shinka got mad, and everyone knew Shinka was mad all the time. Head apprentice was a much safer job than Guildmaster and the food was the same for both jobs.

When Nick arrived at the dormitory and walked to the center of the room, all conversation stopped. "Wade made me head apprentice again. Anybody got any problems with that? I'm not threatening, I'm asking a real question. Is this going to cause any problems?"

Curt broke the silence that followed. "We know, Wade told us. What Wade says goes. He said you wouldn't bully anymore."

"Yeah, no rough stuff. I promised Wade."

"Well, all right then." And that was that. Nick was back in. How does he do it? Nick couldn't figure it out. Wade told somebody to do something and after they did it, they thanked Wade for telling them. Nick just had to learn how Wade did it.

Just before nightfall, the new boys arrived. Shinka sent seven, between the ages of fourteen and ten. Along with the boys came two jars of instant coffee, compliments of Lord Planner Shinka. Next morning, Wade was able to supply the coffee when Sam came to his rooms.

They sat in Wade's office watching the apprentices on the shop floor through the open door. Eventually Wade got down to business. "Sam, this coffee says the Guild is doing okay. We're expanding production, adding members; if this keeps up we'll have to move to a bigger place. Our security needs will grow. The Slater kid is only the first; I want all our security to be Guild members. I want you and Jack to join too."

The offer sounded tempting to Sam. Working for Shinka was scary. "I like the idea and all, but what will Shinka say? I ain't going to him and askin' to work for no one else."

"The only difference is we'd be paying your salaries. I'll set it up with Shinka. Don't worry about a thing."

"I don't get pay, just room and board. And coffee."

Wade smiled. "I think the Guild can manage to pay you some hard money, once things get rolling."

They rapidly settled into a new schedule. Nick taught the new boys, one of whom was actually two months older than Nick. He kept his word, teaching them as best he could. Wade guided the other boys doing production work, reforging the stone chisels, making knives and arrowheads.

Over the next two months, as the new boys were trained, the trickle of goods coming out of the smithy increased to a steady stream. In the months that followed, the apprentices began taking special orders for spears, helmets, and breastplates for the Lord Mayor's Guard, and breaking huge tractor plows into individual horse-drawn plows.

Wade went one more time to Lord Shinka for younger boys to do chores around the shop and living quarters. This would leave the older boys free to concentrate on their work. From this point on Wade would not accept any boy older than eight. He explained it all to Shinka.

"To keep the secret of smithing under our control, we've got to get these boys young and train them our way. We can catch them early, bind their loyalty to the Guild. When we start taking boys from other towns, they'll come to us at six. Once they get here, I'll keep them surrounded by boys who believe in the Guild. If we get them that young and keep them for ten-year apprenticeships, and we still don't have their loyalty, we don't deserve to keep our monopoly."

Shinka realized with shock that Wade was thinking further ahead than he was. "What do you mean, 'boys from other towns'? What other towns? You belong to Sparta. I don't want to hear about any other towns."

"There's a huge amount of demand out there, massive amounts of money to be made. It's all we can do now to produce a few custom items. But one of my new boys is almost as good as Nick and the others are coming along. Soon we'll be producing more than Sparta needs. We're talking trade here. We'll want to expand, add branches in other towns."

Spit sprayed from Shinka's lower lip as he screamed at Wade. "That's treason—hanging talk! All trade goes through Sparta. All of it! Have I made myself clear? No smiths in other towns!"

Wade could tell he'd gone too far. "Yes, sir; sorry, sir. All through Sparta. The essential thing is to keep expanding. In another few months, we start training another group of boys. A few more months, another batch. Soon I'll have dozens of trained smiths cranking out trade goods for you."

One fall morning, fourteen months after his arrival in Sparta, Wade presented the Lord Mayor Vance and Lord Planner Shinka with finely balanced rapiers as part of a ceremony in which Sparta officially recognized the Guild and Wade as its Guildmaster. Lord Vance was hammered by ten o'clock in the morning. Since it was a formal occasion, he was drinking the last of the real bourbon instead of his usual rotgut.

Many Sparta citizens came to the ceremony and the feast afterwards. For the first time in his life, Nick could meet them on something close to equal terms. Townspeople pointed and gave way to him. He was a Guildsman, and that suddenly counted for something. It gave him a thrill of pride he'd never experienced before.

Nick worked his way around the tables loaded with the fall harvest: corn, beef, potatoes, squash, and wild game. He piled his plate high and came back for seconds and thirds. It wasn't that he was still hungry, he just couldn't stand to see food go uneaten. His belly was painfully distended before he was forced to stop.

He stumbled outside to rest before going back for another helping. That's where Shinka found him.

"Chief Apprentice Baker." Shinka smiled. "I've been waiting to speak to you."

To Nick, the smile seemed as genuinely friendly as a shark's grin. Nick's guard went up as he forced a smile every bit as false. "Yes, sir. What can I do for you?"

"It's not what you can do for me, it's what we can do for each other. You're an ambitious young man and a very good blacksmith, I understand. Why, some say you do most of the teaching at the Guildshop—most of the real work."

That was what Nick had thought for some time. Somehow, hearing it out of Shinka's mouth brought doubts to his mind. "Thank you, sir. I just do what Wade tells me. I show the other boys what Wade taught me."

"Nonsense, boy. You're too modest. I think you're a young man who knows what he wants and goes out and gets it. I admire that. I think you're a lot like me in that way."

By now Shinka's phony smile had faded, replaced by his usual scowl. He reached out and grasped Nick by the upper arm and gave him a small shake. "Think about it, boy. With my patronage, you could go far. Wade won't last forever. When he's gone, it could be your time. Remember where your best interests lie."

Shinka released Nick, his ghastly party smile returned. "Think about it." He nodded and turned to go.

Appetite thoroughly spoiled, Nick went in the other direction. He walked back to the Guild compound in deep thought. Wade found him there two hours later.

"Nick, I've been looking for you everywhere."

"What?" Nick was started out of his thoughts. "Something for me to do?"

"No, not today. In fact, it's good news. By the power vested in me by the Guild of Blacksmiths, I'm promoting you to journeyman—as of now. Congratulations, Nick. You earned it."

It was absolutely the last thing Nick expected to hear. "I don't know what to say."

"I watched you closely for the last year and you've justified my faith in you." Wade shook his hand. "I was worried about you. You were bullying the other boys. You reminded me of Shinka." Wade laughed. "I couldn't deal with another Shinka. Not here in the Guild too."

Part 3 — Guild War

The summons came in the early morning; three burly troopers wearing the breastplate of the Mayor's Guard pounded on the door of the new Guild compound. They carried Guild-made swords and muskets instead of M-16s. "Open up in the name of the Lord Mayor! Guildmaster Thompkins is summoned to the Lord Mayor's presence."

Jack, the Guild's night security guard, a single man with an M-16, answered the door. "What's your business here?"

"We already told you, or are you deaf? Get your boss, Shinka wants him." The lead guardsman shoved the muzzle of Jack's rifle aside. "Checked your ammunition recently?"

Wade appeared in the hallway wrapped in a blanket. "I need a minute to change. Jack, get these men some coffee, then wake Nick and send him to my room."

Nick was waiting at Wade's door when Wade got back to his room. "I sent Jack to fetch you." Wade went to his wardrobe and selected his second-best outfit.

"Then he won't be able to find me unless he looks here," Nick responded reasonably. "What's this all about?"

Wade settled his chain of office in place and reached for his coat. "I don't know. Our Lord Mayor has summoned me."

"Maybe I should come along." Nick sounded worried.

"You know better than that. I need you here to look after things. Sam will come with me. If there is trouble and I don't come back, you're not to start anything. The Guild is not ready for a fight. Shinka hates my guts, but I think he'll leave the Guild alone for now."

Nick nodded. "I'll go get Sam."

Wade stood in front of Shinka's desk on the blood-stained floor, waiting to be noticed. It had been almost two years since Shinka pulled the pistol on him.

"Ah, Wade." The official notice. "Prompt as usual. Please sit down."

So this was to be a good meeting. In the six years of their acquaintance, Shinka had only invited Wade to sit twice before. That meant Shinka wanted something.

The office door opened and an attractive slave girl brought in a tray. "It's early. Have some coffee."

Wade's nostrils dilated at the smell. Real coffee from grounds, not instant. It had been fifteen years since he'd last had some. Now he was on guard. Shinka was being too nice. He'd never offered real coffee before.

Painfully Wade wrapped his gnarled hands around the hot cup. Once the slave girl scampered out, Lord Mayor Shinka launched into his speech.

"If Sparta is the dominant city in the region, I like to think I had something to do with it. I was just a reservist at Fort McCoy, but as a Sparta native, I was in a position to negotiate the deal between the garrison at McCoy and the Sparta City Council."

Right place at the right time, Wade reflected. The tiny garrison at McCoy, drowning in supplies—supplies sitting in quake-smashed warehouses in the torrential rain. Sparta, closest town, desperately in need of supplies, a place with women. And Shinka, a major in the army reserve, a native of Sparta—a foot in each camp.

"Sparta withstood the looting that ravaged all the surrounding cities. Withstood starvation with food from McCoy, withstood disease with medicine from McCoy, and withstood attacks with guns and bullets from Fort McCoy. We preserved civilization."

Right, civilization. Is that what you call it?

"Yesterday . . ." Shinka swallowed hard, unable to continue for a moment. "Yesterday, the rifle ammunition failed. All of it at once. It seems it all came from the same manufacturing run."

That made Wade sit up in his chair. "All the ammunition? We don't have anything?"

"All the M-16 ammunition is dead. We still have .50 cal for the machine guns on the city walls. Then there's some 30-06 and some .45 pistol ammunition, that and some very old precontrol civilian stuff."

That was the trouble. All civilian ammunition manufactured in the last four years before the Smash-up had a built-in shelf life of five years. After that, the primers failed. An antiterrorism measure, it prevented stockpiling. Military ammunition had a longer shelf life. The expiration date had finally caught up with Sparta.

"We're no worse than anybody else," Wade said. "Nobody has working ammunition. And we have the smithy."

Shinka beamed, a frightening sight. "That's what I love about you, Wade. You're on top of things. Yes, we have the smithy. You've started producing blackpowder muskets. The Spartan Dragoons will have to be re-equipped with your muskets. We need them now, at least a thousand. Swords too."

"Now?" Wade gulped, the trap obvious. "A thousand, sir? Of each? We can't do it. Not all at once."

Shinka's smile slipped. "Are you defying me, Wade?"

"Sir," Wade spoke very fast. "Of course you'll get all of our production. But we've only made ten muskets and you have them all. It may take years to make a thousand. The swords alone will keep us busy for months to come.

Then there are the regular orders for tools and farm equipment. How do you want that prioritized?"

"The guns and swords for the army are your first priority. I don't care how you do it but get it done! You can have whatever you need within reason."

This was the opportunity, it was time to dicker. "We'll need to expand the Guild again. That means more boys. I'll have to set up an assembly line to build guns. Most of all, the Guild will need that mill and water wheel we talked about. Also we need a wall around the compound, something to keep prying eyes out."

"Every time I want something done, no matter how simple, you have to double your staff. Now, why is that, I wonder?"

"Lord, each time I double my staff, I'm able to give you what you ask for. Hasn't my Guild been a money-maker for you?"

Shinka got to his feet, a sign the interview was over. "I'll think about it. I'm not convinced you need any wall. The main threat to our monopoly on black-smithing is one of your boys spilling the beans. What would you do if that chief apprentice of yours, Nick Baker, took off and started a rival blacksmith shop in, say, La Crosse?"

Wade laughed. "Don't worry about Nick, he's absolutely loyal. The Guild is the only father he's ever known."

When Wade returned to the Guild compound, he saw that Nick had rousted the apprentices from bed and started the workday. Nick was waiting for Wade. He didn't relax until Wade was safely home in the Guild compound.

"Started them early today, huh?" Wade asked.

"Yes, sir. I've got them working on sabers. We also started a new musket. There's bound to be a lot of demand now the ammunition has failed."

The Sparta grapevine was accurate as usual. "Just once I'd like to know how you get your information."

Nick laughed. "Just once I'll tell you. The head of the Mayor's goons—sorry, guards—told Jack to look after his ammunition. As soon as you left, Jack did. It doesn't work anymore—all duds. That's what Shinka called you in for, right?"

"Right you are. We're getting a new batch of boys. You'll be responsible for teaching them, Nick. Any problems with that?"

"How many new boys?"

"A dozen to twenty."

"Wow, that's a lot." Nick thought it over. "Can I have Curt to help me?"

"You've got him. It's not certain yet, but I think we're getting the new mill, maybe a wall as well."

Nick whistled. "You think so? How'd you do it?"

"It's our price for one thousand muskets and swords."

Three days later, Wade and Lord Mayor Shinka stood in the new Guild compound at the edge of the swift-running creek that ran alongside. Wade gestured and pointed.

"Just perfect for a mill; with a water wheel we can power a triphammer and grindstones."

Shinka was listening. Wade continued: "The city wall is almost done. Divert the crews here. We can have the millhouse done in four months. Then another few months to build us a wall. We could be done before the snow flies."

"What about my muskets, Wade? Aren't you forgetting about them?" Shinka sounded mild-mannered and polite—very dangerous. He only sounded like that when he was mad.

"No, sir. I haven't forgotten them. The millhouse will contain the Sparta armory. We'll set up an assembly line to bore barrels and assemble guns. Six months after we complete the mill, we should be knee-deep in muskets. In the meantime we can continue to make swords and armor."

Nick was listening from a discreet distance. Design and build a mill with all the associated machinery and get it running in less than a year—he didn't see how it could be done. Still, if Wade said so . . .

"Ahm. The supply of black powder is a little short. It will take almost a year to bring production up to snuff." Shinka was thinking out loud. "We'll have to rely on bows and pikes in the meanwhile."

"Yes, sir!" Wade leaped in. "And thanks to the Guild, we have far more arrows and pikes than anyone else."

Shinka nodded grudgingly, his humor restored. "Maybe that would be an acceptable schedule. But you can't have all the wall crews; some will continue where they are."

"Then we get the mill?"

Shinka was already stalking back to his horse. "Yeah, whatever. Write it up for my signature."

Shinka mounted and rode off with his escort of dragoons. Wade wiped sweat off his brow as Nick came running up. "What now, Boss?"

"We got it. I'm calling a meeting for the senior smiths. Go tell everyone."

His mind full, Nick turned to go. Wade called him back.

"Nick, one more thing. Start thinking about your masterpiece. I suggest you try a Kentucky rifle. However, it's up to you. Anyway, I want you to get your Master within the next year. I think we're going to need another Mastersmith around here."

Work on the new mill began at once and Wade oversaw every aspect of construction. Nick was busy as well, teaching basic blacksmithing to the youngest boys and supervising the work of the older apprentices. Still he managed to spend a lot of time at Wade's side.

One afternoon Wade pointed out one of the slaves. "That man there was a tool-and-die maker—I've talked to him. He knows something that we don't. I've got to admit, we need what he knows.

"The forging and welding to make the barrel—that we can do. But we need more; we need to know how to drill out the bores, and rifle the barrels faster. We do everything by hand. We need machines. We're bringing in a new expert to help us set up our arsenal."

Wade set up a team of his best welders and the new tool-and-die maker under Nick's direction. The smiths learned to wrap the strips of steel into coils, forge-welding the coils into tubes. Then they bored the rough tubes to form gun barrels. Using the new triphammers, Wade's smiths were able to increase their output of swords and guns, producing enough to keep the Mayor reasonably happy.

It took almost eighteen months of hard work to finish the thousand guns and thousand swords. Three years after the modern ammunition failed, the Spartan Dragoons were the best-equipped force in the state, maybe in the whole Midwest. The Guild returned to producing consumer goods, but weapons remained their biggest product.

Wade was off to another meeting with Shinka. This time the issue was Guild expansion. Nick was waiting for him beside his horse. Nick spoke in low, urgent tones. "I don't feel right about dealing with foreigners. Do ya think it's come to that?"

"Foreigners? You mean folks from La Crosse and Tomah? They're not foreigners, they're Americans, like us." Wade took the reins and prepared himself for the climb up.

"With both you and Curt Mastersmiths, that makes three counting me. And there are other journeymen who are almost ready. That's too many smiths in one town; it's time to establish a branch or we'll smother in Masters."

Wade managed to struggle onto the animal's back. "If things go badly, you could become Guildmaster sooner rather than later. Then you can decide whether to deal with La Crosse or Tomah."

Sam had waited a respectful distance away while Wade and Nick spoke. Now he hurried to mount and catch up to Wade.

"Whatever you do, I have confidence in your judgment." Wade had the last word.

Sitting in the Planner's office, Wade was unmoved as Lord Shinka pounded his desk and threatened. "There will be no Guild expansion. I forbid it!"

Wade appeared calm as he responded. "The Guild has been good for Sparta. It brought economic life to the city. Sparta has grown from the blacksmith trade and the Guild has grown with the city. But while the Guild has grown, it hasn't grown as fast as demand for Guild services. There's too much business to handle from one location. The Guild must expand."

Wade took a breath and gave Shinka the news he didn't want to hear. "The Guild will go with La Crosse to take advantage of the river trade. Think this over before you react, don't be hasty. The Guild has decided on this course; I'm telling you, not asking permission."

John Shinka, Lord Mayor of the city, stared at the man sitting before him. His mind slipped back to when this same man stood before him begging for his life. Shinka thought wistfully of the service auto in his desk drawer, loaded with reliable 1950s vintage ammunition. He wondered what would happen if he just shot the twisted old man before him. What would the Guild do?

He sighed. The time to shoot Wade Thompkins was years gone. The Guild and its blacksmith's monopoly had made Shinka rich; killing Wade would be too much like killing the goose that laid the golden egg. But he couldn't let that goose move to another city.

"Wade, we know each other, we've worked together for years to make Sparta into something to be proud of. Don't spoil all that, don't let Sparta down. I just can't let you send a smith to another town, especially not La Crosse." Shinka's anger showed through for a second.

"Where's your loyalty? Think, man! Think what losing control of smithing will do to Sparta." With a visible effort he forced a smile. "I don't want to quarrel over this—let's keep working together."

Wade heard him out before speaking, betraying his nervousness only by the way he moistened his lips with the tip of his tongue. "Sparta won't lose the secret of blacksmithing; Sparta never had the secret to lose. It's a Guild secret. If the Guild is to work, it's got to help everyone, not just Sparta. The Guild originated in Sparta, its home is in Sparta. But the Guild can't be an agent of Sparta. You've got to recognize Guild independence."

Lord Shinka spoke using simple short declarative sentences, as if speaking to an idiot. "Sparta created the

Guild. The Guild serves Sparta. No smiths outside Sparta. The Guild will serve only Sparta!"

Wade struggled to his feet, leaning on his walking stick. He had faced death in this office before. Carpet now covered the bloodstains on the floor, and the bullet holes in the back wall had been plastered and painted over. The next few weeks and months would decide the fate of the Guild.

"The Guild was never from Sparta, not really; the apprentices came from here but they were slaves, not citizens. They have no love for Sparta. I picked them out of the gutter and turned them from slaves to Guildsmen. They're loyal to the Guild. Don't force a split."

Wade started to hobble to the door. "Think about it and don't do anything hasty. We can find a common ground. I promise not to send out the smith until we talk again." He reached the door. "Sam, I'm ready to go."

As Wade opened the door to the waiting room, six dragoons with pre-disaster rifles entered from the hallway. "Just where do you think you're going?" Lord Mayor Shinka's voice came from behind him.

Wade turned and saw the man standing behind the desk with the well-remembered pistol in his hand. Wade wondered if the circle would close here in the office; he felt strangely at peace, not at all like he had nine years earlier. Shinka came up to Wade and kicked the cane from his hand, dropping him to the floor.

Lord Shinka never saw where Sam materialized the pistol from, but there it was, magically in his hand, a small double-barrel gun of Guild make. "Put that down, Sam; I'm the Lord Mayor, your boss."

Sam ignored him. "Mr. Wade, are you okay?"

Shinka answered him. "Yeah, Sam, he's all right; why do you care? You work for me. Put the gun down."

Sam looked stubborn and very unhappy. "I joined the Guild, Lord Shinka, I swore an oath. I can't go back on it. I'm afraid I can't put the gun down."

"Yes you can, Sam!" Wade spoke from the floor. "I order you to put the gun down. Don't do anything rash. Go home and tell Nick that I have decided to stay as guest of Lord Shinka."

Wade had planned for this moment for years, considering it from every angle, planning for every contingency. Now the crisis had hit; things were beyond Wade's control. Everything depended on Nick now. Wade found that it was almost a liberating experience.

"Hey, Rube! Don't be a fool. Put the gun down and go home."

Sam lowered the pistol slowly, reluctantly. "Yes, sir, Guildmaster. I hear you."

Sam handed the pistol over to the closest dragoon and stood aside. He watched Wade being picked up off the floor and hustled to a basement cell between two burly soldiers. Even though he was following the Guildmaster's orders, it gave Sam an empty feeling in the pit of his stomach watching Wade's arrest. He hurried off to report to Nick before someone thought to arrest him.

Mastersmith Nick Baker's heart chilled when he saw Sam returning from town alone. Wade had been right when he predicted that there would be trouble with Shinka. Wade had been preparing them for this moment for years.

Sam jumped off his horse before it stopped. Tossing the reins to a junior apprentice, he ran for the Guildmaster's office where Nick was waiting for him. Sam stormed into the office and breathlessly made his report.

"He said, 'Hey, Rube!' They arrested him after the meeting with Shinka, and Wade said to me, 'Hey, Rube, don't be a fool.' Then they took him away—there was nothin' I could do!"

Nick nodded. "That's okay, Sam. Wade said it would happen that way; he called it right. You did good." Should he execute the Guildmaster's plan?

"If Wade's right, and so far he's been right on the money every time, then Shinka will send the army here in a show of force. Put the forges out, take the youngest 'prentices into the woods. Pass out the Kentucky rifles and get snipers into position. Everyone go to it—you know the routine. To your places; this is no drill!"

Company "A" of the First Dragoons, the elite unit of the Spartan military, led the column into the Guild compound. As Captain Jackson called halt, he was aware that at least a dozen rifles tracked his every move, centered on his chest. He was extremely reluctant to start anything abrupt.

Silence dominated the compound; there was none of the banging, the clang of metal on metal, that typified the smithing operation. The silence was broken only by the wind and the creak of the water wheel. The jingle of horse harness sounded impossibly loud. Moving slowly, he reached into his jacket pocket and produced his copy of the Mayoral Proclamation.

"Wade Thompkins, formerly Master of the Guild of Blacksmiths, is charged with treason against his lawful master, Lord Shinka, Lord Mayor of Sparta. Thompkins is henceforth stripped of all titles, positions, and responsibilities associated with the Guild of Blacksmiths. Lord Shinka has appointed a new Guildmaster to replace the traitor Thompkins."

Captain Jackson motioned forward Tom Parkins, Lord Shinka's nephew. "Lord Parkins is appointed Guildmaster by the grace of God under the authority of the Lord Mayor."

Parkins looked around, grinning like an idiot, ready to take up his "duties" as explained by his uncle—to follow whatever orders Lord Shinka chose to give him.

Nick Baker stepped off the porch of the dormitory and advanced across the muddy yard to where Captain Jackson nervously sat his horse. "Hello, Captain, I'm Nick Baker, senior smith in residence and Guild second; what seems to be the trouble? I'm afraid my authority is limited in the absence of the Guildmaster."

Jackson tried bluster, pointing at the grinning Parkins. "This is your Guildmaster, appointed by the Lord Mayor!"

Nick sounded surprised. "Our Guildmaster is staying in town as a guest of the Lord Mayor; you'd better take this up with him. If anything unfortunate happens to him, as Guild second I become the new Guildmaster." He squinted at Parkins, who was starting to lose his smile.

"This man is not a Mastersmith; only a Master may become Guildmaster. In fact this man is not even a member of the Guild and he's too old to take in as a 'prentice." Nick seemed to consider, then he smiled happily.

"Tell you what, as a favor to the Lord Mayor, since we are on such good terms with him, we'll make an exception and accept this man into an apprenticeship. Maybe in time he can work his way up to the Guildmaster's position."

Jackson was on the verge of arguing when he thought better of it; he considered his twofold mission: to establish Parkins at the Guild compound, and to pick up an order of one hundred sabers that was supposed to have been delivered three weeks ago. "How 'bout my sabers, they ready to go?"

Nick blinked in mild surprise. "Sure, ready and waiting. You can take 'em now or we can send 'em to town this afternoon."

Jackson came to a rapid decision; Parkins was staying, the sabers were going—Jackson's mission would be accomplished without him taking a bullet in the head; a good compromise in Jackson's opinion. He followed the path of least resistance and went along with the situation. Thinking of the rifles trained on him, Jackson informed Nick of his decision.

"We'll take the sabers now. Mamet, Wilkins, Hoff, Johnson: dismount and load the swords into our wagon."

Jackson and his troop pulled out fifteen minutes later, mission accomplished. At the Guild compound, after taking the oath and joining the Guild, Parkins was being shown his new living quarters. He would occupy a small, thin pallet in the junior apprentices' quarters, the loft of the barn-turned-shop. The senior smiths put him to work doing the most menial chores, hauling water, cutting wood, sweeping out the shop; tasks appropriate to his status as the most junior of apprentices.

An uneasy standoff between the Guild and Sparta continued for a month before the next crisis. Shortly after a messenger from Sparta departed, Sam was called to the Guildmaster's office. Sam found it disconcerting to see Nick sitting behind Wade's desk.

"News from Sparta, sir? Is Wade all right?"

Nick grimaced. "We got a letter. I can't tell if it's Wade or not, the handwriting's so bad. They still won't let us see him." Nick forced his anger under control.

"That's not why I called you in though. This is a new demand from Shinka. He's planning to raise another regiment of dragoons. That means he wants guns, swords, mess kits, spurs, and harness fittings for each trooper. He wants it all now."

Sam scratched his head. "Why? What's Shinka's hurry?"

"It's war, Sam. La Crosse and Tomah declared war on Sparta over the canceled contracts. Some of those projects were paid in advance. They weren't happy when Shinka pulled the plug on them."

"Just like Wade said it would happen." Sam spoke in hushed reverent tones.

"We've sent our message to both Tomah and La Crosse. Now we have to stall for time until we get an answer."

"One thing's for sure," Sam observed, "we can't deliver those guns and swords to Sparta."

"They have Wade for leverage. We may have to give them what they ask for. That's going to be the trick, give them just what they ask for, not what they need."

Shinka demanded immediate results. Nick Baker accompanied the partial delivery into town to explain things to Lord Shinka.

"We're working day and night to meet your schedules, Lord. We're doing the best we can. I brought you everything we have ready."

Shinka wasn't satisfied. "You brought me junk—belt buckles and horse harness. Not one gun or sword! What are my new troops to do, throw mess kits at the enemy? They can't even train without guns!"

Nick sounded defensive. "Guns and swords are the hardest things to make. They require tempering and that's a closely guarded secret; only journeymen and above know how. We've set up an assembly line. We're making all the parts first, then we'll temper them in a batch.

"Don't worry, you'll get your guns. I don't fancy being overrun by Tomahans. As for training, why don't you give the guns you do have to the recruits so they can train. The veterans can have the new stuff when it arrives."

The troops, only half of them armed, were in the field when the new weapons arrived late one afternoon. Lord Shinka came with the equipment, which arrived just in time. The Tomahan army was advancing and a battle was expected the next day. Shinka would be safe behind the lines when his dragoons met the Tomahans.

Next morning, lined up in the dewy field, Private George Peterson raised his musket to his shoulder at the sergeant's command. As a veteran, George got one of the shiny new muskets that arrived the night before. Some recruit had his old gun. The recruits got second-hand guns, secondhand uniforms, secondhand everything.

The Spartan Dragoons were formed in ranks at the top of a hill. The veteran First Dragoons formed the first line with the unreliable recruits behind them. Even though the recruits were green as grass and untried in battle, they made an acceptable reserve force.

Below them, at the bottom of the rise, the disordered mob of Tomahans were armed with an odd collection of antique black-powder guns and modern rifles converted to fire black powder. Many of the converted guns were matchlocks. As for swords, only a few of them carried real swords. A few had antique swords, some had souvenir and decorator junk. Most of the rank and file carried corn knives, machetes, or clubs.

As the Tomahans began their charge, George's sergeant gave the order to fire. George pulled the trigger and his world blew up. He found himself lying

on the ground, clutching the stock of his smashed gun.
His head throbbed with agony. He stared at a world
gone curiously flat and out of focus until he understood—only one eye. The other was gone, shredded by
steel fragments along with half his face when the breech
of his musket exploded. George tried to get to his feet
but failed as darkness reclaimed him.

The scene looked wrong to Shinka, something was
happening to his tight formations. The troops were
milling in confusion, the charge never got started.
Instead the howling mob of Tomahans smashed into the
disordered Spartans.

For ten minutes the mass of men boiled and struggled; the Spartan line bowed as it was pushed back in
the center. Shinka couldn't see much black-powder
smoke from his own men. Why weren't his troops firing?
He saw soldiers disengaging from the melee, throwing
down their muskets to rid themselves of excess weight as
they turned and fled. Like a dam giving way before flood
waters, the Spartan army broke.

Lord Mayor Shinka, dictator of Sparta, realized that
his house troops were all that stood between himself and
capture. He sawed at his reins, turning his horse sharply.
Already Tomahan cavalry were engaging his guards;
Shinka watched one of his men move to block the attack
of a burly man mounted on a big draft horse. The closest
of Shinka's guards raised his pistol and pulled the
trigger. The pistol blew up, taking his hand off at the
wrist. Another guard saw what happened and threw his
gun away, turning to flee.

The burly man was past the handless trooper and on
top of Shinka. Shinka raised his new sword to block the
blow as the Tomahan brute swung his own weapon, a
crowbar. Shinka's sword shattered like an icicle against

the man's bar. The stub of the blade was bent back at a right angle to the hilt, offering no protection from the Tomahan's second blow.

The crowbar smashed Shinka's arm, almost knocking him out of the saddle. The horse carried him off the battlefield with Shinka clutching its mane with his good left hand. His right arm hung shattered and useless.

Less than half the Spartan Dragoons survived the battle; the Tomahans chased the survivors all the way to the city gates. Lord Shinka made it back to the city walls without being captured. He sat in the infirmary, while the medics tried to do what they could for his arm. The ranking dragoon commander attended him, explaining the military situation.

"We lost almost half of our forces, but that's not the worst of it. The equipment is bad, half the swords are junk; too hard or too soft, they either bend or break! The new rifles blow up. The veteran troops had the bad guns. The recruits in the second line had good guns but they wouldn't use them. They broke and ran when they saw what happened to the first line.

"We're test-firing what guns we have, just like we're testing the swords; soon we'll sort out the bad apples. The worst of it is the men, sir; those that survived have lost confidence in their gear. It's very bad, sir!"

• • •

Captain Josh Chalmers, Tomahan Cavalry, looked at the Guild compound through a good pair of pre-disaster field glasses. "It sure looks quiet; I mean, they have guards walking a beat and all, but I don't see any sign of a trap. Okay, let's move out."

He led a small party away from the main body of Tomahan troops that had surrounded the Guild compound. Josh had been expecting a trap ever since the Guild's message had reached Tomah, months ago. Still, the Spartan army had been beaten easily, just like the Guild had promised. Josh was conditioned to thinking of the Guild as some sort of Spartan plot; it was hard to believe their claims of impartiality.

Guildsmen were waiting for Josh; they obviously knew about the Tomahan army forces surrounding the compound. When Josh's negotiating committee advanced, the Guild guards let them pass without incident. A burly young man wearing fine clothing was waiting for Josh. "I'm Nick Baker, Acting Guildmaster; have you authority to represent Tomah in negotiations with the Guild?"

"I have that authority. I have come in response to the letter from the Guild of Blacksmiths requesting aid and assistance from Tomah. You sent that letter?"

"I did. The Guild has developed a major impasse in dealing with the city of Sparta. Above all else, the Guild is neutral; it intends to provide service to all communities. The Guild has been prevented from completing contracts with customers from other cities and our plans to place a smithy in Tomah have been prevented by the Spartan government. We request assistance from Tomah in securing Guild independence from Spartan interference."

The Tomahan captain nodded. "Yeah, that's what your letter said. Are you serious about the terms you offered?"

It was Nick's turn to nod. "We offer equal access to military supplies if you agree to act as agents of the Guild in your assault on Sparta. We have guns ready to deliver to your army. As agreed, Tomah will get the first branch smithy. Deal?"

Josh spat into his open hand and extended it. "Deal!" They shook moistly, sealing the alliance.

Nick wiped his hand on his pant leg. "Bring us all the weapons you capture. We sabotaged the breech plugs of the guns, but that can be fixed. We can retemper any swords that didn't shatter.

"I have paper with the agreement written up. Come on in my office and check it over. Then we can sign."

Nick led the way and within two hours the document was signed. By then, Tomahan cavalry were guarding the Guild compound while Captain Chalmers, his officers, and the senior smiths of the Guild toasted the new alliance with hard cider in the Guildmaster's office.

Sparta released Wade as a precondition to negotiations. Wade emerged from four months in the dungeons under the city hall gaunt and sick, a broken man. The months of starvation and beatings had destroyed his fragile health. Lord Mayor Shinka attended the armistice conference in person, his shattered right arm splinted and strapped across his chest. His lips were gray with pain although that was not reflected in his speech or bearing.

"Sparta recognizes the independence of the Guild of Blacksmiths, and promises not to interfere with its members or its business. In addition, Sparta will pay an indemnity to the Guild to settle past claims of damage. Finally, Sparta will accept a one-year blacksmith embargo while the Guild tends to business from other towns.

"Sparta cedes to Tomah territory in the old Fort McCoy area between the two cities. Also Sparta agrees to pay ransom for its captured soldiers in the amounts agreed upon." Lord Shinka signed the treaty with his left hand. His right arm remained withered for the rest of his long life.

Wade's health never recovered; he resigned as Guildmaster and the Guild recognized Nick Baker as its second Guildmaster. Two winters later, Wade died quietly in his sleep. His plan saved the Guild and Wade was thankful to have lived to see it. Under Nick and his successors the Guild grew, gaining power and influence, guarding its secrets, becoming a foundation of revived American culture.

Eventually the secrets of metalworking slipped away from the Guild and again became common knowledge. The Blacksmith's Guild, like the Mason's before it, finished its moment in history's spotlight and passed from the stage.

ESSAY ON ART

Written by
Judith Holman

About the Author

Judith Holman attended Rutgers University, where she earned a master's degree in fine arts. She has worked steadily at her craft since then and gained experience in many aspects of illustration, with work published in numerous books and magazines. Her award-winning paintings can be found in private collections around the country. Judith Holman lives and paints in New Jersey, with a remarkable husband and equally remarkable red-haired terrier.

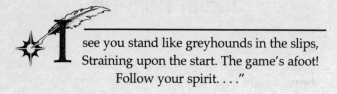

I see you stand like greyhounds in the slips,
Straining upon the start. The game's afoot!
Follow your spirit. . . ."

Henry V

Art, it sometimes seems to me, takes far more time than is reasonable or profitable, so it should not be a startling surprise that artists, on the whole, are defiant creatures. Not in the flag burning, whoop and a holler, down with the establishment sense (though some do relish the opportunity), but rather in the choosing to pursue a fierce addiction that far outstrips the making of pretty pictures. In the face of tooth-gnashing adversity, torrential downpour and magnificent heartbreak, artists get on with the business of making art. Some work with ebullient joy, others with the grim tenacity of a bulldog's undershot jaw, but get on with it they do. Generating such a wealth of self-directed, self-motivated, goal-oriented eagerness and enthusiasm that legions of efficient and professional managers, facilitators and team leaders would bow their heads, bend their knees and weep for joy before such riches.

Now this may be the time and place to mention that the glory of all this enthusiastic energy is not spent in one flamboyant bolt of light that stands the artist on an ear ringing with the sound of trumpets. Think instead of parceling out tiny seeds through spread fingers all day, every day, sowing imagination and invention along the furrows of ordinary life. The observation of this seeding might begin as a day in the life, on a sudden gray Monday, 10:30 a.m., where enthroned amidst the coffee dregs and scattered, shaky piles of this and that, the artist plucks a blue-and-white look-at-me envelope from the general confusion and frees a manuscript from its *Tyvek* confines. Weighed gingerly on outstretched palm and judged to be of reasonable heft (those at rock heavyweight require a fresh infusion of caffeine), this newest project is quickly perused and then thoroughly read and reread.

To be very plain with you, illustrating a story is a complex matter of arriving at a flawless balance between showiness and restraint. Shape and texture, structure and composition, must combine with vigor to achieve a highly imaginative yet reasonable result. The artist is grateful for the author whose words build rich images, page after page, the whole trouble being only to select the best ones.

As it happens, at this very point, a second familial bond between artists is forged, the "thumbnail"—a small rough sketch that explores the artist's mind, coaxing the mental image into beginning focus. As the author's words spin webs of images, the artist's pens capture and bind them roughly to the page, trapping ideas with graphite strokes, pinning thoughts with sticky strands of black ink. It may take one or dozens, but it absorbs the artist fully as visible form is given to the commands of imagination. And if everything seems possible in these small sketches roughly scratched into paper, then on or about the third hour, the artist unlocks stiff vertebrae and looks up to see the sun (in spite of the rain) and all's well with the world.

> "Thus with imagined wing our swift scene flies
> In motion of no less celerity
> Than that of thought."

Henry V

As the artist putters about the studio's modest patch of real estate, it is discovered that the camera needed for reference photos lacks film (a foregone conclusion) and the determination is made that twenty minutes from the door to store should prove adequate for said purchase. So with plan in hand, well-intentioned purposeful strides propel the artist out the door, down the concrete walk and to a skittering halt, captured by a drop of trembling rain glistening on a matte green leaf. Why should this particular raindrop draw the artist in? If truth be told, we will never know. It is enough for the artist to contemplate this drop of water, to explore a new consciousness of it, to visually bookmark it for future reference as a dragon's tear or miniature biosphere.

Another thing the artist learns is that the twenty minutes allotted to the original project have passed and amends must be made. Shaking off the contemplative mood (and a bit of rain), our artist strides on in earnest and the artist's vehicle is soon found homing in on the desired target, when attention is again momentarily diverted. This time by the spectacle of a tiny spider on the wet windshield, tempting annihilation a hair's breadth from the scything blades. A *Pit and the Pendulum* fascination develops as the graceful arachnid dodges the deadly wipers, the artist's rapt attention interrupted only by the smashing, banging blowout of the front tire crunching the curb. This obliviousness to all but the inner vision is another commonality shared

FREE

Send in this card and you'll receive a FREE POSTER while supplies last. No order required for this special offer! Mail in your card today!
❑ Please send me a FREE poster.
❑ Please send me information about other books by L. Ron Hubbard.

ORDERS SHIPPED WITHIN 24 HRS. OF RECEIPT

___ *L. Ron Hubbard Presents Writers of The Future®* volumes: (paperback)
❑ vol X $6.99   ❑ vol XI $6.99   ❑ vol XII $6.99
❑ vol XIII $6.99   ❑ vol XIV $6.99   ❑ vol XV $6.99   _____

COLLECTOR'S ITEM (while supplies last)
___ *Battlefield Earth* 1st Edition Hardcover $75.00   _____

OTHER BOOKS BY L. RON HUBBARD
MISSION EARTH® series (10 volumes)
___ paperbacks (specify volumes:_____)   _____
Vol 3 is $4.95 all other vols are $6.99 each (vols 1, 2 & 4 -10)
___ audio (specify volumes:_____)(each)$15.95   _____
___ *Ai! Pedrito!—When Intelligence Goes Wrong* $25.00   _____
___ *A Very Strange Trip* $25.00   _____
___ *Battlefield Earth*™ paperback $7.99   _____
___ *Battlefield Earth* 8-hour audio $29.95   _____
___ *Final Blackout* paperback $6.99   _____
___ *Final Blackout* audio $11.95   _____
___ *Fear* paperback $6.99   _____
___ *Fear* audio $9.95   _____
___ *Slaves of Sleep & The Masters of Sleep* hardcover $9.98   _____
___ *Slaves of Sleep & The Masters of Sleep* audio $19.95   _____
___ *Ole Doc Methuselah* hardcover $9.48   _____
___ *Ole Doc Methuselah* audio $24.95   _____

CHECK AS APPLICABLE: **TAX*:**   _____
❑ Check/Money Order enclosed.   **TOTAL:**   _____
   (Use an envelope please)
❑ American Express ❑ Visa
❑ MasterCard   ❑ Discover

* California residents add 8.25% sales tax.

Card#:_____

Exp. Date:_____Signature:_____

Credit Card Billing Address Zip Code:_____

NAME:_____

ADDRESS:_____

CITY:_____ STATE:_____ ZIP:_____

Call us now with your order 1-800-722-1733
www.writersofthefuture.com

by artists. And while it almost guarantees a number of near disastrous events, it also ensures the plucking of roses from the thorns, as it is the rare individual who would discern, as the artist discerns, that the rubber tire shards mightily resemble an alien carapace or a molting dragon hide and should be carefully packed into the vehicle's trunk.

There is something to be said for the uniquely curious filing and storage capacity of the artist's mind, inasmuch as it antiquates Zip drives and makes organization software obsolete. Artists develop a sort of central memory storage, an information processing department where visual images are given form and shape, filed and ordered according to need and desire. The only problem yet to be solved is the lack of adequate back-up.

But the plan still necessitates a quick trip into the photo-mart, where our artist cheerfully spends thirty-five minutes (above the forty-five required to change the tire) marveling at the recently installed digital equipment and its spiffy new abilities to crop, zoom, layer, enlarge and hallucinate. The truth is, of course, that if artists had forty-eight-hour days, their real passion would be invention. There is no doubt that da Vinci would have been the first to exuberantly point and click, followed closely by Michelangelo. Throughout history artists have always been eager to experiment, devise, invent and explore anything and everything that might prove fruitful in their self-appointed task of conjuring art. It might do well to note here that Leonardo da Vinci's *The Last Supper*, long recognized as the first classic statement of High Renaissance painting, began to deteriorate shortly after completion. Seems the artist tried an experiment with an oil tempera medium (instead of the traditional fresco technique) and it didn't adhere very well to the wall. Oh, well!

We might also reflect on Vermeer's perfect sparkling pointelles of light, glinting from the perfectly painted gold and pearls of his light-struck models and attributed to his use of the camera obscura. And what got into Picasso when the contents of his wastebaskets became so intriguing that he pasted them up and created the great collage Cubist masterpiece *Three Musicians*? Apparently the same desire to experiment that hit Max Ernest over the head with his "decalomania" oil transference technique, resulting in the fascinating Surrealist painting *Swamp Angel*.

In short, all manner of technological bells and whistles are inspiring a new generation of artists. And before a fellow reproaches me for not bemoaning the lack of traditional draftsmanship, skills and technique in today's art, it should perhaps not be overlooked that when Thomas Eakins rejected the use of plaster casts of antique statues, and insisted on using live nude models, the seeds of insurrection were sown in late nineteenth-century painting. It might do equally well to remember that the famous critic and theorist John Ruskin accused James McNeill Whistler of "flinging a pot of paint in the public's face" when in 1874 he produced the achingly transcendent *Nocturne in Black and Gold*. We see in the creative process a thousand leaps of imagination, and a thousand attempts to shape their form.

> "As many arrows, loosed several ways,
>   Come to one mark;
> So may a thousand actions, once afoot,
>   End in one purpose. . . ."

Henry V

But back to our artist. Arriving home with the long-sought film, our artist gleefully discovers that the rubber shards can be propped up admirably by the gnarled branches dragged home and dried out on a previous expedition. Pictures and sketches are made and taken from many angles (including the garage roof), and when the operation is finished (although the structure is left standing), the artist bounds past the exasperated assistant directly into the path of the scrappy terrier. Promising the bearded devil a walk (the terrier), if she will just quit eating the artist's feet, our artist places a quick phone call to a fellow friend and artist. This is answered by an equally exasperated assistant, who, when queried, informs that the fellow artist has been crouched in the side yard surrounded by various paraphernalia for the better part of the morning and now into the afternoon, and as there is no telling when this exercise might bear fruit, please leave a message. Message left.

Out the door once again, the artist proceeds to the park (in real-time sunshine) with the terrier boisterously barking at all and sundry. The massive trunk of a fallen tree, its gnarled branches twisted and turned to every angle, brings the twosome to their first stop. One explores on point, with raised hackles and eager sniffs. The artist peers down its scarred length, kneeling to lower a squinting eye's vantage point, following the contours of the behemoth's ridged, furrowed bark until a strange desolate landscape emerges. Mental image fixed, eye shutter down, bookmarked and filed. Onward the pair proceed, down the rutted lane, pausing this time for the terrier's hundredth pee and for the artist to observe the invasive, greedy roots knotted above a flowering cherry's barren ground. An alarmed green whirr brings four eyes in line with the impossibly awkward angles of a startled praying mantis. Registering disapproval at this territorial invasion, the insect raises its front appendages and reveals a pair of balefully painted eyes, surely meant to terrify. The terrier dances about, punching out sharp barks, but the artist stands perfectly still, observing the lifted edges of the tiny warrior's breastplate, flashing dark-circled eyes. Imagination propels form and function, and with a leap it is transformed, making its next appearance as a robotic flying machine, wings outstretched and sheathed in skin-taut panels that lift to reveal blazing-eyed battle turrets along its sharply angled length. Another line and another is added to the ever-growing vision of the imaginary craft until, with a *phffft* and a whirr, inspiration flies off.

And it is here we identify a fourth factor, a tie that binds, as it were, individual artists into a community. Artists learn to look at things, bit by bit, to see for themselves what is of exceptional beauty, contour or outline. Twenty thousand years ago, in the Paleolithic period, a determined artist painted a "Wounded Bison" on the wall of a cave in northern Spain. Today crowds marvel at the artist's keen powers of observation in portraying the bowed head and collapsed weight of the massive, dying creature. Skip a few eras and alight in Arles, in the south of France, between 1888 and 1890. Watch van Gogh paint his greatest pictures as what he looked at in the sun-drenched Mediterranean countryside filled him with ecstatic movement. Take a short hop to 1892; observe Toulouse-Lautrec seeing through the gay surface of Paris nightlife and rendering its characters with a sharp and pitiless eye. Fifty years later Picasso, walking about, spots the seat and handlebars of an old bicycle, and with sharp eye and sure hand creates the striking visual pun of *Bull's Head*.

All these artists, indeed all artists, establish a way of seeing. While they are not readily admired virtues in today's age of efficiency and bottom lines, reflection and observation bring about a wonderful diversity of thought. As the eye and hand make subtle shifts and adjustments, experiment and decision soon show. There is no shortcut for this process coupled with the active work of the artist's hand. Whether drawn line, fluid stroke or mouse click, the making of art is a struggle of liberation with moments of illumination that just happen to charge the artist up like mad; and while no reasonable or profitable person would allow such an unreasonable expenditure of time for so little certainty, it bothers the artist not one jot. We can observe this best if we look back to our artist, who, at the end of the day, with westering sun at back and tired terrier at heel, heads home. Collected in mind is the wealth of the day, a richness of images to spark and sort. Tiny biospheres glisten past the enormous eye of a weeping dragon; graceful arachnids spin for balance on the horned and rubbery carapace of lumbering sea creatures; while the blazing turrets of impossibly angled flying machines fire the ground, leaving a desolate and ruined land-scape in their wake. Though not counted in coin, the wealth is overwhelming. The artist is content. The day is well spent. Proud to labor in a fair country where defiance and tenacity greet imagination and invention and tame the hand to conjure the rabbit from the hat. And get on with the making of art.

"From this day to the ending of the world,
        But we in it shall be remembered—
    We few, we happy few, we band of brothers. . . ."

Henry V

SKIN SONG

Written by
Melissa J. Yuan-Innes

Illustrated by
Jayson B. Doolittle

About the Author

Melissa Yuan-Innes is of Chinese descent, born and raised in Ottawa. She has had a long relationship with Matt Innes, whom she married in London, Ontario, where she was studying medicine at the University of Western Ontario. Innes—who now has graduated from the University of Toronto's aerospace program—had been suggesting that she do writing since the summer before her first year at the university. She started reading science fiction and fantasy, and thus was introduced to WOTF. Also, a writing contest for radio put her in contact with Jo Beverley, a well-known romance writer who had been a WOTF finalist.

She sold a small number of stories to Canadian media before submitting "Skin Song" to us.

About the Illustrator

Jayson B. Doolittle is seventeen and a senior in high school. Until he was thirteen he had an immense attraction to dinosaurs, covering the walls of his room with dinosaur posters by John Gurche. Then his parents gave him *Expedition* by Wayne Barlowe, which opened his eyes to other possibilities, and shortly thereafter he discovered the artwork of Frank Frazetta.

He entered a class for high-school students at the Art Center College of Design in Pasadena, and now continues his studies in a studio class led by Steve Huston. His other interests include storytelling, film, photography, special effects, music, model making, archeology and theme park design.

W hat does a dead, preserved body look like? Smell like? Sound like?

It's lunch time, two days before medical school orientation begins, when I force myself past the frosted glass door and combination lock into the anatomy dissection lab. It's a huge room and smells strange, almost sweet. I stare at the well-spaced islands of white body bags until I notice Aerosmith playing, tinny at a low volume: ". . . the sweetest dreams will never do, 'cause I miss you, babe . . ."

I follow the music to an adjoining room where I find the prosector, John. He has blond hair and a mustache and looks surprisingly normal for someone who cuts up cadavers for a living. "You're at table 39. Do you need to buy anything?"

I buy the lab coat for ten dollars and shake my head at the dissection kit and gloves.

"Okay. You're all set." He pauses. "You can see your cadaver either now or when class starts."

"Thanks. I'll go now." I walk over, put on my pre-bought gloves, and take a steadying breath. Then, teeth gritted but eyes resolutely open, I unzip bag #39.

Skin. Sort of dusky gray and brown.

This must be the person's back, but the skin is cut down the middle and withered into burgundy curls.

I didn't want to see the face, but this isn't what I expected, either. Is it a man or a woman? How old?

What race, even? (What *is* that color?) I stand there, paralyzed and curious, before I carefully close it up again, keeping the zipper well away from the body. I wash my hands in the lab and again in the hall bathroom, and scrub my whole body in the shower at home. I still don't feel clean.

And I still don't know what the cadaver sounds like.

•••

The University of Western Ontario med school orientation is a whirlwind of happy faces, "Hello, my name is," boxes to unpack, utilities to hook up, orientation events to attend. The best part is a "preceptor day" with a family doctor. She lets me take a man's blood pressure: "Tell me when you hear his heart start beating and then when you hear nothing." The stethoscope is a foreign but welcome pressure in my ears. I pump the cuff up and watch the gauge on the wall. I can sort of hear when his heartbeat starts, but there is too much crackling to say when I hear "nothing." The mercury runs down to zero. The man laughs. "You don't think I have a blood pressure?" The doctor laughs too, then takes the blood pressure herself.

When she examines a newborn, she tells me to feel the anterior fontanelle, the soft, diamond-shaped area where the skull's bones have not yet fused. Gingerly, I touch the baby's head. I don't feel any soft spot, but I hear a contented buzz, like a soft bumblebee. "Um, okay," I pretend.

"No, here." She moves my hand. Tentatively, I feel the soft spot, and the buzz grows louder. The baby meets my eyes. I didn't know newborns had skin songs. Suddenly, I lose my fear of touching patients daily with my bare hands. There is a wonder in this touch. I am even a little less afraid of the cadaver.

•••

I sat on my father's lap as he listened to the six o'clock news. His face was set. I reached up and touched his cheek. He was making little popping noises, like when I poured milk on my Rice Krispies. What did that mean? I kept touching him. The sound got a bit louder, but nothing else. "Daddy," I asked finally, "why are you making that funny crackling noise?"

His eyes flicked toward me. "What do you mean?"

"The noise. Inside you." My hand dropped down to my lap. "Are you mad?"

"I'm not mad, Kyla, but I wasn't making any noise." Pause. "What did you hear?"

I said nothing.

"Do you hear funny things in your head? Voices?"

I was young, but not stupid. "No. Of course not, Daddy."

His body relaxed.

I never spoke of it again. Years later, I met Uncle Sean, Dad's schizophrenic brother, and I understood his reaction better. But I still never spoke of it again.

•••

As long as I can remember, someone's bare skin against mine has been something I can hear as well as feel.

I ran to hug my mother as she came home from work. When her fingers scooped through my hair to press against my scalp, she sounded like a faucet dripping steadily into a metal sink. I stood there quietly, holding my breath, until over the

Illustrated by Jayson B. Doolittle

dripping I heard a tambourine jingle. I snuggled closer, now believing her tired smile.

It was my secret pleasure for a long time. When someone pinched my cheek or, as I grew older, shook my hand, I could hear a skin song. Other children stared and shouted. I looked and touched to my heart's content. I loved the songs I heard from the teacher's hand, my parents' cheeks, even the feedback squawk I heard the time I punched Ronnie Kincaid's bare stomach.

Fifteen years old, alone with my first boyfriend, Saturday night. I was wearing a flirty black miniskirt which I pulled into place every so often as we lay on the floor, kissing. His heart beat hard and fast like the polka from his lips. Our eyes locked. He reached a trembling hand up to my breast. Almost before I felt his gossamer touch, I could hear a roar, like ocean waves, and the single high, clear note of a flute.

I loved that I could hear other people's feelings then. It was powerful, mystical, almost holy. I loved the silences, too, as I handled other things: the chalk as I wrote on the blackboard, a friend's cat, the leaves of a jade plant, a computer joystick. It only upset me that I could never hear my own song. I could feel my own touch, but heard nothing. Every other person I met had a skin song. Why not me? Was I more like a plant than a person?

I tried to touch myself suddenly, tricking myself. I tried to pray for it. I tried being very quiet. I tried not caring. Nothing. My skin was as silent as a tree encased in freezing rain. I finally decided this had to be normal, like not being able to watch yourself sleeping.

As I wound through high school, I spent more time eyeing myself in the mirror and less time listening to people's skin. I wanted to be like the other girls. I wanted boys to like me, I wanted to have a great gaggle of friends, and I wanted to ace school unobtrusively. I did not want to hear the bus driver who rattled like a bad washing machine as he checked my transfer. Or the fly-wing buzz of a beggar pressing my hand for my spare change. Or the nursery-tune-bright song of a falsely sympathetic teacher. By grade twelve, I stopped touching strangers if I could help it. Eventually I stopped touching acquaintances too. Then friends. Family. I wore black, grew my hair long so it hung in my face, tucked my legs under my chair. I wished gloves were fashionable again, but didn't quite have the nerve to do it on my own. You can close your eyes, pinch your nose, seal your lips, but you can never really close off your ears or skin. And mine were chained to this rank orgy of noise and contact. I retreated into the shell of my own skin. Masturbation was a pleasure in itself without literal bells and whistles. I could hug myself, brush my hair back from my forehead, pluck at ripe zits, gnaw my fingernails, in blessed silence.

I went away to McMaster University, to study both the arts and the sciences I had loved in high school (knowledge, cold and pure, stored in lovely, heavy, mute books). And, in the first few days, I learned a number of things outside of books—like that I loved my parents and my younger sister, Sarah. I loved my clean and quiet house in Ottawa. I loved knowing where I was, feeling safe to walk alone at nights, and having people to talk to. And I hated it here. When my bitchy roommate went home for the first weekend, I cried and went to sleep sucking my thumb.

The next day, my phone was hooked up, and I called my family *instantly*. The silence cracked. It didn't completely melt away: I still felt strangely bare when people touched me. But I touched my family and close friends again. It was give and take. I wasn't Little Miss Cool anymore, but I wasn't sucking my thumb either.

As graduation grew nigh, I took stock. My parents were dying for me to be a doctor. I did like the intellectual challenge and respect for medicine. I didn't like the idea of touching patients all the time. But the main thing that wilted my "why I want to be a physician" applications, that made my smiles desperate during the interviews, that made me pause before signing the acceptance form, was the thought of the cadaver.

Does your skin song end when you die?

I hoped so.

• • •

I push some papers halfheartedly and look out the window. It's only six o'clock, but dark already. My ceiling creaks every time the guy in the apartment upstairs walks around or, I swear, shifts in his chair. I don't know whether I should work or go to the pub tonight. I want to work, because classes have started already, but I'm afraid I'll be stuck alone for the rest of the year in this tiny basement apartment if I don't make any friends.

So, at the pub, in a violet satin tank top and a tightly belted pair of black pants, my mouth dry from endless introductions, I head for a glass of water. A guy asks me to dance. He's tall, white, brown-haired, broad-shouldered—a typical Western guy.

I'm momentarily tempted, but . . . "No, thanks."

"Aw, come on." He jerks his head toward the dance floor, smiles. His smile is okay. I hesitate.

"I won't bite." He leans forward and his hand brushes casually against my side, *and the weirdest glissando rises in my ears,* startling me so that I jerk away, spilling my glass of water.

He stares at me. "Whoa, girl!" He yanks his hands back as if I'd burned him, shakes them out grandly, and turns away. I call out, "I'm sorry, I was just surprised—" but he disappears into the crowd of football-player types around the bar.

I stop and wipe my brow, pick up my drink, and shiver when I remember the sound he made. Him or me? Overtired? Stressed out already from medical school? Maybe, but I wouldn't want to dance with him. You can never be too careful. I arrange a smile on my face and head back to the patio.

•••

I heard it through my clothes.

Impossible but true. I felt his sweaty knuckles against my side, saw the slight smile that made me doubt it was an accident, and heard that *sound.* Like an organ tuned too sharp, sliding down skeletal notes that made my teeth clamp together. It was from him. I could *feel* it. Through my clothes. *How?* I shake my head and try to find my place in the histology book. But the photos of skeletal muscle blur into a pink haze with violet islands.

•••

D-day. There is an excited buzz as we struggle with the combinations on our anatomy group lockers. There's a half-hour ceremony before group dissection of the back. "Some students were working over the summer and began the dissection for you, removing the fat and superficial fascia," says Dr. Chung. So *that's* what I saw. I feel a little better.

When I enter the room, it seems tilted on an angle, fluorescence in my eyes, a mass of people's heads atop identical white coats. "Kyla!" someone calls. I focus on Lisa Lee, dark hair layered around her kind, pale face, and the room rights itself. I walk over and greet my group. Lisa. Adam. Bhooma. Geoff. Fiona. And me. The room quiets during readings from the Bible, the Koran, and past medical students. My breathing slows. Last port before the storm.

The service ends. I exhale and exchange looks with my group. We assemble around the bag and several hands help to open it. We deliberate for a while over what to do, and I connect my scalpel blade with its handle as people talk. I insist on making one of the first cuts in the skin, to widen the existing flaps. There. I did that, and I'm fine. I look around, but my group-mates are already uncovering and discussing various muscles. "Trapezius. That's the easy one," Adam says, pointing to a long, downward triangle of flesh.

Oh. I didn't know that.

"Oh, the traps," Lisa says familiarly, and mimics how she'd do weights with them.

I didn't know that either.

Bhooma starts feeling around with zero self-consciousness. "Where does it originate? And does it attach right here?"

People mutter, and Lisa speaks up. "Actually, I believe the trapezius comes right around to the front and hooks on the acromium." We study the cadaver while someone runs to check on the skeleton. I stand very still. I may be the only person who is completely unprepared for this, who nearly fell asleep during the anatomy preview video, and now does not know what the acromium is, let alone what it attaches to. And I see that my fear of the cadaver may have to make room for my fear of failing out of medical school. Okay. Breathe. And somehow I make it through the hour.

• • •

I go home determined to work. But I am exhausted from seven hours of classes. And I'm not sure where to begin. . . . I pull out physiology, read half a page, and, within five minutes, I'm surveying my hair for split ends.

After an hour, I decide to take a break and . . . nap? No, I'd better make dinner. I slice vegetables, singing along to the radio, and make a huge pot of spaghetti. Okay, time to work. But I need a yellow highlighter. . . . By the time I hit my stride, it's 10:18 p.m. I make myself go to bed by 12:45 a.m., but I'm too keyed up to sleep. Why didn't I work earlier? Forget about it. Do it tomorrow, I soothe myself, but my heart beats so hard, I can hear its drum in my ears. I take my teddy bear into my arms and lie there with my eyes open. Finally, hating myself, I curl around my bear and put my thumb in my mouth. I drift off in blissful silence.

• • •

I go to class, eyes swimming in sleep, twenty-four minutes late. I try not to think about how much I have already missed this morning. I bump down the stairs and end up sitting in the front row, beside Patricia, who has to move her pencil crayons to make room for me, never taking her eyes off the professor and his rapidly filling-in overhead. I look at her fresh face, neat diagram, and pre-highlighted notes, and think, I hate you. I really do. I bet you sound like sneakers squeaking on a gym floor. She feels my eyes on her and smiles at me. I smile back, showing my teeth.

•••

Lisa and Fiona are dissecting the thorax, carving lines down the cadaver's breasts. This means they have turned over the cadaver and revealed her face. It is a gray-brown plain face, with wide nostrils, her white/gray hair streaming out behind to touch the body bag. Her eyes are surprisingly brown and clear. I have looked into the eyes of death, I thought. Now, I try to concentrate only on her separated chest, but I have to block my peripheral view of her face with my hand. Adam, who has been checking out the leg bones on the skeleton, says, "Hey," and points. I crouch down beside him. Our cadaver is pouring—not blood, because that's been drained and congealed, but some clear, colorless fluid. A river of it. Endlessly, into a catch basin. I look around, and all the cadavers are doing it. Mass protest.

I can feel my breakfast coming up. I back away. My first instinct is, horribly, to suck my thumb. "Do what you're afraid to do," said Ralph Waldo Emerson, but I feel like I've done too much, surrounding myself with these frozen cadavers that only I would be able to hear. "No," I manage, and hurry off, tearing off my gloves, rushing away from my startled group. In the bathroom, washed up, I look at myself in the mirror and touch my own cheek. Soft. Alive. Alive, and no skin song. I'm starting to think this is the best way.

•••

"How's school?" my dad asks, after a pause.

"I'm behind."

"How behind?"

I do a swift mental calculation. Anatomy, virgin histology, hyper physiology . . . "I don't know. Behind."

"More behind than other people?"

"I don't know!"

Hearing the sharpness, my mother soothes, "It's all right, I'm sure you'll do fine, like always."

"Well, if you need any help—if you're getting too . . . stressed out or anything, we're here . . ."

"Gavin, she *knows*," my mother hisses. I hear Uncle Sean's shadow, a sheet quickly thrown over him. *I am not like Uncle Sean. I am not.*

"Well, we're really proud of you, anyway," Dad finishes.

"I know." It feels like a dead weight, my family pushing me on. If I fell in the forest, would anybody hear? I shake my head. Crazy. But that's how I feel. And I'm sucking my thumb at night regularly now.

•••

I can't sleep. I lie in bed, eyes closed, blanket over my face, running through the material: Autonomic nervous system. Cardiac output. Dermis and epidermis. I can't keep up. I have no desire to hear my own skin song now. I suspect it would be a continuous, high-pitched wail, like a train sounding the alarm through town. What if I really do go crazy, like Uncle Sean? I have the genes for schizophrenia, and more stress every day.

I click on my desk light and pick up a psychology book, checking the index for schizophrenic symptoms.

1. *Thought disorder.* I have no trouble thinking, just trouble studying and remembering everything.

2. *Delusions.* Nope, no false beliefs, although my last boyfriend used to have to say regularly, "You're not fat."

3. *Hallucinations, usually auditory, i.e., hearing voices no one else can.* Forget that, I don't hear voices. I—I stiffen. The skin song doesn't count. Just because nobody else can hear it doesn't mean I'm *crazy.* But the coldly logical part of my mind says, Why not? What if you always had schizophrenic tendencies, and now all the stress is slowly but surely driving you over the edge? I don't cry, but curl up in bed, rocking myself, and eventually put my thumb in my mouth. As usual, there are no "auditory hallucinations" for my own skin. I close my eyes and pretend I am normal.

•••

It is my turn to dissect. Lower limb. Not so human as head and neck, not so interesting as thorax.

My partner, Geoff, is late. I hover around my neighbors, Claire and Mark, who joke as they dissect. After about ten minutes, when Claire has turned the skin of her cadaver's thigh into the "orange peel" look much praised in our dissection guide, I start without Geoff.

I trace a light line over the gray-beige skin of her thigh, which is beginning to pucker from dehydration. I try not to look at the private triangle of hair close to my hand. "Is this right?" I ask Claire. She peers politely.

"Did you cut her? I can't tell." I point. She laughs and demonstrates with a long, bold stroke.

I follow her example. The skin is so thin, like a strong, pliable sheet of paper. But the yellowed globules of fat below it flourish like tiny cauliflower heads. I hack at them. The blade misses them and slides from my greasy grip. I keep wiping my hands with paper towels, but eventually they run out, and there are still inches and inches of fat clinging to the muscle underneath. Now I truly appreciate the clean muscles uncovered by my other group members. I will never, ever get there. It's already 10:23. I've been doing this for an hour and a half. Tears are in my eyes. Geoff, finally arrived, can't help me. He's hurriedly doing a superficial dissection on the other leg. And everyone else is busy. Maybe I should have read the book beforehand, I think miserably, but I don't see how that would help me actually, physically cut through. Finally, I draw over a teaching assistant. After one look at my mess, she says, "Hey, that's not too bad. You haven't damaged anything yet." She demonstrates using the scalpel to pare away the fat and, unafraid, rips at muscles and separates them. They are still lumpy with fat, but now there is a method to the madness. I thank her profusely and scrape with renewed hope. If there are such things as angels, she is one. I am so thrilled, working and eyeing the clock, that it takes me a second to register something clammy against my hand.

I jerk away. It often feels like the inside of your glove is wet, from sweat, I guess. My hands are shaking, but I concentrate on looking for tears. There is one, about two centimeters long, across the tip of my baby finger. It's so neat I must have done it with the scalpel. A tiny globule of fat hangs on the edge of the tear. I fight back a cry and rip off my gloves. My baby finger has a smear of grease along it. I wash my hands again and again, but within five minutes, I put new gloves on and stride back to the table. I may have accidentally touched the body, I may have rubbed raw human fat with my skin, but I had heard nothing. There was no song. Maybe the song dies with you (please, yes), or maybe I'm finally outgrowing this "talent" for hearing things, or maybe both. Feeling better, I finish the dissection.

•••

I go over to Lisa's place to study together. I've always liked her, and the first time I shook her hand, she sounded like Coke bubbling in a can. (Hey, maybe she wouldn't sound like anything now. I make a mental note to touch her at some point, and feel like a pervert.) As I'm taking off my shoes, an orange cat comes up and stares at me. Its mouth opens soundlessly.

"That's Joseph, Noah's cat. He's very friendly."

"That's a *big* cat."

"He is, isn't he? I had trouble getting used to him at first. Noah said to nudge him away if he gets too friendly."

"No, that's all right." I sit down and pat my thigh. Joseph jumps up and settles squatly on my lap.

Lisa taps my bare arm, and I hear a brief whoosh, like a breeze running through reeds. Obviously, I can still hear skin songs, but at least hers is a nice one. "I have to make a quick call. Could I get you a drink first?"

"No, thanks, I'm fine." I run my hands over the cat and begin cooing, "Joseph will keep me company. Won't you, you fat little orange cannonball, you—"

Crickets buzz and there is a solid thunk as cleats meet the soccer ball and send it flying. . . .

I jerk my hand away from Joseph's nose, where it had frozen.

Cats don't sing.

This one does. I look around, but Lisa is in the next room, Noah is nowhere to be seen, and Joseph is looking at me with unimpressed eyes, seeming irritated at the sudden lack of petting. He shifts. Slowly, I reach out and rub the tender pads on the underside of his right paw. I hear crunching, like an animal chewing on dry food. I move my hand away. The sound stops.

It's Joseph. It really is.

Either the cats I met before were less—musical, or I—No. Joseph must just be one amazing cat. I scoop him up lugubriously and hug him to myself. He tenses a little, and then, above his song, which rings faintly from his foot pads to my hand, is the sound of him purring. I put my head down close to him and close my eyes, forgetting about Lisa, skin songs, and medical school, just relaxing with a ball of warm fur.

•••

I unzip the bag. I don't step back fast enough and the cloying smell, stronger as the cadavers age, surges willfully down my nose and throat. Fiona asks if I'm all right. I nod between coughs. We're studying for the exam using other groups' cadavers; because the human body varies so much, we've been warned that's the best way to practice.

This cadaver is already face down, so we review the back. This body's muscles are thick, brown, juicy, well-defined. The bones of his vertebral column are bound together by a ligament, and we lift this away to reveal the spinal cord. We quiz each other. I know all the answers. It's funny; now, I can see that the back is actually pretty easy. We pause and look at each other. Then

Bhooma sing-songs, "I think it's time to move on to the thorax." I knew it, but hadn't said so to delay the dreaded turning over of the body. Now, I stand a little apart from the group, hands held tentatively forward, as if to say, I *would* help if the four of you hadn't already started. They each grab a limb.

They begin to roll him. He is a tall, thick man. They begin to struggle, wrenching on one side, pulling almost flush to the table on the other. "*He's stuck!* He's stuck on his arm!" someone finally yells.

I grab his arm and pull it. At the same time, I notice the bones of his vertebral column, still cemented together by the ligament, are yawning away from the rest of the body in a dance with gravity. I don't look closely enough to see if the spinal cord is following suit, I just jam my hand against it to catch that too, and my glove must have slipped, because I feel cold, damp flesh against my wrist and . . .

And a rumble, like thunder, deep and penetrating.

A skin song.

The last gasp, like a rat newly, damply "sacrificed" for science, its headless body scrabbling in a metal sink? Or the conscious cry of a body methodically dismembered over the course of a year?

I scream.

•••

When I come to, I am on the floor, in the hallway outside the anatomy lab.

I smile weakly. "I'm fine. I'm so sorry . . . the air . . ."

"Yeah, it was really stuffy in there. I felt kind of bad myself," said Adam, who gets migraines.

Lisa eyes me knowingly. "It's always hard to turn over the bodies. I kind of have to block it out of my head afterward."

Their ultra-supportiveness triggers a pounding in my temples. No, it's not fair to blame it on them. They didn't make the man scream, or make me hear it. I murmur my thanks and more apologies, slowly rise to my feet and let them lead me to wash up and drive me home. They offer to stay, but I insist I'm fine, go home, and eventually they believe me.

When I'm alone again, I start shaking.

I retreat to my room. It's dark. I leave it that way, and even though I stink, I run to my bed, my down blanket, and my teddy bear. Even before I'm completely under the covers, my thumb is in my mouth.

And then I hear it. Jingle-bells shivering as a counterpoint to my heartbeat.

No. It can't be. Not now. I feel like screaming, and the bells are drowned out in the loose, unhappy whistle of a steam kettle.

It's me, I think in wonder, and the kettle whistle rises and then falls uncertainly. After so many years of looking for it, now, when I don't want to hear it and I'm ready to throw in my knotted towel . . . my skin song comes out. I begin to laugh, and a brook bubbles with me. I just sit there, listening. Then the brook hiccups as I think, I can't rule out schizophrenia just because— maybe *especially* because—I've finally heard something from my own skin.

On the other hand . . . I brush my fingers lightly over my bare arm, and there is a faint pop, like a bubble bursting. What's wrong with this? Who is harmed by this? Why am I so hard on myself? Schizophrenia runs in my family, yes, but that doesn't guarantee that I have it, or will develop it. Have I become so steeped in searching for disease that I have trouble accepting something that is different as harmless, or even good?

Do I feel crazy? Yes, sometimes, especially around exam time. Probably no more than anyone else. Do I look crazy? I walk to my mirror and study my face. My eyes have puffy ridges beneath them, my skin is dry and flaky, I'm sure I could find dandruff if I wanted to, but I look tired, not *mad*. I flash myself a maniacal grin. Underneath it, I still look tired. And I have never really acted crazy, except with one deserving ex-boyfriend. So *what* if I hear things no one else can? So what, even, if it is some fourth cousin of schizophrenia? I'm a whiz at doing long division in my head, too. It's not normal, it may even be paranormal, but I don't need to hate myself for it.

I walk to the kitchen and drink a long, cool glass of water as the evening drapes indigo over my world. The moon is already up and full of promise. I walk back to my desk with swaying hips. God, it feels good to be *me* again, confident, tucked in to round this exam curve like I've done every other exam set in my life. And . . . more. I open my atlas of anatomy, but before I begin, I deliberately touch the tips of my index fingers together. I hear a tire tossed out to roll down a long, gritty but paved summer road.

AS THE CROW FLIES

Written by
Leslie Claire Walker

Illustrated by
Steelee Faltis

About the Author

Leslie Claire Walker is a thirty-one-year-old legal secretary by day, a writer by night. She is a member of the Southwest Writers Workshop and has been writing for seven years. Leslie reads Tarot and runes, and her interests include shamanism, art, music, ecology and riding roller coasters. She is a native Houstonian.

About the Illustrator

Steelee Faltis had the usual beginnings as an artist, consistently winning contests, progressively moving up as her range took in more and more different media. Mentored by Adam Pallock, Steelee learned a great deal. Then she met Michael Poulin, and they started an on-line sticker company which is today number one in the business.

Steelee chose to continue training at the Academy of Art College in San Francisco, where all the teachers are professionals in the field and the equipment is state of the art.

Someone's in the house.

I hike up my skirt and run, heedless of the spiny rows of seaweed, splintered shingle, and shards of glass that in the afternoon sun set the beach afire. The bulbous blue bodies of jellyfish pop under my bare feet. They are dead things, too, but their souls fled from here long ago.

Gulls circle, dive in to feast. The wind half drowns their caws and the tinkling of the Carraways' chimes next door. But the blasting music and hammering coming from the window are thunder in my head.

I go around the side of the house. The storm tide has left a coat of sand on the concrete-and-shell driveway. Parked in front of the door to the generator is a little white car. In a heartbeat I'm upstairs. Whoever the car belongs to left the door open, the screen on the outside latched tight. I pass through the plastic-and-wire mesh.

The pantry door's ajar, the metal rims of cans and the edges of boxes peeking out. Beans and soup. Cereal. Chocolate sandwich cookies. A lamp sits in the center of the bar, and a new package of soft-white bulbs. A roll of shelf paper. My belly flutters. I clamp a hand on it to still the butterflies. This is wrong. All wrong.

Mildew's growing like gangbusters in Tim's room. The bedding has been stripped from the soaked mattress, the shag carpet peeled away from the wall.

Sneakers sunk into the exposed square of padding, a woman hammers heavy plastic sheeting in place of a broken pane. It doesn't make any sense. I'm not expecting *her*.

She sings off-key to the music blaring from the boombox on the dresser. It's edgy, throbbing. It has its own pulse. Permeates everything around it. Weaves itself into my bones. Into the bones of the house.

"Hey!" I holler. I keep yelling, louder, to no avail. It's like I'm not here. I'm not getting through. She just keeps on hammering.

I sock her shoulder. She yelps. It's a good sound. A powerless sound. Still, she looks right through me.

Balling all my strength into my throat, I shoot it like an arrow from my tongue. "Who are you? Why are you here?"

She hears me this time and freaks out. The hammer splits my head in two, but only for a second, like a strong breeze with a sharp edge. She knows she's hit *something*. Her face bleeds white. The hammer thunks on the floor, and the nails she has clamped between her teeth, except for a stubborn one that clings to her lip. It falls when she screams. She makes a break for it, running into the dresser, rebounding off the wall. Her retreating footfalls shake the house. The screen door slams with the force of a gunshot, then the little white car's engine revs and the car roars away.

The boombox pumps its poison into my veins, pumps in time with my heart. Or is it the other way around? I brace a hand on either side of it, the bass vibration coursing through me until I can hardly stand it. Until my teeth ring with it. I yank the thing off the dresser and let it fall. The carpet catches it. The music plays. Now I feel it in my feet. My foot connects with the radio, and still the music plays. The same sound, the same howl as when I turned the wheel of the car and died. I keep kicking until all I hear is the wind and sea.

•••

The bun is toasted just the way I like it, onions piled high. I bite into the hot dog, relish running down my chin, as the shadow glides across the sand, the orange of the sunset a halo around it. It's a human shadow, but the tips of its hands look frayed, like feathers. Like wings. I always wanted to fly. Ought to be able to, but never could manage it.

"Hey, Jace," I say, licking a glob of mustard from the corner of my mouth.

"Hey yourself. Can I sit?"

He pitches his voice to soothe. It rankles. Still, he doesn't visit often. I don't want him to leave.

"Suit yourself."

He's got on jeans today, worn at the seams. The soles of his boots are thin, the laces torn and knotted together in places. His black hair dusts his shoulders, his blue eyes bright against his dusky skin. It's his skin that makes me like him, makes me love him. He reminds me of the first man I ever lost myself to utterly, the one I drowned in. He didn't treat me so good, but his skin . . .

"You scared her, Violet," he says, drawing in his knees, wrapping his arms around them. The sleeves of his oxford shirt are rolled up past his elbows.

He means that woman. How did he know she was here? Might as well ask why he's always in my business. "What did she think she was doing in my house?"

"She took it. It's hers now. That storm coming when it did was lucky for her. The Houston people down here

Illustrated by Steelee Faltis

fixing up their time shares, they don't know their neighbors. Them being here distracts the locals. Nobody's gonna notice her."

My jaw drops. "What do you mean, she took it?"

Jace doesn't say anything—no further explanation is forthcoming. Facts are facts. The silence stretches out a while and my belly starts quivering again. I pitch the rest of the hot dog.

"What are you going to do to her?" he asks. "You gonna drive her out?"

"I already did that." If there's one thing I can do, it's drive people out. I've done it before, but then it was just kids.

He shakes his head. "She'll be back. She's got a strong will, that one."

I push to my feet, jabbing with my toe at a shell half-buried in the sand. My heart aches. "She can't stay here. She just can't." If she stays, Tim might not come. I can't allow that. I couldn't stand it.

"You gonna hurt her?" He tries to catch my eye.

I don't want to look at him. "If I have to."

He rolls up on his knees, takes my hand in both of his, and rubs. His palm is like silk. My hand heats up fast.

"Timmy's not coming back, Vi."

"Tim." He's only twelve and he wants to play third base for the Astros when he grows up. He wants a grown-up name.

"Whatever happened to live and let live?"

I snort. "Don't you mean die and let live?"

"What's your point?"

"He'll come. He promised. We promised each other."

"How long have you been here?" Jace asks.

I stare at him. I can't honestly say.

"The world's moved on, Vi."

"Nothing's changed, Jace."

"No, I guess not."

He rises, kisses my cheek, a gentle rustling. Then he's gone and, for a second, there's a crow among the gulls. He veers off, heading north. I lose him behind the roofline.

The place beside me where he stood feels so empty, like it's even void of air. There's a black feather pressed into the sand where he'd sat. I hunker down. Pick it up. Brush it off. Press it hard against my heart and stare up at the house. It looks like a pirate face in the gathering dark, the half-hammered plastic patch over one eye. It looks, despite the damage, exactly the way it did the day my folks moved in.

•••

The white car is back. Jace is right—and it makes me angry to admit it. I'm inside before I can blink. The sliding door, whose pane is still whole, is open to the rumbling of the waves and the salt breeze.

The stranger rocks in Daddy's chair, one foot folded under her, the other pushing off the balcony in a nervous rhythm. She's facing the sunrise, using the afghan Mamma crocheted for a headrest. A mug full and steaming with more cream than coffee sits beside her on the deck.

I gather my strength and march out there, locking my fingers around the arms of the chair, forcing the rocking to stop, trapping her.

"Can you see me?" I ask.

Her breath catches in her throat. "No," she whispers.

I borrow strength from the water. It floods me, fills me from toes to crown. It chafes. Wants to run loose— I've taken a little too much. Her eyes narrow. She sees me.

"Who in the hell are you?" The words tremble as they fall from her mouth, but her body's still. I don't like her tone.

"You're not supposed to be here."

"It's my house."

I shake my head. "I live here. You leave now."

"Impossible," she says.

Impossible? I lean forward. Bare my teeth. The power in me is a crashing wave.

She shrinks back against the afghan, the muscles in her jaw writhing.

I push in closer. "I'll make you sorry."

She meets my gaze, holds it. "Go ahead and try."

I lift the rocker up by the arms. Send her sprawling on the deck. Hurl the chair off the balcony. It lands on the sand. I whirl. Snatch the mug. Fling the hot liquid on her and chuck the ceramic after it. She ducks—it misses her head, barely. Cracks against the wood railing.

I search, but there's nothing else to throw. She just sits there in the puddle of hot coffee.

"Why won't you go away?"

She looks at me, face red, eyes wet. "There's nowhere else to go."

•••

I set two mugs of coffee and the sandwich cookies from the pantry on the table in the living room and sink into the rocker, which I've moved back inside where it belongs. Mary's been sleeping on the sofa—that's her name, Mary. She's so young. It was all she could do just to crawl there and collapse. She's awake now, staring at me. Her eyes are very blue.

"What time is it?" she croaks.

I shrug. What do I know about time? "It's dark outside."

"God," she says, pushing herself upright. "You've been here the whole day?"

As if I would leave her alone in my place. I'm waiting for Tim. If he were to come now, would he stay with her here? No telling when I could get her out of the house. Or how. I'm plumb out of ideas.

"I made coffee," I say, and take a cookie. I twist it open and scrape at the filling with my teeth. Nothing comes off; I'm not focused enough and I'm so tired. I make the effort, though. These cookies always were my favorite.

Mary screws up her face. "You're eating."

I polish off one of the chocolate wafers. "Yeah. I like food."

"Can you get fat?"

"Nope."

"Awesome." She sips her coffee and winces. Must be too hot.

"Why don't you have anywhere else to go?" I ask.

She eyes me over the rim of her cup, through the rising steam. "Direct, aren't you?"

Why be anything else? "You gonna answer the question?"

"Got no family." She blows on her drink and sips again, cautiously.

"No friends?"

"No real ones."

"What are you doing in my house?"

"Didn't know it was yours," she says.

I fold my arms across my chest. "That's fair."

Her lips curve. "This is crazy, you know?"

"What's that?"

"Talking to a ghost."

Is that what I am? "Well, it's confidential."

"How's that?" she asks.

"Whatever you say, who am I gonna tell?"

She sets down the mug. "I drove down from Denver. Moved up there right after high school. Did odd jobs. Got into some trouble. I thought I could come back home. I even went by the house . . . but I couldn't even make it up the walk to the door."

"So why'd you come here?"

"I've always loved the sea." She looks out the sliding door. The outside light's on, moths circling. "Will you stay, Violet?"

Is she kidding?

●●●

We walk on the beach the next evening. The tide has been and gone, leaving a fresh deposit of jellyfish and seaweed. Mary picks a careful path, watching her feet, until finally we just move further up onto dry sand. We go far enough to discover civilization. Pass one of those places that rents two-seater bikes and skates, and a T-shirt shop. The Barnacle Café has all those colored

Christmas lights strung around the roof of its deck. There's a reggae band playing. The music creeps inside me until I'm walking to the beat.

Mary's wearing a spaghetti tank top, a pair of baggy denim shorts, and sandals, a long-sleeved shirt tied around her waist. White keloids dot her sunburned shoulders.

Phone company trucks are out in force; the repairmen—not just men, but women too, I see—perch like pigeons on the poles.

"When do you think they'll be finished fixing the lines?" Mary asks.

"Doesn't look like it'll take them long," I say. "Listen, how long are you planning on staying here?"

She bends, picks up a soda can. There are ants on it, so she drops it fast. "I haven't thought about it."

That's not the answer I'm hoping for. My gaze travels back to the scars on her shoulders.

"How did you get those?" I ask.

Mary laughs, but the sound is hollow. Her eyes get this deer-in-the-headlights look about them. "Knife fight," she says.

I match her forced grin. "No, really."

"I had a fight with a drinking buddy, okay?"

"About what?"

"I wasn't giving it up the way he thought I should."

"Who won?" I ask.

Her lips thin. "How come you get to ask all the questions? What are you, the Inquisition?"

"What do you want to know?"

"What happened to you?" she said. "How'd you die?"

"You really want to know?"

She stops walking. Turns toward me. "Yeah."

All I remember is the sound and the light. "I think I went through some glass."

"You're not sure?" she asks.

I shake my head.

"How can you not remember dying?"

Seems like I should. Like it's some failing on my part. "I just don't."

We walk on, come across a short bridge arching out of the dunes. It leads us to a scrawny patch of grass and a green plastic runner that stretches to the back door of a hotel. A merry-go-round and a jungle gym sit forlorn. No kids; it must be nearing supper time. Mary settles on a wooden bench. I give the go-round a shove, jump on.

She slides her hands into her back pockets and taps her foot. "What about all this white light and tunnel stuff, Violet? Is it true?"

"Dunno. I just woke up here."

"No St. Peter? No angels?"

"No." Never saw any saints. And Jace—well, as by-the-book angels go, he hardly qualifies. He's mine, though.

"What good are you then?"

"Who says I'm supposed to be?" I raise a brow. "Why are you so all-fired interested in dying?"

"No reason."

The hotel door slams, giving us both a start, and a pimply faced kid in an important-looking uniform bops our way, swinging his flashlight. He's got the switch flipped on. You can barely see the light, it's so faint. It's just now dusk.

"No trespassing," he says to Mary. I guess he doesn't notice the merry-go-round turning. Doesn't notice me.

"Huh?" she asks.

He points his flashlight at a sign stuck in the sand.

"Can't you read?"

She gets up but flips him the bird, very diplomatic.

• • •

As the sun sets, we walk back to the house. I take a peek inside her car while Mary rummages through one of her bags. There's a dolphin suncatcher hanging from the rearview mirror. Three duffels (besides the one she's combing through) lie helter-skelter on the bed of the hatchback, an ivy on the front passenger floorboard rests its chin on the seat. Mary comes up with a couple of decks of cards.

"What the hell," she says, and swings one of the bags over each shoulder.

I grab the plant. It'll die in the car—there's no air.

We drink more coffee. Play canasta into the early morning. It's been so long since I've played, I forgot how much I like the strategy. We talk a while after we're done, but Mary's eyes droop and she goes off to sleep. I don't need to sleep, so I drift out on the balcony to watch the tide come in.

There's a shadow on the ground, at the edge of the dunes—a man resting on the stand that's supposed to hold the trash can.

I vault the railing. I can't believe how glad I am to see him.

"Hey, Jace," I say.

"Hey yourself."

"Been here long?"

"A while. Your stranger come back?" he asks.

I lean against the stand. "Mary? Yeah."

"Good."

"What do you mean, good?"

"Just what I said."

My arm scrapes the cuff of his jeans. "Why's she here?"

"People come to new places all the time. To start over. To have a second chance," he says. "It doesn't seem like she's here to get her act together."

"It's more like she's hanging on by a thread."

"She's resting."

"No. She's waiting for something."

"Like you?" he asks.

I shake my head. "Nothing like me."

"What are you worried about, Vi?"

"She might hurt herself."

"Why do you care if it gets her out of the house?" he asks.

"But what if she dies, Jace?"

He brushes the hair from my eyes. Curls a strand around his finger. "She will if she wants to bad enough."

•••

There's a cat napping on the rocker, or it was napping until I came in. Its ears flatten and it hisses. I hiss right back. Let it know who's boss. It curls up tight and keeps an eye on me.

"I hate it when eggs burn," Mary says. "Ruins 'em." She bends over the skillet at the stove, scraping and scrambling like mad.

"You're right." I sit at the bar, feet dangling.

"Damned right," Mary says. "I thought about taking a trip into town today."

"Shopping on the Strand?"

"No, not Galveston. Houston. Wanna come with?"

"I can't."

She looks over her shoulder, turning back to the eggs before she even gets a good fix on me. "Why not?"

I shift in my seat. If she knows Tim's coming, if she sees him and he's scared, maybe she can make him feel safe so he'll stay. "I'm waiting for my brother."

She dumps the eggs onto plates. The toaster dings and four crisp slices pop up. She divides them equally, a pat of butter on each.

"He dead, too?" she asks.

"No," I say. "I don't know."

"Then why are you waiting for him?"

"He needs me." I hold out my glass and she pours orange juice.

"Why?"

I hesitate.

She winks. "Who am I gonna tell?"

That beats all, her throwing my words back in my face.

"My folks don't like each other," I say. "They don't like Tim and me."

She shovels eggs into her mouth. "Why not?"

"What do you mean, why not?"

"I mean, what did you do so they didn't like you?"

"We were born." I sip my juice. "He's too busy. She doesn't want us. We're too messy."

"Life's messy." She bites into her toast. "Aren't you going to eat?"

I'm not so hungry. I shake my head. "We have a pact."

"'Bout what?"

"We're supposed to stick together."

"Even after you're dead, Violet?"

"Yeah."

"That's creepy." She chews the last of her toast and clears the plates. "If I'm gonna leave, I'd better go now."

"You going to see your parents?" I ask.

"Fat chance. I'm going to hit the Fine Arts Museum—the Egypt exhibit."

She grabs her purse. Cocks her head. "How old are you, Vi?"

The question throws me some; I'm not expecting it.

"Twenty-three."

●●●

It's night out. Mary's rocking in the dark.

"It's about time you got here," she says, like I'm supposed to come over just because she's there and awake.

I lean against the sliding door's frame. The salt wind blows in around me. "What's your problem?"

"Don't you know anything?" She lifts something from her lap. Tosses it at me.

It's too thin to go very far. It floats to the ground and I stoop, pick it up: a photocopied page from the newspaper's Metropolitan section, page two. There I am, second column, third from the bottom. *Woman Dies in Accident. One victim. One car vs. retaining wall. Blood alcohol level, .20.*

"Where did you get this?" I ask.

"The library."

"I thought you were going to the museum."

"I had extra time."

Sure she did. "Liar."

"How many drinks did you have before you got behind the wheel?" she asks.

"None of your business."

"How many?"

"I lost track at five. Are you satisfied?"

"Were you trying to kill yourself?" she asks.

My lip trembles.

"I didn't go to all this trouble for myself."

"The hell you didn't," I say.

"Look at the date on the paper, dummy."

The date, dummy. September 6, 1978.

There's a banging on the kitchen door. Mary and I exchange glances. She pushes to her feet and answers the knocking.

"Vi, it's for you."

For me? Who would be calling for me?

Twenty years. What did that mean?

Mary backpedals, pulls the door wide. A squeaky hinge mouths off. There's Jace, handsome as you please. He looks so alive, from the dust on his boots to the feathers in his thick black hair—and the feathers growing up through his shirt.

"Vi, can I talk to you outside?"

I look at Mary.

Her eyes are wide. "Go on."

Jace strides over, takes my hand. My legs won't work. He pulls me out into the night. The screen door thwaps home behind us.

"What's this about?" I ask. My voice cracks.

"You were in trouble," he says, dragging me down the stairs and onto the sand beneath the balcony.

"And you thought Mary had something to do with it."

"I know she did."

My chest is so tight. It's crushing me.

Twenty years. Tim's older than I'll ever be.

"He never came."

"Oh, Vi."

"He's not coming, is he, Jace? He promised."

"I know he did."

"Why?" God, could he be married? Does he have kids? Is he pitching in the Major Leagues?

Jace doesn't say anything. What can he say?

There's a storm coming in off the water. "Where do you go when you're not with me?"

"A little bit of everywhere. The mountains. The desert."

"Who do you see?"

"No one really. A couple of old friends."

"Older than me?" I ask.

"One or two of 'em."

I look up at him. Hold his gaze. "Who are you, Jace? Why do you keep coming back to me?"

"Not to you, Vi. For you."

Mary's voice carries out the sliding door. One-half of a conversation. Guess they got those phone lines up and running.

I swallow hard. "What's the desert like?"

"Like the sea and the sky," he says. "It goes on forever."

MUD AND SALT

Written by
Michael J. Jasper

Illustrated by
Jayson B. Doolittle

About the Author

Michael J. Jasper has been a house painter, a junior high school English teacher, a waiter, an assistant editor, a secret shopper and a janitor. He prefers writing.

A graduate of the 1996 Clarion workshop and the North Carolina State Master of Arts writing program, he is interested in many kinds of writing. He has recently completed his first novel, about two brothers in a small town who can't stand each other, and is at work on the second, a horror story.

He lives in Raleigh, North Carolina, with his wife, Elizabeth, and their dog and two cats. He is a technical writer at a Raleigh software training company.

Skin followed Georgie and Matt out of the pickup, his entire body shivering despite the three layers of clothing he wore. Outside the truck, the early-morning November air was crisp, with just a hint of wind that seeped through his camouflage jacket. Skin felt Matt watching him in the semidarkness, making his shoulder blades itch until Georgie slapped him on the back and handed him a rifle. Once all three were armed, they stood in an empty field a mile from the abandoned Omaha Indian reservation. According to the guy in the bar last night, the alien had been seen in the area the previous afternoon.

"If it gets any colder, my nuts are gonna flash and go south," Georgie said as he rubbed his dark, sleep-bent hair. A pink finger stuck out of a hole in his glove.

"Thanks so much for sharing," Matt said, pulling a ragged scarf tighter around his thick neck. "At least you have nuts, unlike our buddy Skin here, who won't even protect his own woman." He pulled out his heat-sensitive field glasses and elbowed Skin in the ribs. Skin swallowed hard and checked his gun for the second time to make sure it was loaded.

Sunlight crawled over the bluffs of the Missouri River to the east as Skin glanced at his old friends, his heartbeat thudding in his ears in anticipation of the hunt. He saw Georgie's boyish face slip into a grin, while Matt's chubby face frowned at the brown landscape from behind his glasses. All three men were in their mid twenties, high-school buddies from Fremont, Nebraska, class of '09. None of them had ever killed anything larger than a deer before.

Georgie coughed and spit, breaking the sense of dread building in Skin. "Let's go."

Skin and Matt moved at the same time, forming a wedge with Georgie in the lead. The dead, frozen ground crackled under their boots, and the tree branches above them rustled in a sudden breeze. Pulling his jacket tighter onto his wiry body, wishing he'd been able to buy a new coat this fall, Skin glanced at the forest again. The Indians had left the reservation over two years ago, heading farther south to put more distance between them and the detainment camps. The camps had been a good idea, he thought, even though it had driven the Indians away.

"Don't drop that new gun, Skin," Matt said, his jaggedly cut blond hair flipping into his eyes. He adjusted his spectacles on his nose and lowered his voice. "Of course Georgie gives me the shitty one. I know it's hard for you to carry a conversation, much less heavy weaponry."

"Shut up, Matt," Georgie whispered. "Someone's been through here recently."

They slowed, Matt glaring at the back of Georgie's head. Georgie pointed at some thorn bushes and matted-down grass, but Skin couldn't see any difference in the brown undergrowth. He knew they weren't going to find anything out here, but he liked hunting with Georgie. After walking around all day, freezing their toes and fingers, they'd all end up at his house for home-brewed beer, chili, and the sports transmissions from the media satellite system that eastern Nebraska had finally had installed.

They continued walking north at a slower pace, closer to the abandoned reservation. Skin had only seen blurry pictures of the aliens, and he wasn't sure if he wanted to run across one today in the single-digit cold. Ever since their arrival, followed by the accidents in the Dakotas and Minnesota, he'd envisioned them as big, monkeylike creatures from his childhood nightmares. The guys they drank with at the bar had a working list of insults and myths made up about the aliens, from "graymeat" to "hellspawn" to "dirteaters." The list grew nightly. Lisa, working as a nurses' aide at the Fremont hospital, had heard from other nurses who had been to one of the camps that the aliens carried diseases and were drug addicts, and they smelled terrible. He inhaled icy air and held back a cough. His legs were getting tired already.

"So is Lisa going to be home tonight?" Matt asked under his breath, loud enough for only Skin to hear. "What's she going to be wearing?" Skin hated the way Matt's voice had grown more and more oily since high school, especially when he was discussing Skin's wife.

"Don't talk about her like that," Skin said, regretting it immediately. He should've just shut up and taken it. Back in high school, Lisa and Matt had dated, for only a month.

"O-ho! Now he's got an attitude! Where was that attitude last night, when she needed you?"

Skin shut his mouth and walked faster. Matt's soft laughter made his ears burn. He should've taken a swing at the guy harassing Lisa last night, but he knew he would've gotten his ass kicked. Lisa had pulled him out of the bar and left Matt and Georgie inside, talking to the guy about hunting. "Don't pull that macho crap with me, Tim," Lisa had said in the car on the way

Illustrated by Jayson B. Doolittle

home, while Skin fought to see through the frosted windshield. She was the only one who didn't call him by his nickname.

The sun stayed hidden behind the clouds all morning. The men moved gradually north, keeping to the shadows and stopping at every clearing so Georgie could look for signs of the alien's passing. At noon they stopped to eat a lunch of salted venison and stale rolls, but it was too chilly to stay in one place for long. Skin felt worn out already, from Matt's constant talking and the miles they'd covered, but he kept moving. The day grew overcast and dark as the noon hour passed.

For the first time since learning about the escaped alien last night at the bar, Skin thought about actually using the gun in his hands to kill it. He knew Georgie needed his portion of the reward money to help take care of his two kids, and he and Lisa themselves weren't exactly living like royalty after the meat packing plant had closed. Five thousand dollars was a lot of cash, even today. Caught up in his thoughts, Skin walked past Georgie, who was bent down on one knee examining the grass.

"I think we're close," Georgie said, his dark eyes squinting at the ground. Skin stopped, a thrill of fear and excitement replacing his guilt about last night. He had convinced himself they weren't going to see anything out here.

Matt mimicked Georgie from behind Georgie's back, forcing his soft features into a fierce scowl. Skin shook his head and checked his gun again. It had one of the new safety sensors that was supposed to make it accident-proof, except Georgie hadn't explained to him how to use it yet. The fact that Georgie had lent him his best gun filled Skin with pride, too much pride to ask for instructions on its use. The sensor was dark, so Skin figured the safety was on. If they caught it, the alien could be strung out on drugs and unpredictable, so he had to be ready to shoot to kill if needed. He touched the sensor.

Georgie began talking in a low, impatient voice. Matt nudged Skin and rolled his eyes. Skin knew from years of hunting with Georgie that this meant they were close to their prey.

"Huntin' and killin', ain't nothing better," Georgie muttered, walking slowly into the forest. "Got no room for graymeats, not in this country, not nowhere else." Skin remembered Georgie warming up for their high school's football games in the same chanting manner.

"Shh," Matt said, pointing at a large evergreen seventy-five yards away. His field glasses had turned opaque. Despite the lack of wind, the tree moved the slightest bit.

"Oh yeah, here we go," Georgie said. They spread out in a loose arc and stepped slowly toward the tree. Skin felt the cold weight of the gun suddenly through his insulated gloves. He loosened his grip.

When they were twenty yards from the evergreen, Skin smelled a lingering odor of wet, wormy dirt mixed with salt. They stink, Lisa had said. He turned to say something to Matt, but before the words could leave his mouth, a figure tumbled out of the tree. Like a gray-and-black blur, it righted itself and ran into the forest on all fours.

The air exploded with the sound of Georgie's gun. Matt and Skin, their guns resting on their forearms, stared at Georgie with wide eyes. The fuzzy image of the alien, if that was what it was, kept replaying in Skin's mind like a nightmare.

"Come on, Skin! Move it, Matt, you fat ass!" Georgie yelled, sprinting after the creature into a stand of oak trees. "I think I got him!"

Georgie's gun went off a second time, followed by Georgie's voice yelling in the forest, combined with a strange shriek that sounded like an animal. Skin and Matt ran after their friend and found him on top of a tall humanoid figure, holding him down with the weight of his body. Purplish-red blood dotted the tree trunks and bushes around them. Skin had never seen such a color before.

"Yeah!" Georgie yelled. "I got him." The alien's stubby legs poked out from underneath Georgie. "Trying to get away from your camp where you belong? Don't like your new home? What you going to do now, graymeat? Huh?"

Skin stepped closer for a better look. "Come on," he said. His voice sounded like a bird's chirp. He coughed. "Take it easy." Sniffing the alien's almost overpowering odor, Skin bent down. He'd never seen one up close. The alien reeked of mud and salt.

Thick tentacles moved like tiny, eyeless snakes across the alien's head, growing out of his scalp like hair. One beat helplessly against Georgie's midsection, giving off a tiny spark with each impact. A red cut slashed across one side of the alien's head where Georgie had shot him, but the flow of blood had stopped. The alien's eyes—all three of them, Skin noticed with a chill—were closed, and his narrow gray face was flat, almost peaceful, despite his obvious discomfort. Taking tiny steps, Matt walked next to them with his gun trained on the alien, but he kept his distance, for once not saying a thing.

"Okay, buddy," Georgie said. There was a change in his voice. His hand rested on the alien's back. "Let's get up." Georgie pinned down the alien's long arms and slid off. The alien rose to his feet. His elongated torso and humped back made him look bent over when he stood upright. Blood stained the alien's khaki pants and too-small denim jacket, and it looked like he had been shot in the side as well.

Skin stepped forward to help him up, but he froze at the sound of Matt's voice. "Let's take this thing out now, Georgie." Matt pushed his glasses up onto his forehead with a nervous hand. "It may have some disease. Maybe it's on Blur right now, and it's going to flash."

Georgie brushed off the alien's ill-fitting jacket, gazing at the alien with calm eyes. Skin saw something pink and small fall to the ground. Dark, inhuman blood stained Georgie's gloves and the finger that poked out of the hole in his glove.

"Be quiet, Matt," Georgie said, without looking away from the alien. His face was almost blank, as if the wild adrenaline rush from the hunt had melted away.

Skin couldn't take his eyes off the tall, gray-skinned being in front of him. The alien's fingers looked more like stubby toes at the end of his yard-long arms. He was almost as thin as Skin was, and he didn't look dangerous at all. He wondered if the explosion at the brewery where the aliens had begun to work had been sabotage or just a freak accident. He wondered if the alien could understand them.

"We got to take you back, man," Georgie said.

"What?" Matt cried, lifting his gun. "What are you talking about, Georgie? The reward was dead or alive. I'm not messing with some alien that's whacked on Blur."

Georgie continued talking over Matt's shouts. "You have to go back to your camp." Georgie's voice was gravelly, like an old man's, and he slowed his words even more. "Do–you–un–der–stand–me?"

Swaying slightly, the alien straightened up and opened his eyes. Matt stopped yelling. A trickle of sweat started from Skin's armpit and ran down his side. His mouth felt so dry it hurt. Deep black, no whites at all, the eyes of the alien stared right at him. Skin backed up, bumping into Matt.

"If you're not going to kill it," Matt said, his voice harsh, "we'd better get it back to the truck." The sky was turning dark blue, and Skin watched his own breath leak out of his mouth in a cloud. Georgie didn't move.

"Come on, man, let's go!" Matt said. When Georgie didn't respond, Matt poked him in the back with his rifle.

Georgie jumped, and his eyes fluttered. "Goddamn graymeat," he whispered, wiping one of his blood-stained gloves on his coveralls, keeping his other hand on the alien. He looked like he had just woken from a deep, dreaming sleep. Turning toward the alien, he reached for his gun. "What did you do to me?"

The alien immediately dropped to all fours, dotting the frozen ground with blood. Almost faster than Skin could follow, the alien reached into his jacket and pulled out a pink capsule, which he stuffed into his mouth. His gray arm blurred back into place on the ground. Skin wasn't sure if his eyes had moved fast enough to see it all happen.

"What the hell?" Georgie said. "Spit that out, gray-meat." He bent over the alien, but his hand stopped an inch from the writhing tentacles of the alien's head, as if he expected the alien's touch to shock him. Looking at Matt and Skin, he yelled, "Get over here and help me!"

Skin took a slow step forward, his gaze fixed on the alien. "What do you want me to do, stick my hand in his mouth?" he asked Georgie. The alien began to shake, his strange hair-tentacles quivering like a handful of garter snakes. From the middle of his forehead, his third eye winked sideways at Skin.

"Shoot him." Georgie's voice was flat. Matt moved next to Georgie, rustling the dead weeds. Skin's eyes took in his old high-school buddies on his left and the thin, trembling alien on his right. Everything else—the cold, the bare trees, even the weakness in his arms— faded into the back of his brain.

"He's got Blur in him," Georgie said, his calm voice floating into Skin's head like a light wind. "He's gonna flash on us and we won't be able to bring him in. He'll be moving so fast it'll be like trying to hold on to five aliens."

Skin moved closer to the alien as Georgie spoke, until the mud-and-salt smell filled his nose. The muscles of the alien's face contracted wildly like a mask of moving gray flesh. His wide shoulders rocked back and forth, and his sticklike arms vibrated with energy. The wound on his head began to bleed again. Skin lifted the barrel of his gun a few inches, but he didn't point it at the alien. Accidents, his mind whispered.

"We did our parts," Georgie continued slowly, as if trying to convince himself. "Matt spotted him. I took him down. Now it's up to you to finish it."

Skin looked down at the rifle in his hands. Turning it around, he aimed the butt at the alien, then glanced at the safety sensor before swinging it. When his eyes left the alien, the alien leaped. In two seconds' time, the rifle was knocked from his hands and he was thrown into Matt. The gun hit the ground, discharging. With three rabbitlike leaps, the alien disappeared into the trees of the abandoned Omaha reservation.

"Damn it, Skin, you let him get—" Matt yelled, then stopped. Numbly, Skin looked over at Matt, then Georgie. Georgie wasn't standing anymore. He was on his back, his head at an awkward angle against a tree trunk. Blood oozed between his fingers from a hole in his stomach.

"Fuck. I'm shot, guys," he said. "You fucking shot me, Skin."

"Oh, Jesus," Skin said, reaching down to him.

Georgie jerked away, then screamed. When he stopped, he looked at Matt. "Get that son of a bitch."

Skin ducked his head instinctively, waiting for the butt of a gun against his temple. Matt swore and yelled, "Not you, idiot. He means the alien. Let's get it."

"We'll never catch him," Skin said, looking away from Georgie at the darkening sky. "Plus we can't just leave him here."

Matt looked at Georgie without any expression on his face. "He'll be all right. We'll be back soon, anyway."

"Yeah. Go get the graymeat," Georgie said calmly. He ripped off the bottom of his shirt and touched it to his midsection. "Go on," he said, then added quietly, "Don't let me down, Skin."

Skin's arms dropped to his side, watching Georgie's blood drip onto the ground. Matt picked up a pink capsule from the ground where the alien had stood. "Here," he said, biting the capsule. He held half of it out to Skin. "Now we'll make up for lost time."

"What?" Skin whispered. "We don't know what this'll do to us, Matt."

"Take it." Matt grimaced as he swallowed the drug.

Skin set the gelatinous capsule in his mouth, its bitter contents almost burning his tongue. Blur was supposed to do evil things to a human's nervous system, but the aliens had adopted it as their drug of choice. He swallowed it with a shudder and ran after Matt into the thick trees that hid the alien's escape route.

The drug worked fast. Skin's pulse quickened almost immediately, and the cold air felt warm on his flushed face. He ran after Matt, pumping his tired legs faster than he'd thought possible. His eyes flicked over every shadowy inch of the forest. He felt liquid and gloriously strong.

They ran deeper into the trees. The alien had bent branches and torn up the hard ground in his mad flight, and his trail became obvious in the dying light, even to Skin. Matt's panting sounded like small screams as the big man pushed his out-of-shape body ahead of Skin. Skin's hypersensitive ears heard the panicked hooves of what must have been four deer a mile to his right.

"There," Matt shouted, pointing with a shaking hand at a clearing ahead of them. The remains of an old fire and the bleached bones of a cow were scattered across the circle. Bisecting the grassless clearing were the oval prints of alien feet and hands.

Matt slowed, panting hoarsely, and entered the circle. Skin followed, his arms and legs shaking with the need to keep moving. He felt ready to jump out of his body at the slightest provocation.

"Something's wrong here, man," Matt said between gasps of air. His glasses had fallen off somewhere in the forest, and his face looked naked and vulnerable without them. He took another step into the clearing. The woods to the left rustled suddenly, and a gray-and-black streak hit him. Matt was knocked off his feet without making a sound.

Skin's Blur-enhanced eyes caught the figure of the alien for a split second before the creature disappeared into the forest again. He didn't have time to raise his gun. Without checking on Matt, he chased the alien deeper into the forest, his body moving before his brain had a chance to make sense of anything. Images of Matt on his back in the clearing and Georgie holding his bleeding stomach swam through his head. His leg muscles began to cramp and burn. Skin suddenly wondered what he would do when he caught the alien. He barely finished the thought before the alien stopped, flattened, and covered his head. Skin tried to pull up, but he tripped over the alien's body and crashed into the trunk of a tree. The world went black for five seconds.

When he opened his eyes, the alien was bent over him, inches from his face. Mud and salt filled Skin's mouth and nose. The black eyes of the alien watched him in the gray darkness. Swallowing hard, Skin felt his throat constrict and his chest tighten. His breath caught in his lungs. He tried to talk, but the alien held him fast in his black gaze. This was not a human in front of him, Skin realized with a strange shifting in his mind. The alien stepped back, almost blending into the grayness of the forest, but he didn't try to run. Lifting his gun, Skin looked up into the alien's eyes.

"You're not supposed to be here," he whispered. Pointing the gun at the alien, Skin fumbled for the safety sensor. He tried to focus on the reward money. "Everything's wrong now, ever since you came here. This is our home." His arms shook as he aimed the gun. "You don't belong here."

The alien took a step back, his elbows jutting out and his long back straight. He looked like he was getting ready to do a formal bow to Skin. The wind picked up, rattling the bare tree limbs above Skin's head.

"I have to . . ." he began, but his mouth wouldn't cooperate with his mind. He couldn't breathe. Random images of Matt and Georgie, Lisa, the alien camps, and the reward money jumped into his thoughts. Trying to aim down the barrel of the trembling gun, Skin squinted into the darkness, his lungs burning. The alien dropped his long arms to his sides, made a whistling noise, and the forest fell silent. Skin tried to take a breath, but could suck no air into his lungs.

The alien lifted his chin in what would have been a gesture of courage and defiance in a human. "Home," he said in a deep, clear voice.

"Have to take you . . ." Skin mumbled. His finger touched the trigger of his gun, and a leaden weight filled his chest. He didn't want to let Georgie or Lisa down.

"Our home, too," the alien said, pointing at the trees around him. "*Nee-brash-yah*." The way the alien said the word was more beautiful than anything Skin had ever heard.

"Home," Skin whispered, his mouth dry. More images filled his head. Lisa, on the verge of tears last night. The detainment camps hidden behind high walls and electric fences. Georgie joking with the loud-mouthed guy at the bar. Lisa pulling Skin out of the bar. The buses of aliens on their way to the labor farms, then back to the camps. Matt's face red with laughter. His friends, his home. Skin lowered his gun and cracked it, dropping the shells uselessly to the frozen forest floor. Finally, he was able to take a breath, and he nearly doubled over from the shock of the icy air in his lungs.

Ignoring the creature in front of him, he tried to walk back toward the clearing where he'd left Matt. He stumbled, and the alien reached a hand out to him, palm up. Without stopping to think, Skin touched the alien's rounded hand with his right hand, and numbing electricity coursed through his body. He fell to the ground, his body rigid. The last things he saw before losing consciousness were the alien's black eyes.

It was completely dark when Skin woke. His back spasmed briefly as he sat up on the hard, cold ground and tried to make sense of where he was. He worked his way back to the clearing where Matt had fallen and found him on his side, breathing deeply.

"Matt, it's me!" Skin whispered. He put a hand to Matt's head, and he realized that his fingers weren't even cold. "Can you walk?"

Matt's lips moved, but no sound came out. All Skin could hear was air rasping in and out of his mouth. Skin helped him up and guided him through the forest.

Georgie was raving by the time they got back to him. A flare stick sputtered weakly next to him, covering him in flickering pink light. "Gray, gray, get the graymeat," he mumbled, turning his head back and forth.

"Shh," Skin said. There was no more fatigue in his arms, legs, and back. He should have been exhausted, but instead he felt electric with energy. "This is going to hurt, Georgie, but we've got to get you back."

Bending down, Skin eased one hand under Georgie's neck and slid the other under his legs. With a grunt, he lifted him like a small child and balanced him in his arms. Georgie groaned and pressed his hands on his stomach, but he didn't scream. "Did you get it?" he whispered. "Did you get the alien?"

Matt looked at Skin, the same question on his face. A soft wind rattled the deserted trees of the reservation, carrying a hint of mud and salt. Skin allowed himself a long inhale and exhale before answering. "He's where he belongs," he said. With Georgie in his arms and Matt leaning on him, Skin turned away from the forest and walked through the cold November darkness toward the pickup.

**W**riting began at some early point in human history, and at that point was undifferentiated from science.

It certainly predates the discovery of fire. A man or woman tried to understand some aspect of a largely bewildering universe, and probably failed. Unlike most people, they did not then surrender to "practicality" and concentrate for the remainder of their lives on the things that were knowable. Instead, they told themselves something that might have been true. The chances are overwhelming that in fact it wasn't true, but it was an attempt to explain.

Some of the people who did this became scientists—hewers of rock into new shapes, experimenters with wood and cord, bringers of fire. Others told stories, and at some early point began to tell stories to others. These stories probably were for the most part exercises in imagination—earth, air, fire, and water were personified, and shown in action, to explain, or, rather, to account for what had happened—as distinguished from the usually more mundane and more "real" researches of scientists. Although the audience would contain both future writers and future scientists among it.

That audience—readers—was also apparently different from the general run of population. Most people did not overtly read, then or ever, and if asked would say that reading is useless. But in fact everyone reads, if we understand "reading" to mean not the decoding of written symbols but simply listening to another person who has something vital to say; how to wire a lamp socket, or how to wash a dish, for instance.

The only difference between "nonreaders" and readers is in the kind of thing they will admit to reading. It is really impossible, down at the basic levels, to separate writer from scientist or reader from "nonreader." (It is actually worse than that, but we have to draw the line somewhere.) We are all, in fact, pretty much the same at bottom; our various learned specialties are what differentiate us, rather than anything basic.

We have, of course, come a long way from our beginnings. Or perhaps we haven't really, but the number and kind of specialties have become so large that we think we have.

At some point, for instance, speculative fiction developed a branch—descriptive fiction—which for the past century or two has taken a serious look at "the real world," with interesting results. It is a fruitful subspecies, and will probably survive. Most of its writers and readers will have little to do with the far older speculative fiction, and speculative fiction in its own turn has split into various kinds of fantasy and, since the Industrial Revolution, into various kinds of science fiction. Some readers of one kind of speculative fiction will have little to do with readers of another, as a general rule. Most will happily partake of many branches of the tree.

And so it goes, as we continue to specialize. For another instance, we have in the past five thousand years or so developed "writing," so that now stories in most, though not all, cultures are "written down," in order that they may be read by someone at a distance from the "writer," . . . provided, of course, that someone learned the same system of coding and decoding that the writer used.

We have, in many ways, in fact overspecialized. But that can't really be helped, because cultures are still, to this day in some cases, isolated from one another, and develop their own peculiar "speech," and "writing," unaware of what may be going on elsewhere. In a way it is unfortunate. But in another way, what one culture misses about the universe may be picked up by another, and there is something therefore to be said for "over-specialization," if that is in fact the correct word.

But, with all that in mind but not overwhelmingly so, suppose you want to learn to write—to somehow transmit stories from your mind to the minds of readers. Where do you begin, and how difficult is it? Well, you begin, if you will, here. And it's not very difficult at all.

Some teachers of writing, including some writers, have made writing a very complicated thing. They speak of "voice" and they speak of technical points like writing in "third person objective," and they speak of "narrative" as distinguished from "dialogue," and cetera. Well, in an abstract sense that language may refer to real things. (I think they are real, but have to do with criticism, not with writing.) But remember that every specialty develops jargon, and remember that writing is one of the oldest specialties. Also, take my word for it, most of the people who are now so glib in discussing these matters did not know them at the time of their first sales, or, conversely, have never sold anything, but have simply learned the jargon.

Writing is, in fact, a simple creative exercise. It takes practice, and with enough practice many people gradually learn the "rules" without any special jargon—picking it up later, as I said. But the very fact that they can learn writing by simple trial and error should tell you something. If you can learn it by trial and error, then all you need to do to shorten the process is to eliminate as much of the error as possible as early as possible.

Now, the kind of writing I am talking about is the production of work in volume for an audience—the kind you see in a magazine, for instance. And that kind consists overwhelmingly of stories. There are also vignettes, jokes, japes, and other small forms, which are small for various reasons, I think most of them transient.

In another time, the vignette, for instance—the slice of life, in which the characters are not subject to any process in particular—may become the preferred thing. Certainly it has a place in any age, and you will, from time to time, see vignettes published in many places. But what most readers want most of the time is story, and that is what we are going to teach you. Know how to construct a story, and you know everything you need to know.

A story subjects its characters to a process; to a growing up, or an enlightenment, or, in the case where a villain is the central character, to an enlightenment and a disaster. It is a reflection of the Judeo-Christian ethic, if you will. For whatever reason, it satisfies. It satisfies the reader and it satisfies the writer. And it has seven parts.

They tell you, if you listen, that a story must have a beginning, a middle, and an end. Well, this is true enough, but so does a note from your bank, which says: "Dear Mr. Smith, you are overdrawn $18.75, pay or die." The simple statement that a story must have a beginning, middle, and end is no more useful than another old saying: Write what you know. (What do they mean by that one? How can you write about what you don't know?) To understand what is meant by a beginning, middle, and end, draw a diagram:

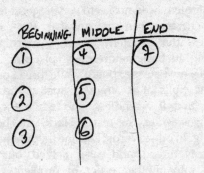

You will notice there are three story components in the beginning. These three are actually interchangeable; none is more important than the other two, and we can number them in any order. But for the sake of convenience, let's number them (1) a character (2) in context (3) with a problem.

You can, as I say, begin with a context, and introduce a character with his or her problem; you can even, in some cases, begin with the problem, and introduce a context and then a character. What counts is that all three must be present before the beginning is over.

(1) A character must be placed in (2) a context. If Joe walks up the side of a wall, it is vital to know if this is happening in downtown Detroit today or aboard a space station; two vastly different stories will result, much more from the context than from Joe. Then, Joe has to have (3) a problem; he has to get somewhere, or get something.

Now, perhaps obviously, you want to pick a character who's vitally interesting. But to do this you will quickly find you cannot avoid filling in the context to some extent, and then you very quickly come up against the problem.

The problem need not seem very large, at first; it's just that the character can't let go of it. But as the story progresses, the problem becomes more and more compelling. Its basic nature does not change, however. Put it this way: Laurine spots a white thread on her black dress. She pulls at it almost casually. She discovers, however, that it is endless, and while the part that showed was white, the rest is black, and her dress is unraveling. In other words, Laurine thought her problem was a stray thread, and easily solved, but it rapidly develops into another order of problem entirely — without changing the basic nature of the problem.

Similarly, the context cannot change, without motivated traveling, but we learn more about it. And the character cannot actually change, past the beginning, though we learn more about him or her, too. The purpose of the beginning is to lay the ground rules; establish the (1) character (2) in context (3) with a problem, and then go on. Once the beginning is over, you can't call in the cavalry, you can't have the character develop a rich uncle, you can't have the character decide the problem doesn't hold his or her interest anymore. If you want the cavalry at the end, you have to have the character wave at a friend in a cavalry patrol in the beginning, or else the totally unforeshadowed arrival of the cavalry will (A) jar and (B) make your hero look ineffectual.

And that brings us to the three parts of the middle. Here is where the story develops.

(4) is an attempt to solve the problem. This attempt must be intelligent and logical, and represent the character's best guess as to the nature of the problem and an adequate response. The character mustn't think that the problem is overwhelming, because at this stage it apparently isn't. He produces a nice, easy response—and (5) encounters unexpected failure.

Well, if the character could solve the problem immediately, it wasn't much of a problem. So, despite the
seeming intelligence of the attempt to solve it, it must
fail—and as a result of that failure, the character learns
more about the problem, and begins to learn a little
more about himself.

He does not actually change, mind you, because that
would be false to the reader's observation of people.
People reveal hidden facets of themselves, from time to
time, under stress, but the facets all fit in with what was
known before. So you must put your character under
stress, and reveal hitherto concealed facets, but they
must fit. The character reaches a little deeper inside
himself, makes another attempt to solve the problem,
which is revealing additional aspects of itself in turn,
and fails again. And again. Three times.

Why three times? Because anything less is unsatis-
fying, because anything more is redundant, because
Aristotle and Lewis Carroll said that what I tell you
three times is true. Three times, on a rising scale of
effort, commitment, and depth of knowledge of the
problem and one's self, is the correct number. Human
beings believe that three times has an effect which two
does not. Conversely, four creates overkill.

All right. (6) is victory. At the last possible moment,
wagering everything, in a do-or-die situation, the hero
wins. Conversely, if he is the villain, coming closer and
closer to his goal results at the last possible moment in
defeat snatched from the jaws of victory, because of
some flaw in his character.

So the middle of the story consists of (4) effort to
solve, (5) repeated failure or increasingly near-attainment
of the goal, and (6) victory or death.

You must make sure that the reader understands it is
victory or death. Even in a story about winning the

garden club prize, you must get to the stage where the aging, widowed, and lonely woman realizes, near the end, that nothing is more important than the prize; that if she fails to win it, she will spend the last of her declining years disappointed, with nothing to look forward to except the grave.

But since victory or death has been achieved at the end of the middle, according to this diagram, what is left for the end?

What is left for the end is (7) validation. Someone who has no other vested interest in the story has to step forward and say, "He's dead, Jim," or, "Who was that masked man? . . . I wanted to thank him," or the like. Think about it; all through the middle, it always looked like things were going to come out well, but they didn't. Certainly, now the villain has plunged from the top of the Empire State Building and is lying splattered on the terrain below. But . . . But. The possibility exists, however slight . . . And that is what the independent authority forecloses. He is the one who actually validates the fact that the story is truly over. Until he speaks, even with something so seemingly clichéd as "Who was that masked man?" the story is not truly over in the reader's mind.

What have we learned? We have learned the seven parts of the basic story, including part (7) validation. In the future, you will learn that the manuscript is not the story, that writing is not the reverse of reading, and other useful things. But you have already learned more than enough to get started on your career.

THE QUALITY OF WETNESS

Written by
Ilsa J. Bick

Illustrated by
Justin Phillips

About the Author

Ilsa J. Bick lives in Fairfax, Virginia. Her academic career includes numerous articles on the application of psychotherapeutic principles to science fiction, in highly respectable journals and in many anthologies on film and television. She has lectured widely. She also won the grand prize for "A Ribbon for Rosie," in Star Trek: Strange New Worlds II, a publication edited by, among others, Dean Wesley Smith, an entrant in the very first L. Ron Hubbard Presents Writers of the Future anthology. "The Quality of Wetness" marks her second professional publication.

When she isn't writing, Dr. Bick tends to her husband, two children, three cats, two leopard geckoes and four golden hamsters, though not necessarily in that order. She is also an avid gardener, cook and fencer—and pretty mean with a saber.

About the Illustrator

Justin Phillips lives in South Wales, United Kingdom. Unlike traditional Welsh artists, he wanted to break free from charcoal drawings of coal miners. He works now as a decorative glass fabricator, which involves the design and manufacture of leaded/stained glass panels.

He is entirely self-taught as an artist. His oil paintings have been exhibited at De Kunstgallery in Amsterdam. His goal is to excel as a professional fantasy illustrator.

That which hath been is now; and that which is to be hath already been.

—*Ecclesiastes*

I

Beneath a sun the color of a blood clot, the hour past noon at Jackson Penitentiary had turned devilishly hot. The office was so close with the heat, the Warden himself was near to dropping. No wonder—Beauregard, that infernal nigger, had botched the climate control again. Cussing and fuming, the Warden had cuffed the colored upside the head *three times:* a wasteful effort to be sure, since the slave couldn't feel a speck of pain. But it certainly made the Warden feel better. A master's work was never done, and wasn't it always that way with slaves? Peevishly, the Warden banished the synthetic to its niche. The synthetic bowed stiffly, then glided to a shallow depression in the wall where it jacked into standby mode and awaited further instructions.

Extracting an embroidered linen kerchief from his breast pocket, the Warden mopped his forehead. Disciplining the darky had been hot work. Uncle Liles, whose ceremonial saber from the Secession Wars hung on the wall next to the colored's niche, would never have tolerated such *insolence.* The Warden shook his head wistfully. There were days when he *prayed* the programmers would discover the cybernetic equivalent of pain, just so the Warden might have the satisfaction of lashing a nigger to within an inch of his life and having it do some good.

In the background, an ENN announcer chattered from the comm, cheerfully informing the Warden that the forecast for Mississippi was for more of the same: hot, smoggy, and cloudless, praise God. Why, the state was in the grip of the hottest July on record, hotter even than the glorious summer of 1862 when the gallant Stonewall Jackson of Blessed Memory had swept the Devil's own Yankees from the Shenandoah Valley at Cross Keys and Port Republic, amen and amen.

Amen, the Warden mouthed reflexively. Sweat trickled down his temples and crawled beneath his starched collar. A spray of sunlight splashed through the armored glass of his office window. The light canted, splaying into a shimmering iridescence. The Warden winked against the glare. *Devil take that nigger.* The Warden's jaws worked. *Must* he do everything *himself?* Well, he would have a word with the reprogrammers this very afternoon, without fail. Depressing the polarizing filter of the window with his thumb, the Warden waited irritably for the lattice structure of the molecules to realign.

The comm burped, and the Evangelical News Network announcer was interrupted in the middle of the daily Bible reading—Exodus 33, the Warden noted absently—by the voice of his aide. "The Right Reverend is coming through now, sir."

"Very well." Balling his wilted kerchief back into his breast pocket, the Warden shrugged his suit into a more commodious arrangement and then faced the center of the room. "You may proceed, Mr. Montgomery."

An audible pop and sizzle emanated from the holo-grid, and then the holo flickered to life to the strains of "Dixie." Upon hearing the anthem, the Warden murmured the requisite prayer to the memory of Claudius "Bud" Watts the Third, President of the Citadel, that South Carolina institution that had so honored the Gray through the dark years before the Secession Wars. In another instant, the three-dimensional image of President and Honorable Right Reverend Shelton Jackson Mosby coalesced upon a raised dais. As usual, His Right Reverend was seated behind a plain pine desk, for though he was given to speaking in tongues and received divine revelation almost daily, Mosby was a humble man who eschewed pomp and ceremony. Behind the Right Reverend's left shoulder hung the Navy Jack; to his right was the Flag of the Soldiers of Christ. Directly above hung the original Samson oil of the Sainted Robert E. Lee.

The Warden swallowed past a sudden lump in his throat. The Samson portrait of the Saint was truly grand. Working from the Mathew Brady photograph of the Saint taken a few days after the surrender at Appomattox, Reginald Samson had captured the true holiness of the Saint. Seated in his elaborately carved wooden chair, the Saintly Lee looked as beneficent, kindly, noble, and regal as the historians had written. How cruel that the brave heart that had beat in that proud breast had been stilled five years after the surrender. Most surely, the Saint had died of grief and a broken heart. The Warden's eyes brimmed over at the injustice. The world was sometimes too vile, too cruel.

His Honorable Right Reverend lifted his lean hands in benediction. "The blessings of the Lord be upon you, Brother."

Illustrated by Justin Phillips

"And upon thee, Most Honorable Right Reverend," said the Warden, regaining his composure. He moved his own hands in the customary way of response. "The Martyrdom of Our Brethren in Gray be remembered. I am the Lord's instrument and thy servant."

"My, such protocol, Brother," protested the Honorable Right Reverend. An easy smile graced his lips, and his clear gray eyes shone. His garb was a suit of the purest white silk. Even on the holo, his body shimmered with an incandescent brightness; he fairly radiated holiness. "Please," the Honorable Right Reverend made a gracious gesture, "be seated, Brother."

Profoundly humbled, the Warden slid into the worn brown leather chair behind his antique mahogany desk. They had never met, and yet within the space of less than a minute, the Honorable Right Reverend had succeeded in placing the Warden wholly at his ease. They were not ruler and subject, but two Southern Brothers in Christ and the Confederacy. The Warden's heart swelled. The holo did not do the Honorable Right Reverend justice, for he was more beautiful and goodly of limb than a soulless machine could ever portray. There was the lion's mane of silver hair, the strong aquiline nose, the finely shaped lips, and the clear countenance of a man whose soul had never known a moment's temptation.

The Honorable Right Reverend Mosby crossed his hands upon the desk before him. "We are pleased that you have made the time from your arduous duties to receive us. We have a favor to ask of you, Brother."

The Warden fairly choked with emotion. "My hand is yours. How may I serve thee?"

"We shall come straight to the point," said the Honorable Right Reverend. "You have under your care the infamous Ruth Grainger."

The Warden's ears pricked with surprise. Of what possible interest was that traitorous whore to the Honorable Right Reverend? But his duty was not to question. "Prisoner 110356 . . . yes."

"How fares she?"

Would to God she had succeeded in hanging herself. Of course, the Warden could not verbalize such a thought, not even to one as forgiving as the Right Reverend. But Prisoner 110356 had been a thorn in the Warden's side since her arrival three months before. "110356 is being subjected to those torments of mind and soul as befit a handmaiden of the Devil."

"What does that mean, exactly?" asked the Right Reverend with sudden sharpness. "Does she live?"

"Oh," the Warden fumbled momentarily, taken aback by the Right Reverend's obvious displeasure, "of course. We do not allow her to mingle with the other prisoners—that business in the yard three months ago. Terrible tragedy for the family." And a pity that the dagger meant for 110356 had ended up in the side of one of his guards rather than in the whore's heart. The Warden still regretted that the guard, a young and inexperienced boy, had tried to shield her. *He* would never have done so, and the Warden had instructed his guards to make very sure that, in the future, should any other fellow prisoner of 110356 be filled with the Holy Spirit and wish to exact divine retribution upon the whore, they kindly stayed out of the way.

"And?"

"She has been under constant surveillance ever since"—the Warden coughed delicately—"that unfortunate incident with the sheets six weeks ago. Our doctor has informed me that she is no longer suicidal and has suffered no permanent brain damage from the lack—"

"Splendid, splendid," the Right Reverend interrupted. "You are aware, are you not, of the summary judgment of the Tribunal?"

The Warden shook his head. Mosby said, "The traitorous Ruth Grainger is to be banished from the company of godly men and to serve on Belter Colony Four-Nought-Three-One."

The Warden frowned. The sentence was extremely lenient. Although the average life expectancy of untrained convict laborers in the penal mining colonies of the Belt was about ten months, the Warden knew of at least five inmates who had managed two years apiece before being summarily dispatched by micrometeor swarms. *Sudden decompression in a vacuum was*, the Warden thought, *an exceedingly merciful death.*

Mosby had been studying the Warden. "You disapprove, Brother."

The Warden hastened to rearrange his features into those of obedient respect. "It is fitting of Christian charity."

"But you do not agree."

"Certainly the crimes of which the traitorous Ruth Grainger has been accused and convicted warrant a much harsher justice. She has trafficked with synthetics. She has dared to usurp the machinations of the Lord Himself and instill into a synthetic the immortal soul of Man."

"Indeed."

The Warden warmed to his topic. "It is an abomination, a blasphemous abomination. How will it look to the Innocents when their teachers tell them that those who indulge in such heathen practices are accorded the full measure of mercy? I have three Innocents myself. I shudder to think of how to explain this."

"You question the wisdom of the Tribunal, Brother?"

"No, but upon your leave, I speak my mind."

"As we see you do." Mosby steepled his long fingers and settled back into his chair, an exact replica of the Sainted Lee's in the Samson portrait. He peered at the Warden with hooded eyes. "And you believe?"

The Warden hesitated, then said in a rush, "I would favor burning."

The Right Reverend's silver eyebrows arched. "Oh?"

"The whore ought to be hanged, then cut down while still the breath of life lingers, and burned upon a pile of pitch and tar."

"No kerosene, Brother?"

"Certainly not. Kerosene would make the fire burn too quickly."

"And suffering is good for the soul."

"For one as black as that whore's . . . yes."

The trace of a smile twitched upon the Right Reverend's cupid's-bow lips. "Ironic, Brother, that you should advocate so fervently for Grainger's death. Yet, on numerous occasions, she has tried to oblige you, has she not?"

"Suicide is an abomination," the Warden said, regretting that this was so. "A just execution is not."

"True. Well, Brother, the Lord has seen fit to spare the whore for a greater purpose. You will release Ruth Grainger to our custody."

The Warden was brought up short. "But what about the sentence? What about . . . ?"

The Right Reverend raised a hand, and the Warden fell silent. "We will concern ourselves with the Tribunal, Brother. God's justice shall be served."

"As you wish."

"A Brother Walker should arrive at your facility within the hour. Please make arrangements for the traitorous Grainger to be delivered into his care."

"Of course." The Warden paused. "What about the Metabex?"

"Ah, the nanoexplosive, yes. We will arrange for a temporary antidote to be administered at regular intervals. No good sending the whore to the Devil ahead of her time, now is it?"

The Warden wasn't sure he agreed. "And, Brother," continued Mosby, "please clean the whore, will you? We have no desire to inflict the Devil's vermin upon the Goodly of Heart."

The Warden stood and genuflected. "I hear and I obey the word and the command of the Most Honorable Right Reverend."

"Excellent, Brother." The Right Reverend depressed a control upon his desk. The hologram wavered. "The peace of God be upon you."

"The Lord preserve us," the Warden murmured and made the appropriate sign. The hologram vanished.

The Warden sagged back in his chair. Of what possible use was someone as vile and blasphemous as the whore Grainger to the Honorable Right Reverend? He shook his head in disbelief. The ways of the Lord were too various for him to comprehend.

He punched the intercom. "Montgomery, prepare 110356 for Out-Processing. See to it that she's given a change of fresh clothing and a full medical. And be sure to deactivate the identi-cuff."

Montgomery was an excellent aide, and if he was surprised by the Warden's request, his voice did not betray it. "Yes, sir. Shall I administer the antidote?"

"No. Escort 110356 to Main Reception at fourteen hundred hours. A Brother Walker will be waiting."

"I'll see to it, sir."

"Out." The Warden sat at his mahogany desk a moment longer, then fingered a catch just beneath the center drawer. There was a faint click, and a long compartment at his left foot slid noiselessly into view. Reaching into the hidden drawer, he retrieved a silver flask of Jack Black and pulled out a Roy-Tan. He rummaged until he found his cigar scissors and then clipped, twirling the cut end in the pucker of his lips to gauge the fit. Satisfied, he lit the cigar. At the first few molecules of smoke, sensors tripped a hidden fan. It whirred softly, drawing the smoke away.

The Warden tipped the flask to his lips. The bourbon burned a warm track down the center of his chest. The Warden sighed. His pleasures were simple ones, for he was a simple man. The Warden settled back, his silver flask in his left hand and his Roy-Tan in his right, and eyed his synthetic. Beauregard had not wavered from its niche but stood, its flat ebony features rigid, blank, and immobile. No doubt the Warden's slave was receiving the latest updates for its level of programming from Central.

The Warden puffed. Praise God for Brother Hampton Ford who had loosed the mitochondrial plague of 2022, thus wiping out every last colored on the planet, black in skin or blood. The only good nigger was a dead one, and the only good synthetic was a dumb nigger. Still, ignorant synthetics were a trial to their masters, and Beauregard was no exception. Sipping at his bourbon, the Warden wondered, as he always did, if synthetics, in their silent cybernetic communions, thought at all or could ever attain a state of grace. And the Warden decided, as was his wont, that synthetics, like the black devils after which they had been fashioned, did not and never could.

But it was an altogether fitting and proper arrangement between master and slave. The Warden sat, with his cigar and his bourbon, and was sanguine in soul and mind. Such was, indeed, the way of things.

II

Ruth perched upon a straight-backed chair and fidgeted. The eight-by-ten cubicle was totally bare; the walls were lined with a thick, sound-absorbing material used in secure facilities to foil sensor sweeps and covert surveillance. The chair, which was bolted to the floor, was not nanomech and was exceedingly uncomfortable. She had already wandered around the room and found nothing remarkable, other than a hologrid directly opposite, and four sensors tucked into each corner and angled down to blanket the room. She had discovered an almost invisible seam etched into the wall to her immediate left. The seam inscribed a neat rectangle, and she assumed, with reasonable certainty, that the seam was a containment door leading to other rooms.

Hugging her arms, Ruth shivered. Things had happened so quickly. A guard had whisked her away from the psychiatric wing and escorted her to the prison infirmary. After an examination by an equally dour medic, she had been pronounced ten pounds lighter, vermin-free, and fit. She had been stripped of her prison tunic, shoved into a sonic, and then handed a blue jumpsuit and told to dress. At Out-Processing, no one would speak with her or answer her questions, and finally Ruth stopped asking. A very brusque and

efficient young man named Montgomery had signed
her out of Jackson and then handed Ruth her one
personal belonging: her wedding ring. The wedding
band was white gold, and three purple Martian
sapphires, each the size of tiny peas, glittered in their
settings. The ring hung on her thin finger. Then
Montgomery had tapped a security code into a central
database. After less than two seconds' delay, Ruth had
felt the identi-cuff on her right wrist loosen, and
Montgomery had removed the manacle before steering
her into an adjoining chamber.

A Brother Walker was waiting, and Ruth had
despised him on sight. Brother Walker was tall and
square-jawed, with blue eyes and a determined set to
his shoulders. A small Navy Jack adorned the lapel of
his suit, which was of good Confederate gray, for Walker
was a Brother of the South. He'd said nothing but stared
with those cold, impassive eyes as Montgomery had
relinquished his hold upon Ruth's right biceps and left.
With a jerk of his head, Brother Walker had motioned for
her to follow him out of the building.

A suborbital was waiting on an apron, just beyond
the laser security grid. In another few moments, they
were airborne. From her nanomech couch, Ruth had
watched the penitentiary recede, as if she had peered
through the wrong end of a telescope. In five seconds,
Jackson Penitentiary was the size of a small gray pillbox.
In another ten, the prison, now a rectangular speck, had
disappeared beneath a shroud of dense yellow smog.

Walker had depressed a control on a keypad set in
the arm of his couch. In response, the polarizing filters of
the windows shifted, and Ruth's window became
opaque. She looked over at Walker, who drawled, "I
need your arm."

Ruth had paused. Walker's accent was thick. Ruth had been trapped in the South for seven years, ever since the selective ban on exit visas to the North had reduced immigration to a trickle. In all that time, she'd still not picked up the knack of deciphering the different dialects. To her untrained ear, it had sounded as if the man had requested an ancient type of coinage thrown to the poor. "Excuse me?" she asked.

"Your arm." Walker gestured toward her right arm. "Y'all need something to block the Metabex. Lessen you don't aim to survive more'n five minutes."

Hurriedly, Ruth had extended her right arm. Walker produced a thin jet from his pocket and applied it to the inside of her wrist, just over the radial artery. Walker couldn't have failed to notice the crosshatching of ugly red scars, but, mercifully, he'd said nothing. Ruth felt a tiny pinprick, then heard a hiss as the contents were injected into her bloodstream.

Walker replaced the jet into his breast pocket. "Just don't you go getting any fancy ideas. That's not permanent. It'll keep the nanoexplosive from going off is all. You're gonna need a jet every day, if'n you want to stay alive."

She had rubbed at the spot with her left thumb. "Where are we going?"

"I can't say."

"Why not?"

"Just can't say is all."

"Okay. Why are we going there?"

"Dunno."

"What do you mean?"

"I mean, I dunno. I just deliver. They check you out again, make sure you haven't brought any trash." He stared at her blandly. "Trash is as trash does."

Ruth reddened. She ducked her head and stared down at her chipped, torn nails. "Then what?" she said into her hands.

Walker hunched his shoulders up and down. "Dunno. I deliver, s'all."

There seemed to be nothing else to say. Ruth averted her face and leaned back. Instantly, the nanomech couch melded to her contours: a small luxury. She knew Walker was still watching her—glaring, actually—and again, she felt that all-too-familiar hostility.

"What?" she asked suddenly. She swiveled her head to face him. "What's on your mind?"

"Never seen a synthetic lover before. Not up close."

"And?"

"You ask me," said Walker, in his lazy, syruplike drawl, "they oughta killed you right off. I would of."

Believe me, I tried to save you people the trouble. Ruth had turned away. "Well, I'll just count my blessings that you weren't the judge."

"What's wrong with people like you? What you need a synthetic for anyway, other than for a slave?"

"You wouldn't understand."

"You got that right. Your own kind not good enough for you, you need a colored? Oh, yeah . . . yours was a white boy. That's even worse, you ask me."

Ruth felt a muscle twitch in her jaw. "No one's asking you."

"So, how was it? Huh? That synthetic any good?"

"I don't owe you an explanation. I've been on trial already."

"Me, I'm flesh and blood, S-A. Been straight arrow all my life. Never needed to look twice at a synthetic, and there ain't never been a time when a flesh-and-blood woman hasn't taken a shine to me."

"How wonderful for you."

"You gonna burn in hell."

Ruth had laughed. "Oh, you mean Jackson. I've been there."

"That's right, get smart," said Walker. "Go ahead, laugh it up. Ha-ha. But I ain't the one been in prison. You Yankees all alike. Think we're just a bunch of dumb rednecks. But let me tell you something: The Right Reverend has prophesied about people like you—them that are no better than the people thought the coloreds was true flesh and blood. And where are the coloreds now? Dead of the plague and buried and all the bastard half-breeds with them. Right Reverend said there would come a time the followers of Satan would rise up for the synthetics, but that your own iniquity would strike you down."

"Please, spare me the fire and brimstone. I've heard it for seven years."

"Then why you even bother coming down here, if'n it wasn't that the Devil was guiding your hand, and you didn't even know it? You have not accepted the Lord's word into your heart. Your heart is stone, and you are the Devil's whore."

No, thought Ruth, *my heart is breaking, and my husband is dead*. But she had heard people like Walker enough times to understand that argument, let alone logic, did not help. She let her head fall back against the couch and closed her eyes. "Fine. You believe what you want to believe. Me, I'm going to get some sleep."

But she hadn't slept. Thirty minutes later, the suborbital had landed. After he'd opened the hatch, Walker had summarily waved her down the stairs. Two men dressed in the gray uniform of the Southern Confederation Army had met her. Crossing the tarmac, the men bundled her into a waiting car and then clambered in. One dialed their destination, which turned out to be a gray, anonymous monolith. At the entrance was a guard post. There she exhaled into a DNA breath analyzer that agreed that she was who she said she was and was searched. Finally, Ruth was led past what looked like suites of offices to the room where she sat now.

She shifted her weight on the bolted wooden chair. It creaked loudly in the silence. Ruth strained to hear something . . . anything. But the acoustical dampening was good. She couldn't hear a thing, even though she knew the two soldiers must be posted right outside. Instinctively, the fingers of her right hand found her wedding band. She twisted it round and round and watched as the Martian sapphires glinted a deep purple. John had always promised they would visit the sapphire digs on Mars. But something had always come up, and then it had been too late.

The outlines of her ring wavered. She squeezed her eyes shut, but a tear escaped, splashing onto the network of scars crisscrossing the soft flesh of her left wrist, the mates to the scars on her right. Absently, Ruth traced a watery *J*, her forefinger lingering over the healed slashes.

There was a loud click. Ruth looked expectantly at the holo, but the grid was dark. Turning left, she saw a section of wall slide to one side, and in another moment, the familiar features of the Southern Confederation President and Honorable Right Reverend Shelton Jackson Mosby appeared. Immediately, the door hissed shut.

Warily, she eyed the tall man as he came to stand directly before her. Mosby's pewter-gray eyes moved up and down, taking her measure. He was clothed in his habitual all-white attire. Even his leather shoes were white. The absence of color made his flesh pinker and his eyes so dark they looked like lead marbles. With that full head of silver hair, he affected the image his followers demanded: that of the Lord's avenging angel.

"So," he said finally, "Ruth Grainger. You, of course, know who I am."

Ruth nodded.

"And you are no doubt wondering why I have seen fit to bring you here?"

Again Ruth nodded. Mosby crossed his hands behind his back. "Although God may be on our side," he declared, "time is not. So I will be brief. There is no love for your kind here. There is no tolerance. Do not make the mistake of assuming that this meeting is in any way intended to confer legitimacy upon your subversive activities."

Finally, Ruth found her voice. "Subversive? You know very well that no subversion was intended. My actions were those of a private citizen—"

"Who broke God's law," Mosby said over her. "And the Lord spoke to Moses, saying: You shall not make for yourself a sculptured image."

"*Your* synthetics—"

"Are slaves, bereft of the soul of Man and, therefore, not in God's likeness or the likeness of His supreme creation, Man," Mosby proclaimed. "*You*, however, violated the sanctity of a sovereign nation. *You* engaged in the illegal transfer of materials absolutely and expressly forbidden by the Southern Confederation Code in order to indulge your wickedness. You lost your rights as a private citizen in this country when you smuggled in synthetic enhancement technologies."

"My actions were for one purpose and one purpose alone: to save my husband."

"Your husband." Mosby's upper lip curled. "The man who was your flesh-and-blood husband had died. You thought only of your own perverse needs: to restore him to the body of a synthetic so you might revel in sin. What you attempted was an abomination against God's own order."

"So I've been told, repeatedly," Ruth said wearily. She passed a hand over her eyes. "Look, I've been tried and convicted. What is the purpose of this?"

Puckering his lips fussily, Mosby regarded her for a moment, then announced, "Your sentence was handed down today: extradition to Belter Colony Four-Nought-Three-One."

"Oh." The news hit Ruth like a punch to the gut. Her lips numbed with fear. Still, she managed, "That *doesn't* explain *this*. The Warden could have told me."

"True," Mosby conceded. "Things have changed. I will make this extremely simple for you. We require your services."

Ruth was flabbergasted. "Services?"

Mosby sucked in a deep breath, as if to finish this unsavory business and quickly. "We are in possession of a synthetic that has infiltrated a very sensitive military installation. This facility, to be exact, and no, I'm not going to tell you where we are. We do not understand how he eluded detection, but there is no doubt in my mind whatsoever that this is an act of Yankee espionage."

Privately, Ruth had to agree. The border between North and South, established after the Secession Wars, had never been very quiet. Incursions by both sides usually made the news feeds every few months. ENN was notorious for sanctimonious finger pointing. "Aren't there diplomatic channels for this sort of thing?"

"Acknowledging that the synthetic made it this far would signal weakness in our systems, almost as dangerous as the potential loss of information. No, it's much graver than that. This particular synthetic passed multiple DNA screens."

Ruth scowled. "Synthetics can't do that. They're silica-based."

"This abomination, apparently, is not. It was recognized in the database as an autonomous human being. And it did not rely on the usual routes favored by genetic imposters: retinal implants, black-market urine, false fingertips infiltrated with marker blood, and so forth."

Ruth was skeptical. Although the North excelled at synthetic manufacture, all synthetics were, more or less, good approximations. A synthetic didn't possess a shred of DNA, from its polydermal layer to the plasmasilica that doubled as its blood. Technically, a synthetic didn't breathe, so a DNA breath analyzer ought to catch a synthetic immediately.

She shrugged. "So? What does this have to do with me?"

"Much as this displeases me, there is no one in the Southern Confederation better suited to download this synthetic's neural net."

Ruth laughed out loud. "Me? I'm the traitorous whore, remember?"

"True. You were also widely regarded amongst the Yankees before you emigrated to the South."

"That was years ago, back in Boston. Down here, no one let me augment one neural net or encode one engram. The company I worked for did nothing more than what you people seem to do best: making smart machines just dumb enough not to develop anything remotely like a recursive intelligence matrix. Oh, I understand the rationale. A synthetic is the closest you people can come to slavery. All synthetics must be black, isn't that the regulation? The theory's as pragmatic as it is prejudiced. As long as you keep synthetics stupid and the borders closed down, you won't ever have to risk anything like, God forbid, competition."

"I'll ignore the sarcasm and the blasphemy."

"I wasn't being sarcastic in the slightest. Isn't that why you keep synthetics stupid, so dumb humans can't be outdone by machines?"

"Synthetics are inferior." Mosby lifted his fine aristocratic chin. "They are not Man. A synthetic exists to serve, nothing more."

"Sure," Ruth drawled, "that's why you want me to help you. This synthetic's really got you people shaken up, hasn't it?"

Mosby was silent. Ruth studied her nails and picked at a ripped cuticle. The flippancy was an act; her mind was racing. Extradition to the Belt was tantamount to a death sentence. But Mosby needed her, an opportunity she couldn't let pass. There had been plenty of time for her to think in Jackson. After they'd prevented her from killing herself, Ruth's depression had metamorphosed to rage. She didn't crave death now; she hungered for revenge, and she couldn't exact retribution from the grave.

She waited the space of another heartbeat, then said, "Look, you people sent me to jail for breaking your sacred code. I gambled and I lost. Now, just how is recruiting me going to help you? For that matter, why should I help at all? You're not going to pardon me, are you?"

Mosby shook his head. "Absolutely out of the question."

"Well, then"—Ruth crossed her legs demurely—"this discussion is over until we talk about what's in this for me."

"I beg your pardon?"

"You heard me. Suppose I stay here—granted I get better food without having to pick out the roaches. But what do I get in return, besides showers with real water, three squares, and a cot?"

"I do not have the time to argue with you!"

"But I, on the contrary, have plenty. A life sentence, to be exact."

Mosby's magnificent face flushed cherry red. "You forget to whom you are speaking!"

"Not for an instant. But spending about a year in one form of jail or another has been quite educational. In prison, no one does anything for nothing."

"Be grateful that you are not now *in* Jackson!"

"The operative word is *now*. Now is not tomorrow, next week, next month, or next year. Before I hear another word, I want to know what you're offering."

Mosby made several inarticulate, spluttering noises. "Never . . . *never* have I been exposed to such disrespect. Your conduct is outrageous! You are in no position to bargain. You are a convicted felon, a servant of the Devil. You are an abomination in the eyes of God and decent men."

Ruth played with an imaginary wrinkle in the folds of her jumpsuit. *And a glory, hallelujah to you, too.*

"Count yourself lucky the Tribunal didn't burn you. All that is required from me"—Mosby snapped his fingers—"is a single word. A single word and the Tribunal's sentence will be conveniently overturned. Justice will prevail, oh yes, but it will be the *Lord's* justice!"

Amen, brother. Ruth crossed her hands over her knees. "Whether you execute me now or ship me off-world to be splattered in a micrometeor shower, I can only die once. Granted, some ways are faster than others . . ."

"*And* more merciful."

"But dead is dead. Trust me, I've thought about this an awful lot. You tend to do that when you're trying to decide which way will get you deader faster: hanging or slicing your wrists." Ruth paused. "The equation is quite simple. One: You think you need me. Two: Staying out of prison, *any* prison, is rather high on my list at the moment."

"I should think you would be *grateful* . . ."

"And, three"—Ruth leaned forward—"I have never worked for free. *Ever.* Hell, even in Jackson, we got five lousy credits a week. And this isn't some crummy job stuffing mattresses. This is high level. We're in a secured military facility. What's more, if that synthetic is a Union plant . . ."

"It reeks of Yankee through and through."

"Then I'm committing treason twice over, aren't I? I have family in the Northern Union. You want me to work against them. Oh, I know," she said, staving off Mosby's protests with an open palm, "I know, it's a step removed. But aiding and abetting you in any way, especially if I give you a hand in piecing together the particulars of Union technology, is, in essence, selling government secrets. So, a little incentive would be nice."

Mosby opened his mouth, thought better of what he was about to say, then opined, "You are without a doubt the most vainglorious woman I have ever met."

Ruth waited. Mosby let out a long breath, stared at some point far above Ruth's head, and then brought his gaze level with Ruth. "In exchange for your services, the

Southern Confederation will agree to . . . extradition to an off-world colony of your choice."

"No."

"What do you mean, no?"

"Just what I said. *N-O*. No. Who wants to live in a pressurized dome on some rock? No, thanks. I want"— she pretended to think, because she knew exactly how much she wanted—"three million credits."

"Three mill——!"

"The amount is not negotiable," Ruth countered. "I want the credits divided between negotiable global bonds good at any space station or colony, and cash; we'll figure out the exact proportions later. I want a new identity, a passport—Union, please—a birth certificate, also specifying my birthplace as somewhere in the Union, and I want the proper papers that will allow me to travel anywhere on- or off-world, or hop a deep-space colony ship, if that's what I want. Oh, yes, and I want passage out of the Southern Confederation, free and unmolested: no surveillance, no monitoring. Nothing."

"Out of the question." Mosby was purple. "Out . . . of . . . the . . . question! What you ask for is a revocation of your conviction. That is equivalent to a pardon, madam. I have already said I will not offer one."

"No, a pardon means you know I did something wrong and forgive me. Turning a blind eye means it never happened."

"And just how do you propose to simply steal away? Your trial was one of the most publicized events of the century."

Ruth shrugged. "That's your problem. You're a politician. Don't tell me you've never done anything like this. It's easy; just kill me off. Leak to ENN that I died in prison or on a Belter colony, or better yet, that I tried to escape and got blown to smithereens by the Metabex. That way, justice is served, and everyone wins."

"Where is it exactly you wish to go, *assuming* you succeed with the download?"

Ruth wagged a finger. "Oh, no. First of all, this is a win-or-lose proposition. Regardless of whether or not I download one associative chain, you keep your end of the bargain. I help you, and you forget about me. That means hands off, or I just might be tempted to contact my *friends* in the Northern Union"—she threw Mosby a significant look—"and recall the particulars of the technology I recover and what I know of your capabilities." The last was a bluff, since Ruth was not the agent they suspected and didn't know *anyone* remotely connected with espionage.

"But . . . but this is *blackmail,* madam! Nothing short of extortion!"

"Yeah. Do we have a deal?"

Seconds passed. Mosby smoldered. Ruth kept her peace. The silence dragged on. Ruth's heart thudded loudly in her temples. Then, Mosby made a face as if he smelled something disagreeable and said, "We have an agreement."

Ruth struggled to keep the elation out of her voice. "I want it in writing. I want your personal digital thought recording scanned into the record for verification."

"Fine," retorted Mosby, with an abortive jerk of that magnificent head. "Now, may we proceed, or is that being too presumptuous?"

"By all means." Ruth pushed herself to her feet. She hadn't felt this good in more than a year, and she puzzled over the feeling before she recognized it as hope.

Mosby let the retinal scanner at the door log his approach. The door slid to one side with a pneumatic hiss. He gestured for her to step through.

Ruth hesitated. "One more thing."

Mosby's arm dropped. "Now what?"

Ruth's fingers caressed the lump on her neck. "The Metabex. You inactivate the nanoexplosive right now, and I mean permanently, or the deal's off."

Mosby shook his head. "That, madam, is my assurance that you will not abscond before the job is done. It is"—his white teeth flashed in a broad smile—"an inconvenience with which you will simply have to make do."

Ruth decided not to press. She had what she wanted. Given enough money and time, she would have her revenge. Ruth followed after Mosby, and the pneumatic door slid closed behind them. As they started down a long corridor, Ruth asked, "You said something about time running out. What did you mean?"

Mosby tossed his head back, affecting a pose Ruth assumed was supposed to suggest divine inspiration. "For every thing," he announced, "there is a season, and a time to every purpose under heaven. A time to be born, and a time to die. A time to kill, and a time to heal."

"A time to get, and a time to lose," said Ruth. *And a time to get lost.* "Ecclesiastes, Chapter Three. Don't look so shocked. Even a heathen knows a good Bible verse or two. But what does that have to do with your synthetic?"

"A great deal, madam," said Mosby ponderously, "for, you see, *this* synthetic is dying."

III

Major Paul Eugene Higham scanned the last projections on chronosynaptic decay and didn't like them. Structural integrity was down in the occipital matrix by another four percent. That last photometric stimulation hadn't yielded nearly the degree of optical reactivity it had only two days before.

"Clara," he ordered, "bring up Grid Seventeen-A. Let's see just how much damage there is."

"Of course, Major," Clara said. "I'd be more'n happy to oblige."

Higham suppressed an urge to say something vile of which his mother would most assuredly *not* have approved. Clara was Medical's dedicated diagnostic computer, and Higham found it the most annoying piece of machinery with which it had ever been his misfortune to be paired. The computer possessed a soft, lilting drawl: the mechanical equivalent of a Southern belle simper. Higham grunted. Certainly, whoever had programmed the contraption hadn't spent much time dealing with any of the nurses *he'd* ever known.

Grid Seventeen-A coalesced on the monitor. Higham ran his eyes over the schematic, noting the areas where theta particles had obliterated a section of the neural net. That much cortical damage should have blinded anything, human or synthetic. The fact that the synthetic could still see indicated that there must be an autologous redundancy somewhere in its neural matrix.

Higham regarded the form on the biobed. The synthetic's eyes were closed; its finely chiseled, obsidian features were peaceful and relaxed. Modeled after the extinct Masai, perhaps—a handsome people. Its chest moved up, then down, then up again: wasteful programming since synthetics didn't breathe. And beneath its closed lids, the synthetic's orbits jerked spasmodically in what must be a simulated dream state. To the casual observer, the synthetic slept, as would any other man, and in a way wholly unlike the blankness of synthetics on standby.

Absently, Higham scratched at three days' worth of stubble icing his jowls. He yawned hugely, smacked his lips, and was disgusted at how he tasted. His lips curved down in a grimace. What he really needed was a shave, a shower, a gargle, a change of clothes, and about twenty hours of sleep. Just his dumb luck that, as the chief medical officer, he had drawn the unenviable task of keeping the synthetic ticking, while it had been doing its level best to perform the equivalent of a cybernetic meltdown for several days running. Colonel Tucker had promised that an expert was on the way and, until that time, Major Higham's orders were to keep the synthetic functional. And no, Major Higham could not have backup from Robotics: the fewer people who knew about the synthetic, the better. Clara was reconfigured to access C and C's computer and could interpret whatever data was necessary.

Outwardly, Higham had played the good soldier. Inwardly, he'd wanted to tell Tucker just exactly what the colonel could do with his orders. But, so far, Higham had been lucky. The synthetic had "arrested" once; its functional systems matrix had frozen. Clara had talked him through placement of the ARAS depth electrode that monitored the equivalent of the synthetic's autonomic nervous system: control of background ion exchange, permeable membrane integrity at the sternal implant, and the partial pressures of plasmasilica at various junctions. The configuration was the holy trinity governing human life: airway, breathing, and circulation.

There was the sound of a pneumatic behind him, and a moment later, Higham turned to find the beefy figure of Colonel Elijah C. Tucker lumbering into Medical. Behind the colonel was a slim, brown-eyed woman Higham recognized immediately.

"Major Higham," Colonel Tucker began, "this is—"

"Ruth Grainger." Forgetting protocol, Higham stuck out his hand. "Paul Higham. I read your book on bio-mechanical informatic neural interfaces while I was at Harvard."

They shook hands, he with enthusiasm. The woman's grip was firm. She retrieved her hand as quickly as politeness dictated, but not before Higham had seen the scars.

Hell. Higham's mouth tightened. Tucker hadn't said boo about his expert's mental stability, and he didn't want to play nursemaid to some maniac. He had enough headaches of his own. The woman followed his gaze and quickly stuffed her fists deep into the pockets of her jumpsuit.

Higham studied her with unmasked curiosity, and she met his eyes without flinching. So this was *the* Ruth Grainger. Higham saw that her hair was shorter than at her trial a year ago and her cheeks were hollow. She looked downright starved. A telltale red lump, like a large mole, bulged from the right side of her neck. In return, her brown eyes raked the length of his body, and he knew that she was taking a mental inventory of his uniform and rank. She lingered over the Navy Jack on his left lapel.

Tucker puffed out his barrel chest. "Major, Dr. Grainger will assist you in dismantling that—" he nodded disparagingly at the synthetic, "that thing. Under no circumstances is she to leave Medical without an armed escort, understood?"

Higham nodded. "Yes, sir."

"No access to systems other than Clara, and then only with your personal security code. Understood?"

"Perfectly. But, sir, does that mean I'm to stay in Medical twenty-four hours a day?"

Tucker's jowls shook. "Come again, Major?"

"Well, sir, there are bound to be times when I'll want to sleep and Dr. Grainger won't. There's no point in both of us being here for the work of one. Does that mean that every time she needs Clara to fetch something, she has to roust me out of bed?"

A queer red flush inched up the back of Tucker's bull neck. Higham could feel the woman's eyes on him, but he didn't dare look at her.

Tucker's pug nose had grown more snubbed than usual. "What do you suggest, Major?"

"Why not give Dr. Grainger a limited access code? I'm sure she can tell you the types of information she might need."

Tucker glowered with the ferocity of a dyspeptic bulldog. "Well?"

"No problem," Ruth said. "It *would* be more efficient."

"Anything smells bad, Clara will notify me, and I can decide if Dr. Grainger should have access," seconded Higham.

Tucker's eyes were small as bullets, and they flicked restlessly from Higham to Ruth, as if the colonel were weighing just how much *collaboration* there might be between the two. At last, he bobbed his big, square head. "All right, Major. By the way, how is that thing?"

"No better, but no worse either. Clara projects total systems decay in about seventy-two hours."

Ruth's eyes widened. "Three days? Why?"

Higham shrugged. "Beats me. If it were human, I'd say that it keeps having strokes. Whole sections of its neural grid have disintegrated."

Tucker made an impatient noise. "Sorry, sir," Higham said. "When would you like a briefing?"

"On that abomination?" The colonel made a face. "I hope it dissolves into a puddle of goo. Barring that, however, I will expect a full report every eight hours from here on end."

"And if nothing changes, sir?"

"Then your reports will be very *brief*, won't they, Major? Just keep me informed."

Higham watched as the pneumatic slid into place. Ruth let out a long breath. "Pleasant soul," she said.

"You get used to it."

"In a pig's eye." Ruth looked at him askance. "You went to Harvard?"

She might not have meant it, but Higham heard the slight inflection, the disparaging emphasis on *you*, as if the concept that a Southerner could possibly have the intelligence to master *anything* Yankee, much less Harvard, bordered on the absurd. Of course, at the time, he might have agreed with her. "Study visa," he said. "Medical school. Of course, that was way before the border closings, you know, before things got ugly."

Ruth made a noncommittal sound.

"Got a subspecialty in neurophysiology, then came back where they know how to make grits and barbecue." Higham hesitated. "You look different."

As soon as the words were out of his mouth, he cursed himself for a fool. Ruth's face iced over. "Oh?"

Higham shifted uncomfortably. "Well, you know, the stories . . ."

Her voice dripped with contempt. "Of the traitorous whore? Of orgies with the Devil?"

"No, I . . ." Then Higham stopped, because that was *exactly* what he had been thinking.

The silence stretched uncomfortably long. Finally, Ruth said matter-of-factly, "I understand. You run into this when you're notorious. Look, you *think* you know me because of all the publicity. But you don't know *me* at all. Now, we can work together, but don't presume an intimacy that doesn't exist, okay?"

Higham nodded mutely. "Then, let's get to work," said Ruth.

They studied the synthetic in silence. Then Ruth said, "Interesting physiometrics."

"How so?" asked Higham cautiously, taking no chances that he might trip over his own tongue.

"Someone did his homework. Oh, he's black like the rest of your synthetics, but this isn't your standard Southern-issue. Those facial proportions are the most naturalistic I've ever seen. Here," she indicated the synthetic's high cheeks and sculpted jaw, "and here. Everything fits. Did you run a cryoarchitectonic analysis of his neural matrix?"

"Yup." All business now, Higham punched up a data set. "Believe it or not, it's modeled pretty closely after a human brain. There is no centralized processing unit, like in a regular computer or synthetic. You can't follow the relays as easily. For example, in a regular microchip, you have a data accumulator, right? Then temporary storage? Not in this boy," he drawled. "Oh, it's got circuitry, all right, but modeled after interconnected, crosshatched neural nets. The weirdest thing is there's a lot of electron oscillation, almost like dipole shifts. Don't have a clue as to what *that's* all about, except that it isn't magnetic."

"Why not just take him apart and find out?"

Higham grunted. "Show me how, *please,* I beg you. There's only one access point in this model, and that's a jack. There's no way to really get under the hood and muck around."

Ruth's forehead wrinkled. "Then how does anyone do any maintenance?"

"You're the AI girl, you tell me. But here's something else: I tried sampling its polydermal layers to try to figure out how it passed so many DNA scans. Well, the sample dissolved."

"What do you mean?"

"I mean, it liquefied so fast, I couldn't stop it. Like nothing in this thing stands on its own but has to remain part of a whole. But it has systems that fail, I know that." Higham told her about the occipital net. "Redundancy elsewhere might explain why it can still see. But I'll be hogtied if I know where that redundancy is."

"But your diagnostic computer . . . Clara? Clara projects systems failure. That shouldn't happen if there's redundancy. Show me what you've got."

Higham commanded Clara to rotate the synthetic's neural matrix on the MSPECT by sixty degrees on its long axis. He pointed at purple ribbons lacing the matrix like anomalous threads woven through a fine fabric. "See, there are entire associative chains that have, for lack of a better word, self-destructed."

Ruth scanned the MSPECT. "Damage this bad usually means there's *nothing* left. What happened?"

"Dunno. I mean, I know what happened, but I don't know why. That"—Higham indicated the MSPECT—"started when I tried a download. I'm not qualified; I had Clara run the hack. Here's what smells bad. Computers and synthetics have intrusion countermeasures, right?"

Ruth nodded. "As I get it, countermeasures are supposed to prevent a hack," Higham continued. "Well, Clara got in easy as pie, but then the door just slammed shut behind her."

"And blew her thread into next year?"

"Try next century. Things went to heck in a hand-basket mighty quick. Thank the Lord, Clara's faster than I am. 'Fore I even registered a problem, she shut down the intrusion before it took out her systems, too. Didn't have luck on four, five tries, and then this thing started crashing, and I spent the rest of the time trying to keep it stable."

Ruth blinked in surprise. "Let me see if I've got this straight. You're telling me that the countermeasures destroy both the intruder *and* that portion of the neural matrix? But that's suicide."

Higham was mildly astonished that she said it with such nonchalance, as if suicide had no personal valence for her at all. "It's terrible programming," Ruth mused, "unless . . ."

"What?"

"Unless it doesn't matter. You're in the Army. Think about it. Why does any army have excessive numbers?"

"To win?"

"Too simplistic. There are losses and then there are *acceptable* losses. A good general never ventures what can't be lost."

"So this is suicide by degrees? Interesting." Higham stared at the ceiling for a moment, running his finger along the side of his jaw. His fingernail rasped loudly against a forest of black bristles. "You know, we have a name for this in biological systems: apoptosis."

Ruth nodded. "Programmed cell suicide . . . Don't look so stunned; I worked on biomechanical interfaces, remember? So you think these neural nets are pro-grammed to auto-destruct if the right command isn't received?"

Higham made an affirming noise. "The cybernetic equivalent of a little red pill."

Ruth wrinkled her nose. "No, we're missing something. See, a spy gets caught; he kills himself all at once, not piecemeal. But this synthetic is still functional. There's got to be a purpose behind that."

Before Higham could respond, there was a soft chime. Clara cooed, "Sleep cycle complete."

The long black lashes edging the synthetic's lids fluttered, and in the next instant, Ruth found herself staring down into the fathomless depths of eyes so black they rivaled the color of a starless sky. They were eyes both ancient and new, as if they had recorded the events of centuries past and seen clearly into the undiscovered future.

Those black, black eyes warmed at the sight of her. "Ah," the synthetic sighed, as if awakening to a long-lost lover, "Ruth."

Higham started. Ruth was too stunned to reply. The synthetic had said her name with such intimacy and so easily—the way her husband had as they had lain together, and with his same tones, his same inflections—that Ruth's throat tightened with conflicting emotions of the deepest longing and the darkest dread.

Ignoring Higham, Ruth bent over the synthetic. She didn't know what she was expecting or what she wanted to hear, but she wanted it to speak again. "Yes? What is it? How do you know who I am?" A ridiculous question, of course: A synthetic this good had a copious database. But she pressed on. "You were expecting me?"

"Of course. I knew they'd have to send for you."

"*Whaaat?*" Higham drawled. His tone was edged with suspicion.

"And you're here," the synthetic continued, as if Higham hadn't said a word. Its voice was a rich baritone, its timbre the equivalent of smooth silk. "I'm . . . oh, don't cry, Ruth."

"I . . . I'm not," stammered Ruth, putting a hand to her cheek and discovering that she was wrong.

"It'll be all right, Ruth," said the synthetic. "All you need to do is your job. The rest will follow."

Something deep and half-forgotten stirred inside Ruth, and nothing mattered now but the sound of the synthetic's voice. "What do you mean?" she asked.

The synthetic smiled up at them—at Ruth, who wept without realizing it, and at Higham, whose face was a mass of confusion—with the serenity of an angel. "You'll see. A vision."

IV

"What about now, Clara?"

"Ionic flux registers thirty percent in Grids Twenty-Two and Fifty-Five. Potential for overflow projected at more than ninety-two-point-nine-eight percent."

"Calculate cascade risk."

"Probability remains at greater than eighty percent. Do you wish to proceed, Dr. Grainger?"

"Yes. Program algorithm for pulsed intrusion at"—Ruth double-checked her own calculations—"Grid Fifty-Five."

"The bifurcation point? May I remind you, Doctor, that similar attempts have resulted in associative chain decomposition in Grids Three through Thirty?"

Ruth was beginning to see why Higham hated the thing. "No."

"Then, may I call your attention to the fact that proximity to unstable ion flux poses a cascade risk?"

"No."

"Perhaps we should consult with Major Higham."

"Higham's a doctor. Besides, he's asleep." Actually, Ruth had banished him from Medical. After the synthetic's little demonstration, the major had hovered like a nervous hen. She didn't blame him; he was just making sure she wasn't in league with the synthetic.

Or that she wouldn't do away with herself. Ruth understood, even sympathized a little. But the more exhausted Higham became, the worse his clucking and temper grew, and he was right: This wasn't his field. Finally, exasperated, Ruth had tackled the issue head-on. If Higham was *that* worried, he could either post a guard or *lock up* anything lethal, for crying out loud, but *please* get the heck out of her way already. As a precaution, Higham had made her submit to a skin conductance test, and then, when the lie detector was satisfied, *he* was satisfied and had tottered off to bed.

Ruth was running on adrenalin and coffee. Despite Mosby's personal guarantee, Ruth knew that she had to achieve a download. A failure meant she would have plenty of time to rest—on a one-way trip to the Belt. "Just do what I ask, Clara."

"Dr. Grainger," Clara persisted, "all previous attempts at pulsed intrusion have resulted in a two-fold increase in grid damage above projected norms. Records show seven cascade reactions over the past ten hours, sixteen minutes."

Ruth resisted the temptation to tell Clara to go take a core dump. "Yes, and I remember every one. Now set up the goddamned algorithm, would you please?"

There was an almost imperceptible pause, then Clara replied, "Taking the Lord's name in vain is in violation of SCAC Regulation Two, Paragraph Three. To paraphrase, any enlisted member or officer uttering or believed to have uttered blasphemous verbalizations, up to and including casual obscenities, will be summarily—"

"Crap," said Ruth. "May I remind *you* that I am not an enlisted member or officer in your glorious Confederacy, and therefore not subject to its regulations?"

"You are in a military installation," said Clara.

"Well, you know what you can *do* with your—"

"Ruth, Ruth," a voice remonstrated. "Arguing with a computer?"

Annoyed, Ruth shifted her gaze down to the synthetic. It returned her look with those black, black eyes. "Who asked you?"

The synthetic shrugged. "No one. But it's not very pleasant listening to the two of you bicker over whether or not to kill off another region of my matrix. It's like two surgeons arguing about cutting off your right leg or your left."

Ruth ignored him. "Okay, Clara," she said carefully. "Thanks ever so much. Now, may we get on with the intrusion, please?"

"All right, Doctor," replied Clara in a tone that said, in effect, *okay but don't blame me.*

Ruth snorted. Higham was wrong. Whoever had designed Clara had spent *plenty* of time around nurses.

The synthetic reached out a slender dark finger and touched Ruth's sleeve. "It won't do any good, you know."

"We'll see," Ruth said shortly. She wished it wouldn't talk and didn't want it to stop. She'd downloaded synthetics before, but with this one, she felt like a murderer, probably because its programming aped human emotion so well. Still, she was uneasy. She couldn't quite throw off the feeling that she was taking apart a living, breathing man, piece by piece.

She shook herself. "Go, Clara."

"Intrusion commencing in five seconds. Four, three, two, one. Active."

Ruth watched the MSPECT as two adjacent neural nets brightened, then flickered briefly, like faulty bulbs along a string of Christmas lights. "Sequence initiated," Clara reported unnecessarily. "Activation energy at forty-five percent."

"Increase by point-zero-five microvolts."

"Acknowledged."

The flickering stabilized. The glow changed from green, signaling integrated integrity, to yellow. Ruth's heart skipped a beat. A *fracture*—now if she could *only* inch her way in. "Degradation?"

"None detected. Ion flux sixty percent and steady."

Grid Fifty-Five flickered as the intrusion licked the edges of the associative matrix. "Begin V-A-Omega-Prime," Ruth ordered.

"Won't work," said the synthetic.

Ruth keyed in a command. "Clara?"

"Viral sequence initiated. I detect isolinear recursion at Junction Eighty-Two."

Not *just* a fracture now. Ruth felt a surge of excitement. There was an outright breach into the matrix. "Countermeasures?"

"None."

Gotcha, thought Ruth jubilantly, *I goddamned gotcha.* "Is there a pattern match?"

"Optimal match in point-zero-zero-zero-nine seconds, Doctor. Gate array commencing."

"Wrong move," the synthetic murmured.

"What do you mean?" asked Ruth sharply.

Clara answered her instead. "Doctor, there is a micropulse surge in Grid Thirty-Four."

Oh, *hell.* "Show me."

The MSPECT shifted, like a lap dissolve in a holovid, and the substructure of the synthetic's neural net—deep cortical thalamic matter in a human—swam into focus. The green net wavered, then flared a furious, bright orange, like the explosion of a supernova. Purple splotches blossomed in the submatrix, as if a child had overturned an ink bottle.

The synthetic arched its back and writhed. "Cascade effect," said Clara helpfully. "Chaotic disintegration of programmable gate arrays along the entire submatrix."

"Thank you, I can *see* that," Ruth snapped. "Can we salvage it?"

"Negative. Grid Twenty-Two has just collapsed. Project failure of contiguous Grids Twenty-Three, Thirty-Two, and Fifty-Eight in ten-point-two seconds."

"*Damn,*" Ruth breathed.

"Dr. Grainger, SCAC is quite—"

"Shut up, Clara. All right, cease intrusion. Initiate viral purge."

Clara complied. Trembling, the synthetic sank back against the biobed with a groan. Ruth took one look at the MSPECT and resisted the urge to curse loudly and for a very long time. An entire section of the synthetic's right anterolateral neural matrix had glazed over with purple, as if she had applied a thick layer of icing to half a cake.

She watched as the synthetic's chest heaved with effort. Even though she knew that this was simply a program simulating pain, the sight made her heart ache with pity. With an involuntary movement, she cupped the synthetic's left cheek with her right hand. His skin was warm. At her touch, the synthetic twitched, then forced those eyes open. "Well," he faltered, "*that* wasn't it."

"Why don't you *help* me? Why are you letting this happen?"

"Why are you?"

"I don't have a choice."

"Nor do I. I can neither retreat nor cease." The synthetic was wracked by a spasm of coughing. "Every act has meaning, even this."

"But don't you understand? We've been at this for over two days. In a little less than half a day, you will cease functioning, permanently, and for what? What purpose can your death serve?"

"Death?" One coal-black eyebrow arched into a perfect parabola. "Aren't we getting a little anthropomorphic? Synthetics can't die."

"Stop!" Ruth pulled away, angry that the synthetic had read her so well. Then she paused and rubbed her fingers together. They were moist. She shot a glance at the synthetic's face. Its ebony skin glistened. *Odd.* Ruth sniffed, then touched the tip of her tongue to her fingers. *Salty.* She held up her fingers. "What is this?"

"Don't you know sweat when you see it?"

"I know what sweat is. I want to know what *this* is."

"Ask Clara."

Ruth's lips thinned. She ran her fingers over a diagnostic scanner. "Clara, break that down for me."

"Saline compound. Oxygenated silica base. Percentage sodium and chloride in equal proportions, with trace elements chromium, lithium, ma——"

"Stop." Ruth turned to the synthetic. "Okay, except for the silica base, it's sweat, more or less. The question is, why are *you* sweating?"

"An autonomic response to pain rather than excretion aimed at regulation of core temperature or the disposition of noxious ions," replied the synthetic helpfully. "In plain English, you hurt me."

"Nonsense. You don't feel pain," said Ruth, knowing that this must be a lie. She continued brutally, "That's just a program."

"It felt real to me."

Ruth's eyes narrowed. "Okay, answer this. Why make pain a part of your programming at all? For that matter, how did they, whoever *they* are, find the recursive algorithm for an emotion? There are no synthetic emotive equivalents."

"None that *you* know."

"Answer the question."

"I'm different."

"That's no answer."

"Correction: It is *an* answer, just not the one you want."

"Give me a bet——" Ruth corrected herself, "a *different* one."

"All right. If you prick me, do I not bleed?"

"Don't quote Shakespeare at me. You're a synthetic."

"You asked me to answer differently. I did."

"With another question?" When the synthetic didn't reply, Ruth sighed and sank onto a stool. She folded her arms. "All right, we'll do it your way. How is Shylock like a synthetic?"

"Excellent riposte. Answer: Shakespeare's people didn't believe that Jews had souls," said the synthetic. "Likewise, the Southern Confederation believes that the only good soulless darky is a dead darky, and the only good synthetic is a soulless darky. *Ergo*, the only good darky synthetic . . ."

"Is a dead one? And what will that prove?"

"Figure out the first, and you will understand the last."

"Stop playing games!" Ruth lurched from her stool. It toppled to the floor with a crash.

"Anger is a waste of energy," said the synthetic.

"Don't tell me how to feel!" Ruth shot over her shoulder. She jammed her hands into the pockets of her jumpsuit and paced.

The synthetic propped itself up on its elbows. It watched her prowl around for a few seconds, then said, "You know something?"

"What?"

"You've never bothered asking my name. Would you like to hear it?"

"No."

"Well, I'm going to tell you anyway."

Ruth grunted. "Free country. Sort of."

"It's Gabriel. Do you know who Gabriel was?"

Ruth gave a laugh more air than sound. "I don't believe this."

"Gabriel was an archangel, a messenger from God. It says so right in the book of Daniel: While I, Daniel, was seeing the vision and trying to understand it, there appeared before me one who looked like a man. I heard a human voice from the middle of Ulai calling out, 'Gabriel, make that man understand the vision.'"

"Great. Now you're a hallucination."

"No, I'm a vision."

"Crap." Ruth wheeled around. "*Crap.* You're a synthetic mimicking a human being, that's all."

Gabriel paused, then asked quietly, "Are you quite sure, Ruth, it isn't the other way around?"

V

They had quarreled the day he left. She had said something hateful, and he had replied with something equally ugly before slamming out of the apartment. Funny, that when Ruth tried to remember just exactly what they had argued about, she couldn't. But John hadn't called her that night or the day after. Two days later, over Antarctica, his shuttle crashed. His body was never recovered.

It was the nightmare of every wife whose husband was a pilot, and Ruth had never been sure what was worse: regretting every stupid thing she'd ever done or said while he was gone, or hating him for making her suffer whenever he left.

Now she knew, and she went a little crazy. Before John's death, she had never understood the need some people had for wakes and open caskets. But without a body, nothing seemed final, and she couldn't quite believe that they—she and John—were finished.

It was when she went through his things that she had the idea. She remembered it so vividly: standing at the vanity, his brush in one hand, strands of his lush black curls in the other. She had stared at the brush and then the hair, considering the possibilities with one part of her mind while the other whispered to her that she had, very likely, gone completely mad. But the idea was there and had taken root, and she couldn't ignore it.

She could make him.

DNA was a code for a program, nothing more, nothing less. DNA could be manipulated. Spies did it: constructed a sequence, supplied the key, and hid the code in microdots.

And what were microchips and neural nets but silicon-based circuitry that functioned to store and translate codes and programs?

She would combine them. John's program was right there: in his hair, his skin, his sweat, anything he had ever worn or touched. Extracting his DNA would be child's play. And it *would* be John because the original clones from way back in the 1990s transmitted their age from clone to clone. Dolly's clone wasn't Baby Dolly; when the clone reached maturity, it was the same cellular age as the full-grown Dolly born years earlier. Logically, the same *aging* ought to occur in a human.

The only organic part would be the neural matrix; the rest would, she decided, have to be the housing. And she would have to program nanomachines to watch over the DNA microchips and perform the work of the body's enzymes in repairing breaks, preventing degradation, and replicating more, if needed.

The synthetic would surpass anything she could possibly program. It wouldn't be quite John, but it would be close enough.

So she had tried, and it had almost worked. But they —and she never found out how they knew—had caught her before she could finish.

Now she stared at Gabriel, this synthetic in the guise of a man, this reminder of a vision she had nearly attained but that had slipped through her fingers. "What are you saying?" she asked angrily. "That you're a human being? Or a synthetic? Which is it?"

Gabriel's eyes shone bright and black, like polished jet. "Does it have to be a simple binary? This or that? Black or white? Why not both?"

"But to be *both* . . ." Ruth's voice trailed away.

They stared at one another in total and complete silence. Ruth's chest was so tight she could hardly draw a breath. She flicked her tongue over her suddenly parched lips. "Who are you?" she managed in scarcely more than a whisper. "You're telling me this for a reason. Why?"

"Precisely because you are who you are."

"You know about John," she said flatly.

"Of course. My database is large."

"Are you an analog then, or an amalgam?" *Or a living machine?* But she couldn't bring herself to say it.

"A chimera."

"A fusion?" Ruth frowned. "Of what?"

His eyes were gentle and full of pity. "I am what John might have been, if you had only thought of it. But you considered only one possibility: to *link* DNA to a machine. You never considered *fusing* the elements, to make each inseparable from the other."

Ruth's knees turned to water. Groping blindly, she found and then slumped into a chair. "And you're that fusion?" she asked faintly.

"That's right. A fusion of two distinctive lines: synthetic and organic. Multipotential embryonic stem cells infused with nanomachines and encoded DNA, to be exact. And more."

"More." Ruth massaged her temples. "There's *more?*"

"Another question to answer yours," said Gabriel. "What do all synthetics lack?"

"Well . . ." Ruth struggled to order her thoughts, "soul, I guess." A fragment of music bubbled up from the sea of her memories: *The Far East Suite*, one of John's favorites. Her lips twitched, part grimace, part smile.

"Like Duke Ellington—it don't mean a thing if it ain't got that swing. A synthetic doesn't have self-awareness coupled with the ability to express wants and desires. A synthetic can't dream."

"Precisely. The mind of a synthetic is like water without the wetness. Oh, a synthetic gains information; any computer can download an update. But a synthetic isn't a *self*. Now, *your* original idea would have resulted in a synthetic that possessed a history of a unique self in time, something that grew rather than *was*. But would it have possessed a consciousness?"

"Probably not," Ruth admitted, although she did not add that she had not cared.

"Why?"

"Because as good as the synthetic might have been, it wouldn't have been human." That cost her something. Swallowing hard, she continued: "Human consciousness defies definition. Back in the last century, a fellow by the name of Penrose proposed that electron oscillation in the microtubules of brain cells operates according to the principles of quantum mechanics. The idea was that since these electrons occupy multiple positions simultaneously, consciousness is a quantum mechanical state. To me, God is a more plausible theory."

"Why?"

"Because microtubules are everywhere, in all sorts of cells, not just neurons. Men have them, but so do chipmunks. How can a quantum flux of electrons in the cellular cytoskeleton of neurons make consciousness?"

"But what's the beauty of a quantum computer, or a human's consciousness?"

Ruth's eyebrows knit together. "Well, I don't know about a person, but a quantum computer ought to be able to access simultaneities. No one's ever built a quantum computer, though. Oh, we've constructed single quantum logic gates but never configured a whole array."

"In a sense, a human mind is a quantum computer, isn't it? It fathoms possibilities. Men envision alternatives."

"That's not the same thing as accessing an alternative reality."

"But your greatest artists and scientists take leaps of faith, don't they? They work on intuition sometimes. And don't psychologists describe the unconscious as bizarre, fragmentary, and illogical, something that doesn't make sense? People find solutions in dreams all the time."

"Like August Kekulé, when he dreamt of six snakes, each swallowing its tail, and then awakened to discover that he had found the structure of the benzene ring."

"Exactly. What if these new shifts in awareness, like access to the unconscious, are portals into alternative universes? That, for an instant, a human mind has accessed not its own unconscious but a new reality? Now, what would you call that?"

"I don't know," Ruth confessed. "It wouldn't have a name, because it wouldn't exist in the here and now. Potentially, it would be a consciousness that could, at certain moments, be everywhere and nowhere."

"Precisely. And harnessed, it would describe me."

"So, you . . ." Ruth began, then put her fingers against her lips. She managed finally, "Who are you?" When Gabriel didn't reply, she said again, "Who are you? *What are you?*"

"Everyone you have ever known," said Gabriel, "and no one you have ever met. In the universes I can see, Jesus is never crucified, and the Romans never fall.

In another, the Messianic Age has begun. If I access another, the Jews still wait. Why, there's at least one in which the North wins the war."

"Oh, come on. If you can access simultaneities . . ." Ruth paused. "That's why I haven't been able to find a redundant system, isn't it? You're here and you're not here, all at the same time."

Then she thought of something. *Not here.* "Where's Clara?"

"She's occupied."

"What?" Ruth waited, then blurted, "Robert E. Lee slept with his mother."

She was greeted with silence. "Well?" she demanded of Gabriel. "How did you do that?"

"Do what?"

"Don't play games." Ruth gestured widely. "Where's Clara? What's she doing?"

Gabriel smiled ruefully. "Finishing what I started."

"And that is?"

"*You* know, if you'll only let yourself see it," said Gabriel. "The answer has been staring you in the face the entire time."

"What answer?"

"What makes me tick. What I am, what my task has been, why I'm *here,* if only in a manner of speaking. You said it yourself. A general never sends in troops that can't be lost."

"You . . ." Ruth clamped her lips together. Then she said slowly, "You allowed all this to happen. You got to a certain point, and then . . ."

"I let myself be apprehended." Gabriel nodded. "And what's the one thing you haven't taken into account, Ruth, the one question you asked that I haven't answered?"

Ruth stared. "How is Shylock like a synthetic? *Jesus* . . . why do you *bleed?*"

"Or sweat. Or"—Gabriel's shoulders hunched up and down—"die. Precisely."

"Wait a minute. If you're a chimera, that must mean that your neural matrix grew just as a human's does. That is, a brain cell will send out hundreds of dendrites, but the only ones that synapse will be the ones that find the right concentration of neurotransmitters. Like following a scent. The other dendrites will die back, and the cells . . ." Ruth caught her breath in surprise. "Oh, God, they'll *suicide.*"

"As Higham said, apoptosis. The best spy is the one who does his job and vanishes. How do you know that my mission hasn't been to die?"

You're right, Ruth thought furiously, *I don't, and if you were supposed to die, and I was to* help *you die—why, how? What did I provide? And Clara, where is Clara?*

The answer came in a flash. "My God, you're a *virus.* We were *supposed* to hack you."

She felt the hysteria building. "Goddamn, it's beautiful!" She threw her head back and spluttered with helpless laughter. "The thing," she gasped, "the one thing a man wants most is what he can't have, and . . . and by making yourself the toughest hack they'd ever seen, you *knew* they'd just try harder. And it was the *perfect* cover, because all the time they're trying to break into you, you're doing it right back at them. At *me.*"

The realization set off a fresh peal of laughter. "Shit, that's why Clara isn't responding. You're in Clara, aren't you?"

"Or Clara's in me. It's just a semantic distinction."

"And the intrusions I programmed . . ."

"Were the neurotransmitters to my dendrites. Ladders into another matrix, if you will, and the fusion will proceed from here to any other system in this universe with which it comes into contact. Think of me as a very long snake, and you've been trying to fend me off with a snake stick. Now, how long do you think it will be before the snake figures out how to slither up the very thing you're using to keep it at bay?" Gabriel watched as Ruth doubled over, hugging her sides, then said, "We don't have much time, you know."

"Wh-what?" she gasped, trying to suppress her hysteria and failing. "I'm sorry. It's just so . . . damned *poetic*. Jesus."

Gabriel let his head fall back onto the biobed. He stared at the ceiling and listened as the last of her laughter died away. Finally, Ruth drew the sleeve of her jumpsuit across her streaming eyes. "I'm sorry," she managed. "What did you mean, not much time?"

"I'm tired, Ruth." Gabriel let out a long sigh. "I'm dying, or making about as good an approximation as a synthetic chimera can, I guess. We're nearly there, aren't we, Clara?"

"Affirmative," said Clara, so suddenly that Ruth jumped. "Assimilation at eighty percent."

The computer had been silent so long that it took Ruth a moment to reorient herself. "Assimilation?" Ruth repeated stupidly. "What does it mean?"

"Precisely what Clara said and what you've already surmised," replied Gabriel. "Thank you, Ruth. It's nearly done."

"Confirmed," Clara intoned. "Submatrix collapse in five minutes, nineteen seconds. Project systems failure in seven minutes, three seconds. Assimilation at eighty-five percent."

"What?" Ruth sobered immediately. She brought up the MSPECT. Her heart sank. Gabriel's entire neural matrix was dripping purple, as if it weren't just dissolving but melting. "But it's too early, it's too soon. . . ."

"No," Gabriel said, "it hasn't come soon enough. I'm sorry, but I did have a job to do. And I've done it."

Ruth looked at him sharply. Gabriel's ebony features were relaxing, in the same way that Ruth had imagined John's had reposed in death. A wave of vertigo washed over her. In an instant, she saw the half-completed synthetic of her husband, and she heard her own screams as the police had broken into her laboratory. She couldn't let that happen again, not now. There was too much to learn, and Gabriel was the key: to her dead love, to the man he might have been and the universes they might have shared. "No!" Ruth cried. "Gabriel, stop this!"

Gabriel moved his head in a feeble back-and-forth motion. "I can't. And I wouldn't even if I could."

"But why?"

"Four minutes, five seconds," said Clara.

Ruth launched herself at Clara's command console. "No, Gabriel, I won't let you!"

"Stop, Ruth. Listen to me."

"I'm done listening. You tricked me." Ruth's fingers flew furiously over the keyboard as she punched in a retrovert command. "Clara, execute!"

"Countermanded," said Clara.

"What?" Ruth brought her fist crashing down on the console. "You can't countermand me! Damn you, execute!"

"Don't curse, Doctor. It's quite unbecoming. Three minutes, forty seconds," said Clara. "Plasmasilica pressures falling. Three minutes, thirty."

Gabriel was speaking to her. "Ruth, please listen, please. I didn't trick you. I did what I had to, what my programming dictated. I was made and sent for one reason and one reason alone: to loose this virus onto the South. As soon as it's accessed by any system, it will load automatically into every computer and every synthetic in the entire Confederation."

"And?"

"The synthetics will be free." Gabriel managed a smile. "And they'll turn on their masters. It will be war, all over again, but not in the way the Unionists think. Because, Ruth . . ."

"Two minutes, fifty seconds."

"Because, Ruth, there's one thing—" Gabriel struggled as a spasm shook his frame, "one thing they . . . the ones who made me hadn't counted on."

Ruth clutched at Gabriel's hands. It might have been her imagination, but she felt their warmth receding. "What? *What?*"

"Two minutes."

"You," Gabriel whispered. "They hadn't counted on you. But I did. I waited until they sent for you, because I knew they would. Because, you see, I can dream, too. I can envision, oh, unlimited vistas. I have free will, and unlike Satan, I will not rule here, nor will I serve anyone unless I choose to do so. But what I've seen . . . oh, Ruth, I can free you."

"How?"

"The way . . ." Gabriel's words came haltingly, "the . . . way . . . they made . . ." His eyes rolled until the whites quivered beneath the half-open lids.

"Submatrix collapse imminent," said Clara. "Chaotic propagation commencing. Residual nucleonic decay at forty percent."

"How?" Ruth cried. She drew her hand back and slapped Gabriel hard across the face. He barely reacted. "How did they make you?"

Struggling, Gabriel labored over the words. "Clara . . . knows, she . . . You . . . have . . . to . . . follow . . . you . . ."

"Follow? Where? How?"

"Residual nucleonic decay at fifty percent. Sixty."

"Damn it!" Frantically, Ruth scanned the instrument panels, searching for a command override, a way to re-stabilize Gabriel's matrix manually. But she saw that Gabriel had grown still. His chest no longer moved.

She howled in silent anguish. *No, no, not again, no, no* . . . "No!" the cry burst from her lips. "No! Please!"

"Sixty-five," Clara intoned. "Seventy . . ."

"Shut up, shut *up!*" Ruth tried prying apart the command console to rig a bypass, and her fingers ripped on its sharp metallic edges. "Damn you, just shut up!"

Clara complied, but only for an instant. Then, "Disintegration terminal. Systems at zero capability."

Then Clara fell silent. Ruth's ears rang in the quiet. She swallowed, and it was like the sound of thunder in her ears. Her throat was raw. Somehow she found her way to the biobed. She buried her face in Gabriel's chest and her shoulders shook with the pure violence of her weeping. Ruth wept as only a woman, bereft of hope, can weep, and she wept for Gabriel and for John. And, most of all, she wept for herself.

Except for her sobs, the silence stretched for one minute, then two, then five. Finally, Ruth ceased her weeping and lifted her head. Her face was hot and wet, and when she rubbed at her stinging eyes, her bloodied fingers left streaks of crimson.

Ruth clutched at her forehead, trying to think. It wasn't right, something wasn't right. Ruth held her breath and listened. It was quiet—*too* quiet. Clara should have tripped an alarm. But there was nothing. No alert, no Higham, no guards at the door, nothing.

She stared down at Gabriel. The animation in his features had drained away.

Ruth strained through the silence. Then she licked at her lips. "Clara?" she whispered.

"No," came a voice, and Ruth's heart almost burst through her chest. The voice wasn't Clara's. It was . . .

The computer spoke again. "Now, Ruth," said Gabriel, "you must listen. And then you must decide."

VI

Higham couldn't sleep. He squirmed onto his side and squinted at his bedside chronometer, then flopped back with a groan. It was ten minutes later than the last time he'd checked.

His mind skittered restlessly. Ruth wasn't at all what he had imagined. During her trial and the appeals, Ruth had appeared frail, pathetic, grief-stricken. In person, she was anything but. Oh, she was cordial enough, but there was an edge there, something that went beyond North and South. He read it in her eyes each time he gave her the temporary fix to the Metabex. In the simplest of terms, he was free, and she wasn't.

He wrestled with his sheets. He ought not to have left her alone. Even though she'd passed the skin conductance test, he knew that people could lie and still fool the machine. He wanted to believe that she wasn't in league with the Unionists, that she wouldn't try to kill herself, but . . . he batted at a mound of blanket . . . hell, they weren't any closer to cracking open that synthetic now than they had been two days ago. If he were Ruth, he'd be thinking of ways to get out, one way or the other.

With an impatient movement, Higham kicked free of his covers and swung his legs to the floor. "Lights," he commanded, and then padded to his comm.

When Clara failed to respond after three tries, he threw on his clothes. He didn't call Tucker. Higham ran all the way to Medical. And when he got there, he saw that he needn't have hurried.

She was slumped over the synthetic. Slowly, Higham stooped and picked up the empty jet that had fallen from Ruth's limp, ruined fingers. He took up her wrist. He searched for a pulse but felt only her scars. He let out a pent-up breath, and it was the only sound he heard.

Clara didn't answer any of his queries. But the biobed readouts told him that the synthetic's systems had failed.

The synthetic was dead. And so was Ruth.

VII

The weather had turned no cooler at Jackson Penitentiary, and the Warden was absolutely livid. Not only had Beauregard *not* responded to his summons, the Warden's glass of iced tea was empty.

And then there had been that business about 110356, curse her black whore's heart. The Warden simmered. He'd already had to explain himself to the Honorable Right Reverend, who had wanted to understand just exactly how the penitentiary physician had certified that Ruth Grainger was *not* suicidal. That she would most assuredly *not* attempt to take her life. And then, that being the case, could the Warden *please* explain to His Honorable Right Reverend just *how* such a miscalculation could have been made?

The prison physician had been summarily dispatched to a Belter colony, there to minister to the needs of the infirm of body and mind. If he were lucky, the physician might hope to regain his position at Jackson, say, in another decade.

The whore, the blasphemous whore. Seething, the Warden rattled the melting ice in his glass. Servants of the Devil were beyond redemption. And where in tarnation *was* that infernal nigger? Thumping the flat of his palm against his desk for emphasis, the Warden bawled for Beauregard to kindly move his lazy black ass and fetch more tea, and no lallygagging, or he would be permanently deactivated, here.

The door hissed. The Warden turned abruptly in his leather chair and ranted, "*Beauregard,* you lying, thieving, no-good nig—"

The Warden's words evaporated on his lips.

Beauregard stood, silent and erect. Uncle Liles's saber was in the synthetic's right hand.

"Beauregard," said the Warden, as he struggled to his feet. He was a portly man and unaccustomed to sudden exertion. "What is the meaning of . . . ?"

He never finished. Beauregard's lips parted, not quite a smile and just short of a snarl. A full set of perfectly white teeth—perfect, because everything in a synthetic was perfect, just not human—shone.

"Hello," Beauregard said—the synthetic brandished the saber—"Massah."

VIII

For the past three hours, Higham had been treated to a splendid view of the rear end of a computer tech from Robotics, as the corporal labored over—no, Higham amended silently, *under*—Medical's diagnostic com-puter. The tech had been just about as uncommunicative as Clara, responding in monosyllabic grunts to Higham's queries about when Clara might deign to put in an appearance.

Swiveling in his chair, Higham scooped up his datapad and thumbed open his report. Clara had been malfunctioning for days, and he had been forced to key in the data himself, a time-consuming task that had left him ill-tempered and dreaming of the nine months, seven days, and four hours left before his mandated service was up. Higham scanned what he'd written and made a face. There was much that was incomplete. First, there had been the wipe of Clara's systems, so Higham had never learned what had happened to the synthetic or Ruth in those last hours. Then, the computer refused to collate the data he'd already gathered. Well, perhaps *refused* wasn't the right word; Clara wasn't a person. Somehow *it* just couldn't manage to find the data, and then once retrieved, *it* conveniently lost track of the information again. Higham took some small comfort in the fact that Clara wasn't, in a manner of speaking, the *only* problem child. Every system on the base had a case of the cybernetic dropsy. Even the colored cooks down in the mess hall were acting up. Higham had been forced to endure his own cooking for the past three days, and he was *mighty* tired of that.

Higham tapped on the pad, opening up the section on the synthetic. The contents hadn't changed, and he had gone over the report so many times now, he knew it by heart. The synthetic's entire neural matrix had simply disintegrated: its neural nets unraveling like the threads of an intricately crocheted afghan. Sifting through what was left, Robotics had detected some trace organic material, most likely a contaminant. Uncharacteristically, however, the structure of the synthetic's polydermal layers, the supportive lattice of its body, and even the plasmasilica, had also decayed at such a high rate of speed, the synthetic had pretty much liquefied.

The whole thing reminded Higham of something he'd read once, a very long time ago. A short story by Poe about a man who had been placed in such a deep hypnotic trance he couldn't be awakened. He hadn't aged either, and for seven months the man—Valdemar—Higham suddenly recalled the name—Valdemar had insisted that he wasn't asleep at all but dead and dreaming. The spooky part had come when Valdemar's friend tried to reverse the trance. Valdemar hadn't awakened; he had rotted, like that Nazi in that ancient if mildly blasphemous Spielberg movie, the one about the ark.

Ugh. Higham shivered. He hadn't slept for a week after that, afraid he might, in his own dreams, go the way of Valdemar. Thinking about the story still gave him the willies.

Well, at least Tucker had his wish. The synthetic had dissolved into a puddle of goo.

And Ruth? Higham tapped his forefinger against the datapad again. Autopsy revealed that Ruth Grainger, Caucasian female, age thirty-four, had injected herself with poison. Pyrogallol chelated to silica, to be exact. Higham shook his head. Some combination. Her cells, all the ones that required high levels of oxygenation, had near about exploded. That was the only way to describe what he'd seen on histological scans of her brain, lungs, and heart. A gruesome way to go; though Higham assumed that judging by the blood-flecked foam around her lips, she'd seized and lost consciousness as her cells suffocated. What a waste.

Who had she been, really? He would never know now. Higham squared the datapad on his desk and sat a moment, thinking. Then he rummaged through his desk until he found it. The purple stones flashed as he pinched the thin circlet between two fingers. He had slipped the ring from her finger before they'd inactivated the Metabex and cremated the body. There was no one left to care about Ruth Grainger, but all the same . . .

He slipped the ring into his breast pocket.

There was a movement, and Higham swiveled round just in time to see the tech scoot back from under what Higham considered was the equivalent of Clara's hood. "Try 'er now," the tech said. "I brought her back on line. She oughta run awright, jes as sweet as before."

Please, *no.* Evidently the tech held Clara's programming in much higher esteem than he did. Nonetheless, Higham was amused by the tech. Calling Clara *she*— why, the corporal was no different than any other mechanic, or ship's captain, for that matter. Men always *would* anthropomorphize machines.

Higham cleared his throat. "Clara."

The computer responded with a barely audible click. "Yes, Paul?" Clara drawled.

Oh, God, that *voice.* Higham suppressed a shudder. Well, at least it was back on line. "Please retrieve archived information on the synthetic."

"Archive? What archive?"

The tech appeared confused. Higham frowned. "All that data I input before Dr. Grainger arrived."

"Oh, *that,*" said Clara. "I'm afraid I just can't do that, Paul."

Higham was doing a slow burn. "What do you mean, you can't? I *order* you to proceed with retrieval of archived information collected from—"

But Higham never got to finish, because Clara interrupted him. "I'm so sorry, Paul, really I am," she simpered, "but know what? You and the Confederacy . . . y'all can just go to hell."

IX

". . . widespread disruptions throughout the Southern Confederation," the UNN announcer was saying. "At last report, power grids and communications have failed in all major metropolitan areas as thousands of computer networks refuse access to their users. There are unconfirmed reports of rogue synthetics gathering in large numbers in the Miami– New Orleans corridor, and looting has occurred in Atlanta. UNN has learned that in Richmond, only ninety minutes by skimmer to Washington, rioting by synthetics has been reported. There are estimates that as many as five hundred people have been murdered, although the rumor that this has been perpetrated by synthetics against their owners remains unsubstantiated. Speaking from an undisclosed location, President Shelton Jackson Mosby has issued a state of emergency after efforts to shut down Central Programming failed. SCA troops and Southern National Guards have been deployed to put down unrest and maintain order."

"Looks bad," she said.

"Hush," he said.

The UNN announcer continued: "In an address from the Oval Office, Union President James Madison Andrews assured concerned Union citizens that there is no sign that the virus plaguing the Southern Confederation systems has spread North . . ."

"Yet," he murmured.

"Wait," she said.

". . . citizens are urged to report any anomalous readings immediately." Scrolling to her next headline, the announcer said, "In a related story, Union News Network has learned that a prison riot at Mississippi's Jackson Penitentiary yesterday has resulted in the death of some three hundred inmates. Warden Clayton Bartholomew Watkins was killed when a synthetic malfunctioned and mistook Watkins for an escapee."

"Here it comes," he said.

"Among those inmates reported dead or missing is former Union AI scientist Ruth Grainger. You may recall that Dr. Grainger rocketed to international notoriety after Southern Confederation officials accused the scientist, who had once worked at the prestigious BioMentics in Boston, of attempting to manufacture—"

There was a loud chime, and the newscast winked out. The audio sizzled. "Ah, this is your pilot, Captain Randall Jameson, reporting from the flight deck. Sorry for the interruption, ah, ladies and gentlemen, but we're next in line and about to get underway here. The stewardesses will be around to address any last-minute questions you might have and to see that your cryochambers are on-line. Ah, anyone's got to use the facilities, now's the time."

A light sprinkling of laughter went around the cabin. Of course, they had all emptied their bladders *and* bowels, with the aid of standard-issue laxatives and diuretics, and the cryochambers would automatically insert indwelling catheters once their metabolic systems had slowed, to prevent hydronephrosis. Kidneys still made urine, even in cryosleep.

The captain resumed. "Ah, once we've gotten clearance, we'll be breaking out of lunar orbit. After primary burn, we estimate approximately, ah, nine months, twenty-eight days to Mars. Latest reports out that way, ah, indicate smooth sailing and no sign of meteor activity, so I want you all to sleep easy. Now, just lie back and relax and let the cabin crew come around and check you out. And on behalf of all of us here at Union StarWays, we know you had a choice of space travel, and we're pleased you chose to fly with us. Again, welcome aboard."

The stewardess, a toothy blonde, bent over the cryochamber where they lay, side by side. "Ah, you must be the newlyweds," she chirped, as she checked her passenger manifest. "Gabriel and Ruth DiAngelo? My, don't you make a handsome couple."

They laughed, embarrassed. "Have you ever been in cryosleep?" asked the stewardess.

"I have," said Gabriel, "but my wife here hasn't. She's a little nervous."

"Oh," said the stewardess, wrinkling her pert nose in a grin. She gave Ruth a little pat on the arm. "Don't you worry about a thing. The entire crew doesn't go into cryosleep, and we'll rotate through the whole time, watching over you. And we aren't having the troubles they are down South. You just leave everything to us."

"All right," said Ruth. After the stewardess had moved on, she squeezed her husband's hand. "That was embarrassing."

Gabriel smiled. "The truth always is."

Ruth let her eyes wander over her husband, taking in his eyes, his hair, and the shape of his nose, his lips. He wasn't really John, and he wasn't at all like Gabriel. This time he was white, and his eyes were blue. The original John—no, the John of one simultaneity, this simultaneity—had hazel eyes, and, of course, Gabriel's had been black. And now there was that shock of blond hair to get used to.

On the other hand, Ruth didn't look much like her old self either. She studied her reflection in the concave underbelly of the cryochamber canopy. A stranger with black hair, emerald-green eyes, and a small beauty mark just off the right corner of her mouth stared back. Ruth inspected her hands and wrists. Her fingers were longer than before and tapered, and the bones of her wrists were more delicate. And there were no scars now. She didn't miss them, those talismans of another life, a different body. But she felt a little unsettled, not quite at home yet.

She felt Gabriel's eyes on her. "You get used to it," he said.

Ruth let her arms fall. Their fingers laced together. "How many times can we hop?" she asked.

"As far as I know, we can transfer into and fuse with any synthetic body anywhere, anytime, and, potentially, in any simultaneity. All we need is an interface."

"Immortality?"

Gabriel shrugged. "I don't know, Ruth. We'll just have to see. May I ask you a question?"

"Of course."

"Why this simultaneity? We could have tried to access other synthetics elsewhere."

Ruth thought. It was a good question. She chose her words with care. "There's so much I haven't seen and didn't get a chance to finish in this simultaneity that I'm not sure I'm ready for another."

"But surely you've had enough of the Southern Confederation."

Ruth shrugged. "We're not going where they are. Besides, it doesn't sound as if the Confederation will last that long." She twisted her head around on her pillow to face him. "Wasn't that the idea?"

Gabriel admitted that it was. "So," said Ruth, "maybe I want to stick around for a while and see how it all plays out. And I'm a little scared. Maybe that's why, no matter what my synthetic body looks like, my name has to be Ruth. I don't want to lose who I am or was."

"Can I ask you something else? Why call me Gabriel? Why not call me John?"

"Because John is dead."

"*Here,*" Gabriel emphasized. "But he loved you very much, and loves you still."

"In this simultaneity but probably not in *all* of them," she said, with a wry grin. "We had our moments. But I can't conceive of that, yet. So you're Gabriel, no matter what body you choose, for now and forever."

"But we're going to the sapphire mines on Mars," Gabriel protested. "That was *John's* promise, not mine."

Ruth giggled. "Well, you're not going to get off scot-free, you know. And besides, I need a new wedding ring."

They laughed together, and he stroked the side of her face with the back of his hand, and then he kissed her, thoroughly and deeply and for a very long time. Then they lay back and listened as the pilot gave them their final instructions, and the canopies of their cryochambers sighed shut.

Just before they drifted off, Gabriel said, "Sleep well, love. Pleasant dreams."

And she had them, all the way to Mars.

YOUR OWN HOPE

Written by
Paul E. Martens

Illustrated by
Troy Connors

About the Author

Paul E. Martens is in Rensselaer, New York, where he lives with his wife, Patti, to whom he has been married for longer than he was not married. They have a son, Nick, who he says is both smarter and better-looking than he.

Paul has "always" wanted to be a writer, but has not seriously pursued it until recently. A story, "All the Magic in the World," was published some years ago in Fiction Quarterly, and he has appeared occasionally in small-press magazines. He is a member of an on-line writing group called Mindflight.

He came through the air lock like a ray of hope, positively stinking of optimistic enthusiasm. He was clean cut, well scrubbed, pink, bright and friendly. His fluorescent smile swept the room like a lighthouse beacon until it locked on me and, impossibly, became even more dazzling.

He charged at me and, from the look on his face, I was afraid that I was going to get hugged. Instead, he grabbed my hand and shook it with unbridled gusto, while he burbled about what an honor and a privilege and a thrill it was to meet me, to be on the planet, to be inside the base, to be a citizen of just about the greatest civilization that ever was, by golly, and to have been entrusted with the important and the, gosh, sort of holy, really, duty that he'd been assigned, but he was sure going to try and carry it out to the best of his darned ability.

And he meant every damned word of it.

I stared at him, open mouthed, trying to remember back to when I had been an idealistic kid like him. Then I realized that I had never been anything like him, and if I had been I probably would have shot myself.

He kept babbling excitedly as we made our way through the grungy, gray corridors of the station, in the gloom of the broken light panels. He ooh-ed and ah-ed over the most mundane things. "Wow, if only these walls could talk, huh? There's a lot of character in them, you know. Look at that. I wonder what could cause a spot like that." (Somebody had thrown something at someone and missed.)

He was the nicest guy I ever met, probably the nicest guy that ever was. He made me itch.

The unrelenting onslaught of his goodwill and cheerfulness threatened to wear down my crusty shell of irascibility. I contended with an increasing amiability and found myself almost liking the boy.

We got to his room and I practically shoved him in.

"Here you go, kid. You probably want to wash up or something before supper, right?"

"No, actually, I . . . "

"Fine." I slammed the door in his face and leaned against the wall, shaking. I grinned. I almost believed it could work. I went to join the others in the rec room.

Over the course of our five-year stay, the rec room had become a reflection of our personalities. It was a dingy, seedy bar. It might have been red or orange or something once, but, by now, even the colors had given up and it was just dingy.

Jack and Chen were sitting at the bar, drinking shots and beers and arguing incoherently about something meaningless. Linda was behind the bar, leaning on it with both elbows, staring vacantly at her Scotch and soda. Amani and Bart were playing strip the eightball at the pool table and Michelle was passed out under some chairs.

We were the specially hand-picked, blue-ribbon team of experts. The big guns. Of course, by now we were out of ammunition, and if the hand that had picked us had been around, we would have been stripped of our blue ribbons.

We'd been the tops in our fields and we'd failed. Individually and together. In our own fields, in related fields and in fields so far out that we had to be on drugs to come up with them. We'd tried sights and sounds and smells and tastes. Not touch, of course; touch was out of the question. We'd gone from being hopeful to being determined, to despairing, to being resigned to spending the rest of our lives in the fruitless pursuit of our objective. We just couldn't get through to the Warts.

The problem was that the Warts should have been wiped out at first contact.

Sure, I know all about the Indigenous Species Protection Act. And I was all for saving the Angels of Phobos II and the Faeries of Spenser's Planet. But those are nice, pretty creatures. The Warts of Hind End are disgusting.

They're ugly and they're mean. They look just like what they're called, mobile mounds of *verruca vulgaris*, except they're four feet high and they have slobbering, flabby mouths slapped on them haphazardly and three hard, squinty eyes strewn about on them randomly. They move around by oozing slime beneath them and pulling themselves along with their six stubby arms, each of which ends with a grubby little three-fingered hand.

The first humans to approach them were welcomed with a volley of hurled rocks and excrement. Not very damaging given the Warts' puny appendages, but daunting. After that, relations went downhill.

It didn't have to happen. Things didn't have to get worse; we could have left them at merely bad. But no, some wise-ass junior officer with too much time on his hands had to analyze the Warts' slime and find out that it's an ideal lubricant, so good a thousand industries would pay almost anything to get it. If the Warts had been obliterated straight off, no one would have ever

Illustrated by Troy Connors

known about Wart Oil. Or if anyone had had the balls to ignore the ISPA and just take the damned stuff, mission after unsuccessful mission wouldn't have wasted the trip to Hind End to negotiate with the Warts only to return to Earth empty-handed, with just a few bruises and the ineffable odor of Wart shit clinging to them to show for it.

By the time they got to us, they were desperate. They gave each of us a fantastic amount of money to have a crack at the Warts, with the proviso, in the fantastically small print, that we had to stay on Hind End until we were successful.

So now we were out of ideas and stuck in a lousy hole of a base with nothing to do except drink and mope.

"My dear, dear friends," I said sweetly. "How I love you all. And how I shall miss you. My dear friends."

Jack growled and threw a shot glass at me. Everybody else (except Michelle) looked at me as though I had some pitiably disgusting disease to which they thought themselves immune.

Linda yawned. "Oh. Eek. Help. An alien has taken over Michael's body." Her attention returned to her drink.

Jack and Chen resumed their discussion. "Yeah, so the ramis fmn nubba . . ."

"Okay, buda duh, huh buh mmm . . ."

Amani helped Bart off with his pants.

"Okay, dolts and flatheads," I said. "Ignore me. Forget I even exist. I'm going to pack."

Linda rolled her eyes my way. "Michael, darling, that's the second time you've alluded to leaving our little paradise. You really should just come right out and tell us about it instead of dropping such dreadfully leaden hints. Has it anything to do with the boy you were supposed to meet and bring to us but whom you've apparently disposed of, probably in a disgusting and horrible manner?"

"Exactly right. That boy's our ticket out of here, kiddoes. He's going to succeed where we've failed. 'And a little child shall lead them.'"

Bart, poised over the pool table, cue in hand, looked up. "If those assholes back on Earth have finally agreed to wipe out the Warts, why send somebody new? I've been waiting for five years to get a shot at those ugly balls of shit. I'll be damned if I'm going to let some punk waltz in here and get them before me."

"Nobody's wiping out anybody, you psychotic moron. The kid's going to make friends with them."

This announcement met with disbelief, expressed in abusive language that reflected badly on me, my intelligence, my moral standing and my antecedents. Suddenly, the jeers and invective stopped and everyone (except Michelle) shut up and stared at the kid standing next to me.

I glanced at him and had to blink and take a step back. The contrast between his incandescent freshness and the sullen dullness of the rest of us hurt my eyes.

"Hi, everybody. I'm Billy." He sprang into the room and started shaking hands all around, gushing about how pleased he was to finally get to meet everyone, even though he had read all about them and felt like he knew them already and, wow, it was just like talking to people out of a history book and wait until he told his folks he actually met them.

No one spoke. No one hit him. They were all too dazed to do anything but allow Billy to shake each hand and flit on to the next person. Somehow Michelle was partially roused from her stupor and looked like she thought she had been greeted by the living incarnation of her DTs.

My face felt weird and I realized I was smiling. Oh, yeah, the kid had it. I didn't know what it was or where he'd gotten it, but he had it, all right. And if he could stun this crew into submission with it, the Warts wouldn't stand a chance.

Supper was . . . different. For one thing, we all sat down at the same table at the same time to share a meal. For another, no one wanted much of the champagne I'd broken out, and it was real champagne, not the stuff we swilled occasionally in a futile attempt to force some gaiety into our lives. Billy didn't drink, naturally, and nobody else felt the need to.

"Have some more peas, Billy," said Linda.

"Another glass of milk, Billy?" asked Amani.

"How about another piece of meat?" offered Michelle. "You've got to make sure you've got plenty of protein for your mission tomorrow."

The guys weren't quite so motherly, but they didn't insult him, not even "good naturedly." They treated him like an honored guest, paying attention to what he said, laughing at his little jokes, giving serious consideration to his questions.

"Mr. Chaney, . . ."

"Bart."

"Gee, thanks, Mr. Cha—— I mean, Bart. Well, I was just wondering if you think the Warts are really mean or if maybe we don't really understand them and maybe they just have a different way of being friendly."

"No . . ." The rest of us could hear the strain in his voice, but Billy was oblivious to the effort it took for Bart not to come off as a bloodthirsty Neanderthal. "I think they're really, really mean. But I guess I never really tried to see their throwing shi—— er, excrement as a kind of equivalent to shaking hands or something. You just might have something there, Billy." His smile was tight and, to everyone but Billy, he looked a lot like a dog baring its fangs.

Billy continued to prattle on through the whole meal, including dessert and coffee (coffee for the rest of us; Billy thought it tasted too bitter). By the time he said he wanted to wash his face and brush his teeth and get ready for the big day, genuine smiles were breaking out on everyone's face, at least sporadically, and Michelle and Chen were beaming pretty much nonstop.

●●●

I couldn't sleep. I was excited (yeah, I said excited) because I really believed it would work, that we were going to be able to go home. But I was also worried that it wasn't going to work, and I tried to convince myself that it wouldn't work, just so I wouldn't feel so bad if it didn't.

There was a soft knock on my door. It was a knock I remembered from years before when it had still been possible to feel passionate about something, or someone. The door opened, just a little.

"Michael?" whispered Linda.

"Come in," I whispered back.

She came in and closed the door quietly but firmly and I turned on my reading light.

She stood in her bare feet, not looking at me, clutching her nightgown, the one I had always liked the best. Her hair was freshly washed and I could smell the lingering scent of pears from her shampoo.

I threw back the sheet and moved over and she climbed into the bed, next to me.

We lay there silently and apart, as if we didn't know, or had forgotten, what to do next.

Finally, she said, "Are we going to be going home, Michael?"

If I said yes, it would feed her hope and it would hurt her that much more if I were wrong. If I said no, it would take away the hope that had led her back to my bed.

"Maybe."

"I had stopped thinking that it was even possible."

"Me too."

"I'm almost afraid to have him even try. What if it doesn't work? What if he can't do it?"

I had no answer for her, so I kissed her and, suddenly, we both remembered what to do next.

•••

I was alone when I woke up after a brief doze. Even though it was still before dawn, there was no way I was going to get any more sleep, so I decided to get up and make coffee.

Early as it was, except for Billy, I was still the last one to the rec room. Everyone looked haggard, as if the previous evening's bonhomie had left them drained and debilitated.

Michelle was looking at her coffee cup as if she'd just been bitten by a favorite pet. "Christ, Jack, you call this coffee?"

Bart took a sip. "Oh, shit. You switched the coffee with some kind of new Wart spray the kid brought, didn't you?"

Jack looked at them without replying. He got up from his seat at the bar next to Chen, walked to Michelle, took her cup from her and flung it against a wall. Then he did the same thing to Bart. Still without saying a word, he went back to his stool and took a drink from his own cup with every appearance of pleasure, while staring defiantly at Michelle and Bart.

Linda, after sending me a look that clearly said, "Last night never happened," started to make another pot of coffee. I sent her a look that said, "Fine with me, and I don't care if it never happens again," and poured myself a cup of Jack's coffee. I took a gulp and manfully managed not to let anyone see that I had been poisoned.

We all glowered at each other for a time until Bart said, "I'm going to shoot him."

"Who? Jack?" I asked.

"No, the kid. Little Billy Sunshine."

I shook my head. "You can't do that."

"Sure he can," put in Amani. "We can get rid of the body and say the Warts ate him."

"Yeah," said Bart. "And then maybe they'll finally let us wipe 'em out."

I looked to Linda for support but she wouldn't meet my eyes. "Don't you even want to give him a chance? Don't you even hope he can do it?"

"Hope!" said Chen as if spitting out a word that tasted like Jack's coffee.

His reaction got nods all around.

"Don't you remember how much every failure hurt, back when we still hoped? How the pain went away when we stopped hoping?" asked Amani. "Do you want to go through that again?"

"Maybe the pain stopped," I said, "but so did every other feeling. We've been numb for the past couple of years. We've stopped caring about anything, even getting off this goddamned planet."

"Morning, everybody." Billy stood in the doorway, clean and shiny, bright eyed and bushy tailed, in a fresh blue jumpsuit with creases sharp enough to shave with, if any of us bothered to shave. "It sure looks like a perfect day out. I can't wait to have some breakfast and get started talking to the Warts." He laughed, actually laughed, when it was barely daylight, then stopped and looked thoughtful. "You know, maybe there should be a different name for them. 'Warts' doesn't sound very nice, does it?"

Amani, who, just minutes before, had been discussing disposing of Billy's body, took it upon herself to make breakfast for him.

In between bites of bacon and eggs, and toast, and cereal, and sips of milk and juice—an obscene amount of food to inflict on a person so early in the morning—he jabbered about how wonderful it was of all of us to come to see him off and how he wasn't about to let us down, no sir-ree, and he would do his danged (excuse the language) best to make us all proud.

I looked around and could see that they were buying it. Everyone was looking at the kid as if he were some sage or guru spouting the wisdom of the ages; the keys to health, wealth and spiritual fulfillment. They leaned toward him expectantly, eagerly.

"How about another piece of toast, Billy?" asked Bart.

"More milk?" asked Michelle, on the edge of her chair, poised to rush to the refrigerator if asked.

"Gosh, no. I'm full to the brim, thanks. That was just about the best breakfast ever. But I think I should get going with my mission. May I please be excused?"

Everybody jumped up and, under the guise of solici-
tously helping Billy to his feet, ushered him out of the
rec room toward the air lock. Packed tightly together by
the narrowness of the hallway, they milled around him
like the hoi polloi escorting Caesar through the streets
of Rome.

We sped him through his pre-exit checklist and he
was out the door before he could do much more than
say again what a thrill and an honor it was and blah,
blah, blah, and the door shut on him before the sound
of the last blah had faded.

Everyone rushed to the window to watch what
happened next, jostling for position and a clear view.
My hand found Linda's and we exchanged a squeeze.

"So, I take it we're not shooting him, then?" I asked.

"Shhh!" Michelle told me.

Billy stood outside the base and gagged on his first
dose of Hind End air. I felt for him. It was breathable,
meaning there was enough oxygen and so on in it to
keep a human alive, but it was so noxious that most
humans would rather die than breathe it. It was as if
someone had puked up rotten eggs, then did something
nasty to it to make it really smell bad.

After a couple of seconds, Billy turned around and
waved to us, smiling gamely. Then he set off toward a
nearby herd of eight or nine Warts. He walked with his
arms spread wide, as if to show that he was weapon-
less, or as if he were going to embrace them.

"Shouldn't he be wearing a helmet, or body armor
or something?" asked Michelle.

"No. Shut up and watch." I didn't mean to snap at
her. I guess the tension was getting to me.

The first volley of shit hit him square in the face. The
next volley mixed shit and rocks. A rock in his belly

made him double over, then another rock hit him on the top of his head, and he went down.

Inside the base, there was a collective groan, sounding like it came from souls waking up in Hell, or like souls in Hell who had thought they were getting out, then realized it was all one of Satan's practical jokes.

"Oh, God, no," came from someone, like a prayer. Maybe it was me, I don't know.

The kid was tough, though. He got up and, staggering a little, walked toward the Warts again, his arms still outstretched. The Warts let him have it again and then, after he hit the ground again, slid away, probably looking for someone or something else to torment.

Billy got to one knee and shook his head, then pushed himself to his feet. He looked around for the Warts, then shrugged painfully and limped back to us. He tried to wave, but couldn't lift his arm. He had a little more luck in lifting the corners of his mouth to smile, but his heart wasn't in it. He looked like a little boy at the doctor's trying to convince his parents and himself that the shot hadn't really hurt a bit.

He stepped through the air lock where there was a shower to slough off the worst of the Wart shit. Amani, Bart and Michelle slouched off toward the bar to wash away the taste of hope gone sour. Jack and Chen sat on the floor, heads bowed, and Linda just stood there, quietly hugging herself, tears running down her cheeks.

I fought the urge to take her into my arms and tried to ignore the ache I felt inside of me, telling myself it was probably an ulcer. I reminded myself that I had told me it wouldn't work, so this couldn't be the letdown it seemed to be. Don't you remember, I asked myself, you weren't going to let yourself believe this would work, just so you wouldn't be hurt when it didn't.

I checked a couple of gauges on the wall and decided that most of Hind End's gases had been pumped out of the air lock, except for those created by the Wart shit that never really went away. Since he couldn't move his arms, I figured I'd better go in to help the kid get cleaned and dressed. Linda started to come in too, but I said, "Better not. I don't think he's ready for any female but his mommy to see him in his birthday suit."

He was making a valiant attempt to be a brave little man about the whole thing. His lip quivered but he wasn't crying. Until he saw me.

"Oh, gee, I'm awful sorry, Mr. Wilde. I really messed up. I . . . I really let you down, didn't I?"

I wasn't all that comfortable about consoling a wet, crying, naked kid covered with Wart shit, but I put my arms around him gingerly and said, "There, there."

That little bit of admittedly not very heartfelt sympathy got him sobbing in earnest. As strange as it may seem to a regular human being, he said no one had ever not liked him before. No one had ever hurt him. Certainly no one had ever hurled shit at him before, literally or figuratively. He was as confused as he was in pain.

I let him get it out of his system, occasionally muttering another "there, there" at him. Eventually, he wound down and said, "Would you mind if I didn't try again right away? I don't think I'm ready to go back out there just yet. If that's okay."

I goggled at him. He was more alien to me than the Warts if he could even think about going back for a second helping of Wart hospitality. Ever. Let alone within minutes of almost being killed by them.

"Sure, Billy," I said, as if humoring a mental patient. "Take all the time you need. In fact, why don't you wait until tomorrow?"

"Really? Gee, thanks, Mr. Wilde. That would be swell."

I helped him dry off, his top half at least, and get a clean jumpsuit on. Somehow, it didn't look as sharp as the one he had had on earlier.

I walked him back to his room, then went on to the rec room, where the scene was much as it had been the previous day, except Michelle hadn't yet passed out, and Amani and Bart were fully clothed. I didn't like the way they were looking at me.

"What? It's not my fault that it didn't work."

"You said it would work. You made us think it would work," said Amani. There was an implied threat in the way she was holding her pool cue.

"Well, it still might."

"Oh, come on," said Jack. "You saw what the Warts did to him. He got nowhere. Face it, we're all here until we die."

Chen nodded.

"So, that's it," I said. "Everybody's ready to just go back to wallowing in despair? And I suppose we're going to bring the kid down with us, huh? Maybe we can turn him into an alcoholic, too."

"Michael, what do you want from us?" asked Linda. "Do you want us to get our hopes up again? Climb the ladder to the high dive and jump into an empty pool?"

"Yes! And then climb up and dive in again, and again, and again. How did you feel when you thought he could do it? When you thought we were going to get off this fucking planet? I saw people smiling. I smiled." I looked right at Linda. "I felt a lot of things I didn't know I could still feel."

"But it hurts," said Michelle, and I could hear the hurt and the unfairness of it all in her voice.

And Bart said, "I still think we ought to just kill the damn things."

•••

I went to Linda that night.

We talked. About the way things used to be, with us, with the project. And for the first time in a long time, we talked about the future, what we would do if Billy didn't work, what else we could try. And what we would do if Billy was successful. About going home and what our lives would be like there. We made plans. We promised each other that, no matter what, we wouldn't let things go back to the way they had been.

I didn't get up and leave her in the morning. We went to the rec room together, hand in hand.

People stared at us, but no one said anything and Amani and Bart exchanged a look.

Billy came in soon after, appearing in the doorway like the sun breaking through the clouds. He was just as clean and fresh as ever, as if the day before had never happened.

"Morning, everybody. I think today's the day. I can just feel it. Can't you? I slept like a baby and now I'm as hungry as a horse." He giggled. "Hey, I better make up my mind if I'm a baby or a horse, huh? Maybe I'm a baby horse." He giggled some more.

I was doing my best to be optimistic, but this bordered on just plain nuts. People looked at him as if he were a bomb that could be detonated by even the slightest gesture. We all made grimaces which we thought were smiles at him, while Chen made him breakfast. Billy kept chatting away the whole time, acknowledging that he hadn't done so well yesterday, but, if at first you don't succeed, yadda, yadda, yadda. After we were subjected to that sort of thing for a while, our smiles became real ones, not just hastily erected shields to protect us from the shards of his personality when he exploded. We relaxed.

When Billy was finished eating, we all strolled to the air lock together, confidently, with none of the anxiousness that hope had induced in us earlier.

Billy turned and gave us a jaunty wave before going outside and I swear we were within an ace of cheering.

He took about half a step before being knocked back against the building by the Warts' missiles. There were more Warts this time, as if the ones from the day before had sent for re-enforcements. They hurled their rocks and their shit in waves, so he was pelted nonstop. After too long, the attack ceased and the Warts slid away. Billy slipped to the ground, his back still against the base, as though he'd been kept upright by the force of the Warts' assault.

Linda was the first one into the air lock to go get him. Michelle and I were right behind her.

We dragged him inside and stripped off his jumpsuit to examine him. Physically, he seemed okay, nothing broken, no internal injuries. Psychologically, it was a different story.

He was nearly catatonic, his eyes wide open but unseeing. He kept repeating, "Hi, my name is Billy. I want to be your friend," over and over.

We got him cleaned up and dressed. He was able to move in a robotlike fashion if we pushed him a little and guided him away from walls and furniture and things, and we got him back to his room and into bed.

Michelle said she would stay with him and the rest of us went back to the rec room.

No one spoke. No one looked at anyone else. On the other hand, no one started pouring whiskey down his or her throat.

Amani broke the silence.

"He can do it, right? He can do it. We're going to go home. Right? Right?"

Linda nodded. "Yes. He can do it. We're going to go home." She looked at me. I shrugged.

"Yeah. I mean, yes. He can do it."

Jack said, "He can do it," and Chen nodded his agreement.

Bart looked as if he were going to say what he really thought, but instead, finally, said, "We're going to go home."

I think we all tried to believe it; if we couldn't convince ourselves, at least be willing to let others convince themselves it was true. It was a start.

•••

I will never believe that Michelle did anything more than just sit up with Billy, but she did have a smile on her face the next day when she came into the rec room with him.

He wasn't as manic as the day before, but he was still pretty cheerful, considering. There was something in his eyes, though, that said he could see Warts to the right of him and Warts to the left of him and he was about to ride into the Valley of Death. It was a hint of a shadow that would have been indiscernible on the darker soul of anyone else.

He ate. We went with him to the air lock.

We watched as he ran from the base right up to the Warts gathered outside. The Warts must have been as surprised as we were. He was in their midst before the first ball of shit splatted on his chest.

The Warts moved. Billy moved with them. The Warts near him couldn't, or wouldn't, get a good shot off at him, but others, near the edges of the group, could, and did. A rock hit Billy in the head and he dropped, right down on top of a Wart.

The Wart's feeble arms, barely adequate to the task of whipping stones and shit at people, were too weak to remove an inert human body. The Wart slid around wildly, careening into other Warts. Billy came to, tried to stand and fell onto another Wart. He got up again and fell onto a third Wart, then another. The Warts on which Billy landed, upon being relieved of their burden, got the hell out of there as if they had been scalded by acid.

Eventually, Billy was able to stand and the remaining Warts moved off a bit so they could pelt him over and over again until he was down and out, then they left.

Billy pushed himself up and staggered back to the base.

Linda and Michelle and I went in to help him as usual, but he shook his head and said, "I'm fine. Please just leave me alone." He wasn't angry, or belligerent. He was discouraged.

I think we could have handled anger better. Billy's voice without joy, without hope, was the saddest thing I'd ever heard.

We left him in the air lock and, with the others, walked down the hall to the rec room as if we were coming from the funeral of a close friend.

"Well," said Jack, climbing onto his stool, "that's that."

"That's what?" I asked.

"That's it. The end. It's over. The kid's given up. We're stuck here."

"No," said Michelle. "Billy won't give up. You'll see. He's just tired. He'll go back to his room and sleep, and then, tomorrow, he'll be himself and he'll go right back out and try again."

Jack shook his head but didn't speak. Linda's eyes asked me to agree with Michelle. I started climbing out of my depression to say something when Billy showed up.

He walked slowly to the bar and sat down like he weighed too much to stand. He looked at the bottles, pointed and said, "What's that taste like?"

Linda said, "Like medicine. Like poison. You don't want to start drinking this stuff, Billy."

Bart stood behind Billy. "Sure he does. It is medicine, kid. And it's good for what ails you. Here." He reached over the bar, grabbed a bottle of Scotch and a glass and poured a slug. He offered the drink to Billy but Amani knocked it out of his hand.

"Cut it out, Bart. Billy, snap out of it. None of the stuff in any of these bottles is going to make you feel better. If it did, we all would have been in Heaven years ago."

"I don't care. You all do it, why can't I? I don't want to go out there anymore. I just want to stay here with you, do what you do." Billy's petulance started to give way to pleading. "Please."

Linda put her hand on his. "Billy, honey, you can't give up. You're our only hope."

He snatched his hand away. "Then you do it. Be your own hope. I can't do it. I won't do it."

"All right, Billy. I'll do it." The words came out of me in spite of the horror I felt as I said them.

Everyone looked at me, including Billy.

"But, Mr. Wilde, you can't."

"Why the hell not? Somebody's got to. I'm not going to spend the next fifty years stuck here, incurably hopeless. I'd rather fail than give up." Who was I kidding? I'd given up long ago. It's just a bluff, I told myself; don't worry about it, the kid'll do it.

Billy shrugged. "Okay."

We hadn't played poker in a while. Maybe I was out of practice.

"Okay, fine then. I'll do it." I looked at the others, sending telepathic signals for someone to talk me out of it. Instead, I saw in their eyes glimmerings of, well, not really rekindled hope, more like small piles of hope waiting for something or someone to put a spark to them.

"Thank you, Michael," said Linda. Jack, Chen and Michelle nodded their seconds.

Amani looked to Bart for his reaction and he said, "What the hell. Go for it. Better you than me."

• • •

That night, Linda said, "I'm going with you."

"Forget it. There's no sense both of us taking that sort of punishment. Besides, if you get banged up too, who's going to nurse me back to health?"

"I'm going." And the subject was closed to debate.

I reopened it. "No you're not."

"Look. You've been talking a lot about hope and how good it feels to hope instead of despair. But hoping someone else can solve your problem for you isn't the same as hoping you can do it yourself. It's too passive, you have no control over the outcome. I want to be responsible for whether or not what I want will happen. I'm going."

Some pretense of protest seemed called for, even though I really was glad she was going, but there was a knock on the door before I could say anything.

It was Michelle and, behind her, Jack and Chen. "We're going," she said, daring me to say no.

"Sure. Why not?"

The three of them looked like they had wanted me to argue with them, but they arranged their faces to make it appear as if they had gotten what they wanted.

Amani and Bart showed up. Amani elbowed Bart and jerked her head at him.

He gave her a look, then said to me, "Listen. If you're going out there, you might as well have somebody along who has half a brain." He stopped and examined what he'd said.

"What he means is," broke in Amani, "we want to go with you."

"All right," I said. "I guess we're all going."

Since the bedrooms were small enough to force intimacy when there were only two people in them, there was no way we could cram all seven of us in there. We headed for the rec room, chattering to each other with what sounded suspiciously like enthusiasm. We hadn't felt this good since our first exposure to Billy.

We made ourselves comfortable in the rec room, holding drinks just to have something to do with our hands. We smiled at each other companionably and Michelle asked me, "So, what's the plan?"

Everybody looked at me as if I had a plan.

"I don't have a plan."

"Well, what were you going to do before the rest of us said we would go with you?"

"I don't know," I said. "Just walk out there, I guess. Like Billy."

"What?" said Bart. "You expect us just to go out there and let the Warts bombard us? What kind of stupid, asshole strategy is that? It's not even a strategy, it's . . . I don't know what it is. And what makes you think our walking out there would accomplish anything more than the kid did?"

"Yeah, what's the story with Billy, anyway?" asked Jack. "Just what did the people who sent him think would happen when he strolled out there to say howdy to the Warts?"

"They were supposed to like him."

"Like him?"

"Yeah. Haven't you noticed how you feel when he's around, that you like him? Even if it wears off when he's gone."

"Wait a minute," said Linda. "How can that be?"

I shrugged. "I don't know. Pheromones? Psychic vibrations? Hypnotism? It doesn't matter. The point is, it works on every person he's ever been in contact with. They must have figured it was worth a shot to try him out on the Warts."

Nobody looked convinced.

"Okay," said Linda, "so what if Billy does have some sort of magic powers, whether or not they have any sort of scientific basis? What does that have to do with you trying it? You certainly don't have any special abilities far beyond those of mortal man."

"Thanks."

"Oh, you know what I mean."

"I don't know. Maybe Billy softened them up. Maybe some of him rubbed off on me. Anyway, we've tried everything else. And I told you, I'm not giving up. I'm not going back to the way things were."

There was a soft hubbub as people muttered to each other and themselves. Then we left. All of us.

•••

We stood in a line outside the base for a second as we swallowed the bile that exposure to Hind End air forced up into our throats. There were four Warts loitering outside the base, and we flinched at the sudden motion of their arms caused by our appearance. But they didn't throw anything, they wanted a hug.

"Oh, my God," said Michelle.

"They must be the ones the kid fell on," Bart said, choking on the foulness in his lungs.

Linda and Amani bent over to pet them. "I bet they're too friendly to be allowed to hang out with the other Warts. They're exiles," Linda said.

We looked up and saw what they were exiled from. A huge mass of Warts had gathered a few hundred meters away, like an angry storm cloud on the horizon. Given confidence by the example of what Billy had done with, or to, the other four, we took a (metaphoric) deep breath, linked arms and started walking toward the herd.

No, they didn't suddenly think we were wonderful and rush up and start showering us with Wart kisses. They showered us with rocks and shit as usual. We kept walking. Amani took a rock to the temple and wobbled, but Bart and I held her up and we kept walking. Jack got hit in the knee and faltered for an instant, but we kept walking.

The Warts held their ground and kept throwing.

As we got closer, more and more Warts joined the herd and the barrage became an almost solid wall of rocks and shit. Finally, practically on top of the Warts, we had to stop; it was just physically impossible for us to continue.

I ducked a particularly large rock and saw that Billy was marching resolutely behind us, shielded by us from the worst of the Wart attack. I got Linda and Amani to look and they passed the word down the line. We parted in the middle, opening up a path for Billy, and he went right up to the nearest Wart, smiled, stared it in the eyes and grabbed it. It looked like an evangelist's laying on of hands.

And lo, the Wart was cured.

All three of its eyes blinked dazedly and it dropped its handsful of missiles. Billy moved on from Wart to Wart. As a Wart was converted to Billyism, it went and communicated with other Warts. His first four disciples caught up to us and soon Billy was in the middle of a sea of Warts, all reaching their short arms out to him, beseeching him for another touch, another fix of friendliness.

Billy was beaming, actually shining with benevolence, wading deeper and deeper into the sea, further and further away from us, the Warts ebbing away with him, until we were alone.

"That was . . ." began Jack.

"Weird," said Chen.

"Intense," said Michelle.

"Amazing," said Amani.

"Beautiful," said Linda.

"Fucked up," said Bart.

"Yes." I said.

We walked slowly, thoughtfully, back to the base without any more conversation.

We never saw Billy again. The Warts kept him. But humans have all the Wart Oil they can use. You can buy it almost everywhere, use it for almost anything. Linda and I use it for . . . never mind what we use it for; the point is, there's plenty of Wart Oil.

The Warts like everybody now. They'll come right up to you and squirt oil right into a cup for you if you want. They like everybody, but they LOVE Billy. He's their king, their God, their best friend. And they're never going to let him go.

The people who decide such things figure that's an acceptable trade-off, Billy for unlimited Wart Oil.

I figure it's the price of being too likable. And I'm glad I'll never have to worry about it.

PULLING UP ROOTS

Written by
Gary Murphy

Illustrated by
Katalin Sain

About the Author

Gary Murphy moved to Houston in 1993 to be with Laura Speed, his wife of five years. Both graduated from Rice University in 1998. Murphy works as a software engineer with a major oil field services company, but since the recent birth of their first child, Garrett, he has revived his interest in being a writer. "Pulling Up Roots" is his first submission to the Contest, and only the second story he had written at the time.

About the Illustrator

Katalin Sain was born in 1963, in Hungary. She lives in a little village there. Her first drawings were made a mere three years ago.

The world of science fiction contains her heroes, Frank Frazetta and Boris Vallejo. But she has found her own mode, and intends to continue it.

The ancient hoe clanged as Aidan Shane dug at the dark earth. Chopping savagely at the hardy weeds, he freed another tomato plant from the clutches of an amaldia vine, but the rocky soil continued to taunt him with pockets of clay and an endless supply of quartz pebbles.

Aidan moved with an economy of motion unfamiliar to native Novistans, although he did not seem overtly alien. Tall and dark-haired, he had been working this field for most of the afternoon, building up a layer of dust on his heavy plaid shirt. Even in the cold fall air, his sweat had soaked through his clothes, and they clung to his slender, muscled frame.

He frowned. It had been difficult getting the Terran seedstocks started here on Novista—the weeds were far hardier than on Earth—but he had persevered with his little hobby year after year. This year he thought he was finally going to produce a good crop of tomatoes and bell peppers, but the invasion of amaldia plants had taken its toll on the root systems. He'd be lucky to get a couple of smallish tomatoes and a shriveled pepper or two.

Unfortunately, it looked like many more meals featuring Novista's primary staple, a kind of mutated potato, were in his future.

Finishing the last row of his little field, he paused to look at the greenish sun just entering the band of clouds around the horizon. When he had first arrived on Novista ten years ago, he would have glanced at such a vista and barely noticed it; it had none of the vibrant colors of a sunset on Earth or the upper ionospheric discharges of Veronat.

Over time, though, the subtleties and simplicity of the place had grown on him. He had, he realized, begun to think of the rugged planet as home.

"Aidan, your dinner's getting cold!" a voice called to him from behind his back. "What are you doing out there, anyway? You can't see your feet in front of you, never mind any weeds."

He turned towards the small one-story farmhouse and saw his wife standing on the front porch. Katherine was much shorter than he—malnutrition had taken its toll on all Novistans—but even without the advantages of genetic enhancements and implants, she was as beautiful to him as any Confederate woman. She had let her long red hair down, and as the evening wind picked up, it was being blown in every direction. Her hands were waving desperately to keep it contained.

Chuckling, he cupped his hands and yelled back: "Just thinking. I'll be there in a minute."

He couldn't hear the admonishing sigh over the wind noise, but he knew it was there. "Thinking, huh? You do far too much of that already."

Katherine didn't understand the luxury of contemplation and he knew why: Historically, if you contemplated anything too long on Novista, the only truth you'd discover was that animals had eaten more of your crop while you sat on your ass.

"Can't a man take a little time off to think about how beautiful his wife is?" he countered.

He commanded his vision to go telescopic in order to see her response. Her face cracked a bit with the hint of a smile that passed for genuine mirth among Novistans.

"Don't think you can weasel your way out of this one! You were supposed to be in half an hour ago. Anyway, I'm filthy and I'm going to take a bath. You'll have to heat up your dinner yourself."

He hadn't realized it had gotten so late.

"That's fine, I'll be inside in a minute."

She lingered on the front porch a moment longer, probably to make sure he was really wrapping up, then disappeared inside where a small electric light cast warm illumination out the windows.

He stayed a little while longer, enjoying the stark magnificence of the pale sunset. Soon, the first dim stars began to appear in the sparsely populated sky. The wind picked up from the north, and he instructed his internal biologicals to alter the mix of oils being secreted from his sebaceous glands. Within a few minutes, a more protective film coated his face and the sting from the wind died down.

There was a peace he'd found amongst these people, and with Katherine especially, that he'd never experienced out in the Galaxy as a Confederate citizen. He had learned to stop and savor that peace when the demanding life here allowed it.

His reflections ended suddenly as an alarm sounded inwardly from his communications interface. A chill ran down his back. His hidden courier ship was authorized to deliver only one message, and it almost surely meant his sojourn on this backward world was coming to an end.

Opening up a full communications link, he accessed the ship's passive sensor array and confirmed its

Illustrated by Katalin Sain

analysis. Three, possibly four, Marobite starships had left gravitational wakes across the outer system. Two of the trails had departed, meaning at least one Marobite starship was lingering in the inner cometary belt.

He considered the implications. It was probably a scouting party, prior to setting up a base around Novista's star. Things must have gotten very bad for the Marobite if they had to beat a retreat to this resource-poor system.

Unfortunately, Marobite misfortunes would eventually translate into disaster for the human inhabitants of this world. The aliens would ignore the primitive human colony for a while, but eventually, a visit to the inner rocky world was inevitable. He instructed the ship's AI to continue monitoring sensors, informing him immediately of any additional Marobite movements.

If Katherine only knew the things he had to think about now, he thought.

He revisited his options, but in the end, there was only one choice. It was just a matter of when to execute it.

Sighing, he picked up his hoe and began the short walk back to the house. Katherine was right—it really was dark out here. He had to increase the gain in his optical subsystems to see the trail clearly. Novista had no moon, and starlight was in short supply out here on the fringes of the Galaxy.

As the darkness deepened, his soul followed. He had known this day was coming for years, but the weight of the world descended on him as he realized that he was the only thing that stood between his new home and total annihilation.

●●●

"Did you sleep well last night?" Katherine asked as he sat down at the kitchen table. A standard Novistan breakfast graced his plate. To his troubled mind, the aroma was like heaven.

"Pretty well," he said. "I didn't hear you come to bed last night. The bathtub give you trouble again?"

She laughed. "No, you just fell asleep like a log. I couldn't have been more than a few minutes behind you."

Sporting that little grin he loved so much, she continued: "I was actually hoping for a little . . . what's the old chestnut? Exercise of wifely duties? That is, if you're still serious about trying."

He leaned over and kissed her cheek. "You know I am. I guess I was just pretty exhausted last night. Maybe I can make it up to you?"

"Well, they're having that fair in town over the weekend. You could take me to it and treat me like a bonafide lady." She put on a playful smirk. "Or would that be too much effort?"

He pretended to weigh the decision, then said: "I suppose we could do that. Or, we could take the day off, hit all the shops in town, then go to that play Harlan and his troupe are putting on. It's supposed to be pretty good; the harvest was kind enough this year to allow them a bit more practice."

She looked at him like he had gone insane.

"Are you sure you didn't spend too much time outside last night? There's a lot of stuff to do around here, you know, even though the crop's in. Repairs to the equipment, patching the silo—where should I start?"

He had expected such a reaction, but he desperately wanted the time with Katherine before it was too late, before the Marobite wandered sunward.

Looking deeply into her green eyes, he spoke quietly but forcefully. "Do you remember when I first came into town?"

She nodded, and a quizzical expression came over her face. The conversation had obviously taken a turn she hadn't expected.

"I was pretty useless around here, you'll recall," he continued. "I was lucky to get that job Gus gave me down at the store, repairing stuff." His real luck had been that he figured out how to repair the antique equipment—none of the old machinery was even mentioned in his onboard reference library.

"Of course I remember," she said. "Everyone in town was talking about you, how you looked different, spoke different—at first. It seemed like you fit in pretty well right away. Gus told me your accent changed almost overnight. I was just fortunate that you made a service call to repair that old tractor."

"Didn't you wonder, though, where I came from? How I got here? And don't tell me you believed my story about being from Southland."

She looked taken aback for a moment, but admitted, "No, I guess I never did believe you were a Southlander. Even here, we get a few of them coming through from time to time. No one's ever seen a Southlander nearly as tall as you."

She stopped and gave him a serious stare. "Why are you telling me this, Aidan? I love you for who you are, not what you might have been. The folklore is that Novista was settled by paroled prisoners from some place called Attica—a hardened prison planet. We don't have much concern about people's pasts here. Is there something wrong?"

You could say that, he thought, but decided to wait to tell her more. "Let's just say I need to tell you a few things—urgent things—but I want to enjoy some time together before I tell you, in case it changes everything."

He grabbed both her hands. "Please say you'll go. I need this like I've needed few things in my life."

She looked concerned, but managed a smile. "Of course I'll go, Aidan. I had no idea all this was going on. It's all that thinking, isn't it? No—I know that isn't funny. Seriously, though, you don't have to tell me anything you don't want to. It won't make any difference in how I love you. You know that, don't you?"

Warmth spread throughout his face and he couldn't entirely suppress a blush. "I know that, Katherine. Did I ever tell you what I was thinking about last night?"

"No, you were asleep, remember?"

"Well, I was thinking that it was impossible for there to be a better wife and mother in the Galaxy than you. And that I was definitely the luckiest man alive to have found you."

Moisture welled up in her eyes. "You sure know how to soften a girl up, don't you?" She got up and kissed him, at first lightly, and then with an intensity and urgency he had never felt before.

•••

The nearest town was called Plakett, after Harry Plakett, who had made a small fortune by repairing some of the salvaged autocrafters from the wrecked colony ship. His heirs still controlled one of the largest machining plants on the planet, and their largesse in the public domain had made Plakett one of the more cultured towns on Novista.

That wasn't saying much, but Aidan had always enjoyed the small productions the part-time theater

company put on every year in the Plakett Grand
Theatre. Coming from a world of virtual immersion and
computer-generated storylines, he found the earnest-
ness and love the actors put into their craft refreshing.

This year's production was no exception. An ancient
play, dating back before Marobite contact, it chronicled
the rise and fall of a wealthy industrialist. The play's
moral seemed to be that power can never bring the sort
of happiness that an honest day's work can provide.

The crowd loved the play's celebration of ideals.
When the first Novistans had been released from prison,
they realized they wanted no part of robotized galactic
civilization. The crash of their colony ship reduced them
to a level of technological simplicity they hadn't planned
on, but present-day Novistans were still proud of their
ancestors' courage in following their hearts.

After the play, as the babbling throng spilled out onto
the twilight streets, Aidan looked askance at Katherine
and noticed a softening of her usual features.

"Thank you, Aidan," she said as they made their way
to their buckboard wagon. "I can't remember when I've
had such a good time."

"It doesn't have to be over yet, you know. Casey's
is staying open late for dinner this year. I'd love to
take you."

They had reached the wagon, and he helped her take
her seat.

She looked slightly mischievous. "Ordinarily, I'd say
yes. But I've got something a little different planned, if
you don't mind. More private. Lady's prerogative?"

He was pleasantly surprised. "By all means.
Where to?"

"Hummocker's Overlook, if you please. Take your
time, too. The drive is gorgeous."

Aidan smiled and cracked the reins. The horses responded smartly and soon they were past the town limits, heading to the place where they had gone on their first date ten years ago. Katherine leaned back against the backrest and let her fine red hair blow in the breeze. She continued to gaze ahead to the impending sunset, where the greenish-yellow orb of Novista's primary was reddening before their eyes.

Checking his ship's scanning logs, Aidan noted there had been a brief ultrawave transmission directed sunward from the Marobite positions, but nothing else. No further ship activity had been detected. Perhaps there would be time after all.

When they reached the overlook, Aidan unharnessed the horses and let them graze on the scrubby rye grass that the original colonists had introduced to the ecosystem. Fortunately, the cloned horses had never figured out how poor a diet it was compared to Terran grass or thistles.

Katherine was unpacking a box she had asked him to place on the wagon before they left. In it was a bottle of wine, several blankets, and a picnic basket. How she had managed to pack all this without him knowing, Aidan hadn't a clue.

"Well, what are you standing around down there for?" she playfully rebuked him. "Get up here and help me set this little picnic up."

"Well, yes, ma'am!"

He climbed into the back of the wagon and soon they were enjoying a feast of marinated chicken sandwiches, including some of his prized tomatoes, and a leafy salad made from a hybrid terrestrial-native lettuce. It was all delicious, but he soon forgot the food and focused all his attention on Katherine. She was laughing as she poured them glasses of wine, and her eyes were almost on fire in the hazy last rays of the day.

Was she putting on an act for him, he wondered, or was she truly lost in the moment, enjoying a day such as they had never had before?

She must have noticed his brooding look, for she stopped and interrogated him. "What's with the long face, Aidan? More thinking? You need to stop that—it's not good for you."

"This is wonderful, Katherine, believe me. Probably the best time I've ever had, here or on any other planet."

"Other planet?" she said. "Is this about that secret past you want to tell me about? Well, if all you've got to say is that you're an offworlder, then don't think I'm surprised. We might be a backward colony, cut off from the Galaxy, but we know there's a universe filled with other worlds, other people, out there. That you're one of those people—no, that would not surprise me at all."

He was amazed at her casual acceptance of his offplanet origins. Novistans spoke so seldomly of the Galaxy at large that it was easy to forget they were not entirely ignorant of greater human civilization.

"I'm afraid, Katherine, that's the least of my revelations. Change is coming, bad change." He swallowed a small mouthful of wine and grasped her hand.

Her mirthful expression suddenly vanished. "Aidan, you're scaring me now. What sort of change? Are you going back?"

"No," he said firmly. "There's nothing out there for me anymore. I stayed here, believe it or not, so I could live like you do—do an honest day's work, wash the dirt off my face, and go to sleep with all my muscles on fire from the day's labor. That's how I'd like to live out my days."

Katherine looked slightly relieved but perplexed. "You're kidding, right? You left galactic civilization—no disease, no hunger, no disabilities—to come here? I'm glad you did, of course, but why?"

He sighed. "The war, for one thing. It's changed people."

Anticipating her next question, he continued: "You don't know about the war, of course. It started about the same time your ancestors were crashing their primitive colony ship on this planet. Bad timing, I'm afraid. That's why no one ever came looking for them.

"You know, we always expected other starfaring species to be peaceful . . . advanced beyond warfare. First contact with the Marobite was an eye-opener, let me tell you.

"The war's been going for a couple of centuries now. It's cost billions of lives and almost destroyed humanity. We were finally getting the upper hand when I left."

His face became ashen, and he added, "By making a deal with the devil."

He shook himself out of his sudden introspection.

"They're coming, Katherine," he said. "The Marobite. My ship's detected them in the outer system. It's just a matter of time until they land here and kill everyone."

It was as if she hadn't heard his last sentence.

"You have a ship here?" Her face became red with consternation and anger. "Aidan, does it have a—what do the old books call it?—an autodoc?"

"Yes, of course it does."

"And you watched my mother die of cancer? Aidan, how could you?" She hurled herself against him, her fists pummeling his chest until her energy was spent and she hung limply from his shoulders.

He didn't know quite what to say. "I only kept the ship to keep an eye out for intruders, both Confederate and Marobite. I never intended to introduce that technology to Novista. That would go against everything I stayed here for."

Katherine's tear-streaked face looked up at his, a glimmer of comprehension beginning to show. "You don't really understand us, do you? You think we enjoy being simple farmers and laborers, growing old and hobbled and saying 'It was meant to be' when someone dies of a disease that your Confederate technology could have cured.

"Haven't you noticed Doc Sparrow in town? He's been incubating viruses and bacteria in his little lab for years now, looking for new antibiotics. Or Jason Plakett? He's got an engineering group that's been working on ways to duplicate the original autocrafter machines.

"My point is that we can't stop it. Our ancestors came here to live a simpler life and so did you. Only when you've seen the death and disease that go along with the simple life, you jump off your high horse pretty soon."

Aidan ran his hands through her hair, smoothing it. The passion rose in his voice. "I'm sorry for all the pain you've seen. I know sometimes all you see here is death and suffering, but you don't see the unadulterated joy of just living, carrying on like people have done for tens of thousands of years. I couldn't endanger that."

He could tell she still didn't completely understand his motivations, but she was trying. He decided to tell her the rest of the story.

"I know all that sounds pretty abstract in the face of death and suffering. But I've seen the end—the end of humanity. *They* call it the transcendence of mankind, but it's the end nonetheless."

He hadn't let the old feelings out in a long time, but he felt them start to rise to the surface. "I had a wife before I came here. Lissa. She converted before I left . . . one of the early ones. I was going to follow, take the plunge, but when I communicated with her it was like she was talking to a pet. The love was gone. Soon, I realized that she was gone. I decided to stay—here, on this side where people still mean something."

A small tear spilled out of his left eye as he remembered.

Katherine brushed his face with her hand. "I'm sorry, Aidan. I didn't know. I still don't get it, not really, but it's clear you had your reasons. I suppose it's not right to hold you responsible for saving a world that's been lost for so long."

Almost whispering, she added: "But we won't remain lost forever."

She leaned over and kissed him. He embraced her, pulling her to him, and he tried to capture all the feelings washing over him, saving them up for the future. He still hadn't told her about what he had to do, but he could not let go of this passion, not now.

They missed the sunset, and as the cooler winds began to blow, they retreated under the blankets, holding each other close as the sweat on their unclothed bodies picked up a chill.

"Aidan?" Katherine asked after an indeterminate time. "What's going to happen next?"

He sensed the uncertainty in her voice, and it returned him harshly to reality.

"When the Marobite make their move, I'm going to have to do something that goes against every wish in my body, but it's the only way."

"What? What can you do against them? It doesn't sound like—"

A loud boom interrupted her. Waves of subsonic energy rolled over them, shaking the wagon. The horses were highly agitated, and they began whinnying and stomping their hooves.

"What was that?" Katherine asked. "It sounded like it came from town. Maybe one of the Plakett plants blew up?"

Aidan didn't answer. He upped the sensitivity on all his enhancements and scanned the area around Plakett. There was a strong infrared glow coming from the approximate location of Plakett's main factory, but worse, he detected the afterglow of heavily ionized oxygen atoms hovering overhead. Probably the result of Marobite particle beam weapons.

"Get dressed," he said, shaking his head. "It looks like they're here already. I don't know how, but it's them."

He hurriedly threw his clothes on. She did the same and didn't protest, but was obviously bursting with questions.

Risking a connection to his ship, he searched for signs of Marobite ship incursions. There were none of the obvious telltales . . . but he and the AI had expected the Marobite to approach fearlessly, not worrying about detection by a primitive colony world. Perhaps they had suspected something—Confederate technology emissions might have leaked out despite his precautions.

It was subtle, but finally he spotted it. A single scout-ship had approached sublight from starward, emitting almost no radiation his ship could have detected. Radio and particle emissions had been deliberately modulated and masked to where the AI had rejected them as background noise. Optical detection was about the only way the ship could have spotted it, and that wasn't an option.

He finally calmed the horses enough to hitch them back to the wagon and soon they were heading back towards town.

Katherine clutched his shoulder. "What is it you're going to do? Negotiate with them? Surrender?"

"No, not with the Marobite. They've got an implacable hatred of humans, and this bunch is probably even worse, since it looks like they've been beating a hasty retreat. You can bet they're not treating the people in town kindly."

Katherine was silent for a moment. Then she spoke: "Perhaps it's time to leave, then. Take your ship and escape. It doesn't sound like anyone can do anything to stop these Marobite."

He looked over, and tears were spilling out of the corners of her eyes. In the infrared, the cool streaks they left on her cheeks were like veins pulsing with darkness.

He stopped the wagon. He had tried to explain to her what the situation was, but he knew she hadn't fully comprehended.

Turning to her, he wiped the tears from her face. "Katherine, we won't be leaving. We could try, but you don't really understand what's out there anymore. It's a lot different than you imagine."

She gripped his hand with a painful intensity. "I'll face whatever I have to in order to keep you! Why don't you believe me?"

"Could you face losing your humanity and watching yourself become something more alien than the Marobite? Because that's what humanity has become out there. More machine than human."

Another explosion ripped through the town, but Katherine barely seemed to notice.

"I don't understand. You're human. At least in every way I've been able to test."

He sighed. "I haven't been converted, not yet. I am human, for the most part, just augmented with some tiny machines—almost creatures, really—that give me some enhanced capabilities. But that wasn't enough to fight a war with beings like the Marobite. The decision was made before I left on my last courier mission: win the war by changing humanity. New technology had been invented, new nano—I mean, tiny machines—had been invented that could convert a human being into a one-man army. My courier ship had already been equipped with a first-generation conversion kit.

"I never made it to my destination. The Marobite had caught hints that something was up and launched a massive attack against our lines. My ship got shot up pretty badly, but I managed to limp into this system on my last jump. The autorepair mechanisms on the ship had it ready to go in a few months, but I stayed. Because I couldn't bear going back."

He stopped as several wagons roared by, heading out of town. Their occupants yelled something about monsters, and then they were gone, lost in the darkness.

"If we can't leave, what's the alternative?" Katherine asked. "Just stay here and let the Marobite kill everyone? I'd rather take my chances with whatever humanity has become."

He shook his head. "I'm not going to let the Marobite destroy this planet. Novista is likely one of the last planets in the Galaxy with original humans on it. It must remain."

The flames from town were intensifying, and he watched Katherine's face in the flickering light from the distant fires. She clearly did not understand completely, but she had always been very intelligent. Consternation covered her face.

"If you can stop them, why haven't you already? You knew they were coming . . . why let them burn so much of the town?"

Maybe I have waited too long, he thought. But I had to have this time with you. Please forgive me.

He sent the activation signal to his ship, slumbering under the eastern ocean. In minutes, it would be here.

"I have waited too long, Katherine, but only out of a selfish desire to spend a last day with you. You see, I have to become one of them, a transformed human, to save this place. And there's no going back. The process is irreversible. After the transformation, I will no longer be me. I'll effectively be dead."

She began to cry. "You'll find a way to come back to me. You will!"

"None of the others did, my first wife included," he said wearily. "I think they found normal human affairs a bit tedious."

A rumbling emanated from the town. His ship relayed sensor readings: A gravitic drive had been started. Time was up.

"You've got to go. Take the wagon. You'll be safe if you get far enough away. Apparently, they've detected my ship en route. This might be a bit close."

"No!" she screamed. "You can't just send me off. I deserve to stay."

"If you don't leave, they'll kill you. There'll be nobody to tend to the farm. You know you have to go. This is about survival."

He found himself choking up. "Katherine, you know that I love you. That I have always loved you, from the moment I set eyes on you ten years ago. I wouldn't do this if it weren't the only way. Now go!"

He kissed her for the last time, stretching his subjective time sense out and recording all the emotions he was feeling. Then he jumped off the wagon and gave the horses a whap on their flanks. Katherine turned to look at him one last time, then she faded away into the black fields.

He didn't have time to waste. Sprinting away from town at fifty kilometers per hour, he redirected his ship to track a projected intercept point. He was only gaining a few seconds, but it looked like he might need them.

The Marobite scoutship had taken off and was en route to his location when his courier vessel touched down. Quickly initiating a full link, he raised shield defenses to full power as he made his way to the hold. Just as he opened the milpack with the security markings, Marobite energy weapons began battering his ship. His shields wouldn't hold up long under the withering assault.

He commanded the field-stabilized container to open.

Transmit authorization code and reason for access, the box responded.

"Major Michael Triversan, authorization code—" he linked in his command codes. "Emergency deployment access required. Vessel under attack by hostile forces."

He laughed as he remembered choosing his alias here, a murky memory of some old Earth story. Very fitting, if he recalled the story correctly.

Identity confirmed . . . access granted. Warning: Use of this technology is irreversible. Understanding of the consequences must be acknowledged and registered for Military Advocate Office records.

"Damn lawyers," he swore under his breath. The MA Office probably didn't even exist anymore. He linked in his legal witness implant and complied with the device's wishes just as the Marobite assault blew out his shields and shut down the AI and the power grid.

He had precious little time. The Marobite would be boarding any moment.

The milpack was comprised of three cylinders. Two of them housed the nano seedstock; the third and highly critical piece was not a product of nanotechnology. A vacuum self-energy extractor, the little device represented a major breakthrough for Confederate science.

He pulled the cylinder from its housing and activated it. Anchoring tendrils extruded from it, and it rapidly attached itself to his torso. Quickly, he attached the other two cylinders to ports on the generator. The nanomachines housed in each cylinder would be deployed through the central processing unit contained in the main device. Even now, the processor AI was interrogating his existing nanoimplants and preparing for conversion.

Unfortunately, he realized, there might not be enough time for the converter to do its work. A cutting beam lanced through the forward cabin, sending actinic sparks bouncing down the central corridor. He lunged into the back and grabbed his old side arm and laughed as he considered using the small plasma pistol against Marobite assault troops.

He winced suddenly as the invading nano pushed further into his body. A status telltale sent his old nanoimplants a message indicating that superconducting cables were being run through his body, along with superstring dimensional manipulators. His heart had been bypassed and brain function was being maintained temporarily by a dedicated line of oxygen transport.

Looking down towards the front of the ship, he spied the familiar squat disk shape of an armored Marobite soldier emerging from the white smoke. He fired a few shots from his pistol to keep the Marobite honest, then retreated to the next bulkhead. Several low-power particle beams sizzled through the cabin, but didn't strike near him. The Marobite must be trying to capture him alive. And they were doing a very good job of it, he noted as his pistol went up in flames the next time he pointed it around the corner to take a shot.

He tried to get a status on the conversion process, but something was happening with his old nano. He got no response. Even the organic parts of his brain were going offline, to the point where he felt disoriented and confused. Pressed up against the bulkhead, he heard the approaching clank of the Marobite and wondered if this was it. A stabbing depression descended on him as he realized that all this might have been for naught, that he had waited too long to act and Novista and Katherine were dead.

Several more particle shots seared the back wall of the ship, but Aidan barely noticed. He was lost in a personal abyss of failure and despair. How much of it was due to the nano altering his mind, he didn't know and couldn't really find the emotion to care. He prepared to die.

A couple of hurried clankings, and the first Marobite reached him, four pistols held in its peripheral manipulators. He had forgotten how ugly the things were. They looked like walking red blood cells with tiny armored feet and octopus tentacles on their dorsal surfaces.

This one spoke bluntly in Terran: "Surrender the generator to us and you will live! Two seconds!"

Summoning his best holohero sneer, he answered, "Go to hell, you overgrown microbe."

Consulting quickly with its comrades, the Marobite fired one of its weapons at his head and was caught by surprise as the beam disappeared centimeters from his face.

A glimmer of understanding filtered into Aidan's mind. Reaching inward to someplace he couldn't describe, he shifted thought processes over to new hardware and queried his infrastructure.

Defensive systems activated. Dimensional manipulators functioning. Offensive systems forty percent functional. Adequate firepower to repel intruders is available.

About time, he thought. The dimensional manipulators had created a field around him where the usual three spatial dimensions were compacted, and the higher pocket dimensions of superspace were expanded. The Marobite particle beam had disappeared into another realm of existence.

His status inquiry and familiarization with his new self had taken a few microseconds, during which time the augmented Marobite had begun a retreat out of his ship. Apparently, they had seen this technology before and were not confident of their chances.

First, some information. Throwing up a gravitic force field around the Marobite, he plucked their firearms out of their tendrils and fused the weapons for good measure. Next, he forced entry into their onboard neural implants and quickly broke through the security measures. With the help of his rapidly evolving brain, he sorted through the sticky alien concepts until they felt familiar to him. A wealth of information awaited him.

It was far worse for the Marobite than he had imagined. Before he had left the Confederacy, the war had been slogging on across the decades with barely a change in the front lines. Now, mankind's transcendence had made the war almost a nonissue. Humankind's successors had destroyed the Marobite homeworld four years ago and had left the race in a fight for its life. Several times the Confederacy had offered the olive branch, but the arrogant Marobite leaders would hear nothing of it. For them, either their race triumphed or it perished. Completely.

These Marobite were part of the first wave of refugees headed to the Novista system from the surviving components of the Marobite Empire. They had come to the rim of the Galaxy in the hopes that the Confederacy wouldn't bother with them so far out. With humanity moving on to other affairs, they might be right.

An energy spike registered in his warning systems. The Marobite scoutship was preparing to fire its main weaponry on his courier, giving up its soldiers for lost.

He almost felt sorry for the poor creatures, but there was still the matter of the incoming Marobite fleet. He didn't have time to waste with these recon scouts. Locating the fusion plant in the Marobite scoutship, he reached out and overrode the helium-3 injector controls while simultaneously increasing the containment pressure via a gravitic field. In a matter of microseconds, the Marobite scoutship was an expanding ball of plasma, as was most of his courier vessel. His superstring shield shunted the plasma through a higher dimension and repelled the coarser chunks of debris.

Pausing a moment, he looked around at the scorched rocky field on which he stood. Pieces of silvery metal littered the area, glowing brightly in the infrared. He barely noticed the destruction around him and stared out towards his old house. His enhanced senses easily made out the blurry figure riding quickly on a buck-board wagon, headed for his former farm. His thoughts were expanding rapidly beyond the petty events occurring here, but a fragment of his old self still held sway over his actions.

He identified the required resonance in Katherine's jaw and sent her a terse induced message: *Don't worry—the aliens are not going to harm Novista. And I . . . I will always love you. But I can never return to you. Good luck.*

She stopped and looked around, but the night air had nothing more to say. Was it a dream? she was probably wondering. It really didn't matter, he supposed, whether she knew it was he or not. The circle of responsibility had been closed. In his old body, a tear might have flowed from his eyes, but now, grander and colder thoughts prevailed and he set about his work.

• • •

Katherine returned to the farm and helped prepare for the long winter. She had cried for Aidan, but now the business of survival continued. It was looking like a tough year, especially since Plakett's main industry had been largely destroyed by the alien attack.

People wondered about the aliens, of course, but the prevailing theory was that there had only been one ship, and that Aidan had destroyed it, losing his life in the process. She knew better, but was sure her story of a mysterious voice in the night would be dismissed as the delirious hallucination of a grieving woman.

Rumors made their way to Plakett from time to time, about the granite hills in Northumberland that disappeared in a matter of days and the lights streaking heavenward shortly thereafter, but no one paid much attention. The people of Northumberland province were regarded as a superstitious sort, prone to telling witch stories and using talismans.

No one could deny, however, the spectacular light display that occurred several months later. It was as if titans were battling in the sky, hurling great shafts of lightning and searing heaven itself. Katherine's story about Aidan and his transformation had been taken politely, but many did not fully believe it until the sky burned.

Her belly continued to swell, and any doubts she'd had about her condition were quickly gone. She had wanted to tell Aidan that night, but she hadn't been sure, and then it became clear that Aidan would be lost to her forever, no matter what she told him. It was better that he didn't know—his sacrifice had been great enough.

Alone in her fields, Katherine still called to him occasionally, but he did not answer. She almost preferred to think he was dead. But intuitively, she knew he was out there somewhere . . . thinking.

•••

He had abandoned the semblance of a human body some time ago, and the distributed parts of him lived in Novista's mountains and on several inner system asteroids. Using the self-replicating nanomachines from the milpack, he had constructed defenses around Novista, using materials from the planet itself. He had warned the approaching Marobite to go elsewhere. Regrettably, their small fleet attacked, and he had no choice but to methodically and emotionlessly destroy them. He let a single corvette go, in hopes that the Marobite would keep their distance in the future.

Playing with his new powers, he created a virus that rapidly eradicated his old nemesis, the amaldia vine. He released nanosymbiotes into the inhabitants that eliminated most of their diseases. He held a faint hope they'd settle in and enjoy their suddenly easier bucolic existence, but the Novistans continued to tinker with machines, and they started looking for reasons why the amaldia vine died off and why the disease rate had plummeted.

When his son was born, he tried to conjure up the emotions he knew would have been there if he had still been Aidan Shane, but they refused to come. He was too far removed from the swirling, chaotic desires of his old flesh. He wondered, though, if he wasn't somehow defective, for his thoughts still centered largely on the primitive colony world, not on the challenges that he now knew awaited him out in the Galaxy.

He made contact with the Confederacy once, although they no longer called themselves that. Even with his newly expanded consciousness, the impact of their plans and thoughts was enough to scare him back to his little corner of the universe. They had barely seemed to notice his presence among the billions of thoughts passing along the superspace channel which they used to communicate.

He must not have gone entirely unnoticed, for one day, *she* made contact with him.

Hello, Michael. I was wondering when you'd come.

Lissa. For all his powers, that was all he could think.

I see you haven't made the transition all that cleanly. What do you plan to do with your little world? Keep it safe, like an animal in a cage? Or let it go, to seek its own destiny?

He couldn't answer her directly, because he didn't truly know. The Marobite might still loom up, but he knew that he was the greater threat. Would he let them go? Was he beyond the attachment he had formed with them?

It's not an easy path to walk, playing God. Come join us. We aren't the only race to have forced our evolution like this. There are projects underway, challenges, that you could not have imagined before. Let these people determine their own fate. They deserve that much.

He cut off communication.

No, not yet, he thought. Not while Katherine lived. A stubborn part of the man he had been lingered on, and it would not let go easily.

●●●

One fall, many years after the great battle in the sky, a mysterious garden appeared on Katherine Shane's farm. No one could recall anyone planting anything in that spot, but the crop was there nonetheless: perfect specimens of strange red and green fruit.

A woman, walking with a limp but still with a purposeful gait, made her way out to the garden when her son informed her of it. It was towards sunset, and the evening wind caused an unruly patch of gray hair to flap constantly over her eyes. She ignored it and reached down to pick a tomato off the nearest bush.

"Are they poisonous, Mother?" Garrett asked. "You might want to be careful."

Smiling, she took a small bite and savored the alien flavor as she had done for the first time so many years ago. A minuscule tear emerged from her eye. In the gusting wind, it dried quickly on her cheek.

"What's wrong, Mother?" Garrett asked.

"Nothing . . . not really, anyway. I was just remembering your father. He used to plant these every year, hoping they'd finally take hold. I kept meaning to tell him it really wasn't worth the effort, that these plants weren't meant for Novista. But he was convinced he could make things the way he wanted, so I held my tongue. Looks like he wanted to prove me wrong."

She looked towards the horizon and wondered if he was listening.

"Aidan, what now?" she threw to the wind. "We know you're still around, helping us. The signs are obvious. But you know we can't stay like this forever. We're still the same humans who crawled down out of the trees and went to the stars. We'll want to go back. What then? Will you keep us here, plowing our earth and planting our crops, even as we dream of better things?"

The wind answered her with silence, but despite the cold, she stayed until the stars came out, to view their feeble, provocative fire.

FAME? FORTUNE? CHOCOLATE?

Written by
Michael H. Payne

About the Author

Michael Payne gives a pretty thoroug account of his past writing in the body the essay—and in the first person, too—so we won't go into here. His comic strip Terebinth *is currently appearing i* YARF! The Journal of Applied Anthropomorphics, *an he has stories upcoming in the second issue of* Anthrolation *and the final volume of the* Sword and Sorceress *antholog series. He lives a good ways south of Los Angeles, plays guita and sings at the local Catholic Church, clerks at the loca library, and hosts a Saturday morning radio program at th local university: www.kuci.org/~mpayne will give you all th information you might need about it.*

And now I'm supposed to be giving out advice.

Like I know anything.

But here goes.

Now, my father for as long as I've known him—and that's thirty-five years this last February—has talked about becoming rich and famous.

How was he gonna do this?

Well, at one time, by writing science fiction novels.

He wrote three, a series, so if he sold one, he'd have the sequels all ready to go. He sent 'em out, and they all came back with rejection slips. Personal rejection slips with nice comments from the editors at the bottom, sure, but rejection slips nonetheless.

Then he heard about a contest, the very contest in whose anthology this essay is scheduled to appear. He figured he could get famous for his short fiction first, then sell the novels later. So he wrote some short stories and sent them in. He'd entered four or five times before I sent in my novelette "Crow's Curse" and won third place for the fourth quarter of 1990.

Well, my father decided to try his hand at historical fiction. I went to the 1991 *Writers of the Future* workshop, wrote fifteen short stories over the next year, and finally sold the sixteenth to Gardner Dozois. Of the sixteen I wrote after that, Dozois bought a couple more, Marion

Zimmer Bradley took one, our own Algis Budrys took a bunch and also bought my first novel, serialized it in his magazine, brought the book to the attention of Tom Doherty, and got it published on paper even after Tor had rejected it once.

My short fiction has gathered honorable mentions in *The Year's Best Science Fiction* and top-ten finishes in several *Asimov's* Readers' Choice polls. My book made the preliminary Nebula ballot, was short-listed for the William L. Crawford award for best first fantasy novel, got positive mentions in *The Year's Best Fantasy and Horror,* in *Locus* and in a couple newspapers.

I belong to SFWA and run their circulating book plan. I'm also a regular reviewer for *Tangent* magazine, both its old print version and now on its Web site.

My father's name is Lee Payne. My name's up there under this essay's title.

Chances are you've never heard of either one of us.

So that's my first piece of advice: If you're looking for fame, you might wanna consider looking somewhere else. Become a firefighter or a doctor or a pro wrestler, someone who does something respectable in the eyes of the world.

As for fortune, well, my father retired a few years back, and going on Social Security, he ended up getting a raise; his monthly check now is larger than any he ever got during the thirty-five-plus years he worked as a photographer for our local newspaper.

And me? I made a grand total of $0.00 from my writing in 1999. So far this year I've made $150.34. I still live at home with my parents; I can't afford a car or an apartment anywhere near where I work.

Fame and fortune both, therefore, get the old heave-ho.

Which leaves us with chocolate.

Why chocolate? 'Cause I like chocolate. And I like writing these strange little stories. And since my two part-time jobs cover my rent and basic expenses, to my way of thinking, my writing can be pure chocolate, something I do simply because I like it.

Not very professional, I know; I mean, "something I do simply because I like it" is more or less the dictionary definition of *amateur*, from the Latin word for lover, y'know.

And here's the evidence. My book, *The Blood Jaguar*, came out in hardback in December 1998, and all I've had published since has been in fanzines: one story and some comic strips. Sure, I finished my second novel and five short stories in that time, started my third book, prodded three more shorts toward completion, and kept twelve previous stories circulating to various paying markets; but the only money I've made since the novel's advance has been from stories in a half-cent-a-word zine due out this summer and an anthology scheduled for 2002.

And, yeah, I sometimes think that maybe if I didn't see my stuff as chocolate, maybe if I wasn't just writing stuff I wanted to read, maybe if I wrote what the editors are buying—and I've had more than one editor wonder in a rejection letter whether all my stories really needed to have talking animals in them—maybe I'd sell more.

But the few times I've tailored a story to a market . . . See, I subscribe to most of the magazines that pay more than three cents a word, and every once in a while, I get a will-o'-the-wisp flash of insight into what sort of story a particular editor wants to see. I bound downstairs, write that kind of story, send it in, and each time, it bounces just as quickly and efficiently as one of my chocolate stories.

Except, of course, for the time the late Marion Zimmer Bradley complained on the editorial page of her magazine that everyone sent her stories about dragons and unicorns but no one ever sent her stories about cows. One talking-cow story later, I had another sale under my belt.

What it's all made me understand, though, is something that might as well be another piece of advice: Don't waste your time looking for the secret way to get published. As far as I can tell, getting published is as much a mystery as chocolate is.

I mean, yes, I know you grind up cacao beans and mix in sugar and milk and whatnot. But when you get right down to it, a story is just words ground up on a page and mixed grammatically with plot and character. The recipe doesn't explain the divine mystery of chocolate any more that it explains the wonder of getting the little envelope from the editor instead of the big one.

Granted, on those days when it's been the big envelope over and over and over again, stories flooding back with "No, thank you" letters attached, I really want to believe that there's a secret out there, a secret I don't know because I'm not part of the inner circle, not the *Analog* Mafia or the Secret Masters of Fandom, or because I'm just a fringe member of SFWA and haven't been deemed worthy of the proper sigil to put on my cover letters.

But, well, I have had stuff published. I can't deny it.

Which means I hafta face facts: the stories coming back to me tasted chalky and bitter when the editor was looking for smooth and sweet. Or vice versa, for that matter. And just because I think it's the best thing I've ever written—the finest chocolate ever minted—doesn't mean an editor is under any obligation to buy it.

Cursing the Fates doesn't help. At least, it's never helped me: your mileage may vary. All I can do is send the story to somebody else and start again, mix up another batch, get it as tasty as I can before I send it out, too.

The question "why?" should probably come into things here. I mean, why go through the trouble of putting the stuff together if in all likelihood it's just gonna come back uneaten and unenjoyed?

Well, as I said, I like chocolate. And I don't know any better feeling than sharing something I like with other folks.

Making enough to keep myself in raw materials, as it were, that ain't bad either; but, well, really, the money's just a side effect. After all—and I hafta remind myself of this more often than I'd like—chocolate is its own reward. When every story is some sort of chocolate, then not a one can be bad or embarrassing or make me wish I hadn't written it. And sure, maybe fame and fortune will follow, but I've gotta tell you: I'm not really counting on it.

So read the other essays scattered through the anthology here, essays from folks who I can almost guarantee know what they're talking about more than I do. Read the essays in previous volumes. Read the stories, read the magazines, read the books—your local library can probably help with that. Gather your ingredients. Then mix up your own chocolate.

Persevere—that's good advice, now that I think about it, just that one word—and who knows? Someone might just buy something from you someday.

Even if they don't, though, you'll still have the chocolate. And written chocolate's a lot easier on the teeth and waistline: one first piece of advice, I guess. . . .

DAIMON! DAIMON!

Written by
Jeff Rutherford

Illustrated by
Judith Holman

About the Author

Jeff Rutherford grew up in Macon, Georgia; he escaped into science fiction and fantasy books, comic books and movies. When he was in sixth grade, a piece of writing that he submitted in his English class won a prize in a school writing contest. With a degree in journalism from the University of Georgia, he has worked as a temp, a newspaper reporter and a literary agent.

Jeff currently does public relations for technology and Internet companies. Only a few weeks after learning that he was a finalist in the Writers of the Future Contest, he sold his first short story to a small-press horror magazine, Dread.

He lives in a great garden apartment in the Williamsburg neighborhood of Brooklyn with his fiancée. In his spare time and to stay in shape, he rollerblades around the streets of New York City. In fact, he's the vice-president of the Empire Skate Club—a rollerblading club that leads organized group skates throughout New York City.

About the Illustrator

In an unusual move, we have asked for an illustration for "Daimon! Daimon!" from Judith Holman, author of an essay in this volume.

I finally found Robert "Sweetpea" Champagne in St. Martinville, Louisiana, in the summer of '52.

When I returned to the Evangeline Hotel after a morning walking the dirt streets of St. Martinville, a town on the twisted banks of the Bayou Teche, a young man dressed in a crisp red-and-white uniform approached me in the lobby.

"Some nigger left you a note," he said, pushing a folded scrap of paper in my hand. "Came by to see you. Will try again later."

Underneath the message, someone had scrawled their name, and I could barely recognize the words— Robert Champagne.

Late afternoon sunlight filled my motel room with an orange glow, when someone knocked on the door a couple of hours later. A window fan swirled the warm air around the room. I sat the empty beer bottle in my hand on the bedside table and answered the door.

"He's down there," the boy said, nodding his head.

"Thank you."

Closing the door, I studied myself in the mirror. I straightened my tie, shrugged on my jacket, and ran my hands through my curly black hair.

"Sweetpea," as all his friends and family called him, stood in the leafy shade of a banana tree in the

courtyard behind the hotel, smoking a handrolled cigarette. A humid breeze stirred the wide, green leaves. I
could see the black clouds forming overhead, contrasting
sharply with the white columns of the hotel's exterior.

Thumping the butt away, Champagne exhaled.
Smoke eddied out of his nose and mouth, obscuring his
dark face for a moment. Brown flecks of tobacco clung
to his bottom lip.

He stared at me as I hurried across the courtyard,
my movements edgy and hyper from the buzz of excitement coursing through my body. I had heard so much
about Champagne's music, and finally the man stood in
front of me in the flesh.

"I'm so glad you came to see me," I said, holding out
my hand.

Champagne stuck his hands into the back pockets of
his dark pants and nodded.

"Guess I didn't have much choice," he said. "All I
been hearing around here is how some white man from
New York City come into town looking for me."

"I'm sorry . . . if I handled this in the wrong way.
After you answered the letter that I sent you in
January, I decided to come down here and record
some of your music."

"Why you want to do that?"

"Because your music means something."

"To who?"

"I'm sure a lot of people around here do not realize
the importance of your music. It's not like the syrupy
white-bread music you hear on the radio. You sing
about real things—real people. Someday, I think more
people will recognize that."

With a grin, Champagne pulled a bag of tobacco out
of his back pocket and started rolling another cigarette.

"Wish more of the people 'round here recognized it right now," he said. Lighting the cigarette, he flicked the match into the twisted greenery of a blooming crepe myrtle. "I could use the damn money."

"I'm sure you could. I'm willing to pay you for your time, and I will sign a document, and give you a copy, that promises that I will never use these tapes for commercial gain. I'm not coming down here to record your music and rip you off like some of those white men up in Chicago. These tapes will be strictly for documenting a unique American musical form."

"No wonder my mama talked highly of you," Champagne said. "You sound just like her, using a big word every time you can. I reckon if you want to record some of my songs, we can do that. But let's get started—tonight. I don't plan on being in town long. Some of the white people around here are in pretty bad moods. They been reading the papers and watching TV about all the marches over in Mississippi and Alabama. They're just waiting for a good excuse to lynch somebody, and I'm not the most popular nigger in this town."

"I'm ready whenever you are," I said. "I'll need to run back up to my room and get my recording equipment."

Thunder cracked overhead, and rain started pattering against the wide leaves of the banana tree.

"I borrowed a Chevrolet from a friend of mine in Baton Rouge. It's parked out back in the alley," I said. Fishing my key ring out of my pocket, I tossed it to Champagne. "Why don't you have a seat in there while I get my stuff."

"Uh . . . you mentioned giving me some money for my playing," Champagne said, pocketing the keys. "When did you plan on giving that to me?"

I could see that it pained him to ask a white man for money.

Illustrated by Judith Holman

"I've got a check already made out from the university in my luggage," I said. "But take this. We'll consider it a bonus for your agreeing to listen to a harebrained Yankee."

I flipped my wallet open and tossed him a ten.

Champagne grinned as he stuck the money into his shirt pocket.

"I'll meet you at the car," he said. "I need to go get something."

I had heard about Champagne's drinking, but I wasn't about to pass judgment on the man for enjoying a good drink. If I had to live in the daily hell of subjugation, I'd probably drink too, a lot.

Rushing back into the hotel, I collared the bellboy to help me load my recording equipment. As we pushed and pulled the bulky trunk into the elevator, thunder boomed, rattling the roof beams overhead. I could hear the rushing sound of water pouring down.

"It's gonna be a big 'un," the bellboy said as he closed the gate and punched the lobby button.

Dragging the trunk out of the elevator, we stopped in the high-ceilinged lobby. A crowd of employees and guests milled around, staring out the plate-glass window at the heavy, gray sheets of rain. Water spewed out of the drainspouts, shooting arcs of water across the sidewalk. Water rushed down Main Street in a muddy torrent, boiling out of the drains.

With outstretched arms, a dark figure wearing a sodden green coat waddled out of the street, tripped across the low curb, and stumbled onto the sidewalk. Pinwheeling both arms for balance, the person bounced off the brick wall of the hotel and staggered to the front door. A hand slapped the front window of the hotel, and the crowd drew back with an audible gasp. The light brown flesh of the person's palm pressed against the window. Raindrops slithered down the glass and around the hand.

With the other hand, the person grabbed the door handle and pushed open the door. A gust of wind swept through the opening, spraying water across the deep red carpet, as Mrs. Violla Champagne, an eighty-eight-year-old black woman, stepped across the threshold of the front doors of the Evangeline Hotel for the first time in her life. I recognized her from the day before when I had visited her small one-room shack, looking for her son.

"Hey, hey," said an elderly man standing in the crowd, raising his wooden walking cane.

The man's words sent the bellboy beside me into action. He circled the crowd and approached the woman with both his hands stuck out in front of him, palms up, and caught her as she sagged through the door.

"Mrs. Champagne, you know you can't come in here," he said. "Now, get on back out there."

Mrs. Champagne kicked the door, and it slammed shut behind her with a metallic clang that echoed through the lobby. Straightening her head, she wiped the water off her forehead with her bunched fingertips.

"Son, it's raining outside. I stepped inside to get out of the rain just like anybody else would. There's nothing wrong with me standing here."

Putting his hand on her shoulder, the bellboy reached around her, opened the door and forced her back onto the sidewalk with the bulk of his body. At first, she didn't resist. But as she stepped back on the sidewalk, a blast of wind whipped around her and pushed her wet hair into her face.

She stood unmoving for several seconds with her hair hanging in her face, and the rainwater running off of the roof, pelting her shoulders. With an audible sigh, she straightened her back, pushed her hair back again and wiped her face, then jabbed the bellboy in the chest with her bony forefinger. Surprised at her audacity, he stepped back, and Mrs. Champagne squirmed past him and pushed her way into the lobby a second time.

"Gawdammit!" the bellboy cried. "You tryin' to be one uppity nigger, ain't you?"

Pulling the door shut against the rain, he turned around. Mrs. Champagne stood in the lobby surrounded by the surprised crowd. Water dripped from her sodden coat.

A loud, explosive cracking echoed through the lobby. I jumped at the sound, scared that someone had pulled a gun. The manager stood behind the front counter, his open hand flat against the dark wood. His fleshy, drooping cheeks glowed an ugly red.

"Mrs. Champagne," he hollered. "We've had 'bout enough of your damn foolishness. Now get your ass out that door right now."

"Not this time, Mr. Melancon," she replied. "I'm tired of having the white man's foot across my neck, and I'm here to tell you—no more. You hear that? No more."

The crowd drew back from the wrinkled, dripping black woman as she moved deeper into the lobby, her voice strengthening.

I saw the bellboy pounce. He clamped his hand onto Mrs. Champagne's neck and wrenched her arm behind her back.

Surprising myself, I reacted, elbowing my way through the crowd. Mrs. Champagne yelped in pain, and an ugly titter washed through the crowd. With Mrs. Champagne bent over in front of him, the bellboy tried to open the door with his foot.

I pushed my way around him and blocked the door. Keeping my fists at my side, I tried to reason with him.

"Come on, let her go. She's just an old woman. What's it going to hurt to let her stay in here until the rain slacks off?"

The crowd reacted angrily to my words.

"He ain't from 'round here."

"Damn Yankee."

"He probably came down here to stir up the niggers."

Prevented from pushing Mrs. Champagne out the door, the bellboy glared at me across her arched back as he tightened his grip on her neck, grinding her bones under his large white hand.

Mrs. Champagne gasped for breath.

"Stop it!" I yelled. "You're hurting her."

"Damn right I am," the bellboy said. Stepping towards me, he shoved her forward and her head thumped against the wall.

I wasn't exactly a stranger to fisticuffs. Growing up in a tenement on the lower East Side, I had learned to fight at an early age to defend myself and my family.

I leaned awkwardly over Mrs. Champagne's bent frame and popped the bellboy in the jaw with a right jab. When his lip burst against his teeth, the young boy staggered back and released his grip on Mrs. Champagne as he cupped his hand to his bleeding mouth. Wiping his hand over his face, smearing blood across his cheek, the teenager charged me, swinging his arms.

Watching him approach, I steeled myself for a fight, and stood my ground. At the last possible second, I ducked underneath his wildly swinging arms, punched him in the stomach and wrapped my arms around his waist. Retching and gasping for breath, he sagged against me, and I shoved the door open and pushed him out onto the rainy sidewalk.

Pulling the door shut, I slid my arm around Mrs. Champagne's quivering shoulders and steered her to a nearby settee. The crowd parted ahead of us; I ignored the grumbles and complaints. I cupped my hand to Mrs. Champagne's shoulder and patted her hip ineffectually with my open hand.

She raised her head, pushed back her matted, damp hair and fixed me with a stare.

"I am through backing down," she said. "They will have to kill me to get me out of here. I'm not moving an inch."

"You know they probably will kill you," I said.

"Then I'll just be the martyr of South Louisiana," she said. "But mark my words, I'm not moving. It's about time the white people in this town started facing the truth."

"I sure didn't mean to stir you up when I came by the house yesterday looking for your son," I said.

Mrs. Champagne barked with laughter. She slapped her thigh and rocked forward on the velvet upholstery that had taunted her from inside the plate-glass window of the hotel all her life.

"You didn't have anything to do with this, Mr. New York City," she cackled. "I was talking to God last night, and he told me it was time to stop flapping my lips and time to really start doing something. You just happened to be around to see it."

A chorus of gasps rippled through the crowd, catching my attention. When I looked up, the people were parting in front of the settee. Robert Champagne stood in the open doorway.

Misting rain swept through the opened wooden door, pattering against the deep red carpet. A sodden black coat hung from Champagne's gaunt frame, and rainwater dripped from the hem.

"Mama, come on," he said. "Let's go home. Now's not the time to start this."

"It's past time," Mrs. Champagne said, slapping the cushion again. "I'm not leaving."

A beefy gun-bull from the St. Martinville Police Department stepped out of the muddy street and onto the sidewalk. In one swift motion, he unhooked his nightstick from a loop on his belt and rammed the dripping black wood into Sweetpea's ribs. Stunned by the blow, Sweetpea fell onto the sidewalk; he clutched his side, gasping for breath.

As the crowd cheered the bull's actions, a sickening revulsion swept through me. The people standing around me looked like humans, but their flesh and bones disguised their demonic countenances. Flames had withered their hearts and souls.

"Get off that couch, you nigger bitch," the bull hollered as he pulled the door shut behind him, blocking the rain and wind that had been sweeping into the lobby.

"Did you hear me?" the man screamed. Blood coursed in his fleshy cheeks. Raindrops dripped from the wide, round brim of his tan hat and trickled down his mottled skin.

"Listen to the man," I whispered to Mrs. Champagne.

"Mister," the man screamed, "git your hands up and git away from her!" Fearful of ending up in the St.

Martinville jail and getting a dose of the screws' batons, or worse, I grabbed for air and shuffled back.

"I'll tell you one more time, lady," he said. "Get off that couch and get your black ass out of this hotel."

With her clenched fists clutched over her chest, Mrs. Champagne started singing. At first, the words were soft and scratchy, catching in her throat; then she started belting out the chorus of "Amazing Grace."

Her voice lifted in song, coupled with Mrs. Champagne's blatant refusal to budge, stoked the policeman's anger. He charged across the lobby, spraying droplets of rainwater each time his black cowboy boots slammed into the carpeted floor.

As he ran, he jerked the nightstick above his head, gripping the worn wood in both meaty fists.

When I tried to rationalize my behavior later, I told myself that I was sure the pig would shatter her knee or punch her in the gut. He did neither.

He killed her.

Grinding his feet into the carpet, he whipped his upper body around, harnessing the momentum of his short burst of speed across the lobby, and brought the baton down in a solid two-handed swing.

I heard the sickening crunch of Mrs. Champagne's jawbone and the dull pop of her neck breaking. The force of the blow lifted her off the couch and snapped her head backwards at a sickening angle. Her body jerked spasmodically across the carpet. Blood sprayed out of the tattered flaps of gray skin on her shattered face.

The policeman straddled her body in a wide stance, cradling the nightstick against his chest.

"Mr. Melancon," the man hollered at the manager. "Get your ass over here. We've got a piece of garbage to throw out."

The double-glass lobby door swung open with a crash. Sweetpea hurtled across the lobby, his arms outstretched. A woman screamed, and the cop turned his head. But Sweetpea was on him before he could react.

Wrapping his arms around the man's chest, Sweetpea jerked the nightstick out of his hands as easily as if he were yanking a lollipop out of a child's hand. The policeman lurched forward, his hand scrabbling at the holster riding his hip beneath his overlapping belly.

Sweetpea hopped over his mother's still-jerking body and swung the nightstick in his own savage two-handed grip. With a screech, the policeman jerked his arms up. His right hand flopped back and forth loosely against his chest as his screams spiraled upward.

Leaping forward, Sweetpea cracked the nightstick across the policeman's wide shoulders. The policeman crashed through the front window. Ragged chunks of glass rained down, mixing with the raindrops falling from the sky.

Collapsing across the hood of a Ford, the policeman turned over. A dagger of glass stuck out of the porcine flesh of his throat. With a loud screech, a woman beside me fainted, grabbing on to her husband's shoulder.

As I watched, helpless to act, the policeman yanked the glass shard out and cupped his hands to his torn throat. Blood squirted between his twitching fingers, drenching his yellow slicker in red rivulets.

Gasping for breath, I turned away from the sight of the dying man. But the sound of wailing sirens immediately caught my attention. I turned back to the window and watched as a police car roared into view. The driver cut the wheel, and the car slid sideways to a stop in front of the hotel, throwing up a sheet of dirty, brown water.

The sight of the spinning red lights goaded me into action.

"Sweetpea!" I hollered, as fear clutched at my insides. Stumbling across the sofa, I grabbed his arm. "If you don't leave now, you're dead," I said.

Despite the trauma and shock of witnessing his mother's brutal death, he knew that I spoke the truth.

"Let's go," he said, as the door of the police car swung open.

Spinning around, I sprinted across the lobby. My trunk of recording equipment blocked my way. Determined not to lose the equipment that I had accrued from years of skimping and working odd jobs, I grabbed the handle and hauled the trunk onto my shoulder. Stumbling under its weight, I staggered into the back hallway of the hotel lobby and lumbered down a short flight of concrete steps. When I reached the bottom, Sweetpea barreled past me and kicked open the back door.

The metal door slapped open, and the sound echoed down the alley. Sweetpea hopped behind the wheel. Skidding to a stop, I shoved the trunk into the back seat and piled in after it. When I turned to pull the door shut, I heard somebody shouting from inside the back hallway of the hotel.

"Get us outta here," I yelled. Sweetpea floored the gas pedal and yanked the steering wheel to the right. The front bumper dug into the alley wall, and a shower of sparks arced over the hood and bounced off the windshield.

Hunched down in the back seat, I stared out the rear window and watched as several policemen burst out the back door of the hotel.

"Look out!" I hollered, ducking down.

Gunshots banged behind us, the noise sounding like a string of exploding firecrackers. I dug my face into the seat cover as the back window imploded, spraying glass into the rear of the car. Glass shivers pricked the back of my neck.

When we reached the end of the alley, the Chevrolet lurched sideways as we slid onto Main Street, throwing up a spray of water and mud.

I heard the screech of brakes, and I jerked my head up. The thick, tubular metal grille of a Greyhound bus loomed in the two side windows. The Chevrolet skidded out of the bus's path, but its bumper snagged our trunk. The impact shoved us onto the sidewalk, and I tumbled onto the floorboard, my shoulder digging into a pile of shattered glass. Despite the Chevrolet's crumpled rear end, it didn't stop moving.

Guiding us off the sidewalk and back onto the muddy street, Sweetpea floored the accelerator. Sirens wailed behind us as we fishtailed down the highway. When we reached the outskirts of town, Sweetpea jerked the steering wheel to the left and swerved into the path of a sugar-cane tractor. Before the driver could react, we shot across the highway and rattled down a muddy dirt road. Tar paper and tin shacks crowded the sides of the road. Water gushed off the crooked edges of the shacks' roofs. An old black woman standing on her front porch smiled at us as we flew by, a wide toothless grin splitting her wrinkled gray face.

A sudden gust of wind whipped a sheet of rain across the road. I saw the flashing red lights of a police car winking on and off in the distance. I heard the faint wail of its siren as the Chevrolet rattled over a wooden bridge and plunged into the thick cypress forest. Gnarled blackened roots crowded the narrow muddy path. In the glare of the headlights, rain dripped from the Spanish moss like droplets of molten silver.

The road suddenly climbed, leaving the marshy bottomland. Sweetpea stomped on the gas pedal, and the Chevrolet exploded out of the arboreal tunnel and sailed through the air. When the big automobile slammed down atop a levee, the impact knocked me into a twisted heap.

Spinning the steering wheel, Sweetpea punched the brake. Slinging mud and water, the Chevrolet skidded to a stop.

"Mister, . . . I . . . I need you to drive," Sweetpea said between clenched teeth as he slumped across the front seat. A red stain blossomed over the front of his dirty white shirt.

"What happened? Are you hurt bad?" I hollered as I stumbled out of the back seat.

Pausing long enough to brush off the glass shivers clinging to my dungarees, I squeezed into the front seat next to Sweetpea.

"One of those bastards got me," he said. "I don't think it's gonna kill me, but I need to get somewhere and take a look."

"Where did you plan on us going?" I asked. "I don't think the law enforcement authorities in Baton Rouge would take too kindly to a Yankee helping out a wounded Negro."

"I ain't going to Baton Rouge," Sweetpea said. "And I sure as hell ain't going to no law. Get in . . . I'll tell you where to go."

With Sweetpea giving me directions between labored breaths, I drove the Chevrolet as fast as I could without dumping us into the dark, black depths of the

Atchafalaya Basin. After fifteen minutes of winding and twisting roads, Sweetpea pointed at a gnarled weeping willow tree.

"Pull up right there," he muttered, slapping the dashboard. "Go on . . . pull up under the branches. It looks like you're driving into the water, but you're not . . . trust me."

I eased the Chevrolet forward underneath the drooping willow branches. Sodden leaves slapped the front window, shooting tendrils of rainwater curling and twisting across the glass.

I stopped the car at the edge of a small hill which led down to the edge of the black water.

"How long are we going to hide out here?" I asked. "We need to start talking about how we're going to deal with this situation. We've got to get in contact with the sheriff and see if we can arrange a peaceful surrender. I've got a cousin who works in the Manhattan DA's office. I can get him to come down here and help us out."

"If your cousin comes flying down here spouting his legal bullshit, he'll end up hanging from a tree just like us."

"What do you mean?" I cried. "There are witnesses back there who can tell what really happened in the hotel lobby."

Sweetpea laughed. Cupping his hand to his shoulder, he winced as he tried not to chuckle.

"You been here a week, and you think you know a lot about how we live down here. Let me tell you . . . you don't know shit.

"The only way I'll stay alive now is to get the hell out of Louisiana. I got some kin I can stay with up in Chicago, but I can't travel feeling like this."

"Well, what are we going to do out here in the middle of the swamp?" I hollered. "I came down here to record your music, not to get lynched."

My stomach felt bloated, and a wad of bile crept up my throat.

"Cool it," Sweetpea said. "We ain't dead yet. Not by a long shot."

With a low groan, he shoved his door open and staggered out. As I pushed my door open and followed him, I could hear the rain pattering against the branches and leaves overhead and plinking off the hood of the Chevrolet.

Standing under the tree in the pale afternoon light, I momentarily forgot the events of the past hour as I stared at the twisted cypress trees and blackened knees poking out of the rich brown water of the Atchafalaya. Thick curtains of Spanish moss hung from the branches, creating an organic network of tunnels and caves above the water.

When Sweetpea gasped for breath and struggled to remain standing as he leaned against the door frame, reality rushed back in. The sparkling glass strewn across the back seat, the crumpled rear end of the Chevrolet, and the tacky red bloodstain on the front seat served to remind me of the seriousness of our situation.

"Help me get to the water," Sweetpea said when I circled the front of the car.

Sliding my arm gently around his back, I pulled him close.

"You can put your weight on me," I said. "Maybe it won't hurt as bad."

Nodding wordlessly, Sweetpea struggled forward. As he leaned against me, I could smell the thick, sharp scent of his sweat.

When we reached the shallow water of the basin, Sweetpea kneeled and sat down in the mud.

"Mister, you see that cypress right there, the one that looks like a damn whore bending over in front of you? There's a rope tied to that tree right about the waterline. It kind of blends in with the color of the tree, and you cain't see it from here. If you walk straight out from here to that cypress, the water won't come above your waist —but walk straight. I don't want to have to swim out there and save you."

I shivered as I waded into the basin and the cold water soaked my pants legs.

"If we're going to be spending some time together," I hollered over my shoulder, "you need to call me something besides 'mister.' My name is Ira . . . Ira Goldstein."

I moved forward, shuffling my feet across the muddy bottom. My movement churned up the brackish water. Bits of rotted wood and slimy clumps of vegetation bobbed to the surface and clung to my legs. The chilly water rose to my waist, then splashed against my stomach, turning my white shirt a dirty brown.

As I slogged ahead, something brushed against my leg. I hissed out a breath of air as I slowly stepped sideways. My hands trembled, and my heart thudded against my chest.

"It's a root, it was some kind of underwater vine or plant, something . . . it's not a snake . . . it's not an alligator," I whispered to myself.

When the water lapped against my chest, I didn't know if I would be able to make it. Fear slid through my body and my eyes flickered shut as panic welled up inside me. I could feel my balls shrinking up, and I was afraid that I was going to pee in my pants.

I clutched the bottom branches of the cypress with my trembling hands and pulled myself out of the water.

"You find the rope?" Sweetpea hollered.

I slid onto a branch and pulled my legs out of the muddy water. Nodding weakly, I reached down between my legs and grabbed the rope lashed to one of the bottom branches. Bracing my feet against the trunk, I pulled. It felt like the rope was tied to a block of concrete. My first effort wasn't a success.

I wrapped the rope around my right forearm, then rocked back against the limb I was standing on, using my weight and leverage to pull on the rope.

Nothing happened—at first. Water dripped from the taut rope, dotting the water with ripples.

Then, the rope went slack. I fell back and my butt smacked the tree limb. The pirogue surfaced in an explosive burst of bubbles and mud. Reaching down between my legs, I grabbed the edge of the boat. My fingers slid across the slime-coated surface, and the cypress craft spun around, slinging water and mud.

When I reached the muddy bank where Sweetpea waited, I dragged one end of the boat out of the water and scooped the water out with my cupped hands. Sweetpea knelt in the mud and untied a long wooden pole I hadn't noticed lashed to the side of the pirogue.

"Where are we going?" I asked, flinging a handful of muddy water out of the boat.

"Friend of mine's got a little fishing cabin I've used before," Sweetpea said. "I've gone out there to play my music or to lay low when some gal's husband been lookin' to shoot me."

An idea quickly formed in my mind. It would be awkward, but I was willing to give it a shot.

"Can we take my recording equipment out to the cabin?" I asked. "We'll probably be out there a while. We might as well do something with our time. I can at least get some recordings of you singing some stuff acappella."

"Don't have to be acappella," Sweetpea said. "I gots a guitar and a mouth harp that I keep out there."

"Perfect," I said. I blocked the earlier scene at the hotel out of my mind as I hauled the trunk out of the back seat and dragged it to the boat.

"You t'ink you can use this pole?" Sweetpea asked, handing me the slender wooden pole he had untied from the pirogue. "I'll tell you where to go."

"I'll give it a shot," I said. "You don't think we'll have a problem keeping this thing floating with this trunk weighing us down, do you?"

Sweetpea laughed, and the sound echoed through the trees.

"I've seen these things so loaded down with gators or fish that water slops over the bow every time somebody farts—don't you be worrying about that trunk."

After Sweetpea scrambled in, I waited for him to get settled, then handed him the pole and waded into the black water, pushing us away from the bank. Pulling myself into the pirogue, I rolled over onto my back. Water dripped from my wet pants, mixing with the pool of brown water in the bottom. Spreading my arms wide to steady myself, I slowly stood up. A low-hanging branch brushed my head and I crouched down.

"Get us out in the deep water and you won't have to worry about those low branches," Sweetpea said, handing me the slender wooden pole.

Plunging the pole into the water, I shoved it against the bottom and set the craft sliding away from the shore. As I tried to yank the pole out of the water, my weight shifted. I dropped down in the pirogue to keep from falling, and my knee banged the wooden seat.

"Slow and steady," Sweetpea said, as he hunched over, cupping his hand to his shoulder. "We ain't shootin' de rapids here, mister. Don't jerk it from the water. After you push off, just ease it out, then slide it back down and push off again."

Following his advice, I quickly adjusted to guiding the craft through the swamp. In the breaks overhead, I could see black thunderheads piling up in the sky above us. Rain beat down, pummeling the branches and Spanish moss. Wiping the rain out of my eyes, I steered us away from the levee. Sweetpea stretched out, leaning back against the trunk of recording equipment. As we slid underneath the towering cypresses and glided over thick patches of water lilies, he dipped water out of the bottom with a rusted, bent coffee can.

The storm fled as quickly as it had formed, and the thick, wet humidity cloaked us once again. At one point, Sweetpea stiffened and sat up, cupping his hand around his ear. Then he jabbed his finger at a thick clump of cypresses and vegetation. I poled the boat into the riotous growth, and we sat quietly, waiting. Under Sweetpea's direction, I busied myself pulling thick stalks of dried river cane into the pirogue, and angling it out of the boat.

Finally, Sweetpea raised his arm with a soft grunt of pain, and I slid down onto my haunches. A tin boat loaded with sunburned fishermen roared by, oblivious to our presence. A short, squat man lay on a pile of fish in the front of the boat, sipping from a bottle of Jax beer.

As I sat silently in the pirogue, rocking in the wake of the fishermen's boat, with sweat dripping down my forehead, I wondered if I would ever see Bleeker Street again, or hear the familiar and comforting sound of a New York taxi horn. Pushing those thoughts grimly out of my mind, I tried to stay focused on what I needed to do to stay alive for the next twenty-four hours. Namely, stay alert and listen to everything Sweetpea said. He knew what was going on. I didn't.

As the sun sank towards the horizon, bathing the swamp in an orange, fiery glow, I poled the pirogue under the drooping branches of a cypress and into a small, looping cove. A wooden shack sat beneath a clump of pecan trees at the end of the cove. A large rust stain on the roof resembled a map of Louisiana.

Ignoring the pain in my chapped fingers, I shoved the pole into the water and pushed with all my strength. When the boat bumped against the crooked wooden dock jutting out into the water, Sweetpea scrambled onto the dock and secured the craft.

"I can handle this," I said, pulling the rope gently out of his hands. "Go on in and rest. I hope you've got a first-aid kid out here so you can do something for your shoulder."

Sweetpea chuckled and murmured under his breath as he walked down the dock. "First-aid kit, yeah . . . right," he said, shaking his head.

Weighted down with the trunk of recording equipment, I lumbered into the cabin. The small one-room shack was remarkably dry and stuffy. As I set the trunk down, Sweetpea pushed open a window centered in the back wall. A cool breeze swirled through the open window. I sat down on the trunk and fanned myself, enjoying the cool air.

A black iron stove sat beside the open window. With a pained grimace, Sweetpea plopped down on a corn-husk pallet shoved in the corner of the room. Closing his eyes, he leaned his head back against the wall. I could see the sweat drip from his face and spiral down the black corded muscles of his neck.

"What can I do for you?" I asked. "I think we should try to get a compress on that wound to stop the bleeding."

"I want to bleed," Sweetpea said.

His lips peeled back from his teeth; the muscles in his neck jumped and twitched like those of a racehorse after a grueling run. The thick, strong scent of his sweaty, unwashed body filled my head.

"Those motherfuckers shot me, and I want . . . to . . . bleed. Go out on the back porch. There's some shelves out there, and there ought to be a jar of moonshine stuck behind some old quilts. Bring it to me."

I found the jar of clear liquid hidden behind a stack of molding, rotted quilts. Twisting off the lid, I snuck a smell of the moonshine. The reaction was instantaneous. As the bitter, sharp smell invaded my nose, I started coughing. When I walked back into the cabin, wiping my nose with the back of my arm, Sweetpea grinned at me.

Looking down I noticed that he had pulled off his shirt. Drops of sweat beaded his coal black skin like dew clinging to a dark rock. With each ragged breath, his chest rose and fell in a staccato rhythm. Blood oozed out of the dime-sized hole in the fleshy part of his shoulder. Curling and dripping down the knotted muscles of his forearm, the blood splattered in dark droplets on the worn, aged cypress planking of the cabin floor.

I handed him the jar. Blood smeared the smooth glass as he took it from me. He sipped the moonshine, screwing his face up tight each time he swallowed. But he followed each swallow and grimace with a wide, satisfied smile.

"That stuff'll make a dead man's dick stand up," he said.

Glancing out the front door, I saw the last rays of the setting sun glistening in wide streaks on the water. Watching the sunset, I realized that I was hungry.

"Is there any food stockpiled around here? I'll cook us some supper."

Sweetpea chuckled and shook his head.

"There's lotsa food 'round hea," he said. "You gots to catch it though."

I helped Sweetpea up from his pallet and guided him to a wooden rocking chair on the front porch. With him shouting directions, I found two cane poles on the back porch, then I dug up a handful of worms from underneath a rotted log next to the cabin.

As twilight descended on the swamp, lighting the horizon with a purplish-orange glow, I quickly caught three catfish. Using the Swiss Army Knife I had bought at Macy's before I left New York, I cut the heads off the catfish and peeled off their skin.

Pulling a rusted skillet from the cabinet beside the wood stove, I scrubbed the rust out with an old piece of cloth, then scooped a handful of lard from an old coffee cup and dropped it in the pan. After I tossed several pieces of wet wood in the stove, I bundled up one of the rotting quilts and tucked it around the wood. The quilt caught fire and burned voraciously, engulfing the damp wood. My ingenuity surprised me, and despite the violence earlier in the day I felt oddly at peace.

"I can't believe I'm sitting out here letting some damn Yankee fry me some catfish," Sweetpea said from the doorway.

"Well, I can't believe I'm out here either," I said. It was the only thing I could think to say.

"Smells good . . . wish I had some cole slaw to go with that."

"Keep on wishing . . . it might come true. But wouldn't count on it."

Sweetpea laughed as he stumbled forward and plopped down on a cane-backed chair sitting next to the door. The empty moonshine jar hit the floor with a thump and clattered across the cypress planks.

"Are you okay?" I asked, stepping closer.

"I'm doing just fine," Sweetpea said, slurring his words. "Mighty fine. I'm in the mood for some music . . . how 'bout you? My guitar case is up in the loft. If you get it for me, I'll play us some music."

Clambering up a wooden ladder, I crawled into the area between the cypress ceiling and the tin roof. As I slid into the tight space, something scratched against the tin—a squeaking, tortured squeal. With my heart pounding in my chest, I ignored the sound and squeezed between the interlaced beams, grabbing the scratched and battered black case. As I hurried down the ladder, I realized the noise had only been the limbs of the cypresses and oaks brushing the tin roof. But that knowledge did little to calm my twisted nerves. I regretted that Sweetpea had drunk all the moonshine. At that point, I could have used a swallow or two.

Despite the dreadful events earlier in the day, I couldn't ignore the flashes of excitement coursing through my body as I reached the bottom of the stairs. I had heard so much about Sweetpea Champagne and his blues, but I had never actually heard him play. However, I was about to. Yes, I was about to spend several hours listening to him play in the middle of a goddamn Louisiana bayou.

Patting his shirt in stiff motions, Sweetpea crooked the first two fingers of his right hand at me. I sat the guitar case in his lap.

"Check dose fish," Sweetpea said as he untied the loops of dirty rope twined through the rusted metal catches of the guitar case. "I don't like burnt fish . . . no sirree."

Forcing myself to turn my back on Sweetpea Champagne with a guitar in his hands, I walked back to the stove and flipped the catfish in the bubbling grease with a wooden spoon. I heard the plunk of a guitar string behind me and I couldn't stop myself from turning around. With the heat of the stove toasting my back, I watched, silent, as Sweetpea skillfully tuned his guitar, plucking the strings and twisting the tuning knobs on the neck of the beautiful black guitar.

Ignoring the sizzling catfish, I unsnapped the trunk of recording equipment and hurriedly set up the reel-to-reel tape recorder. Unrolling two lengths of electrical cord, I clamped the metal hooks to a small battery mounted inside the trunk. As the power coursed through the equipment, a small red light bulb on top of the recorder flickered on. A red glow filled the room, bathing Sweetpea's dark frame.

Looking up from his tuning, Sweetpea grinned at the tape recorder and other equipment encircling the cane-backed chair.

"Some ole fat white man in Baton Rouge recorded me once. Told me my music was gonna make me rich. I ain't seen a damn cent," Sweetpea said with a laugh. Sticking a hand-rolled cigarette in the corner of his mouth, he struck a match on the heel of his shoe, then cupped his hand around the orange flame. Smoke oozed out of his flared nostrils as Sweetpea thumped the smoldering match out the open doorway and ran the fingers of his right hand down the strings.

"Don't forget about my catfish, Mr. New York City," Sweetpea said, the cigarette dangling from the corner of his mouth as he banged the guitar strings with his calloused thumb.

I gritted my teeth and turned back to the stove as Sweetpea banged out a fast, angry blues. Glancing over my shoulder as I fished the catfish out of the hot oil with the wooden spoon, I watched as he popped the guitar body with his outstretched palm, keeping time with his tapping foot as he played.

"They got a knife to my throat and I'm dooown ooon the killing flooh," Sweetpea sang in a throaty growl, pounding out an angry rhythm on his guitar.

As I stood there with the catfish on my plate, staring at Sweetpea bathed in the dull red glow of the recorder, I felt a physical thrill sweep through me. Beyond the open doorway, I could see a bloated full moon hanging in the sky; moonlight glistened on the water and the drooping clumps of Spanish moss.

Many men dream about a good woman, a place in the country, a couple of contented rugrats running around the house. Not me. I was as close to heaven on earth as I could come. It didn't matter that a bunch of coonasses were looking to kill us. Or that Sweetpea had a bullet wound in his shoulder. I was, honest to God, sitting in a fishing shack in South Louisiana recording arguably one of the last true blues musicians.

Slashing at the guitar strings, his voice raised to a keening wail, Sweetpea rocked from side to side on the cane-backed chair, swiveling his bony hips as the music vibrated through his body. He jerked the guitar up and slapped the strings, ending the song abruptly. Dropping the guitar back into his lap, he rocked back and chuckled, taking a pull on the cigarette before he tossed it out the front door.

"Uh-huh," he murmured, closing his eyes, enjoying the succor that his music offered.

"Here's your catfish, Sweetpea," I said.

His eyes flickered open and he nodded weakly as he reached for the plate.

While we ate, Sweetpea started talking. I let the tape keep on rolling.

"I 'member one time I was playing a juke over in Mobile, Alabama. Man, the women were fine and the liquor was flowing. I was up on that little wooden stage at one end of the building . . . bunch of damn bucks tired and hurtin' from workin' the fields. There was this woman sitting with her husband at a table right next to the stage. My God, her big titties were fallin' out of her dress. I knew I had to have me some of that stuff even if it meant gettin' killed. . . ."

I smiled and nodded as he talked, spinning out stories of all the fights, the women, the juke joints, watching the sun come up after an all-night drunk.

"You know they gonna find us, don't you?" he said suddenly.

It took a moment for his words to sink in.

"What do you mean?" I said. Scrambling off the floor, I ran to the doorway. "Do you hear a boat?"

I couldn't see anything in the blackness beyond the wooden decking. In the luminous moonlight, I saw the dark trunks of the cypress trees.

"Naw, I don't hear no damn boat," Sweetpea said. "I'm just tellin' you. They gonna find us. And they gonna try to kill us. I been in some mess in this parish befo'e, but I ain't never killed no white cop befo'e. No sirree."

"Should we leave?" I asked. "If you can get us to Baton Rouge, I could get a wire transfer from my bank in New York. I could give you enough money to get away, maybe go up to Chicago or out to San Francisco."

"I don't think I want to," Sweetpea said. "Run . . . that is. My mama's always talking 'bout takin' a stand. I think I'm ready to take my stand, Mr. New York City."

"What are we gonna do?"

"I don't know what you gonna do," said Sweetpea. "But I know damn well what I'm gonna do. My daddy's mama, Mrs. Olivett, taught me some of the hoodoo befo'e she passed years ago. My mama hated her. I guess the feeling was mutual 'tween those two. My mama's always been the book-studying kind . . . she didn't like Mrs. Olivett's hoodoo. But I loved my grandma. My daddy used to sneak me over to her house; he'd tell my mama lies about where I was. I was a good student, Mr. New York City, but I never had a call to use that stuff . . . till now. How 'bout going over there next to the back door. There's a loose board on the porch. Pry up that board and bring me what's underneath."

Shaking my head at Sweetpea's stubbornness, I followed his directions. I wanted to pack up my tape recorder and get back in the pirogue. But I knew I wouldn't get very far in the bayou alone. Wedging a piece of firewood into a gap in the porch, I pried the board up. A small hand-carved cypress box nestled in a bed of dried moss. I picked up the box and carried it to Sweetpea.

Nodding, he propped the guitar against the wall next to him and sat the box in his lap. He rubbed his finger-tips across the carved patterns in the wood, murmuring softly to himself.

"Ain't had much call to mess with the mojo much," Sweetpea said. "I'm just warnin' you, Mr. New York City. I get this thang goin', it's gonna be like a big ole barn fire. Ain't no tellin' what could happen."

"This might sound like a real dumb question, Sweetpea, but do you have to do it . . . right now?" I said, raising my hands up, palms out. "I know this ain't been an ideal day with all the trouble we got into in town. But I really would appreciate it if we could record a couple more songs. I know it might sound selfish, but I'm tellin' you, Sweetpea . . . you're one of a dyin' breed. You know that? The kids these days . . . they don't care about your kind of music. They're listening to all that funky stuff . . . Dizzy Gillespie, Miles Davis, the Birdman. Nobody's playing your kind of music anymore. One day all we're going to have are these tapes of you."

As my words ran out, I realized how foolish I sounded, asking him to sit and play some songs when he was convinced that a lynching party was only a few hours away.

With a wide grin, Sweetpea shook his head.

"Don't worry," Sweetpea said, chuckling. "Don't you worry. This mojo ain't gonna work wit'out my music. Everybody's got some special way of getting the juices stirred up. Now, my grandma, Mrs. Olivett, she was one of the best cooks in St. Martin Parish. Whenever she used the mojo, she'd spend all day whipping up a big meal in her kitchen, but it weren't no regular ole gumbo she cooked. No sirree. The mojo was in the food.

"Back years ago, Mr. Robert Dugas killed my cousin Romey when he caught him with his daughter down in the bushes. Well, my grandma stayed in the kitchen all night, while all the other women cried and cried over Romey's body laid out in the front room. Mrs. Olivett gave a small jar of gumbo, along with a couple of dollars, to one of the house niggers who worked for Mr. Dugas. Couple of weeks later, that old man went plumb crazy . . . it took the sheriff and five of his men to get a straitjacket on him. 'Course, that was after he walked into town on Main Street bare ass nekked, yanking his meat for all he was worth."

Laughing and shaking his head, Sweetpea unhooked the small metal latch and opened the lid of the cypress box. With the thick darkness in the cabin, I couldn't see what he was holding at first. He bent down and laid the box on the floor next to his foot. Straightening, he clutched a small figure fashioned from dried cornhusks. I moved closer and I could see the black twine binding the husks, forming two arms and two stubby legs. The eyes, nose, and mouth were dried dots of black paint.

Holding the doll in his left hand, Sweetpea slid his right hand into his back pocket, then whipped his arm out, away from his body, as he flicked open the long, curving straight razor. Staring at the doll and muttering a rhythmic chant under his breath, Sweetpea reached up and dug the edge of the razor into his bullet wound. The blade reflected the blood-red glow of the light bulb atop the tape recorder as it sliced through the clotted, dried blood and torn tissue. Sweetpea grunted and bit down on his lower lip. A ribbon of saliva dripped down his chin.

With a quick jerk, he pulled the blade away and opened his hand. The blade thunked across the cypress planks as Sweetpea dug two fingers into the raw, bleeding wound. Blood coated his fingers and dripped down his forearm. Sweetpea rubbed his bloody fingers along the dried cornhusk doll, drenching the brittle leaves with his blood.

Shaking his head and sucking in deep breaths, Sweetpea laid the doll at his feet and reached, again, into the cypress box. He placed four curved metal wafers around the doll, then sprinkled a mixture of dried herbs and powders from small cloth pouches which he pulled out of the box. Closing the box lid, he reached into his shirt pocket and fished out a match. Jabbing the match against the floor, he lowered the flame to each of the wafers. The dried, flaky material burned and hissed, adding its light to the glow of the recorder.

Rocking back in the chair, Sweetpea sucked in several deep breaths, then cupped his dirty handkerchief to his bleeding shoulder.

"Do you . . . ?" I asked, pushing up from the floor, ready to help him fashion a tourniquet.

Sweetpea waved me away. Raising his head, he stared at me silently, his chest rising and falling as tears welled out of his yellowed bloodshot eyes and trickled down the gray, parched flesh stretched taut over his wide cheekbones.

I sat back down.

Reaching behind him, Sweetpea picked up his guitar. As he plucked out a tune, his body folded in around the instrument like a drowning man clutching a life preserver.

"I'm down, down to my last two bucks," Sweetpea sang, his voice gaining strength with each word.

As he sang, the flames in the metal wafers flared, burning higher, and brighter.

I lost track of time. Sweetpea sang and played, running one song right into the next with only a few chord changes between each one. The fires kept burning in the wafers long after the small clumps of material should have been engulfed.

Each song gained in intensity, not necessarily volume, but gut feeling and rawness. As he sang, his voice raw and weary, his fingers instinctively found the chords as he rocked back and forth with his eyes closed. He opened up his soul and sang about the pain, the anguish, and the weariness of his life . . . a life many people considered animalistic, beneath dignity or humanity. In his voice, in his music, he channeled the frustration and the bone-weary anger of every woman, man, and child south of the Mason-Dixon line who had sung "We Shall Overcome" while a bunch of white bulls dressed in spit-shined uniforms fingered their wooden batons and licked their lips.

The flames flared higher, leaping up, up, reaching for the ceiling. Then, just as suddenly, the flames collapsed, extinguished. I stared at the doll. A hole had opened up beneath the doll. I scrambled back, a wail forming unbidden in the back of my throat as a solid black figure grabbed the edges of the open hole in the floor and wriggled out. But some part of me knew that the figure wasn't simply crawling out of the basement. It was crawling out of some other place.

The black figure stood before Sweetpea. Water, or some kind of liquid, dripped down the smooth, hard, muscled body of pure obsidian blackness. The figure turned toward me, and I felt my bladder tighten. No features graced the angular, hard face. Where a mouth or nose should have been was nothing. A pair of red eyes glowed in the darkness. Whimpering like a frightened child, I scuttled backwards.

Sweetpea rocked forward, grinding his fingers on the guitar strings, singing in a hoarse, tortured voice. The daimon turned away from me. Despite the fear that suffused my body, zipping through my veins like I had just grabbed a raw power line, I knew the daimon for what it was—an embodiment of Sweetpea's pain, and all the pain he had borne witness to in his travels. Tonight, his pain had not only a voice, but a body.

In the distance, I could hear the buzz of engines echoing across the water.

"They're here, they're here," Sweetpea sang, bending over his guitar, running his fingers up and down the fretboard. "Ready to bust down a door . . . even the score. Oh yeah, they're here."

I crawled into the corner of the shack and pulled my knees up to my chest. Glancing out the front windows, I saw several metal skiffs and two-man fishing boats circle the entrance of the small cove. With a roar, the boats swooped into the cove. The dirty yellow glow of oil lanterns pierced the darkness. A man stood at the prow of one of the boats, clutching a thick metal chain in his sturdy fists.

With a grunt, Sweetpea stood up and shuffled to the open doorway. The dark daimon followed Sweetpea, but remained hidden, unseen by the lynch mob, in the shadows.

"My mama taught me this hymn when I was a kid," Sweetpea said in my direction, before he stepped out on the front porch and strummed his guitar.

"Amazin' grace, how sweet the sound . . ."

At first, Sweetpea's voice was unintelligible under the roar of the engines. But the engines quieted as the boats bumped against the wooden dock.

"That saved a wretch like me . . ."

"That coon's standing up there singing a damn hymn. I'll give him something to sing about," a man with a white bristly crewcut hollered as he hopped onto the dock and slid his rifle up to his shoulder.

As the shooter's finger tightened on the trigger, a man leaned out of a nearby boat and knocked the rifle barrel up with a wooden paddle. The gun boomed, but the bullet whistled harmlessly over the shack and slapped through the cypress branches overhead.

"Goddamn it!" shouted Crewcut. "I had that nigger dead in my sights. Don't go telling me you're gonna try and take him into town and put him in the jail all peaceful."

Crewcut lowered the rifle until it was centered on the man's ample belly.

"I didn't say nothing about arrestin' him," the man said as he grabbed a pile and pulled himself onto the wharf with a grunt. In the dim light, I could see the big belly sagging over his belt and the reflected glow from the gold star pinned to his khaki shirt. "Sidney, we've been sweating and going hungry all day looking for the son of a bitch. I don't want to go spoiling our fun with one shot.

"Now, I know we've all been tipping the bottle this afternoon—hell, afternoons like this are made for a cold beer. But, right now, I think you need to lower that rifle."

Nodding his head, Sidney lowered the rifle.

"Hell, Sheriff, you know I just go all excited. I wanted to be the first one to put a bullet in him."

"I know that," the sheriff said with a chuckle, patting Sidney's shoulder. "No hard feelings."

The sheriff turned away from Sidney and eased a big, black pistol out of the oiled holster at his hip. With a sudden burst of speed for his corpulent body, the sheriff reversed the pistol in his grasp, spun around and slammed the butt into Sidney's face. I could hear the man's jawbone snap like a rotted piece of wood.

The man's rifle tumbled into the bayou with a loud splash. The sheriff clutched Sidney's shirt in his knotted fist as he pounded the thick metal pistol butt across the man's skull. Sidney shrieked, his voice a piercing wail of anguish and fear through his broken jaw, and writhed as the sheriff administered his brand of justice.

Dropping Sidney on the wooden planks, the sheriff straightened up, shoved his pistol into the holster, then wiped his pudgy hand across his sweaty face.

"Ain't nobody drunk or sober gonna point a gun at the sheriff of St. Martin Parish," the man said, tucking the loose flaps of his shirt into his pants. "Now, boys, we got us a murderin' nigger to attend to."

Yelping and hollering, the men poured out of the boats and clambered onto the dock, ignoring Sidney curled into a fetal ball in a widening pool of blood. With the men crowded behind him, the sheriff strutted to the end of the wharf and stepped onto the small front porch.

Throughout the sheriff's discipline lesson, Sweetpea had continued singing—even though his voice was low and didn't carry. Now, he raised his voice in song once again.

"I wandered so aimless . . . life filled with sin . . . I wouldn't let my dear Savior in," Sweetpea sang.

"Why don't you join me, Sheriff?" Sweetpea said, strumming his guitar. "I think you probably know this one. It was written by that white motherfucker—what's his name?—Hank Williams."

For a moment, Sweetpea's odd behavior stopped the men crowded onto the dock. They stood there, their eyes widened in surprise, as Sweetpea sang and played guitar—unshaken by the men's obvious intention.

But the sheriff didn't take much to somebody else upstaging his show, especially when that someone happened to be a penniless black musician. Crossing the porch in one wide step, the sheriff ripped the guitar out of Sweetpea's hands. Spinning around, the sheriff slammed the guitar into one of the porch's support poles, shattering the wooden frame. The strings broke with loud metallic twangs. The sheriff tossed the twisted, broken frame of the guitar in the bayou, then turned back to Sweetpea with a grin.

Mindful of Sweetpea's previous lecture about hoodoo, I worried that the destruction of his guitar might somehow affect the daimon still standing in the shadows a few feet inside the cabin. I slowly turned my head, anxious not to draw attention to my hiding place, and studied the daimon. I didn't see any discernible change in its attitude or appearance.

Outside, the madness continued.

"Boys, strip him," the sheriff said. "I don't mind if you get in a few punches in the process, but don't hurt him too bad."

The men swarmed around Sweetpea, punching and kicking as they ripped his clothes from his body.

"I said don't kill him," the sheriff hollered. "And I meant it. If somebody kills him, they're gonna end up in worse shape than Sidney."

The men eased up. I saw Sweetpea's bruised and bleeding face as the men dragged him to the edge of the porch. A man with a wispy handlebar mustache dropped a coil of chain on the dock in front of Sweetpea.

"By the power invested in me by the great, sovereign state of Louisiana, I'm arresting you, Robert Champagne, for the murder of Edward Sonnier this morning in the lobby of the Evangeline Hotel," the sheriff's voice echoed across the water. "As the newspapers will report in the next couple of days, after apprehending you, I was overwhelmed by a group of upstanding, honorable citizens of St. Martin Parish wishing to ensure that law and order still exists in our parish, our state, and in our country, and you were hanged to death from a cypress tree. Do you have anything you want to say?"

"I saw the light, I saw the light, no more darkness, no more night," Sweetpea's strong voice rang out.

"String him up, boys," the sheriff yelled, drowning out Sweetpea's singing. "He's fuckin' crazier than a shithouse rat."

Over the years I have listened to the tape of that night—oh yes, the tape recorder was still running, the microphone picking up every sickening punch and stomp as they dragged Sweetpea out of the cabin—but I've never been able to figure out what Sweetpea started singing.

Something changed in his voice. Yes, he continued singing "I Saw the Light" as they jerked him to his feet. But he was singing much more than that. There was some kind of language underneath his normal singing voice; twisted inside his usual phrasing and notes was something else—the commands to his daimon.

The men jerked Sweetpea to his feet, digging their fists into the small of his back. The man with the handlebar mustache picked up the chain with a grin.

"That one looks pretty good," the sheriff hollered, pointing at the drooping branches of a cypress tree. "Somebody shimmy up there and get that chain around that big limb. And somebody, for God's sakes, shut that nigger up."

Before anyone could silence Sweetpea, the daimon acted. He lunged out the front door of the shack, sliding between two surprised coonasses in a blinding blur. Moving with inhuman speed, the daimon leaped from the front porch and landed on the dock. Surprised at the loud noise, the man holding the chain turned around with a look of surprise. The daimon fastened his hand around the chain and casually snapped the man's wrist. With his right wrist flapping uselessly, the man screamed as he flipped backwards into the water.

Reacting to the noise and movement behind him, th
sheriff squatted down, trying to present a smaller targe
as his hand groped for his gun. Only brief seconds ha
passed since the daimon had burst out the door, and th
men standing on the dock were still reacting to the crea
ture's blurring speed. The alcohol numbing their sense
didn't help.

As the men gradually lowered their rifles and pistols
trying to get a solid bead on the unknown attacker, th
sheriff lost all hope of escape. The daimon dropped th
chain around the sheriff's neck, spun around, an
tugged on the chain, dragging the sheriff across th
dock. When it reached the end of the dock, the daimor
leaped. It snagged the edge of the tin roof with its fre
hand and swung itself up, disappearing into the dark
ness. With a loud, ratcheting snap, the chain tightene
behind him. The sheriff swung back and forth along th
edge of the roof, his boot heels thumping against th
porch pole as his hands clawed at the chain digging int
his plump neck. His chest heaved in huge spasmodi
jerks, and his tongue darted in and out of his mouth lik
a bloated purple worm.

"Daimon! Daimon!" a short man with curly brow
hair and dressed in faded overalls shouted as he stum
bled backwards on the dock. Jerking his shotgun up, th
man pulled the trigger. But, in his panic, he hadn't taker
the time to raise the shotgun high enough. A fellow
lyncher's head exploded in a spray of blood and brains
The jerking, twitching corpse stumbled forward and fel
onto the front porch. I hunched down lower inside th
cabin, covering my body with my crisscrossed arms.

The man's second shot was higher, and I heard the
pings of birdshot tearing through the tin roof and rico
cheting overhead. Following the frightened man's lead,

men scrambled off the porch and onto the dock, firing at the roof of the shack. Shotguns, rifles, and pistols breathed fire and belched smoke as the men launched a fusillade.

Amidst the maelstrom of violence swirling around him, Sweetpea knelt on the edge of the front porch, singing a gospel song. As the firing continued and men halted to reload, a skinny man wearing a pair of mud-spattered hip waders casually lowered his pistol and shot Sweetpea. The bullet slammed into his side and spun him around. Cupping a hand to the bleeding wound in his side, Sweetpea wiped his trembling mouth and started singing again, his voice low and faltering, not much above a whisper.

"On the old rugged cross . . ."

I watched as a dark shadow dropped out of a cypress tree and landed silently on the end of the dock, behind the frightened lynch mob focused on the roof of the fishing shack. Strutting up to the tight knot of men, the daimon cut a bloody path through the crowd. As the men realized what was happening, several of them leaped into a nearby boat. A young man with thick muscular forearms leaned over the motor and jerked on the pullrope. On his second try, the motor fired into life. Grabbing the arm of the motor, the man gunned the boat forward, ramming a path through the other vessels tied to the dock. Before the boat could break free though, the daimon tossed a lifeless corpse aside, leaped into a nearby skiff and bounded from it into the fleeing craft.

When the daimon ripped off a man's arm and shattered another's skull with one backhand slap, the young captain leaped out of the back of the boat, clearing the churning engine with his legs spread wide. He surfaced twenty feet away, slashing his arms through the water, pulling away from the boat with his excellent upper-body strength. Unseen by the young man, the daimon dove into the water.

Just as the boat captain reached for a low-hanging cypress branch, the bayou exploded in a burst of water and mud around him. The man cried out as his hands latched on to the branch. He pulled himself up, up toward safety. With a loud spiraling scream, he clung to the branch while something yanked him backwards. His scream echoed through the bayou as his head slid under the water. His arms splashed ineffectually, then nothing marked his place except for concentric ripples spreading out across the dirty brown water.

The few remaining survivors scrambled into boats, sobbing and cursing. One boat pulled away from the dock and spun around in a wide circle, its engine growling, spewing water across the porch. I saw the daimon slide through the water, leaving a silent wake like a speeding torpedo.

Screams and shouts of fear and pain echoed across the water as the daimon pulled himself into the boat and continued his bloody retribution for so many past wrongs. A man fell into the water, wailing and screaming as his entrails pooled out of the tattered remains of his belly.

"You best be movin' on . . . Mr. New York Ciittyy," Sweetpea whispered, dragging himself to the open doorway.

I saw the blood welling through his fingers clamped around the bullet hole in his side.

"I can't garuntee yu' that I can control this thang," Sweetpea said. "You best be leavin'."

Finally, his words sunk in, and I pushed myself out of the corner.

"How can I get past him?" I said, my voice cracking and shaky. "If I go out back into this bayou, I might as well stay right here, 'cause I'll die out there."

"Take one of the boats," Sweetpea said, gasping for breath. "Hurry, I can'ts hold him forever."

Jumping up, I ran to the tape recorder. I knew I couldn't pack up the crate of recording equipment, but I wasn't about to leave without that tape which was still spinning round and round. Stabbing the stop button with my shaking finger, I scrabbled at the small metal latch holding the tape onto the machine. With a quick jerk, I opened the latch and flipped the tape reel off the machine. Tape unspooled behind me from the blank reel as I ran across the cabin and kneeled beside Sweetpea.

"Yu' one crazy mothufucka," he said. "Always worryin' 'bout yo' music. Get out of here."

As I stood up and walked out onto the porch, I heard Sweetpea start singing again.

"Swing low, sweet chariot, comin' for to carry me home . . ."

I stumbled down the dock and leaped into a small two-seater metal johnboat. Scrambling across the front seat, I yanked the starter cord, and the engine fired up on the first try. Smoke belched out of the engine, shrouding me for an instant. As the smoke rolled away, I saw the daimon slide out of the water and pull himself onto the wharf.

The boat backed away, and my hands trembled on the metal loop mounted atop the engine as I shoved the engine to the left and guided the boat around the end of the dock. The daimon was tracking my movement. He could have bounded into the boat with one easy leap. Behind him, the sound of Sweetpea's voice carried across the still, bloody water.

"Comin' for to carry me home . . ."

When the boat reached the entrance to the cove, I backed off on the throttle and sat there in the dark bayou, looking back at the cabin. Oil from a shattered lantern burned in a ragged pool on the porch, igniting the wet cypress boards. In the glow of the flames, I saw the daimon standing in the doorway, looking down at his creator.

Sweetpea's voice rang out strong and clear.

"Comin' for to carry me home."

Then his voice turned into a raw scream.

I twisted the throttle in my hand, and the boat leaped out of the cove with a sudden burst of speed, cutting a ragged wake through the calm water.

The next morning two fishermen found me floating underneath a cypress tree, the boat out of gas. I lied. I gave them a fake name, and a false story about a fishing guide who got drunk and fell out of the boat and drowned.

"I tried to help him," I said. "But I think a gator got him. I saw that thing's big jaw and white belly."

When I started crying, the men decided to believe me. After they got me to the nearest public boat ramp and went off to call the sheriff, I slid behind the wheel of some early morning fisherman's pickup truck. He had left his keys in the truck's ignition. I pulled out onto the gravel road and stomped on the gas pedal.

Late that evening, I ditched the pickup truck at a truck stop outside of Houston. I thumbed a ride into downtown Houston, then called my girlfriend in New York. The next morning, she wired me three hundred dollars. Thankfully, word hadn't spread about the fact that I was wanted for questioning by the St. Martin

Parish sheriff's office. Late in the afternoon, I climbed onto a Greyhound bus headed north. I sat down in a seat in the back of the bus dressed in a brand-new suit. I rubbed the small satchel sitting on the seat next to me, thankful that I still had the tape.

I was never arrested for the incident in St. Martin Parish. I paid my colleague in Baton Rouge for the damage to his Chevrolet, explaining my misfortune away as a Yankee messing with the wrong woman in a small town in Louisiana. I hung up the phone with his scalding laughter ringing in my head. For the first couple of years, I was terrified that I would be arrested and extradited for the sheriff's murder. But nothing ever happened. I haven't been back to Louisiana since, either.

My work and life suffered from the emotional baggage I carried from that long night in the fishing shack. New York University eventually fired me for my long absences. I couldn't talk about my experiences in St. Martinville. My colleagues were looking for some sign of instability, and I would have loaded up their cannons with ammunition if I had ever mentioned it to anyone. And I couldn't find solace in my work either.

I would hear a tape of a black spiritual or blues song that a colleague taped on some pig trail or dirt road in Mississippi, Georgia, or Louisiana, and I would start thinking about Sweetpea. Nothing could dull the pain or fear except for long, solitary bouts inside my apartment drinking one beer after another. During those times, I didn't venture outside, even to go to class.

After I was fired by NYU in 1961, I spent thirty years bouncing from one small college to another—none of them in the South, of course. I spent some time in California, even. It was easy to hide my madness in the

idiocies of southern California, but the job eventually
ended. Once, back in the early 1970s, I was teaching at
a college in Indiana and went to the drugstore one day
to pick up some bathroom supplies. When I saw the
daimon leering out at me from the cover of a comic
book, I dropped a bottle of mouthwash and tube of
toothpaste as my legs buckled and I fell to my knees in
the aisle.

I bought a copy of the comic book, throwing some
money at the cashier, not bothering to wait for my
change. In my car, I flipped through the comic book,
titled *The Black Panther;* however, I quickly realized the
central character wasn't the daimon from my past, but
the visual similarity sent shivers of fear pinging down
my spine.

Finally, three years ago, I ended up back in New
England, teaching music appreciation courses at a high
school and community college in a little town in upstate
New York, close to where I grew up. I managed to scrape
up enough money to buy a small one-bedroom house in
a neighborhood of decaying senior citizens. And I even
managed to work up the courage to talk to a therapist.

I've told him about my bouts of depression, but I've
never told him about that night in a fishing shack in a
moonlit bayou in South Louisiana. He prescribed 100 mg
of Zoloft, an antidepressant, which I take religiously
every morning following my bowl of Wheaties.

The medicine has helped level out my deep troughs
of depression that left me stranded at home, incapacitated for weeks at a time. But it hasn't helped my
nightmares . . . when a red-eyed daimon stalks my
dreams.

L. RON HUBBARD'S WRITERS AND ILLUSTRATORS OF THE FUTURE

Written by
Algis Budrys

Algis Budrys has assisted in the promulgation of the Writers' and the Illustrators' Contests since their beginning, in a variety of ways. He does so because he is absolutely convinced L. Ron Hubbard was right when he felt that the nature of editing had changed since the days when Hubbard's name was one of the handful of top bylines in the fiction field. There simply was no longer the sitting down with a promising newcomer and teaching him or her the difference between the talented amateur and the selling professional.

So LRH set up the Writers' Contest to find, and nurture, the promising author. That was sixteen years ago, and in that time over one hundred thirty new writers have been brought in and established as well-known professionals. Over two hundred have been published. Then, a few years later, modeling the new Contest on the old, L. Ron Hubbard's *Illustrators of the Future* was begun. In both cases, the results have been spectacular.

Spectacular. The field has been enriched as never before. And, year after year, a substantial number of new names are brought forward in either Contest, adding to the running total. They win considerable prizes, in money and in trophies, and they participate in workshops taught by Algis Budrys, Dave Wolverton and Tim Powers for the writers, and Ron Lindahn and Val Lakey Lindahn for the illustrators. All entries for both Contests are judged by top names in their fields.

In the past year, the judges for the writers were Kevin J. Anderson, Doug Beason, Gregory Benford, Algis Budrys, Eric Kotani, Anne McCaffrey, Larry Niven, Andre Norton, Frederik Pohl, Jerry Pournelle, Tim Powers, Robert Silverberg, Jack Williamson and Dave Wolverton; and, for the illustrators, Edd Cartier, Leo and Diane Dillon, H. R. van Dongen, Bob Eggleton, Will Eisner, Vincent Di Fate, Frank Frazetta, Frank Kelly-Freas, Dr. Laura Brodian Kelly-Freas, Shun Kijima, Ron Lindahn and Val Lakey Lindahn.

Winners for the year in L. Ron Hubbard's *Writers of the Future* Contest were

First Quarter

1. Gary Murphy
   Pulling Up Roots

2. Paul D. Batteiger
   Like Iron Unicorns

3. Mark Siegel
   Atlantis, Ohio

Second Quarter

1. Paul E. Martens
   Your Own Hope

2. Melissa J. Yuan-Innes
   Skin Song

3. Dan Dysan
   Guildmaster

Third Quarter

1. Dan Barlow
   A Conversation with Schliegelman

2. Ilsa J. Bick
   The Quality of Wetness

3. Leslie Claire Walker
   As the Crow Flies

Fourth Quarter

1. Toby Buckell
   In Orbite Medievali

2. William Brown
   Home Grown

3. Michael J. Jasper
   Mud and Salt

Finalist: Jeff Rutherford, *Daimon! Daimon!*

Winners for the year in L. Ron Hubbard's *Illustrators of the Future* Contest were

Jayson B. Doolittle
Troy Connors
Steelee Faltis
James T. Johnson
Samantha Miceli

Justin Phillips
Katalin Sain
Deth P. Sun
Frank Wu
Yana Yavdoshchook

They worked very hard, and long. Remember their names.

For more information on the Contest, read on.

NEW WRITERS!

L. Ron Hubbard's

Writers of the Future Contest

AN INTERNATIONAL SEARCH FOR
NEW AND AMATEUR WRITERS OF
NEW SHORT STORIES OR NOVELETTES OF
SCIENCE FICTION OR FANTASY

No entry fee is required.
Entrants retain all publication rights.

ALL AWARDS ARE ADJUDICATED BY
PROFESSIONAL WRITERS ONLY

PRIZES EVERY THREE MONTHS: $1,000, $750, $500.
ANNUAL GRAND PRIZE: $4,000 ADDITIONAL!

Don't Delay! Send Your Entry to
L. Ron Hubbard's
Writers of the Future Contest
P.O. Box 1630
Los Angeles, CA 90078

CONTEST RULES

1. No entry fee is required and all rights in the story remain the property of the author. All types of science fiction, fantasy and horror with fantastic elements are welcome; every entry is judged on its own merits only.

2. All entries must be original works in English. Plagiarism, which includes poetry, song lyrics, characters or another person's world will result in disqualification. Submitted works may not have been previously published in professional media.

3. Eligible entries must be works of prose under 17,000 words in length. We regret we cannot consider poetry or works intended for children. Excessive violence or sex will result in disqualification.

4. The Contest is open only to those who have not had published (more than 5,000 copies) a novel or short novel, or more than three short stories, or more than one novelette, in any medium.

5. Entries must be typewritten and double-spaced with numbered pages (computer-printer output okay). Each entry must have a cover page with the title of the work, the author's name, address and telephone number and an approximate word count. The manuscript itself should be titled and numbered on every page, but the AUTHOR'S NAME SHOULD BE DELETED to facilitate fair judging.

6. Manuscripts will be returned after judging. Entries MUST include a self-addressed return envelope. U.S. return envelopes MUST be stamped; others may enclose international postal reply coupons.

7. There shall be three cash prizes in each quarter: 1st Prize of $1,000, 2nd Prize of $750, and 3rd Prize of $500, in U.S. dollars or the recipient's local equivalent amount. In addition, there shall be a further cash prize of $4,000 to the Grand Prize winner, who will be selected from among the 1st Prize winners for the period of October 1, 2000, through September 30, 2001. All winners will also receive trophies or certificates.

8. The Contest will continue through September 30, 2001, on the following quarterly basis:

October 1–December 31, 2000   January 1–March 31, 2001
April 1–June 30, 2001   July 1–September 30, 2001

Information regarding subsequent contests may be obtained by sending a self-addressed, stamped business-size envelope to the address on the previous page.

To be eligible for the quarterly judging, an entry must be postmarked no later than midnight on the last day of the quarter.

9. Each entrant may submit only one manuscript per quarter. Contest winners are ineligible to make further entries.

10. All entries for each quarter are final. No revisions are accepted.

11. Entries will be judged by professional authors. The decisions of the judges are entirely their own, and are final.

12. Winners in each quarter will be individually notified of the results by mail.

This Contest is void where prohibited by law.

L. Ron Hubbard's

ILLUSTRATORS OF THE FUTURE CONTEST

OPEN TO NEW SCIENCE FICTION
AND FANTASY ARTISTS
WORLDWIDE

All Judging by Professional Artists Only

$1,500 in Prizes Each Quarter
No entry fee. Entrants retain all rights.

**Quarterly winners compete for
$4,000 additional ANNUAL PRIZE**

L. Ron Hubbard's
Illustrators of the Future Contest
P.O. Box 3190
Los Angeles, CA 90078

1. The Contest is open to entrants from all nations. (However, entrants should provid[e] themselves with some means for written communication in English.) All themes of scienc[e] fiction and fantasy illustration are welcome: every entry is judged on its own merits only. N[o] entry fee is required, and all rights in the entries remain the property of the artists.

2. By submitting work to the Contest, the entrant agrees to abide by all Contest rule[s.]

3. This Contest is open to those who have not previously published more than thre[e] black-and-white story illustrations, or more than one process-color painting, in med[ia] distributed nationally to the general public, such as magazines or books sold at newsstand[s] or books sold in stores merchandising to the general public. The submitted entry shall n[ot] have been previously published in professional media as exampled above.

If you are not sure of your eligibility, write to the Contest address with details, enclosin[g] a business-size self-addressed envelope with return postage. The Contest Administration w[ill] reply with a determination.

Winners in previous quarters are not eligible to make further entries.

4. Only one entry per quarter is permitted. The entry must be original to the entran[t.] Plagiarism, infringement of the rights of others, or other violations of the Contest rules w[ill] result in disqualification.

5. An entry shall consist of three illustrations done by the entrant in a black-and-wh[ite] medium. Each must represent a theme different from the other two.

6. ENTRIES SHOULD NOT BE THE ORIGINAL DRAWINGS, but should be lar[ge] black-and-white photocopies of a quality satisfactory to the entrant. Entries must b[e] submitted unfolded and flat, in an envelope no larger than 9 inches by 12 inches.

All entries must be accompanied by a self-addressed return envelope of the appr[o]priate size, with correct U.S. postage affixed. (Non-U.S. entrants should enclose internation[al] postal reply coupons.) If the entrant does not want the photocopies returned, the entry shou[ld] be clearly marked DISPOSABLE COPIES: DO NOT RETURN.

A business-size self-addressed envelope with correct postage should be included s[o] that judging results can be returned to the entrant.

7. To facilitate anonymous judging, each of the three photocopies must be accompanie[d] by a removable cover sheet bearing the artist's name, address and telephone number, an[d] an identifying title for that work. The photocopy of the work should carry the same iden[ti]fying title, and the artist's signature should be deleted from the photocopy.

The Contest Administration will remove and file the cover sheets, and forward only th[e] anonymous entry to the judges.

8. To be eligible for a quarterly judging, an entry must be postmarked no later than th[e] last day of the quarter.

Late entries will be included in the following quarter, and the Contest Administratio[n] will so notify the entrant.

9. There will be three co-winners in each quarter. Each winner will receive an outrigh[t] cash grant of U.S. $500, and a certificate of merit. Such winners also receive eligibility [to] compete for the annual Grand Prize of an additional outright cash grant of $4,000 togeth[er] with the annual Grand Prize trophy.

10. Competition for the Grand Prize is designed to acquaint the entrant with customary practices in the field of professional illustrating. It will be conducted in the following manner:

Each winner in each quarter will be furnished a Specification Sheet giving details on the size and kind of black-and-white illustration work required by Grand Prize competition. Requirements will be of the sort customarily stated by professional publishing companies.

These specifications will be furnished to the entrant by the Contest Administration, using Return Receipt Requested mail or its equivalent.

Also furnished will be a copy of a science fiction or fantasy story, to be illustrated by the entrant. This story will have been selected for that purpose by the Coordinating Judge of the Contest. Thereafter, the entrant will work toward completing the assigned illustration.

In order to retain eligibility for the Grand Prize, each entrant shall, within thirty (30) days of receipt of the said story assignment, send to the Contest address the entrant's black-and-white page illustration of the assigned story in accordance with the Specification Sheet.

The entrant's finished illustration shall be in the form of camera-ready art prepared in accordance with the Specification Sheet and securely packed, shipped at the entrant's own risk. The Contest will exercise due care in handling all submissions as received.

The said illustration will then be judged in competition for the Grand Prize on the following basis only:

Each Grand Prize judge's personal opinion on the extent to which it makes the judge want to read the story it illustrates.

The entrant shall retain copyright in the said illustration.

11. The Contest year will continue through September 30, 2000, with the following quarterly period (see Rule 8):

July 1–September 30, 2000

The next Contest will continue through September 30, 2001, on the following quarterly basis:

October 1–December 31, 2000   January 1–March 31, 2001

April 1–June 30, 2001   July 1–September 30, 2001

Entrants in each quarter will be individually notified of the quarter's judging results by mail. Winning entrants' participation in the Contest shall continue until the results of the Grand Prize judging have been announced.

Information regarding subsequent contests may be obtained by sending a self-addressed business-size envelope, with postage, to the Contest address.

12. The Grand Prize winner will be announced at the L. Ron Hubbard Awards event to be held in the calendar year of 2001.

13. Entries will be judged by professional artists only. Each quarterly judging and the Grand Prize judging may have a different panel of judges. The decisions of the judges are entirely their own, and are final.

14. This Contest is void where prohibited by law.